The most beautiful Bibles

ΑΛΑΙΟ
ΗΜΕΡΩΝ

Österreichische Nationalbibliothek

The most beautiful Bibles

edited by
Andreas Fingernagel & Christian Gastgeber

TASCHEN
HONG KONG KÖLN LONDON LOS ANGELES MADRID PARIS TOKYO

Contents

III. Biblical exegesis from the Church Fathers to Scholasticism

IV. Medieval versions of history in world chronicles and history Bibles

V. The juxtaposition of the Old and New Testaments in typological picture Bibles

VI. Bible manuscripts of the Jewish and Eastern Orthodox faiths

Bible production in medieval monasteries

*"Oh, you lucky reader, before you touch a book wash your hands, turn the pages carefully and keep your fingers well away from the letters! For someone unable to write
Cannot imagine what an immense labour it is.*

*Oh, how hard is writing: it blurs the eyes, squeezes the kidneys and tortures every limb.
Only three fingers write, but the whole body suffers ..."*

This graphic description of the sorrows of a scribe (found in a Visigothic dictionary dating from the 8th century) offers us a glimpse not just of the laborious nature of the work, but also of the precious nature of the manuscripts thus produced. With their minds deeply concentrated and their bodies stooped or hunched, monks or lay brothers devoted themselves day after day to the service of God, toiling for over 12 hours a day in the light-filled summer months, writing out the texts of the Holy Scripture with painstaking accuracy and in a standardized script. As well as complete Bibles, they copied out Gospel Books and Epistolaries containing selected passages from the scriptures, liturgical texts, the writings of the Church Fathers and those, too, of the "ancient heathens". A complete edition of the Bible, extending to some 1200 pages in a folio format, would take a scribe between two and three years to write out single-handedly. Often, therefore, several copyists were engaged upon the same manuscript; in such cases, we speak of several "hands" being involved. Once the text was written out, the next task – performed if necessary by another scribe – was rubrication, i. e. the identification in red ink of the beginnings of sentences or *nomina sacra*. Only after this, as the third stage of the production process, came the illumination of decorative initials and borders surrounding the introductory chapters, etc.

Since daylight was an important prerequisite for the work of a scribe, the room used as the scriptorium in a monastery can often be identified by its numerous, if

Eberler Bible, Cod. 2770, detail from fol. 85r (Daniel, Prologue): The prophet Daniel with banderole inscribed: *LAPIS ANGULARIS SINE. CA(PITULUM) II.* ("A stone was cut out without [hands...], Chapter 2").

▸ **Neapolitan Luxury Bible, Cod. 1191, detail from fol. 3v:** Jerome hands a monk one of his writings.

possessiunculas uendideris · nō hēt xp̄c̄.
unde alat paupes suos · Totum de de
dit · qui se ipsum obtulit · Apl̄i · na
uem tantum 7 recia reliq̄runt · Vidua
duo era misit in gazophylatium · 7
p̄fertur cresi diuitiis · Facile 7 con
tempnit omnia : qui se semꝑ cogi
tat ēē moriturum · 7c̄.

Desiderij mei · desideratas accepi
ep̄las · qui quodam presagio futu
ror cum daniele sortitus ē nomen :
obsecrantis · ut trāslatum in latinaz
linguam · de hebreo simone pētatheu
cum nr̄or auribꝰ tradēm · Periculosuz
opus certe · 7 obtrectatorum latrati

7 flumina de ue
uiue · Et que n
auris audiuit
dit · que p̄parauit
7 multa que p
dant · In trogen
ta sunt · 7 cum
libris hebraycis
testimonium e
ysaya · ttium
p̄ uibus · quntum
multa ignorant
menta sectantu
libris autentia
erroris : nō ē m
denti factum c
ne ptholomeus
am apud hebre
tatem apprehen
io ciuo faciebat
ina cadē uidebat
aliud sēpta tes
aut alr inspirat
runt · ut 7 regi s
fidi nō uulgare
auctor · septua
orie mendatio
diuisi · eadem s
eiusdem ptholo
pt tp̄e iosephi
z in una basili

fairly small windows. In the depiction of two scribes in the scriptorium of the abbey church of Echternach (ill. p. 16), for example, we see – within an idealized and stylized view of the monastery – a long row of small windows and, copying manuscripts beneath them, a layman on the left and, on the right, a monk with habit and tonsure. They are sitting, in the hunched position already mentioned, behind angled desks and are holding their quills with three fingers. This 11th-century miniature adorns an Epistolary produced for Henry III (today in the Staats- und Universitätsbibliothek Bremen, Ms. 216, fol. 124v), a type of manuscript which contains the passages from the Gospels read out during the Mass, arranged according to the liturgical year.

For an entire millennium, between 500 and 1500, monasteries were the chief centres of writing, of manuscript production, of the housing of books in libraries and often, too, the chief centres in which they were used. In the 6th century, after the collapse of the Roman Empire and prior to the rebuilding of secular power centres in Europe, the papacy took over the task of safeguarding the cultural heritage both of Greek and Roman antiquity and of Christianity. Reformist popes such as Father of the Church Gregory I, known as Pope Gregory the Great (reg. 590–604), were supported by the monasteries, within whose strict, hierarchical structure the study of the Christian scriptures and their translation into contemporary modes of expression were the prime concern.

In the *Regula de servis dei* which he wrote for the new monastic communities springing up across North Africa and southern Europe, St Augustine († 430) placed the personal striving for perfection at the centre of monastic community life. To this belonged the reading of the Holy Scripture. Augustine names – as if it were a matter of course – a librarian as guardian of this important monastic office.

Of even greater significance for manuscripts and their use was the Rule of St Benedict of Nursia, who founded the monastery of Monte Cassino in around 530. His philosophy, summarized in the well-known phrase *Ora et labora*, required monks to remain in the same community all their lives and to accept the rule of their abbot, who assigned every member of the monastic community a specific task in the self-sufficient running of the monastery. The Rule of St Benedict also required prayers and devotions to be performed in the rhythm of the liturgical hours and the *lectio* to be read at mealtimes. In idealized medieval depictions of monasteries, the room devoted to the Library is generally located near the church, so that the books required for liturgical use, divine offices and readings were ready to hand. A scriptorium is usually also nearby. Benedictine monasteries spread rapidly across northern Europe; at least 70 were founded over the course of the 7th and the 8th century, 70 in the 9th and the 10th century respectively, and about 100 in the 11th and 12th century respectively. These Benedictine monasteries played an important role in supporting the educational policies of Emperor Charlemagne (crowned in 800), who initiated not only a reform of handwriting (introducing the Carolingian minuscule) but also, and most significantly, a book-learning and library programme whose impact would endure even into the Middle Ages.

The number of books housed in one monastery varied markedly. We can assume a figure of somewhere between 30 and 60 manuscripts, most of them for liturgical use; only in a few instances up to the 12th century did the total exceed 100. One exception, however, was the Benedictine monastery of Lorsch (764–1248), which particularly profited from Charlemagne's patronage of learning and which according to a catalogue dating from the 9th century housed some 590 codices. These included lavishly illuminated

Lectionaries, Epistolaries and Bibles, but also texts by Livy and Sallust as well as others by Greek historians.

Two monastic reforms played an important role in the following centuries, the first introduced by Abbot Berno († 927) at Cluny abbey in France. Berno not only reinstated the strict monastic discipline set down in the Rule of St Benedict, but above all sought to make newly-founded monasteries independent of bishops and secular feudal lords and to place them directly under the authority of the pope. This reform, which was propagated by the monastery of Gorze in Lotharingia as well as by Cluny, contained the instruction - significant for the history of libraries and books - that the scriptorium was one of the most important focuses of work in a monastery. Canon Geoffroy of Sainte-Barbe-en-Auge, writing around 1170, expressed the opinion that *Claustrum sine armario quasi castrum sine armamentario* - "a monastery without a scriptorium is like a castle without an armoury". Drawing its imagery from life in a Carthusian order, the charterhouse in Basle later expanded upon this comparison in its *Informatorium bibliothecarii*:

> *Monasterium sine libris est sicut civitas sine opibus,*
> *castrum sine muro, coquina sine supellectili,*
> *mensa sine cibis, hortus sine herbis,*
> *pratum sine floribus, arbor sine foliis.*
> "A monastery without books is like a community without wealth,
> a castle without walls, a kitchen without utensils,
> a dining room without food, a garden without herbs,
> a meadow without flowers and a tree without leaves."

The Cluny reforms prompted the foundation of several new monastic orders, including the Carthusians in around 1084, the Cistercians in around 1098, the Augustinian Canons in around 1059 and the Premonstratensians in around 1120. The Carthusians and Cistercians in particular adopted a strict, hierarchical organization, with the head of the Order directly subordinate to the pope. The Carthusians evolved out of a colony of hermits established in 1084 by St Bruno of Cologne († 1101) in La Chartreuse, near Grenoble. In addition to poverty and self-denial, their prime emphases lay upon meditation and the reading of the Holy Scripture, accompanied by a strict observance of silence. The copying of books was thereby set down in the Carthusian Rule as the main focus of manual labour, making writing and study essential aspects of service to God. Precise instructions were also laid down with regard to copying, writing materials etc. and even extended to directions about the lending out of manuscripts. Book production took place under the charge of the *sacrista*, who held overall responsibility for the writing utensils and manuscripts and who oversaw copying itself. There emerged from this a preoccupation with textual accuracy, as works of philological scholarship also became important in their monasteries.

The Carthusians proceeded to build up extensive collections of manuscripts, collections rivalling the libraries of the Benedictines. Thus an inventory drawn up at the charterhouse in Mainz (founded in 1308) in *c.* 1470 lists some 1500 manuscripts and incunabula, including not just Bible manuscripts, theological works and devotional tracts, but also scholastic textbooks as well. The library rules stated that all lendings had to be written down and reviewed every six months, that senior monks enjoyed precedence over junior ones when it came to borrowing manuscripts, that a slip bearing the number

ІС ХС
АПО
СТО
Л·ЛУ
КА

of the cell of the borrower had to be put in the place left by a removed book as a "substitute", and that a maximum of five volumes could be borrowed at once. Manuscripts could only be lent out to other monasteries with the permission of the prior.

The new orders being founded in the 13th and 14th century, in particular the so-called mendicant orders, had different requirements of their libraries. The Franciscan Order, founded by St Francis of Assisi in 1209 and granted papal approval in 1223, embraced a life of poverty and itinerant preaching. Although the Franciscans used liturgical books in the Mass, their Rule did not specify a daily reading of the scriptures. Since what possessions the individual houses did own had to be as simple as possible, the few surviving manuscripts from Franciscan monasteries of the $13^{th}/14^{th}$ century are generally written on plain parchment without embellishment. The oldest documented Franciscan library is that of St Emmeran's abbey in Regensburg, where an inventory of 1347 lists 86 manuscripts, primarily works of biblical exegesis and patristics as might be expected, but also including works on jurisprudence and a copy of Ovid. In Amberg in the Upper Palatinate, on the other hand, the number of manuscripts recorded around 1500 is 52, and in Kehlheim 21 – considerably fewer, in other words, than in the case of the so-called "old orders".

The Order of St Dominic († 1221), based on the Augustinian Rule, aimed to convert heretics through the persuasive power of preaching. Since preaching and serving as confessor were central to the Order, Dominic attached great value to theological training. Study and scholarship were an automatic part of Dominican life. No one was allowed to become a preacher unless they had completed at least three years of theological training, and without at least four years' study of theology, no one could teach in public. The monks were permitted a minimum of personal possessions, a restriction which also extended to books. The Dominican Rule laid down precise regulations for libraries. It was the responsibility of the *cantor* to look after the liturgical books, and the scriptorium was headed by a *librarius*. The Rule also included instructions relating to how manuscripts should be housed, looked after, copied, displayed, catalogued and used.

From the Dominican Rule we also learn how a library might grow: firstly, through the labours of its own scribes, secondly, by contracting work out to external scribes, and finally by selling duplicate manuscripts in order to be able to purchase works the library lacked. Libraries also received no small number of manuscripts as donations and might also inherit books owned by monks who had died. Since Dominicans were intended to devote themselves first and foremost to study, waged scribes were employed to take over some of the work of copying. All consultation of books was subject to censorship by the librarian and the prior, in order to prevent any heresy from creeping in. Special permission had to be obtained in advance for each copy. It was advised not to collect too many books, but to concentrate upon manuscripts of a sound content, upon a good selection of authors and upon the accuracy of the text – illumination was largely avoided.

The first Dominican monastery within the German-speaking sphere was founded in 1222 in Cologne. Its members included Albertus Magnus († 1280), Thomas Aquinas († 1274) and the mystic Master Eckart († *c.* 1328). Teaching at the University of Cologne, founded around 1388, was for a long time dominated by Dominican thought: in

Slavonic Liturgical Apostolos, Cod. slav. 6, detail from fol. 4v (St Luke): St Luke the Evangelist sitting and writing, above him the Holy Ghost as a white dove.

a fire which swept the library in 1659, autograph works by Albertus Magnus and Thomas Aquinas were amongst those destroyed. The Dominican monastery founded in Vienna in 1226 still exists today; a catalogue of its library, drawn up in 1490, lists a huge collection of 985 manuscripts. The books were laid out on desks in systematic order, with the first book always being the Bible.

Mention should also be made of the Brothers of the Common Life in the Netherlands and Lower Rhineland, who made an important contribution to the distribution of books during a period when the age of the manuscript was drawing to its close. Founded shortly before 1400, this loose association of laymen embraced as their goal moral perfection through the personal discovery of God. Without taking the monastic vow, they lived a communal life with no personal possessions. They held Scholasticism to be outmoded and wanted to replace monastic piety, with its renunciation of the world, with a new, popular mysticism, a cosmopolitan *Devotio moderna*. They devoted themselves to caring for the poor and sick, but also to providing spiritual welfare through the dissemination of religious texts. Their particular target groups were impoverished students and clerics, whom they wanted to protect from moral dissipation. Copying books was their sole manual labour. Since they also earned their living from it, one might almost speak of a commercial publishing enterprise, even if they were thereby aiming at a higher goal: preaching not through words, but through writing – *Fratres non verbo sed scripto praedicantes*.

Each fraternity had its own librarian (*librarius*), who as well as managing its manuscript holdings also supervised the accuracy of the copies being made and set the

St Jerome, Commentaries on the Bible, Cod. 930, detail from fol. 147v: Portrait of St Jerome.

Utrecht Luxury Bible, Cod. 1199, detail from fol. 1r (Genesis, Prologue): St Jerome.

prices at which they were sold, writing master (*scriptuarius*), book painter (*rubricator*) and bookbinder (*ligator*). The books these fraternities owned were simple and largely plain, but highly legible. The Brothers of the Common Life produced not only Bibles, but also liturgical books, patristical works, prayer books, meditations and collections of sermons, in many cases in the German language. They also compiled their own anthologies, often containing pious quotations from the works of the Church Fathers. The expansion of the Brothers of the Common Life in the 15th century coincided with the advent of printing, which the fraternity was relatively quick to exploit. Mariental monastery in the Rhineland had its own printing press by as early as 1474, Rostock as from 1476. Working as a scribe in Deventer, for example, was Thomas à Kempis, whose *De imitatione Christi* served as a model example of edifying sermons composed in the spirit of the *Devotio moderna* movement. It is thanks to the efforts of the Brothers of the Common Life that German versions of the Bible were published in print in Cologne at a very early date, 40 years before Luther's ground-breaking translation.

In a codex in the possession of Michelsberg monastery in Bamberg (today housed in the Bamberg Staatsbibliothek), dating from the 3rd quarter of the 12th century and largely devoted to the writings of St Ambrose of Milan, we find a pen drawing illustrating numerous stages of book production (ill. p. 15). Appearing in the central field is the Archangel Michael, who is being venerated by four monks at his feet, with the artist himself on the left placing the final flourish, so to speak. The upper and lower medallions in the central axis portray monks reading and teaching with the aid of books, while in the vertical axes on either side we are shown the various activities involved in making a

Greek Gospels and Praxapostolos, Cod. suppl. gr. 52, detail from fol. 75v: St Mark sitting in front of a desk, getting ready to copy (!) his Gospel from a manuscript lying open on a lectern ("Beginning of the Gospel of Jesus Christ, the Son of God").

Slavonic Liturgical Gospel Book, Cod. slav. 7, detail from fol. 5v (St Matthew): St Matthew the Evangelist seated and sharpening his stylus, with desk and writing utensils.

codex. Pictured on the left, starting from the top, are monks sharpening a stylus, writing on a wax tablet, stretching and scraping the parchment and preparing the wooden boards for the covers. On the right, from the top, a scribe (with a quill behind his ear) is sorting the gatherings which, in the medallion underneath, are being laid in a sewing frame. Only then do we see the edges being trimmed and the clasps being hammered on.

For 1500 years after Christ, the main and most important writing material used for precious manuscripts was not the papyrus that had been used in antiquity for centuries, but parchment. Animal skins were first soaked in a solution of lime and water, in order to remove any remaining scraps of flesh and also to make the parchment more durable. It was then stretched taut on a frame and scraped one more time with a knife, leaving a smooth surface. The scribe gave the parchment a final rub with pumice before starting to write.

Parchment was a very precious material, one for obvious reasons not easily obtainable and therefore also very expensive. A codex of 600 to 800 pages required the skins of some 300 to 400 sheep. Figuratively speaking, a large herd of sheep thus had to be slaughtered and skinned for a single work. In addition to sheep, the skins of goats and calves were also used, and occasionally also donkeys, deer and gazelle, and in special cases even camels. Particularly thin parchment, obtained from the skins of young animals, was highly sought-after, and Books of Hours were even written on the skins of animal foetuses. The skins had to be as flawless as possible, free of scars left by insect bites or injuries, for example, or holes where bones had pierced the skin. Small tears and holes were often sewn up, or left in the parchment and simply written around.

Purple parchment was particularly costly, and was written upon with gold, silver or white ink. This luxury format was chosen first and foremost for Bible manuscripts. More common were brown and black inks, which could be made with materials that were generally readily available in a monastery. To make the normal carbon ink (as described by Pliny in the 1st century AD in his *Naturalis historia*), you simply needed lamp-black and gum. This gum could be obtained north of the Alps from the resin of stone-fruit trees. Pinewood soot was the best for ink. The usual ingredient of brown ink, on the other hand, was blackthorn bark, cut in April or May. The dried bark was pounded, peeled, soaked in water and finally boiled down.

Iron-gall ink was also employed. These deep-black inks were wipe-proof, but depending on their chemical constitution could also react aggressively. In damp conditions, in particular, they ate into the parchment and left a number of holes. Iron-gall inks are made out of metallic salts such as ferrous or copper sulphate, binders such as gum, and solvents, for which wine, beer or vinegar might be used. There were countless recipes for such inks, varying significantly in their ingredients.

Pure gold ink was also employed for particular display. Fragments of gold leaf were ground in a mortar and mixed with nitrates. Oxgall and copper bloom were added, and the whole mixed and poured through a sieve. The resulting ink was then applied with a quill and finally burnished. Gold was frequently depicted using orpigment, a yellow arsenic trisulphide which produced a sulphur-yellow colour but which was not with-

St Ambrose, De officiis ministrorum, fol. 1v: Various stages in the production of a codex, Bamberg, mid-12th century. Bamberg, Staatsbibliothek, Ms. patr. 5

out its dangers. It was extracted from mines and sold at a high price. So too was green made from malachite, also known under the name of mountain green after its source. Red and yellow ochre were obtained from earth and were simply ground and mixed with water. Pure ultramarine blue was obtained from pulverized lapis lazuli. Since white was relatively difficult to manufacture, white lead was the usual choice. An old recipe contains the following instructions: "Take lead, shape it into sheets, hang it over vinegar, collect the bloom and wash it until it is clean, then you will get white lead." Verdigris – i. e. copper oxide – was also used. Such paints and inks were thus by no means harmless, and the idea, put forward in Umberto Eco's *The Name of the Rose*, of contaminating an illuminated manuscript with a secret poison is not at all far-fetched. Anyone licking their finger frequently while working with these substances would rapidly suffer their ill effects. Instructions on making medieval inks and paints and on preparing parchment are handed down in numerous treatises and in workshop manuals known as pattern books.

We opened this essay with a description of the sufferings of the scribe, who only receives his rightful reward on Judgement Day. The title page of a manuscript containing the twenty books of the *Etymologiae* by Isidore of Seville, dated to the years 1160–65 and today housed in the Bayerische Staatsbibliothek in Munich (Clm 13 031, fol. 1r; cf. ill. p. 16), shows in the upper half of the picture Isidore in his bishop's robes with a quill in his hand. The scroll bears the words *Fac mea scripta legi que te mandante*

Epistolary of Henry III, fol. 124v: Two scribes in the scriptorium at Echternach, 11th century. Bremen, Staats- und Universitätsbibliothek, Ms. 216

Isidore of Seville, Etymologiae, fol. 1r: Christ Judging the Life of Swicher the Scribe, *c.* 1160–1165. Munich, Bayerische Staatsbibliothek, Clm 13 031

peregi – "Prepare my writings, which I have composed at your behest, for reading." The publisher of these writings, Bishop Braulio, accepts the scroll. In the lower half of the picture, the scribe named Swicher is seen on his deathbed. Opposite him sits Christ, also with a book in his hands, passing judgement on the scribe's life. The angel on the right is holding a set of scales and weighing the scribe's achievements in the shape of a codex, which quite literally tips the balance: the devil is forced to flee, and in the middle of the picture the soul of the scribe is taken up to Heaven by an angel. In this manner, not just writing a devotional treatise but also making a copy of a precious manuscript is shown to be a pious form of service to God.

The term "codex" comes from the Latin *caudex*, a wooden board, and thus simply refers to the external shape assumed by the manuscript, as distinct from the roll. The codex form was adopted in the first centuries AD both for legal codices and for shorter literary texts, such as Martial's *Epigrams* and the books of the New Testament. It is evident that the codex was easier to use than the more awkward roll.

Papyrus continued to be used into the 5th century AD. Paper made its first appearance from AD 1000 in North Africa and within the cultural sphere of Islam, which had emerged in the Orient in the 2nd century AD and had been spreading across the Arab world since the 8th century. The first paper mills appeared in Moorish Spain in the 12th century; the first north of the Alps were those in Nuremberg, established in 1390. This signified an important change of writing material, without which printing could never have achieved its mass impact. Whether parchment or paper, both materials were squared off and folded into gatherings of 2, 4 or 8 leaves. The writing area was then marked out with fine dots and if necessary the pages ruled with fine lines. Writing itself was carried out with a split-reed pen or feather quill, both of which required frequent sharpening. As a rule, scribes also had to prepare their own inks. With the gatherings in front of them, they first wrote on the recto and verso of the first half of the bifolia, then the second half. Each gathering was given an identifying mark of some kind, to ensure that the quires would be assembled in the correct sequence. These marks variously took the form of pen-strokes, letters and numbers. Later it became the custom to use catchwords, whereby a few words or syllables from the opening lines of the next quire were included in the bottom margin of the last page of each gathering.

Two ink-pots are often depicted in front of the scribe, indicating that he carried out the preliminary rubrication himself. As a rule, however, the actual illumination of a manuscript formed a separate phase of production, one demanding its own talent and skill. The scribe would frequently leave spaces to be filled in with decorative initials, writing a tiny letter – a so-called "representative" – in the gap so that the illuminator would know which initial was required. This custom was adopted in early incunabula, in which printed "representatives" can still clearly be seen in copies that were never subsequently illuminated by hand. After the work of writing and illumination was finished, the quires were bound. In earlier centuries they were stitched together, one sewn directly on top of the other; only with the invention of the sewing frame, visible in the miniature reproduced here (ill. p. 15), did it become possible to join together a larger number of quires without actually attaching them directly to each other. Instead, they were stitched to bands of leather or parchment which increased the stability of the whole and could be attached in turn to the wooden boards making up the covers. These sewing frames are documented from the 12th century onwards, and some researchers believe they were in use even earlier than this.

Beech, oak and elm were commonly used for the wooden boards. The spine and boards were first covered with leather and parchment, and the quires attached directly to the spine, which accounts for the notable rigidity of many bindings from the 10th to 12th century. Only gradually did it become possible to make hollow backs, allowing greater flexibility. The leather covering was decorated with blind-tooled lines or stamping, for example with a *supralibros*, an ex libris inscription. Bindings were often further adorned with clasps and bosses, which both prevented manuscripts from gaping open and ensured they lay better – manuscripts were namely housed lying flat on the shelf, not standing up in a row. The metal bosses also offered a degree of protection from damp and allowed the air to circulate through the gap they created between manuscript and shelf. In some libraries whose collections were consulted for study purposes, all the books were physically chained to desks as *libri catenati* (chained books). The chained library in Cesena in central Italy can still be admired today.

Since this short introduction has concentrated solely upon the production of Bible manuscripts, no mention has been made of manuscripts produced in secular workshops, commissioned for the libraries of royalty and the nobility and produced for the universities. At the early universities of the late 12th and 13th century in Paris and Bologna, there arose an entirely new system of copying by lay scribes. In this system, universities drew up standard exemplars of their textbooks and placed them with a *stationarius* (the English "stationer" is derived from this term). Individual gatherings from these exemplars were then lent out to lay scribes for copying and the transcripts subsequently checked by the universities for accuracy.

The quality of the writing materials, the costliness of the inks and illumination and the expensive, ornamented covers of the bindings all reflected the importance attached to Bibles and the respect in which they were held. Their value was ultimately determined, however, by the laborious, skilled contribution of the scribes and illuminators, who thereby – as we have seen – hoped to secure their own place in eternity.

Stephan Füssel

Bible moralisée, Cod. 1179, Cod. 1179, detail from fol. 246r (Apocalypse): King with open *Bible moralisée*; below: an illuminator working on a *Bible moralisée*.

From Royal Collection to National Library

The manuscripts and their provenance

Reconstructing the many paths by which the manuscripts in the collection of the Austrian National Library originally reached the library represents a science in itself. Signposts are provided first and foremost by the codices themselves. Ownership inscriptions, often deleted and written over by subsequent owners, notes which site a codex within a family or broader historical context, together with cataloguing inscriptions, form the most solid pointers. But entries made by readers, and the refurbishment of old manuscripts with "modern" bindings bearing coats of arms and monograms which preserve for posterity the identity of the owner, all yield clues which ideally enable us to trace the entire history of the manuscript from its production to its acquisition by the library.

Information can be gleaned, secondly, from inventories and lists of manuscripts that have passed to the library – for example in the wake of monastery closures. While such catalogues may indicate whether a codex was formerly in private possession or belonged to a religious foundation, the details they contain are often very general and frequently make it difficult to assign a codex to a specific former owner.

Accounts of the library's foundation also deviate all too often from demonstrable fact, and much of the historical research conducted into the origins of the institution is built upon speculation. It concentrates upon the reconstruction of the collections assembled by the titled heads of the Austrian branch of the house of Babenberg, and the Habsburgs who followed them. Only in a few cases, however, is it possible to link surviving manuscripts with concrete names. The title of "founding codex" can only be demonstrably assigned to a luxury manuscript in Habsburg possession in the late 14th century.

St Jerome, Commentaries on the Bible, Cod. 930, detail from fol. 1r: Portrait of King Matthias Corvinus.

▸ **History Bible of Evert van Soudenbalch, Cod. 2771, detail from fol. 10r (Genesis):** Dedication scene with patron Evert van Soudenbalch, the canon of Utrecht cathedral, who commissioned the manuscript.

Only much later, with the appointment of Hugo Blotius (1575–1608) as the first official imperial librarian, do we find tangible evidence of the library developing into an official institution, and only with the building of the Vienna Hofbibliothek in the 18th century was the imperial collection of precious books given a fitting home, one where it could be displayed, administered and consulted (the public was granted limited access to the collection even in those days).

Its function as a Hofbibliothek (Royal Library) – it only assumed the title of Österreichische Nationalbibliothek (Austrian National Library) in 1945 – exercised a strong influence, in its early days, over the library's collection and acquisition policy, and consequently over the character of its first holdings. A large proportion of its precious manuscripts derived from the private collections of leading aristocratic houses. By tracing these manuscripts back to their individual owners and thus reconstructing the latter's holdings, we can identify a collector's particular interest in certain subjects and themes, or their "merely" aesthetic preference for certain epochs in manuscript illumination or binding. Common to all these collectors – in line with their elevated position in society – is their orientation towards the most sumptuous and best that their age had to offer, both in the case of manuscripts intended for private use (such as prayer books) and in codices of a more official and public character, such as those donated to religious foundations.

Serving as a sort of collecting basin for royal manuscripts was the library of Archduke Ferdinand II of Tyrol (1529–1595), which was housed in Ambras Castle near Innsbruck (Cat. II.4, II.5, II.7, II.9, IV.2, V.5). In 1665, following the extinction of the Tyrolean line, the collection was transferred to the Vienna Hofbibliothek under praefect Peter Lambeck (1663–1680). With it came a large number of luxury manuscripts from the former possession of Emperor Friedrich III (1452–1493) and Emperor Maximilian I (1493–1519). In addition to these imperial treasures, mention should also be made of the manuscripts which Count Wilhelm von Zimmern (1549–1594) selected from his rich collection of codices in Old and Middle High German and presented to Emperor Ferdinand II in 1576 (Cat. IV.3).

The Österreichische Nationalbibliothek owes a considerable number of major works of Renaissance illumination and bookbinding to acquisitions from one of the greatest royal libraries of the late Middle Ages, the famous *Bibliotheca Corviniana* built up by King of Hungary Matthias Corvinus (1458–1490; Cat. III.1). Regrettably, this library was extensively decimated over the course of time and its collection scattered far and wide, and only a small proportion of its original holdings still survives.

Before the middle of the 18th century, finally, the Hofbibliothek purchased the library of the bibliophile general and statesman Prince Eugene of Savoy (1736), who had also made a name for himself as a collector through his acquisition of precious illuminated manuscripts (Cat. IV.4, IV.5, V.2, VI.4, VI.10). His collection embraces a fascinatingly wide range of codices, organized – entirely in line with the need for a classification of the "world of books" – into subject areas. Bound at the Prince's behest in different-coloured morocco bindings bearing his coat of arms, the books thereby also presented the imposing appearance their owner desired. Through the visual impression made by their coloured spines, moreover, the *Eugeniana* become an integral part of the magnificent Baroque architecture of the library in which they are housed.

Manuscripts from monastic houses, by contrast, only entered the Hofbibliothek intermittently prior to the late 1700s, for example after being "borrowed" by court historiographers acting on behalf of the emperor. Only in the wake of the secularization linked in Austria with the name of Emperor Joseph II (1741–1790) did the manuscript holdings of closed monasteries occasionally pass to the Hofbibliothek. These included, as from 1780, the libraries of the Augustinian abbey of St Dorothy's in Vienna, the Jesuit colleges in Vienna and Krumau (Cat. V.3), the Benedictine monastery in Mondsee in Upper Austria and the Damenstift convent in Hall in Tyrol (Cat. I.5, V.1). During this period, finally, the Hofbibliothek secured one of its most important acquisitions of monastic manuscripts with the transfer to Vienna of the Salzburg Cathedral library and the Archbishop's library (Cat. II.8, III.3).

The Hofbibliothek also added to its holdings from a third source of manuscripts, namely the private collections of scholars, which at the instigation of its dedicated librarians it began to purchase in growing numbers. In the context of the present volume, particular mention should be made of two acquisitions secured during the early years of the Hofbibliothek through the efforts of its first librarian, Hugo Blotius. In 1578 Blotius purchased from Johannes Sambucus, who was in financial difficulties, the latter's collection of predominantly Latin and Greek classics (Cat. I.3). Shortly afterwards, the no less important collection owned by the imperial envoy Ogier Ghislain de Busbecq, dominated by Greek manuscripts that he had purchased in Constantinople (Cat. VI.2, VI.3), was also acquired for the Hofbibliothek.

The many and varied sources from which the library's holdings are drawn make it possible to paint a comprehensive picture of specific areas of focus – such as the Bible in the Middle Ages under the spotlight here – from a number of different angles. The collections built up by Austria's ruling princes, which centred around luxury manuscripts prized, in many cases, not just for their sumptuous illumination and materials but also for the glory they reflected upon their owners, thereby represent the glittering showpieces. From the monastic libraries, with their more scholarly, theological focus, stem many examples of exegetic literature. The present library is enriched, lastly, by its acquisition of manuscripts from scholars and educated individuals who had themselves acquired them out of a humanist interest in the broadest sense.

Andreas Fingernagel

▸ **Ludolf of Saxony, Life of Christ, Cod. 1379, detail from fol. 1r:** The Gonzaga coat of arms.

t ergo egrotus p[ri]mum et sollicitum
t ueniat ad ip[su]m p[er] profundam
ac sollicitam confessionem et
propositum semp[er] declinandi a
aciendi bonum . Secundo
n in xp[ist]o fidelis eff[ect]us tamq[uam] ipsi p[er]

rgatur no a sordib pecorum . Deus enim
idheret ignis consumens ē purgatoem
ens . Secundo pp sui illuminatoem .
enim cui assistit lux ē in tenebꝭs lucens . au
nne illustratur docetur ordinate disponere
m suam ad xpm et celestia ad seipsũ &

I. Textual traditions and editorial revisions: Bibles from their beginnings to the standardized Bibles of the 13th century

The biblical texts of early Christianity were written, in Greek, on papyrus – in a manner distinctive of Bible production: the papyrus (almost) never assumes the form of a scroll, but is laid out as a codex, corresponding to the modern book. With the embrace of Christianity as the official religion in the 4th century and its acceptance within ever higher circles, Bible manuscripts began to undergo design changes which documented, in visual terms, the importance of the new faith. There was now a demand for luxury Bibles, some of them written and illustrated in gold and silver ink on purple parchment (cf. Cat. I.2). A very different face is presented by the Hebrew Bible, with its deliberate omission of the Septuagint (cf. Chapter VI, Introduction). In line with the 2nd Commandment, biblical illustrations were fundamentally forbidden. The desire to lend splendour to the appearance of the text therefore often found expression in the Masorah, the commentary written out in the margins in the shape of various figures (cf. ill. p. 29, 31, 32, 35), or in the magnificently decorated pages which appeared at the front of individual sections.

In non-Greek-speaking areas, the Bible was gradually translated into the local language (cf. Chapter VI), in the Latin-speaking West from the 2nd century onwards. These very literal translations fell into at least two main categories, the European and the African, and are today grouped under the heading of the *Vetus Latina*, the "Old Latin" version of the scriptures. In the 4th century Pope Damasus instructed Jerome to produce a new, binding translation of the entire Bible (cf. Cat. III.1). In the case of the Old Testament, Jerome thereby referred back extensively to the original Hebrew texts. His new Latin translation, which was completed in 405/6, became known as the Vulgate (*Vulgata*, "the common [version]") and was increasingly embraced from the 7th/8th century onwards.

Bologna Bible, Cod. 1127, detail from fol. 466r (II, III Epistula Johannis, Epistula Iudae): Ornamental initial "S".

▸ **Vienna Genesis, Cod. Theol. Gr. 31, detail from fol. 7r:** Rebekah gives Eliezer a drink from the jug.

Whereas the contents of printed books can be assumed to remain the same, consistency and reliability are fundamentally problematic in the case of medieval manuscripts. The texts they hand down are characterized by diverging opinions as to the validity and authenticity of scriptural books, individual passages and even individual turns of phrase; every time the manuscript is copied, moreover, there is a danger that mistakes or alterations will creep in. If the continuity of manuscript production was broken for any reason, for example in the era of population migration, new originals, often dating from much earlier times, had to be procured and laboriously re-copied. The scribe endeavouring to produce an accurate manuscript was also faced with the additional challenge of compiling a "valid" text from a number of incomplete and differing variations. The problems inherent in ensuring a continuous Latin-text tradition, however, also encouraged scholars to look back to earlier sources, and in particular to Hebrew texts.

It was this challenge that faced the scholars who, as part of the reforms initiated by Charlemagne, embarked upon a grammatical and orthographic revision of the Bible. After a number of preliminary, unfinished efforts, it was in Tours under Alcuin (*c.* 730–804), the Anglo-Saxon theologian who originally came from York, that large numbers of such newly-edited Bibles were copied out and sent to patrons all over the empire. Issued as pandects, i. e. in a single volume, these Tours Bibles became in turn the originals from which further copies were transcribed in other monasteries (cf. Cat. I.4).

Following a decline during the Ottonian era (10th–11th century), the production of Bible manuscripts became the focus of increased interest during the Romanesque period of the High Middle Ages, contributing to the emergence of the Romanesque giant Bibles. Following on from the earlier Carolingian Bibles, this interest was also linked with a concern to uphold established textual tradition. These fresh efforts to produce faithful editions of the Vulgate were sparked by the Gregorian reform movement and are symptomatic of the cultural environment from which they issued. As a rule, they required structured, often centralized forms of organization, such as those provided by the court schools during the Carolingian era, for example, and encouraged during the Romanesque era by the strengthened papacy and the flourishing of monastic orders. Only scriptoria, where manuscripts could be copied out in a reliable and highly sophisticated manner, offered the conditions within which traditional texts that had been researched and declared definitive could be accurately handed down.

From the end of the 12th century, the circumstances within which manuscripts were produced started to undergo a fundamental change. While individual orders – in particular the Dominicans, Franciscans and Carthusians – continued to strive for editorial accuracy, book production shifted away from scriptoria, linked exclusively to religious institutions, and more towards the secular realm and the realm of the universities – with a number of consequences for Bible production. The centre was Paris: here, over the course of the 13th century, the Vulgate (by now "spoilt" by various additions) was improved and reworked into a "standardized" edition that would long remain definitive (cf. Cat. I.5). Once again, this new version drew upon the corrections made under Alcuin.

Alongside Paris, the second major international centre of Bible production and distribution in the 13th century was the university city of Bologna, particularly famed for the study of law. Over the period from *c.* 1230/40 to 1320/30, well over 100 richly illuminated Vulgate manuscripts issued from the Emilian capital. Based on the revised Paris edition, they adopted the text of the Paris Bible, including the variations introduced by *vel* ("or") in the margin, the order of the biblical books, the chapter divisions, the page layout with titles at the head of the page and even, in their initials, the French iconography. The Dominican and Franciscan theology schools in Bologna, in particular, maintained very close links with Paris, as reflected in the manuscripts which records show they exchanged. French scribes and illuminators are also documented in Bologna. In 1249 the Franciscan school already existing in Bologna was granted papal recognition and put on

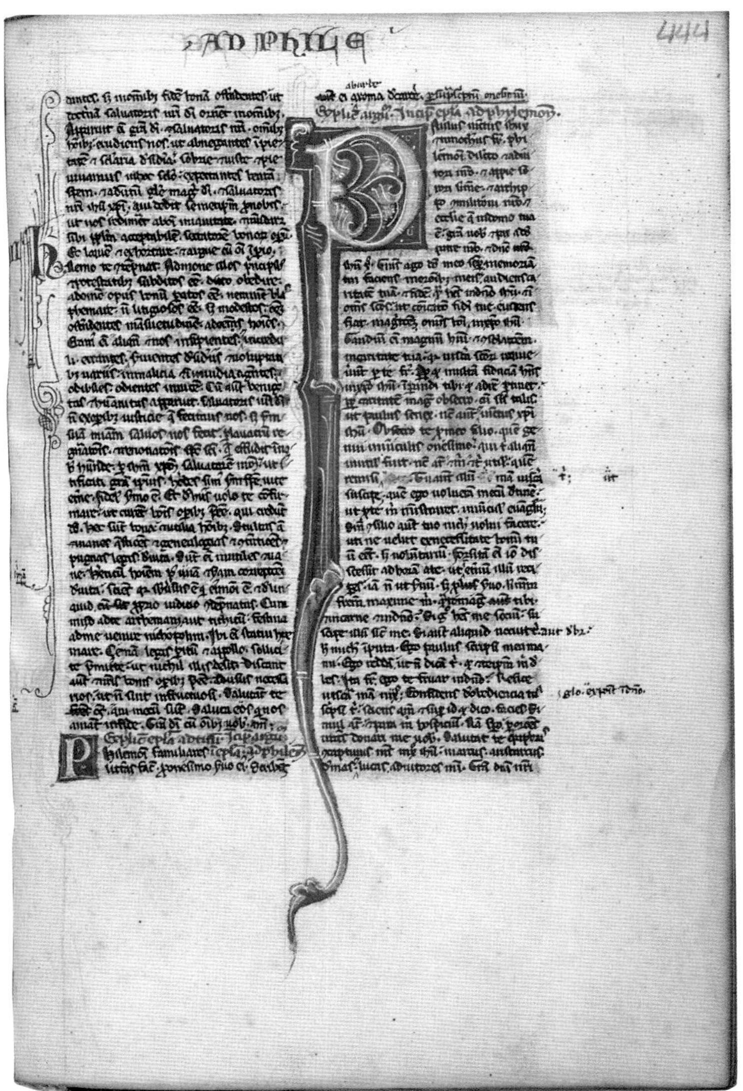

a par with the Parisian school. While the earliest known Bologna Bibles are decorated primarily with ornamental forms, historiated initials appear with increasing frequency from 1240 onwards. One of the earliest Bologna Vulgates with partial illustration is the – up till now, virtually unknown – Bible in Stift Heiligenkreuz (Codex C 7 right). From 1250 onwards, it was usual for Emilian Vulgates to be decorated throughout with historiated initials at the start of the individual biblical books, as seen in the Vienna Codex 1101. It is an interesting fact that, following on from the early pocket Bibles, the format of Bolognese manuscripts subsequently becomes bigger – chiefly, no doubt, to allow space for their ever more lavish illustrations. These reach their high point in the codices executed in the Byzantine manner of the Second Bolognese style, whose chief representative is the Bible housed as Codex 52 in the archives of Gerona cathedral. The workshops which illuminated Bologna Bibles also illustrated legal manuscripts with miniatures.

C. G. / A. F. / K.-G. P.

Bologna Bible, Cod. 1127, detail from fol. 444r (Epistula Pauli ad Philemonem): Ornamental initials marking the start of the Epistle to Philemon.

Torah, Haphtaroth, Megilloth, Cod. hebr. 28, detail from fol. 149r (Leviticus): Large Masorah in the shape of a dragon.

I.1

Torah, Haphtaroth, Megilloth

France (?), before 1348

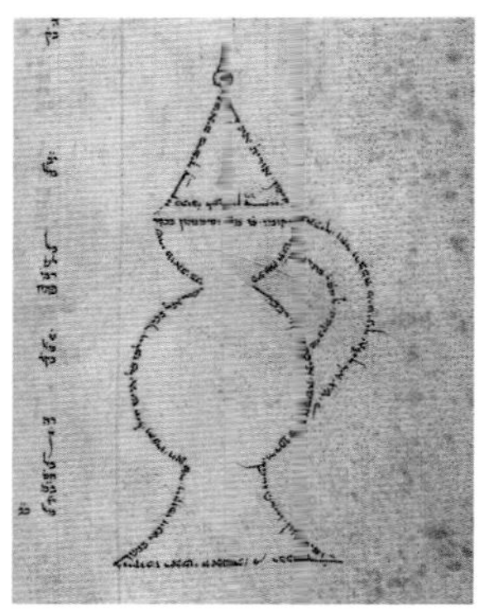

The manuscript, copied by an unnamed scribe (who probably emphasized his forename, Chaim, in the biblical text on fol. 35v), contains the Torah (the Pentateuch), the Haphtaroth (readings from the Prophets which follow the reading of the Torah in the synagogue service), and the Megilloth (the five festival scrolls). The ownership inscription on fol. 362v, which is accompanied by a short poem and blessing, shows that the scrolls, as in other examples in the 14th century, were probably originally bound in front of the Haphtaroth. In their present position at the back of the codex, the scrolls finish on fol. 401r with an abbreviated form of the first line of the colophon found – written out in full – at the end of the Haphtaroth.

From approximately the 8th century onwards, Jewish texts were written in codices, so that the scroll as a form served solely liturgical purposes. As a text designed for study, the Torah in the present Codex hebraicus 28 contains, in the middle of the page, the (consonantal) text incorporating vowel signs, symbols indicating the pronunciation of certain consonants, and markings relating to the ceremonial recitation of the text.

Circles above the words refer to the small Masorah (critical notes on textual forms) in the margins beside the main text. The large Masorah (providing an explanation of the small Masorah and cross-references to parallels via key words) is written above, below and even at right angles to the main text and is often shaped into a variety of figures (ill. p. 29, 31, 32, 35). These figures normally bear no relevance to the content of the biblical text. The Masorah contains information about the occurrence of certain word forms in the Hebrew Bible and thereby ensures that none of the consonants making up the text are lost or changed. It thus enables the codex to serve as a possible model for future copies. A copyist who might otherwise attempt to "correct" the text if faced with an

Detail from fol. 33r (Genesis): Large Masorah (accompanying Genesis 24:54) on the right in the shape of a pitcher – as a reference to Genesis 24:53 (Abraham's servant presents Rebekah with "silver and gold vessels").

▸ **Fol. 186r (Numbers):** Large Masorah in the shape of four dragons, two in the top margin and two in the bottom, linked by their intertwining tails.

לְחֹדֶשׁ הַשֵּׁנִי בַּשָּׁנָה הַשֵּׁנִית לְצֵאתָם
מֵאֶרֶץ מִצְרַיִם לֵאמֹר שְׂאוּ אֶת רֹאשׁ
כָּל עֲדַת בְּנֵי יִשְׂרָאֵל לְמִשְׁפְּחֹתָם לְבֵית
אֲבֹתָם בְּמִסְפַּר שֵׁמוֹת כָּל זָכָר לְגֻלְגְּלֹתָם
מִבֶּן עֶשְׂרִים שָׁנָה וָמַעְלָה כָּל יֹצֵא
צָבָא בְּיִשְׂרָאֵל תִּפְקְדוּ אֹתָם לְצִבְאֹתָם
אַתָּה וְאַהֲרֹן וְאִתְּכֶם יִהְיוּ אִישׁ אִישׁ
לַמַּטֶּה אִישׁ רֹאשׁ לְבֵית אֲבֹתָיו הוּא
וְאֵלֶּה שְׁמוֹת הָאֲנָשִׁים אֲשֶׁר יַעַמְדוּ
אִתְּכֶם לִרְאוּבֵן אֱלִיצוּר בֶּן שְׁדֵיאוּר
לְשִׁמְעוֹן שְׁלֻמִיאֵל בֶּן צוּרִישַׁדָּי
לִיהוּדָה נַחְשׁוֹן בֶּן עַמִּינָדָב לְיִשָּׂשׁכָר
לִישָׂ... נְתַנְאֵל בֶּן צוּעָר לִזְבוּלֻן
אֱלִיאָב בֶּן חֵלֹן לִבְנֵי יוֹסֵף לְאֶפְרַיִם
אֱלִישָׁמָע בֶּן עַמִּיהוּד לִמְנַשֶּׁה גַּמְ
גַּמְלִיאֵל בֶּן פְּדָהצוּר לְבִנְיָמִן אֲבִידָן
בֶּן גִּדְעֹנִי לְדָן אֲחִיעֶזֶר בֶּן עַמִּישַׁדָּי
לְאָשֵׁר פַּגְעִיאֵל בֶּן עָכְרָן לְגָד אֶלְיָסָף
בֶּן דְּעוּאֵל לְנַפְתָּלִי אֲחִירַע
בֶּן עֵינָן אֵלֶּה קְרִיאֵי הָעֵדָה נְשִׂיאֵי
מַטּוֹת אֲבוֹתָם רָאשֵׁי אַלְפֵי יִשְׂרָאֵל
הֵם וַיִּקַּח מֹשֶׁה וְאַהֲרֹן אֵת הָאֲנָשִׁים
הָאֵלֶּה אֲשֶׁר נִקְּבוּ בְּשֵׁמֹת וְאֵת כָּל

לפי חרב ויירש את ארצו מארנן עד
יבק עד בני עמון כי עז גבול בני עמון׃
ויקח ישראל את כל הערים האלה
וישב ישראל בכל ערי האמרי בחשבון
ובכל בנתיה׃ כי חשבון עיר סיחן מלך
האמרי הוא והוא נלחם במלך מואב
הראשון ויקח את כל ארצו מידו עד
ארנן׃ על כן יאמרו המשלים באו
חשבון תבנה ותכונן עיר סיחון׃ כי אש
יצאה מחשבון להבה מקרית סיחן
אכלה ער מואב בעלי במות ארנן׃ אוי
לך מואב אבדת עם כמוש נתן בניו
פליטם ובנתיו בשבית למלך אמרי
סיחון׃ ונירם אבד חשבון עד דיבן
ונשים עד נפח אשר עד מידבא׃ וישב
ישראל בארץ האמרי׃ וישלח משה
לרגל את יעזר וילכדו בנתיה ויירש
את האמרי אשר שם׃ ויפנו ויעלו
דרך הבשן ויצא עוג מלך הבשן
לקראתם הוא וכל עמו למלחמה
אדרעי׃ ויאמר יהוה אל משה אל
תירא אתו כי בידך נתתי אתו ואת כל
עמו ואת ארצו ועשית לו כאשר

לפיתגם דחרבא ויריתו
ישראל ית ארעיה מארנון
עד יובקא עד בני עמון
ארי תקיף תחום בני
עמון׃ ונסיב ישראל ית
כל קרויא האילין ויתב
ישראל בכל קרוי אמוראי
בחשבון ובכל כפרנהא׃
ארי חשבון קרתא
דסיחון מלכא דאמוראי
הוא והוא אגיח קרבא
במלכא דמואב קדמאה
וכבש ית כל ארעיה מן
ידיה עד ארנון׃ על
כן יימרון מתליא עולו
חשבון תתבני ותשתכלל
קרתא דסיחון׃
ארי קידום תקיף כאשא
נפק מחשבון עבדי קרבא
כשלהוביתא מקרתא
דסיחון קטילו עמא דשרן
בלחיית מואב כומריא
דפלחין בית דחלתא רמתא
דארנון׃ ווי לכון מואבאי
אבדתון עמא דפלחין
לכמוש מסר בנוהי עריקין
ובנתיה בשביא למלכא
דאמוראי סיחון׃ ומלכו
פסקת מחשבון עדא
שולטן מדיבן ויצדיאו
עד נפח דסמיך עד
מידבא׃ ויתיב ישראל
בארעא דאמוראי׃
ושלח משה לאללא
ית יעזר וכבשו ית
כפרנהא ותריך ית
אמוראי דתמן׃
ואתפניאו וסליקו אורח
מתנן ונפק עוג מלכא
דמתנן לקדמותהון הוא
וכל עמיה לאגחא קרבא
לאדרעי׃ ואמר יי למשה
לא תדחל מניה ארי
בידך מסרית יתיה וית
כל עמיה וית ארעיה
ותעביד ליה כמא

EXTENT: 401 parchment folios
FORMAT: 195 x 285 mm
BINDING: Vienna Hofbibliothek leather binding with blind and gold tooling, dating from the late Baroque
CONTENT: Torah, Haphtaroth, Megilloth
LANGUAGE: Hebrew (Aramaic)
ILLUSTRATION: figured Masorah (commentaries) and schematic pen drawings (fol. 243v, 244v)
PROVENANCE: The manuscript was formerly in the possession of one "Eliezer" (according to the entry on fol. 1r). Another ownership inscription on fol. 362v does not give a name. According to Schwartz (1925), the codex "probably [came] from the old university library".
SHELFMARK: Vienna, ÖNB, Cod. hebr. 28

unfamiliar spelling, is informed by the notes in the Masorah where else and how often this particular phenomenon occurs, so that he can deliberately preserve the traditional version. The simple presence of the Masorah thus guarantees the integrity of the sacred text.

In addition to the large Masorah, the text is bordered at the top and bottom (and sometimes at the side) by the commentary of the famous Rabbi Solomon ben Isaak ("Rashi", 1040–1105). The Torah is accompanied in the inner margins by the Targum of Onkelos, an Aramaic translation of the Hebrew scripture. This translation may be understood as an elementary commentary and was to be studied weekly in conjunction with the passage from the Torah read out in the synagogue on the Sabbath. Even if the present codex was not actually used in the synagogue, its selection of scriptural texts is based on those recited in the liturgy. Above and below the Targum, written out in a smaller, paler script in the shape of a circle, are more notes on the biblical text.

The ownership inscription on fol. 362v tells the sobering story of someone who saved the manuscript from the flames of a town whose inhabitants were murdered in a pogrom in 1348 (in connection with the plague epidemic of 1348/49?). He himself was able to escape, via Avignon, to Aix, where he was given shelter. In Avignon, which became part of the Papal States that same year, Jews were considered "citizens", and the owner of the manuscript may hence have survived there for some time.

Two readers' notes on the final page (*visto per me Gi[ovanni] Dominico Carretto 1618* on fol. 400v and *Dominico Irosolomi[ta]no 1595* on fol. 401r) point to later users of the manuscript – evidently after the Megilloth had been bound *behind* the Haphtaroth. Domenico Gerosolimitano (*c.* 1552–1621), a Jew born in Palestine who converted to Christianity, lived in Italy and served as a censor of Hebrew books for the Inquisition.

C. L.

Fol. 223v (Numbers): Large Masorah in the shape of a dragon on a slender pedestal.

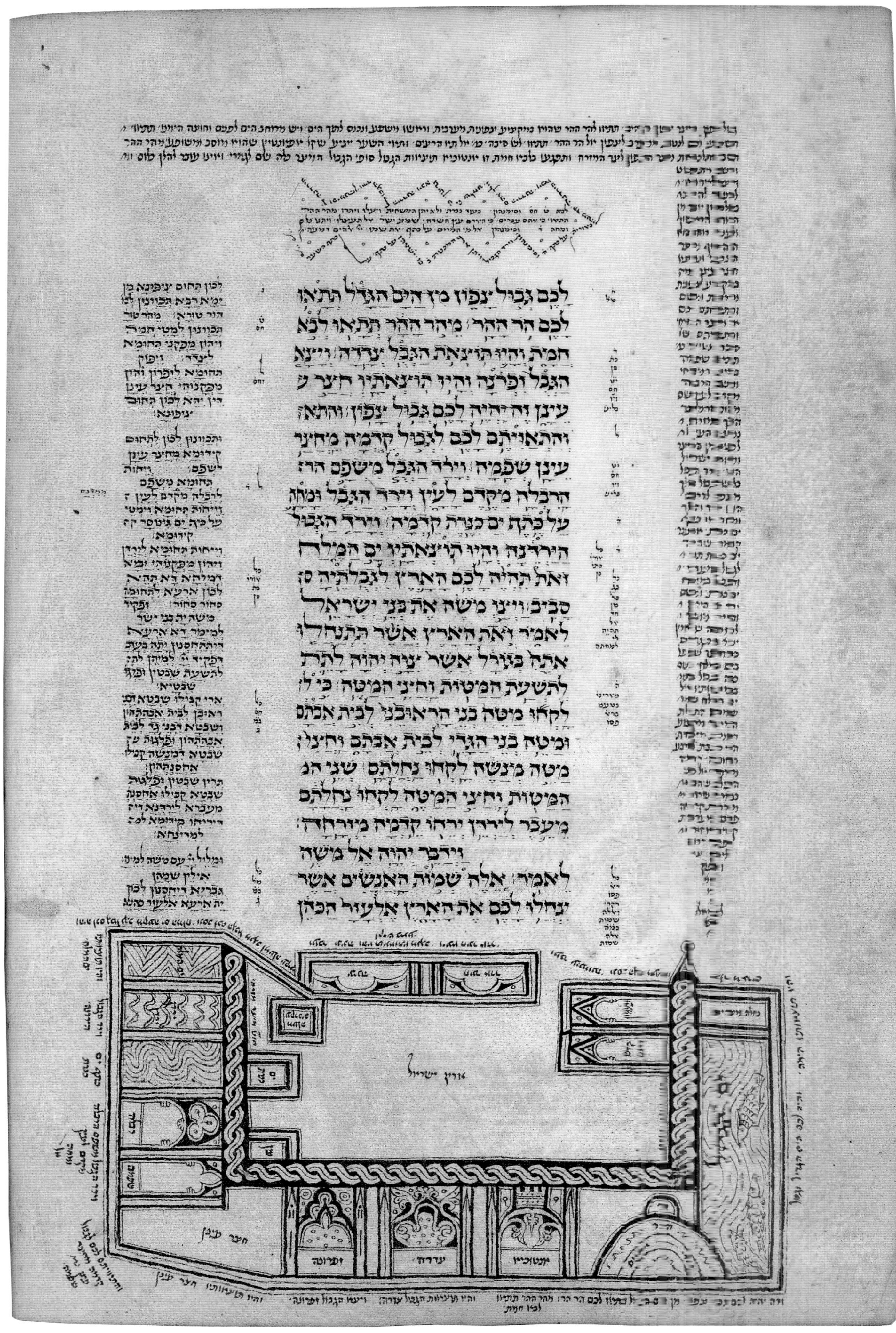

Fol. 244v (Numbers): Drawing of the land of Israel, based primarily on Numbers 34.

▸ **Detail from fol. 102v (Exodus):** Large Masorah in the shape of a dragon.

ויאמר יהוה אל מ
מאנתם לשמר מצו
כי יהוה נתן לכם את
הוא נתן לכם ביום הש
שבו איש תחתיו אל
ממקמו ביום השביע
העם ביום השבעי
ישראל את שמו מן
גד לבן וטעמו כצפי
ויאמר משה זה הד
יהוה מלא העמר מ
לדרתיכם למען יראו
אשר האכלתי אתכם
בהוציאי אתכם מאר
ויאמר משה אל אהר
אחת ותן שמה מלא
והנח אתו לפני יהוה
לדרתיכם כאשר צוה
משה וינחהו אהרן ל

I.2 Vienna Genesis

Region of Syrian Antioch (?), 6th century

The history of Greek Bible illumination currently begins with the Vienna Genesis, which contains the earliest surviving illustrated biblical cycle in codex form. A slightly earlier illuminated Genesis – the Codex Cotton Otho B VI, which dates from the 5th/6th century and is today housed in London – was almost completely destroyed by fire in 1731 and only survives in 129 badly singed fragments.

For Bible manuscript historians, the Vienna Genesis is also the point of departure for a development whose stylistic and iconographic origins cannot be traced to any other surviving manuscript. The inspiration behind its portrayal of successive biblical scenes was probably drawn from a number of quarters: alongside a wide range of heathen sources, Christian motifs could have been adopted from pictorial friezes (such as those in basilicas) or from narrative sequences on tombs or Christian textiles. Although regular attempts are made to explain the heterogeneous nature of the stylistic sources behind the Vienna Genesis in terms of a (now lost) Jewish pictorial tradition, this remains conjecture: no concrete examples of such an art survive, and this line of argument has met with scepticism among experts. The *Vienna Genesis* as a whole has never been cited as the basis for a later manuscript, although its motifs find parallels in Middle-Byzantine ivory reliefs, for example.

The remarkable feature of this manuscript lies in the presentation of its pictures, whereby word and image complement each other. It contains both individual scenes and lengthier cycles (cf. ill. p. 42–43), with pictures being divided into an upper and lower half in order to portray a sequence of events. Successive scenes may equally be found within individual pictures, however. The entire text could be followed from the illustrations alone. The text itself was abridged; different rulings on different folios indi-

Detail from fol. 17r: Joseph in prison with Pharoah's cup-bearer and baker.

► **Detail from fol. 1r:** The Fall in three scenes: Eve and Adam recognize their sin.

EXTENT: 24 parchment folios extant, individually preserved beneath sheets of acrylic glass (also bound with two sheets from another purple codex relating to Luke 24, part of the St Petersburg Codex GPB gr. 537)
FORMAT: 304–326 x 245–265 mm
CONTENT: Genesis 3:4–50:4
LANGUAGE: Greek
MINIATURISTS: A workshop with (at least) 11 contemporary, anonymous miniaturists
ILLUSTRATION: One miniature in the lower half of each page, comprising (with a few exceptions) several scenes in sequence (125 individual scenes in total)
PROVENANCE: The surviving folios may have been brought to Italy (Venice? cf. Cat. IV.2) by Crusaders. In 1662 Archduke Leopold William bequeathed the sheets, which were bound as an appendix to an unspecified Latin codex, to Emperor Leopold I in his will. In 1664 they entered the Vienna Hofbibliothek.
SHELFMARK: Vienna, ÖNB, Cod. theol. gr. 31

cate that, depending on the space available, the text has been shortened to the relevant passages by one or several editors, and then written out by one (of two or three) scribe(s).

With its sumptuous materials (gold and silver ink on purple parchment), the Vienna Genesis marks the inception of the luxury Bible, produced to satisfy the awakening demand amongst the bibliophile aristocracy for aesthetically sophisticated Bible manuscripts. Its lavish format suggests that it was commissioned by a member of the nobility. It is conceivable, too, that it was commissioned by an individual, group or institution for presentation to a social superior, as in the case of the Vienna Dioscurides (Vienna, ÖNB, Cod. med. gr. 1) of AD 512, which was dedicated to Princess Juliana Anicia by the guilds of Honoratae, a district of Constantinople. The lack of all specific reference to this codex in the sources indicates that it must have enjoyed probably a quiet existence in an aristocratic household until passing into Western hands as a prize specimen.

In its present form, the Codex theologicus graecus 31 is just a quarter of its original length; it is calculated that it originally comprised 96 folios, with 192 miniatures illustrating altogether 500 individual scenes. Thorough study of the script and miniatures has revealed that the manuscript was produced in a professional workshop in which calligraphers and miniaturists divided the work between them. The hands of probably 11 miniaturists have been identified in the surviving folios, a number which clearly shows that such luxury manuscripts must have been produced in far higher numbers in those days, presumably in response to much higher demand. Sadly today, just a few examples are all that survive from the era in which production of these sumptuous manuscripts was in full flower, and before it was checked by Persian and Arab conquests.

C. G.

Fol. 2r: The Flood in one scene: Noah's Ark on the waters.

Fol. 3r: God (represented as a hand) makes his covenant with Noah and his sons.

▸ **Detail from fol. 8v:** Abimelech watches Isaac and Rebekah.

▸▸ **Detail from fol. 15r:** Joseph interprets his second dream, in three scenes: Joseph dreaming with the sun and moon; Joseph tells his father and brothers of his dream; the brothers discuss Joseph's dream while watching their flocks.

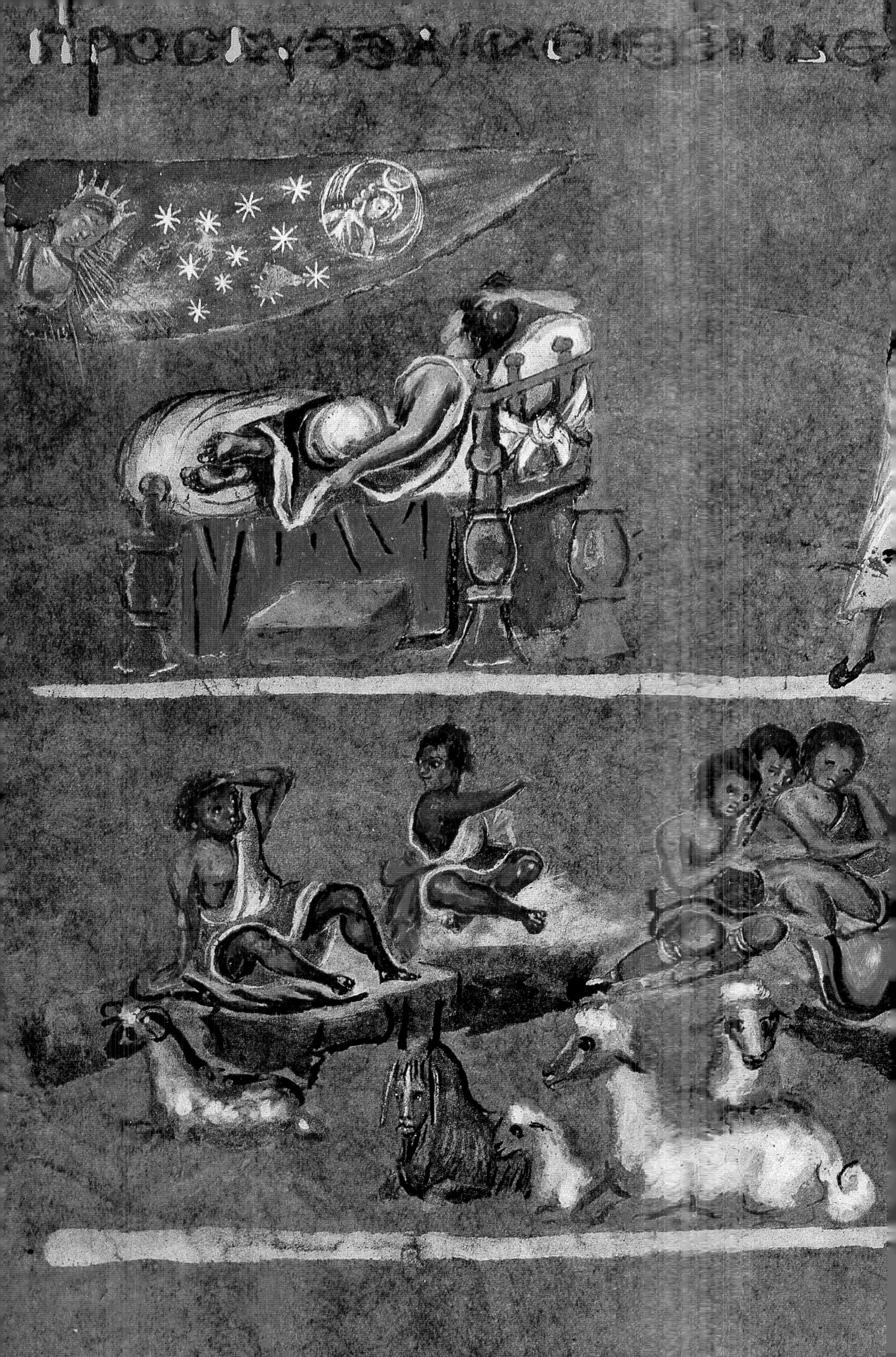

I.3

Greek Gospels and Praxapostolos

Constantinople (?), 1st half of the 14th century

With the consolidation of the Byzantine Empire which succeeded the conquest and appropriation of the city of Constantinople by the Latins (1204–1261), the arts also saw a new flowering, one closely linked with the imperial Palaeologan dynasty (1261–1453). Over the previous decades, and in particular following the seizure of Constantinople by the Crusaders, manuscripts had been plundered and destroyed on a scale whose true extent is impossible to estimate. From their seat of government in Nicaea, the exiled Lascarid emperors (1204–1261) sought to preserve their Byzantine culture and in particular to maintain the tradition of sacred manuscripts, an endeavour in which they were joined by the monasteries.

Following the re-conquest of Constantinople and the return from exile of the emperor and patriarch, book production also underwent a number of changes. The untidy scripts of the 13th century were regulated, for example; popular in theological manuscripts from this era is an "archaizing" style which looks back to the minuscule of the 10th/11th century, a script characterized by clear, even lettering which is attractive to look at and easy to read. During this period, the Hodegon monastery in Constantinople developed its own, easily legible style of writing, the Hodegon style, which survived even after the conquest of Constantinople by the Turks (1453).

The Codex theologicus graecus 300 is a concrete example of such efforts to improve script quality, as demonstrated by the clarity and legibility of its writing and its economic use of abbreviations. Its sumptuous illuminations suggest that the manuscript was produced in a very good workshop, which has been localized to Constantinople. One unusual detail allows us to deduce that the codex was executed in the following sequence: first, the copyist wrote out the scriptural texts, leaving one page at the start of each text free for a full-page miniature. A decorative field – taking up about a quarter of a page – was evidently planned at the beginning of each biblical book, since this

Fol. 134v (St John): St John and his scribe Prochoros, who is taking down the beginning of St John's Gospel ("In the beginning"); above left, a ray of light as a symbol of divine inspiration.

Ο ΑΓ ΠΡΟΧΟΡΟΣ
ΑΓΙΟΣ Ο ΘΕΟ ΛΟΓΟΣ
ΕΝ ΑΡΧΗ

Novum Testamentum
Liber Andreæ Contrarii
Augustissimæ
Bibliothecæ
Cæsareæ
Vindobonensis
Codex manuscriptus
Theologicus Græcus
N.

EXTENT: 361 parchment folios
FORMAT: 189–193 x 137–140 mm
BINDING: Vienna Hofbibliothek parchment cover of 1755 (rebound under praefect Gerard van Swieten, 1745–1772)
CONTENT: Gospels and Praxapostolos
LANGUAGE: Greek
ILLUSTRATION: five full-page miniatures of the Evangelists and the Apostles Peter and Paul

PROVENANCE: An inscription identifies the first owner as Andreas Contrarius (Venice, 15th century); the manuscript was later purchased by Johannes Sambucus (1531–1584; from 1566 councillor, court physician and court historiographer at the Vienna court) for his library; it is documented in the collection of the Hofbibliothek under praefect Sebastian Tengnagel (1608–1636).
SHELFMARK: Vienna, ÖNB, Cod. theol. gr. 300

amount of space has been set aside at the start of all four Gospels and Acts (ill. p. 49). The illuminator has forgotten to fill these fields in, however, and so the tops of these pages remain blank.

In the miniatures depicting the authors of the Gospels, we find a characteristic feature of Byzantine Evangelist portraits, namely a detailed portrayal of all the writing utensils that a copyist in those days would have used. In the portrait of St Mark (ill. p. 48), for example, we can make out on the table a pair of dividers used to mark up the rulings, a pair of scissors for trimming the edges and a knife for cutting the quill nib.

The provenance of the manuscript is particularly interesting. A century after it was produced, it was in the possession of the Italian humanist Andreas Contrarius (born in Venice at the start of the 15th century). Contrarius was in touch not only with the most important representatives of the Italian Renaissance, such as Francesco Barbaro and Lorenzo Valla, but also with the Greek scholars Nikolaos Sagundinos and Theodoros Gaza, and engaged in a dispute with Georgios Trapezuntios. It was probably through Sagundinos that he was familiar with Greek. He may have obtained the present manuscript, in which he had his coat of arms painted as a full-page bookplate on fol. 1r (ill. p. 46), through his contacts with these Greek scholars, more and more of whom were being forced into exile by the Turks. Contrarius is known to have owned other manuscripts, but the present example is thought to have been the only Greek codex in his collection.

C. G.

Fol. 1r: Renaissance coat of arms of Andreas Contrarius (15th century).

▸ **Fol. 58v–59r (St Mark):** Miniature of St Mark the Evangelist, seated at his desk with all his writing instruments (above left, a ray of light as a symbol of divine inspiration), and the beginning of St Mark's Gospel.

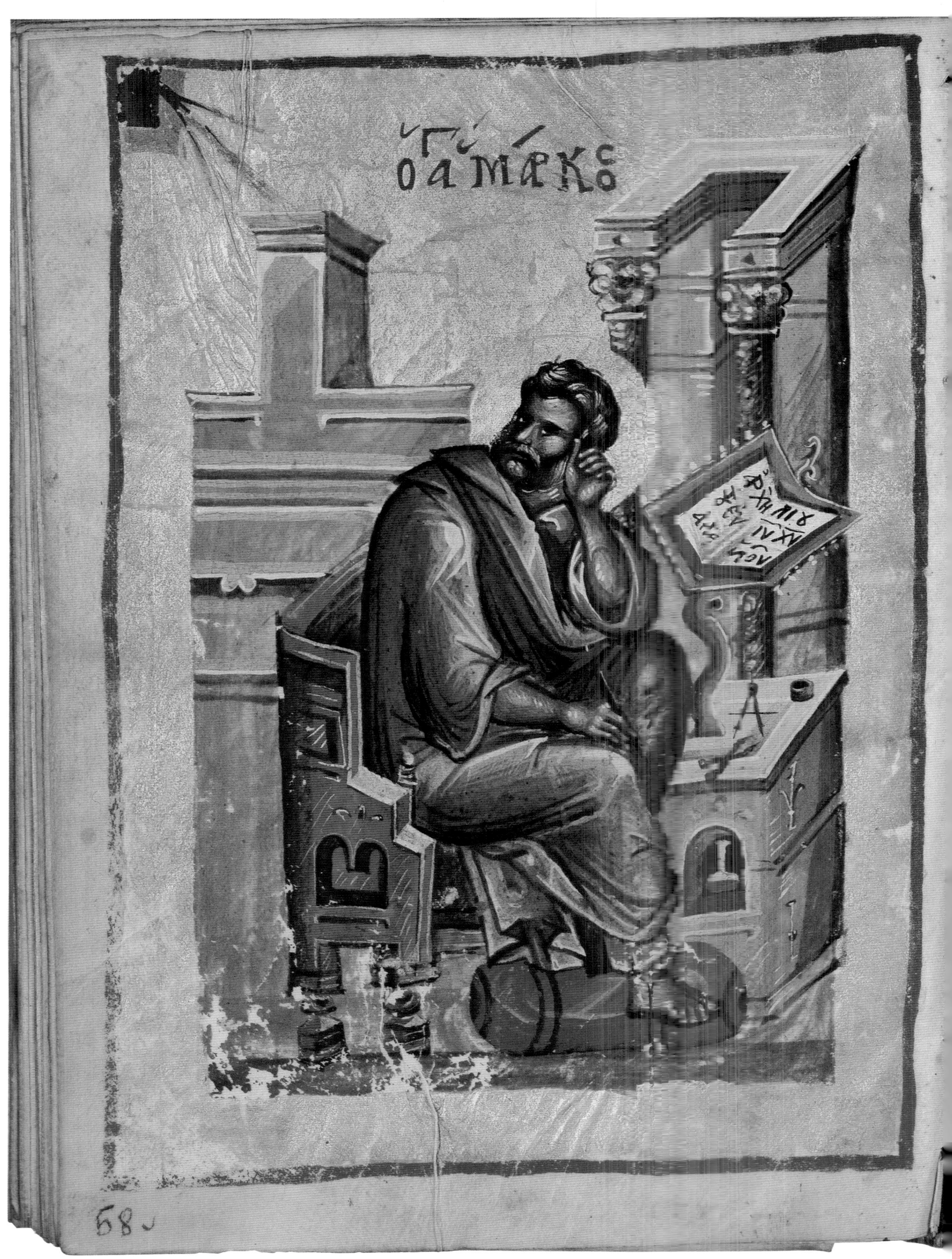

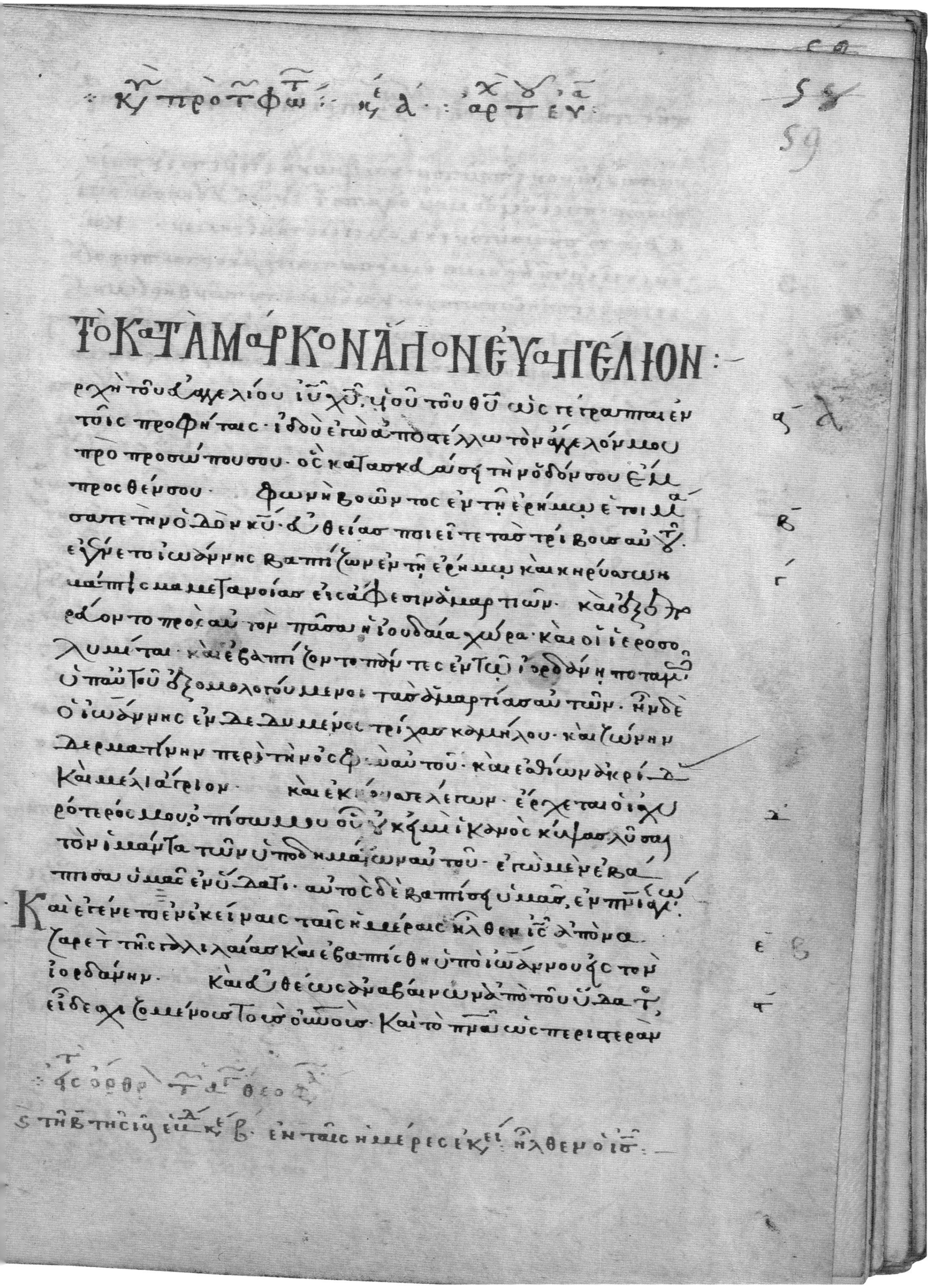

ΤΟ ΚΑΤΑ ΜΑΡΚΟΝ ΑΓΙΟΝ ΕΥΑΓΓΕΛΙΟΝ

ἀρχὴ τοῦ εὐαγγελίου ἰυ̅ χυ̅ υἱοῦ τοῦ θυ̅· ὡς γέγραπται ἐν
τοῖς προφήταις· ἰδοὺ ἐγὼ ἀποστέλλω τὸν ἄγγελόν μου
πρὸ προσώπου σου· ὃς κατασκευάσει τὴν ὁδόν σου ἔμ-
προσθέν σου· φωνὴ βοῶντος ἐν τῇ ἐρήμῳ· ἑτοιμά-
σατε τὴν ὁδὸν κυ̅· εὐθείας ποιεῖτε τὰς τρίβους αὐτοῦ.
ἐγένετο ἰωάννης βαπτίζων ἐν τῇ ἐρήμῳ καὶ κηρύσσων
βάπτισμα μετανοίας εἰς ἄφεσιν ἁμαρτιῶν· καὶ ἐξεπο-
ρεύοντο πρὸς αὐτὸν πᾶσα ἡ ἰουδαία χώρα· καὶ οἱ ἱεροσο-
λυμῖται· καὶ ἐβαπτίζοντο πάντες ἐν τῷ ἰορδάνῃ ποταμῷ
ὑπ' αὐτοῦ ἐξομολογούμενοι τὰς ἁμαρτίας αὐτῶν· ἦν δὲ
ὁ ἰωάννης ἐνδεδυμένος τρίχας καμήλου· καὶ ζώνην
δερματίνην περὶ τὴν ὀσφὺν αὐτοῦ· καὶ ἐσθίων ἀκρίδας
καὶ μέλι ἄγριον· καὶ ἐκήρυσσε λέγων· ἔρχεται ὁ ἰσχυ-
ρότερός μου ὀπίσω μου οὗ οὐκ εἰμὶ ἱκανὸς κύψας λῦσαι
τὸν ἱμάντα τῶν ὑποδημάτων αὐτοῦ· ἐγὼ μὲν ἐβά-
πτισα ὑμᾶς ἐν ὕδατι· αὐτὸς δὲ βαπτίσει ὑμᾶς ἐν πνι̅ ἁγίῳ.
Καὶ ἐγένετο ἐν ἐκείναις ταῖς ἡμέραις ἦλθεν ἰς̅ ἀπὸ να-
ζαρὲτ τῆς γαλιλαίας καὶ ἐβαπτίσθη ὑπὸ ἰωάννου εἰς τὸν
ἰορδάνην· καὶ εὐθέως ἀναβαίνων ἀπὸ τοῦ ὕδατος
εἶδε σχιζομένους τοὺς οὐρανούς· καὶ τὸ πνα̅ ὡσεὶ περιστερὰν

I.4

Carolingian Bible (also known as the Rado Bible)

Northern France (?), 2nd third of the 9th century

Codex 1190 is also referred to in the literature as the Rado Bible, but this name derives from a misconception. The text of the Bible is preceded by two poems (fol. 16r–16v) composed by Alcuin, abbot (796–804) of St Martin's Abbey in Tours. Due to an error in the transcription on fol. 16v, the text was believed to mention one Rado, who was identified with Abbot Rado of St Vaast (795–815) in Arras in France. The codex was correspondingly assumed to date from the period around 800. In fact, however, the manuscript was only compiled in the 2nd third of the 9th century. The original upon which its text and illustration are based has been identified as a two-volume Bible (Cod. lat. 45 and 93 in the Bibliothèque Nationale de France, Paris) written between 820 and 840 in a Paris abbey, perhaps St Denis. It is therefore likely that Codex 1190, too, was produced in northern France.

The illustration of the manuscript consists of initials and canon tables. Eight large initials in gold, yellow, green, red and brown are found at the beginning of biblical books (ill. p. 50). The initials are filled and embroidered primarily with interlace; in one initial *Q(uoniam)* on fol. 250r, the descender has been replaced by a bird grasping a fish in its claws (ill. p. 51). The 48 small initials are decorated with foliate motifs, interlace and other patterns (stepping and zigzag) but are not coloured. The decorative architectural surround framing the canon tables is similarly executed in pen only (fol. 237v–238r).

In its conception as a single volume, the present Bible illustrates how the production of pandects at Tours influenced other abbeys. The text of the Bible itself, however, exhibits a number of different influences, which have yet to be fully explained. Although efforts had been continuing since the time of Charlemagne (747–814) to arrive at a correct, standardized biblical text, the Bibles of the Carolingian era demonstrate a

Detail from fol. 18r (Genesis): Initial *I(n principio)* opening the Book of Genesis.

▸ **Detail from fol. 250r (St Luke):** Initial *Q(uoniam)* at the start of St Luke's Gospel.

non crediderunt. Post haec autem duobus
ex eis ambulantibus ostensus est in alia effigie
euntibus in villam & illi euntes nuntiaverunt
ceteris. nec illis crediderunt. Novissime re-
cumbentibus illis undecim. apparuit & ex-
probravit incredulitatem illorū & duritiā
cordis. Quia his qui viderant eum resurrex-
isse non crediderunt. Et dixit eis. euntes
in mundum universum praedicate evangelium omni creaturae. Qui crediderit & bap-
tizatus fuerit salvus erit. Qui vero non
crediderit condēpnabitur. Signa autem
eos qui crediderint haec sequentur. In nomine meo daemonia eicient linguis loquentur
novis serpentes tollent. Et si mortiferū
quid biberint non eis nocebit. Super egros
manus inponent & bene habebunt.
II Et dns quidem ihs postquam locutus est eis.
assumptus ē in caelum & sedit a dextris dī
I Illi autem profecti praedicaverunt ubique
dno cooperante & sermonem confirman-
te sequentibus signis.

LUCAS SYRUS ANTHIOCENSIS

arte medicus discipulus apostolorum postea
paulum secutus usq; ad passionē ei serviens dno
sine crimine. nam neque uxorem umquam
habens. neque filios. LXXIIII annorum obiit
in bithynia plenus spu sco. qui cum iam scripta essent evangelia p mattheum quidem in
iudea. p marcum autē in italia. sco instigan-
te spu in achaiae partibus hoc scripsit evangelium. significans etiam ipse in principio
ante alia esse descripta. cui extra ea quae
ordo evangelicae dispositionis exposcit. ea
maxime necessitas laboris fuit ut primū
graecis fidelibus omni prophetatione ventu-
ri in carne di xpi manifestata humanitas
ne iudaicis fabulis attenti. in solo legis de-
siderio tenerentur. Ne vel hereticis fabulis & stultis sollicitationibus seducti
excederent a veritate. elaboraret dehinc
ut in principio evangelii iohannis nativi-
tate praesumpta cui evangelium scriberet

in dno pleno. & filio proditionis extinc-
to oratione ab apostolis facta sorte
dni electionis numerus compleretur.
Sicq; paulus consummationē apostolicis
actibus daret quem diu contra stimu-
lo recalcitrantē dns elegisset. quod
legentibus ac requirentibus dm & si p
singula expediri a nobis utile fuerat
sciens tamen quod operantem agricolā
oporteat de fructibus suis edere. vitavi-
mus publicā curiositatem ne non tam
volentibus dm videremur. quam fasti-
dientibus prodidisse.

EXPLICIT PREFATIO

INCIPIT EVANGELIUM SECUNDUM LUCAM

UM

IN NOMINE XPI

UETUS TESTAMENTUM

ideo dicitur quia ueniente nouo cessa-
uit; de quo apostolus meminit dicens;
uetera transierunt. Ecce facta sunt
noua; Testamentum autem nouum
ideo nuncupatur. quia innouat;
non enim illud dicunt nisi homines
renouati ex uetustate per gratiam
& pertinentes iam ad testamentum
nouum quod est regnum caelorum;
hæbrei autem uetus testamentum
ezra auctore iuxta numerum
literarum suarum in xxii duos libros acci-
piunt. diuidentes eos in tres ordines;

legis scilicet & prophetarum. & agiographorum; Primus ordo legis in quinque libris accipitur. quorum primus e[st]
q[uo]d e[st] genesis; Secund[us] hellesmoht. quod est exodus; Tertius uagecra. quod est leuiticus; Quartus uagedaber. quod e[st] nume[ri]
quintus elleaddabarim. quod est deuteronomium; Hi sunt quoque libri moysi. Quos et ebrei thora latini legem appellant
Proprie autem lex appellatur. quae per moysen data est; secundus ordo est prophetarum in quo continentur libri octo; quorum primus. iosue bennun. qui latine dicitur iesu naue; secundus sopthim. quod est iudicum; Tertius samuhel. quod e[st] re[gum]
primus; Quartus malachim. quod est regum secundus; Quintus esaias; Sextus hieremias; Septimus ezechihel; Octauus taresra. qui dicitur duodecim prophetarum; qui libri quia sibi pro breuitate adiuncti sunt pro uno accipiuntur; Tertius est ordo agiograforum. id est sca scribentium. in quo sunt libri nouem; Quorum primus iob; Secundus nabla. q[uo]d e[st]
psalterium; Tertius maloth. quod est prouerbia salomonis; Quartus coeleth. quod est ecclesiastes; Quintus sirasirim. quod e[st] can-
tica canticorum; Sextus danihel; Septimus dabreiamin. Quod e[st] uerba dierum. id est paralipomenon; Octa[uus]
ezras; Nonus hester; qui simul omnes. quinque. octo. & nouem fiunt uiginti duo. sicut superius conprehensi sunt; Quidam au[tem]
ruth & cinoth. quod latine dicitur lamentatio hieremie agiografis adiciunt & xxiiii uolumina testamenti ueteris
faciunt iuxta uiginti iiii seniores qui ante conspectum di assistunt; Quartus est apud nos ordo ueteris testam[enti]

eorum librorum qui in canone hebraico
non sunt; quorum primus. sapientiae liber est;
Secundus. ecclesiasticus; Tertius tobi;
Quartus iudith; Quintus & sextus
machabeorum; Quos libros iudei int[er]
agiografa separant; ecclesia tamen xpi
inter diuinas scripturas & honorat & p[rae]-
dicat; in nouo autem testamento duo sunt
ordines; primus euangelicus. in quo sunt matheus
marcus lucas iohannes; secundus
apostolicus. in quo sunt paulus in xiiii epistolis.
petrus in duabus. iohannes in tribus.
iacobus & iudas in singulis. actus apostolorum
& apocalipsis; summa autem utriusque
testamenti diuisio trifarie distinguitur. id est
in historia. in moribus. in allegoria. rursus
ista tria multifarie diuiduntur. id est
quid a deo. quid ab angelis uel hominibus gestum
dictum quis sit. quid prophetae pronuntiauerint
de xpo & corpore eius; quid de diabolo &
membris ipsius. quid de ueteri & nouo
populo quid de presenti saeculo & futuro regno
atque iudicio

Libros autem sacrarum
scripturarum
quos prescri[psimus]

EXTENT: 292 parchment folios
FORMAT: 365 x 225 mm
BINDING: white leather with blind tooling over wooden covers (Vienna 1707)
CONTENT: Bible (Old and New Testament)
LANGUAGE: Latin
ILLUSTRATION: eight large and 48 small initials and canon tables

PROVENANCE: The manuscript was in Bohemia in the 12th century, and by some unknown route subsequently entered the Vienna Hofbibliothek, where it is documented from 1576 onwards.
SHELFMARK: Vienna, ÖNB, Cod. 1190

confusing variety, not just in the sources on which their individual books are based but also in the order in which they are presented. Alongside the Vulgate, the Latin translation of the Bible completed by St Jerome (*c.* 347–419), we also find elements of the so-called *Vetus Latina*, an Old-Latin version of the Bible, translated from the Greek, which had been in use since the 2nd century but which from the 5th century onwards was gradually superseded by the Vulgate. Since scriptural texts such as the Pentateuch (the first five books of the Bible, i. e. Genesis to Deuteronomy), the Book of Psalms and the Gospels were also available as separate codices, and since it appears that every available text was consulted when preparing a complete Bible, it was possible for very different traditions to find their way into the final manuscript. Thus the organization of the books of the Old Testament in Codex 1190 reveals parallels with a group of Spanish Bibles, while that of the books of the New Testament corresponds to Bibles from Tours. The two Old Testament books of Tobit and Judith, meanwhile, which follow the old-Latin translation, are probably derived from a local, northern French source.

The subsequent history of the manuscript can be reconstructed from annotations found in the text. In the latter third of the 9th century it was probably in Corbie, which in the 11th century lay in the German-speaking realm. In the first half of the 12th century, a member of the Orthodox Church made notes in Czecho-Church Slavonic on a list of readings on folios 239v to 247v; the manuscript must therefore have been in a Bohemian monastery at that time. How it subsequently made its way into the Vienna Hofbibliothek is unknown.

F. S.

Fol. 17v: List of the books of the Old Testament.

I.5

Parisian Pocket Bible

France, middle of the 13th century

At the start of the 13th century, there appeared in Paris a handy type of Bible which proved so popular that, within just a few decades, hundreds of copies were being produced. These "pocket Bibles" played a central role in promulgating a new version of the Bible that was establishing itself between 1200 and 1230 in university circles in Paris. This version can be recognized amongst other things by its inclusion of the Prayer of Manasseh after the 2nd Book of Chronicles and of the so-called *Interpretation of Hebrew names*, an alphabetical dictionary giving the Latin meanings of the Hebrew proper names. Its production no longer lay in the hands of monastic scriptoria, but was organized by booksellers. Having had the Bibles – of which the pocket-size editions were in particular demand – copied out by scribes, these booksellers then passed many of them on to illuminators, who kept to a specific format in their illustrations, as can be seen in the two examples in the Austrian National Library: the biblical books and most of the prologues begin with initials in gold, blue, dark red, red, pink, green, white and gold. Areas of skin are rendered in a pale colour, and the faces in Codex 1151 have been given rosy cheeks (fol. 1r). Initials, figures, the internal fields of initials and foliate branches are outlined in black, while white lines and ornamentation offer a lively contrast to the dark colours. The number of initials containing pictorial fields varies from Bible to Bible: in Codices 1150 and 1151, the prologue to Genesis and the beginning of Genesis itself (ill. p. 56) are visually emphasized in this way, as is also the beginning of the Book of Proverbs in Codex 1150. Ornamental initials and *fleuronnée* initials serve to announce the beginning of the remaining books, the start of prologues and the start of new chapters.

Detail from fol. 2r: Initial with St Jerome, author of the prologue to Genesis.

► **Fol. 1v:** Miniature of the Creation from the beginning of the 16th century.

xiiii in zacharia. Quartum in prouerbi-
is. Quintum eque in ysaia. Quod
multi ignorantes apocriforum delira-
menta sectantur, et hiberas neni-
as libris autenticis preferunt. Causas
erroris non est meum exponere. Iudei prudenti factum dicunt esse consi-
lio, ne ptolomeus unius dei cultor etiam
apud hebreos duplicem divinitatem
comprehenderet. Quod maxime idcirco
faciebant quia in platonis dogma cadere videbatur. Denique ubi-
cumque sacratum aliquid scriptu-
ra testatur de patre et filio et spiritu sancto
aut aliter interpretati sunt aut omni-
no tacuerunt, ut et regi satisface-
rent et archanum fidei non vulgarent.
Et nescio quis primus auctor .lxx.
cellulas alexandrie mendacio suo
extruxerit, quibus divisi eadem scriptitarent, cum aristeus eiusdem
ptholomei yperaspistes et non
multo post tempore iosephus nichil tale retulerint, sed in una basilica congregatos contulisse scribant,
non prophetasse. Aliud enim est vatem,
aliud esse interpretem. Ibi spiritus
ventura predicat; hic eruditio et verborum copia ea que intelligit
transfert. Nisi forte putandus est
tullius economicum xenofontis
et platonis pitagoram et demostenis prothesiphontem afflatus rethorico spiritu transtulisse. Aut aliter
de eisdem libris per .lxx. interpretes,
aliter per apostolos spiritus sanctus
testimonia texuit, ut quod illi tacuerunt hii scriptum esse mentiti sunt.
Quid igitur? damnamus veteres? Minime. Sed post priorum studia in domo
domini quod possumus laboramus.
Illi interpretati sunt ante adventum christi, et quod nesciebant dubiis protulere sententiis. Nos post passionem eius et resurrectionem eius
non tam prophetiam quam hystoriam
scribimus. Aliter enim audita, aliter visa narrantur. Quod melius

intelligimus, melius et proferimus.
Audi igitur emule; obtrectator ausculta.
Non damno, non reprehendo .lxx. sed confidenter
cunctis illis apostolos prefero. Per istorum os michi christus sonat, quos ante
prophetas inter spiritualia carismata c.x.xii
posita lego, in quibus ultimum
pene gradum interpretes tenent.
Quid livore torqueris? Quid imperitorum animos contra me concitas?
Sicubi in translatione tibi videor
errare, interroga hebreos, diversarum
urbium magistros consule. Quod illi
habent de christo tui codices non habent.
Aliud est si contra se postea ab apostolis usurpata testimonia probaverunt,
et emendatiora sunt exempla-
ria latina quam greca, greca quam
hebrea. Verum hec contra invidos. Nunc
te deprecor desideri karissime, ut qui michi
tantum opus subire fecisti et a genesi exordium capere, orationibus
iuves, quo possim eodem spiritu quo
scripti sunt libri in latinum eos
transferre sermonem.

In principio creavit
deus celum et terram.
Terra autem erat inanis et vacua, et tenebre erant super
faciem abyssi, et spiritus domini
ferebatur super aquas. Dixitque
deus: Fiat lux. Et facta est lux. Et vidit lucem quod esset bona, et divisit
lucem a tenebris. Appellavitque
lucem diem et tenebras noctem. Factumque est vespere et mane dies unus. Dixit quoque deus:
Fiat firmamentum in medio
aquarum, et dividat aquas
ab aquis. Et fecit deus firmamentum, divisitque aquas que
erant sub firmamento ab
hiis que erant super firmamentum.
Et factum est ita. Vocavitque deus
firmamentum celum. Et factum est
vespere et mane dies secundus. Dixit
vero deus: Congregentur aque
que sub celo sunt in locum unum

EXTENT: 611 parchment folios
FORMAT: 140 x 95 mm
BINDING: worn black-velvet binding dating from the 16th century
CONTENT: Bible (Old and New Testament, without the Book of Psalms), alphabetical dictionary giving the Latin meanings of the Hebrew names
LANGUAGE: Latin
ILLUSTRATION: one full-page miniature (16th century), three historiated initials, 74 ornamental initials, numerous *fleuronnée* initials
PROVENANCE: In the second half of the 16th century (?) the Bible reached the Damenstift in Hall (Tyrol). In 1783, following the closure of the foundation, it passed to the Hofbibliothek in Vienna.
SHELFMARK: Vienna, ÖNB, Cod. 1150

The English philosopher and theologian Roger Bacon († 1292) bemoaned the inaccuracy of this new Bible put out by Parisian theologians and booksellers, but such criticism did not stop the pocket-size version, in particular, from selling rapidly. Who bought these tiny Bibles, and why demand for them should decline after 1300, are questions on which we can only speculate, since these Bibles rarely contain coats of arms or the names of their first owners. Having issued from the sphere of the university, they would certainly have been bought by teachers and students. Their small format must also have appealed to the monks of mendicant orders, since it meant they could carry the Bibles with them when they left the convent to go out and preach. An indication that the Bibles were indeed employed in this way lies in the fact that a number of them contain liturgical calendars for use by such orders. The early owners of pocket Bibles probably also included wealthy members of the laity, however, who used the text originally designed for theologians and priests for their own private worship, either in place of their existing psalters or in addition to them (the Book of Psalms is absent in some of these Bibles, as in the case of Codex 1150). It is therefore possible that the decline in demand for pocket Bibles was linked with the rise, towards the end of the 13th century, of more user-friendly Books of Hours, compendia of scriptural texts organized into daily devotions for ordinary people to recite at home. These Books of Hours would succeed the pocket Bible as the new and unrivalled best-seller.

Although the production of small Bibles declined after 1300, existing copies continued to be prized. In the 16th century the Bibles of Codices 1150 and 1151 were given new bindings by their owners, and an opening miniature was added to Codex 1150 (ill. p. 55). In the case of Codex 1151, it was probably the priest David Vischer, to whom the book belonged in 1565, who added the missing pagination and the information on the index tabs.

C. B.

Fol. 5v (Genesis): The blessing of creation on the 7th day. The separation of the earth and the water. The creation of Adam.

II. Magnificence and grandeur – Luxury Bible manuscripts

Luxury Bible manuscripts date back to late antiquity and the earliest surviving parchment codices. Their sumptuous format was intended to reflect their importance and was tailored to their function either for private or "public", ceremonial use. At the focal point of the artistic programme stood the Bible codex representing its own complex textual tradition whose form was determined by the size of the page, the materials used, the carefulness of the script and – here most important of all – the illustration.

Depending upon the artistic trend they embody, the illuminations in these luxury manuscripts are characterized by a delight in narrative detail and a striving for realism or – where the emphasis is different – by abstract, ornamental, decorative elements. The gamut of design options spanned by Bibles from the earliest times to the Late Gothic is very broad: from being restricted solely to first letters, the decoration may start from one initial and spread across the whole page, or may illustrate the text in pictorial cycles which unfold within separate, framed miniatures.

In pre-Romanesque times, single-volume pandects bringing together the complete holy scriptures are rare. The luxury manuscripts of late antiquity, written predominantly in Latin, Greek and Syrian, contain for the most part individual biblical books, sometimes combined into groups. The most important example of this type of manuscript is the Vienna Genesis (Cat. I.2). Its use of purple parchment, its writing executed in gold and silver ink and its comprehensive cycle of illustrations identify it as a luxury manuscript conceived as a pictorial codex. The second famous Genesis codex from late antiquity, the Cotton Genesis (London, British Library), is indirectly represented in another manuscript housed in Vienna, the *Histoire universelle* (Cat. IV.2), and its cycle of illustrations also found an echo in the mosaics of San Marco in Venice (13th century).

Neapolitan Luxury Bible, Cod. 1191, detail from fol. 8v (Genesis): Decorative border.

▸ Wenceslas Bible, Cod. 2759, detail from fol. 2r: King Wenceslas and Queen Sophia (?), flanked by the coats of arms of the Holy Roman Empire and Bohemia. (Balaam Master)

ten · Sunder gleich als vns schrei
bet da · Der heiligen schrift hystori
a · Also wil ich euch schencken · V
Vnd mit vreuden trencken ·

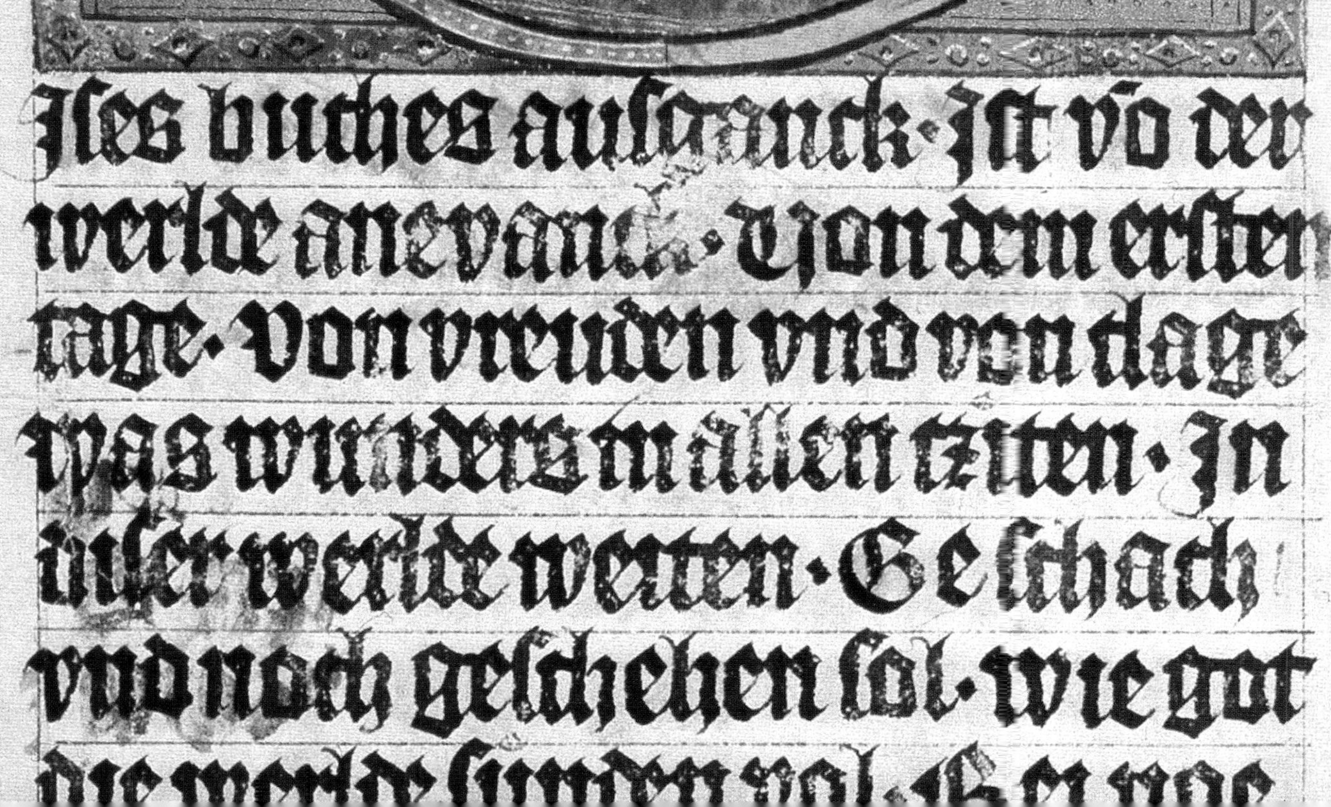

Dises buches ausganck · Ist vō der
werlde anevanck · Von dem ersten
tage · Von vreuden vnd von clage
Was wunders in allen ziten · In
diser werlde weiten · Geschach
vnd noch geschehen sol · wie got
die werlde schuffen sol · ...

The next milestone in the history of luxury Bibles documented here is represented by the pandects produced in Tours abbey in western France during the Carolingian era. The attention paid to the overall artistic design of such codices, combined in Tours with a concern for textual accuracy, may be seen against the backdrop of the Christian kingship of Charlemagne and his patronage of learning and the arts.

The imposing, almost monumental appearance of the Tours Bibles and the design of their text and decoration, in turn provide the point of departure for a path that leads via the large-format Bibles produced in Italy from around 1050 to the so-called Giant Bibles of the Romanesque era. While fragments from Southern Germany and Austria continue to show the influence of their Italian forebears, the Admont Giant Bible (Cat. II.1), which survives almost fully intact, already reveals a largely independent, regional style, making it one of the major works of Romanesque manuscript illumination from the Salzburg area.

Sumptuously illuminated Bibles were also in fashion amongst the Cistercians, otherwise so ascetic in their attitude towards art. After Abbot Stephen Harding († 1134), one of the founders of the Cistercian Order, had one such Bible made in Cîteaux at the start of the 12th century, a number of luxury Bible manuscripts were produced by this Order. The Lilienfeld Bible presented here (Cat. II.2), which despite its "late" date remains firmly rooted in the Romanesque tradition, also aspired to the status of luxury manuscript, as evidenced by the lavish illumination of the initial *I* at the start of Genesis, which fills the whole page (ill. p. 72).

The assimilation of influences from Upper Italian manuscript illumination, coupled with the impact of the Gothic Bibles issuing from France gave rise to new forms of decoration, as already evident in the Krems Bible (Cat. II.3) which arose towards the end of the 13th century. The wider possibilities of Gothic manuscript illumination announce themselves in the relationship between the decorative elements and the text, as the ornamentation of the initials spills across the margins of the page and into the gaps between the columns.

Of decisive importance for the further development of Gothic Bible illumination were the revisions to the Bible undertaken at the university in Paris at the start of the 13th century, since these resulted in the first standardization of the complete Bible. The introductory initial *I* at the start of the Book of Genesis, with its portrayal of the work of Creation, could now advance – despite its relatively small format – to the status of magnificent "frontispiece" to the Holy Writ. Illuminated initials generally marked the start of the biblical books, which were now arranged in set order, while subordinate *fleuronnée* decoration identified the beginning of each chapter.

Highlighting the initials in this way was primarily intended to make it easier to find specific passages in the text. At the same time, however, such initials provided a setting for the most important biblical scenes. Over the course of the 14th century in particular in art north of the Alps, initials increased in complexity and size, and their arabesque extensions provided room for coats of arms and even alternative worlds of miniature figures or scenes from everyday life (drolleries). South of the Alps narrative scenes were popularly staged not only in historiated initials, but also in square miniatures (Cat. II.6), which were often added in the lower margin.

Luxury Bibles were commissioned on both sides of the Alps by members of the royal courts. In the 14th century, moreover, the European aristocracy's desire for self-aggrandizement and its bibliophilic passion for collecting encouraged the invention of extensive pictorial programmes of the highest quality. Vast cycles of miniatures thereby interweave the history of Salvation with a history of the world in which every ruler takes his divinely ordained place. This naturally demanded new pictorial formulae, for which artists, as it has been shown, turned to chronicles of world history.

When, around 1390, work was proceeding in the imperial capital of Prague on the large German Bible for King Wenceslas IV (Cat. II.4), the dissemination of the vernacular translations of the Bible that had arisen as part of the *Devotio moderna* movement had already been banned. Wenceslas' German-language luxury Bible might thus have become, for the first time, a statement of opposition to the Church authorities by a *Rex Romanorum*. It remained unfinished, however.

Over the course of the 15th century, commissions for luxury Bibles increasingly came from prosperous merchants and burghers (Cat. II.5 and II.8). Although the decorative schemes employed in these codices were more modest than those of luxury Bibles destined for the aristocracy, they economized neither on materials nor on the quality of their execution and drew their inspiration from current trends in Flemish and Italian art. Even after Gutenberg started bringing out the first printed Bibles as from 1453/54, handwritten and skilfully illuminated parchment Bibles continued to be produced for many years (Cat. II.9), and illustrations added to printed books. Only towards 1480 was the transition to Bibles produced entirely by typography more or less complete.

A. F. / M. T.

Eberler Bible, Cod. 2769, detail from fol. 171r Chronicles, Prologoue): Depiction of a battle.

Neapolitan Luxury Bible, detail from fol. 1r: St Jerome, dressed in a grey monk's habit, at his desk.

II.1 Admont Giant Bible

Salzburg, around the middle of the 12th century

As in the case of liturgical manuscripts used in services, faithful transmission of the text was a central concern of Bibles. The correction of errors that had resulted from careless transcription or the use of unauthorized sources, coupled with the desire for a modern edition of the text, often made it necessary to alter the existing version. So too in the Admont Giant Bible, in which several sets of changes can be identified. One such set of alterations was probably carried out immediately after the manuscript was first copied: entire passages of text were erased and rewritten (i.e. written over) or corrected in the margin. The same is true of the division of the Bible into individual chapters. The original divisions of the Romanesque manuscript were substituted in the 13th century for a system which can be traced back to the English theologian Stephen Langton (*c.* 1150/55–1228). Even in the case of such a magnificent codex as the Admont Giant Bible, the fact that such alterations impaired the aesthetic appearance of the manuscript was accepted for the sake of having a correct and up-to-date text.

Like other comparable Bibles of this type, the present codex was probably commissioned by a high-ranking individual or – and there are countless examples of this – by a "pool" of donors, and presented to a specific religious institution. Such commissions were frequently prompted by the founding of new monasteries and nunneries.

For whom this magnificent manuscript was originally composed has not yet been established with certainty. Hymns added in the margins have led some researchers (Mezey [1981]) to propose a Cistercian order; historical arguments speak in favour of the Cistercian abbey of Heiligenkreuz in Lower Austria. In its foundation phase, this abbey maintained links with Hungary, where the manuscript was later held. On the basis of

Detail from fol. 241v (Jonah): Historiated initial *I*(*onas*) in the Prologue to the Book of Jonah. Jonah is escaping from the whale.

▸ **Fol. 3v (Genesis):** The story of Creation in six pictorial fields: the Fall of Lucifer and the Creation of light (1st day of Creation). Creation of the firmament (2nd day of Creation). Creation of the sun, moon and stars (4th day of Creation). Separation of the land and the seas (3rd day of Creation). Creation of the fishes and the birds (5th day of Creation). Creation of the first people and the beasts of the earth (6th day of Creation).

INCIPIT PROLOGUS IOHELIS PROPH(ETAE).

IOHEL FILIUS fatuel. DESCRIBIT TERRA(M) XII. tribuu(m) eruca. brucho. locusta. rubigine uastan(ti)b(us) consumptam: post euersione(m) prioris p(o)p(u)li. effusuru(m) sp(iritu)m s(an)c(tu)m sup(er) seruos d(e)i et ancillas: id e(st) sup(er) centu(m) xx. credentiu(m) nomina effusuru(m) in cenaculo syon. q(ui) centu(m) xx. ab uno usq(ue) ad quindeci(m) paulatim et p(er) incrementa surgentes: xv. graduu(m) numeru(m) efficiunt. q(ui) in psalterio mystice canentur. Exp(licit) p(rologus) IOHEL PROPHETE.

INCIPIT IOHEL PROPHETA.

VERBUM DNI QUOD FACTUM EST AD IOHEL FILIUM fatuel. Audite hoc senes. et aurib(us)

236v

EXTENT: 262 (volume 1) and 234 (volume 2) parchment folios
FORMAT: 560 x 400 mm
BINDING: Baroque leather binding by Admont Abbey (dated 1737); stamped decoration (single stamps and rollers)
CONTENT: Bible (Old and New Testament)
LANGUAGE: Latin
ILLUSTRATION: more than 130 foliate initials, predominantly executed in gold and silver; canon arches; 44 miniatures
PROVENANCE: From western Hungary, the manuscript reached the Benedictine abbey of Admont in Styria at the latest in the 15th century. In 1937 it was purchased from the monastery for the National Library.
SHELFMARK: Vienna, ÖNB, Cod. Ser. n. 2701

notes added to the Psalter, however, it is clear that the Bible was still employed in the Romanesque era for specific liturgical functions and was not just a treasury showpiece.

Despite the lack of certainty surrounding its first owner, it can be confidently shown that, relatively soon after its completion, the manuscript was being used in the Benedictine monastery of St Peter's in Csatár in western Hungary. There, a copy of the foundation charter, a list of relics, and records of donations to the monastery were all added to its pages. After being pawned and deposited in the neighbouring abbey of St Adrian's in Zala (Zalavár), the trail of the manuscript goes cold, and only resurfaces with certainty in the 15th century. An inscription added during this period indicates that it was the property of the Benedictine Admont Abbey.

The most striking aspect of the Bible, apart from its size, is its sumptuous illumination, characterized by initials in gold and silver and large miniatures (ill. p. 64). Almost the size of a panel painting, it recalls works of monumental painting. Inconsistencies and discrepancies in its overall decorative scheme may be the result of changes to the original aesthetic programme. The type of decoration and the style of the initials and miniatures bring the work into line with other illustrated Giant Bibles from the region of southern Germany/Austria. The Bible has been specifically linked with Salzburg book illumination of the Romanesque era, and was produced in a workshop that also accepted external commissions. *A. F.*

Fol. 236v (Joel): The vision of the locusts: Leaning slightly forward, the prophet is reaching for the insects, a swarm of brown "beetles" and green "locusts" in the shape of parrots, who are pecking at the flowers or fruits of a bush. God appears as a half-length figure in an opening in the heavens.

Detail from fol. 84r (Joshua): The calling of Joshua. God presents Joshua, who is armed with a sword, with a pennant lance.

Detail from fol. 94v (Judges): The acts of Gideon. Gideon is called by God. This miniature contains two scenes: on the left, Gideon approaches God, who appears in an opening in the heavens, and is instructed to free the Israelits from the yoke of the Midianites. On the right, Gideon is seen laying a ram's fleece on the threshing floor. The wispy "clouds" signify the dew.

▸ **Fol. 227r (Daniel):** Daniel in the lion's den: The lower field shows Daniel sitting in the lion's den amongst the lions, who are resting quietly. Arriving on the left is King Darius, anxious to release Daniel. In the separate pictorial field above, the prophet Habakkuk, guided by an angel who has hold of his hair, is bringing Daniel some food.

Detail from fol. 206r (Ezechiel): Ezechiel's vision: the prophet lying asleep on his bed; appearing to him are Christ, enthroned in a mandorla, and an angel.

Detail from fol. 237r (Amos): The architecture with its gates flung ostentatiously wide is that of the city of Damascus

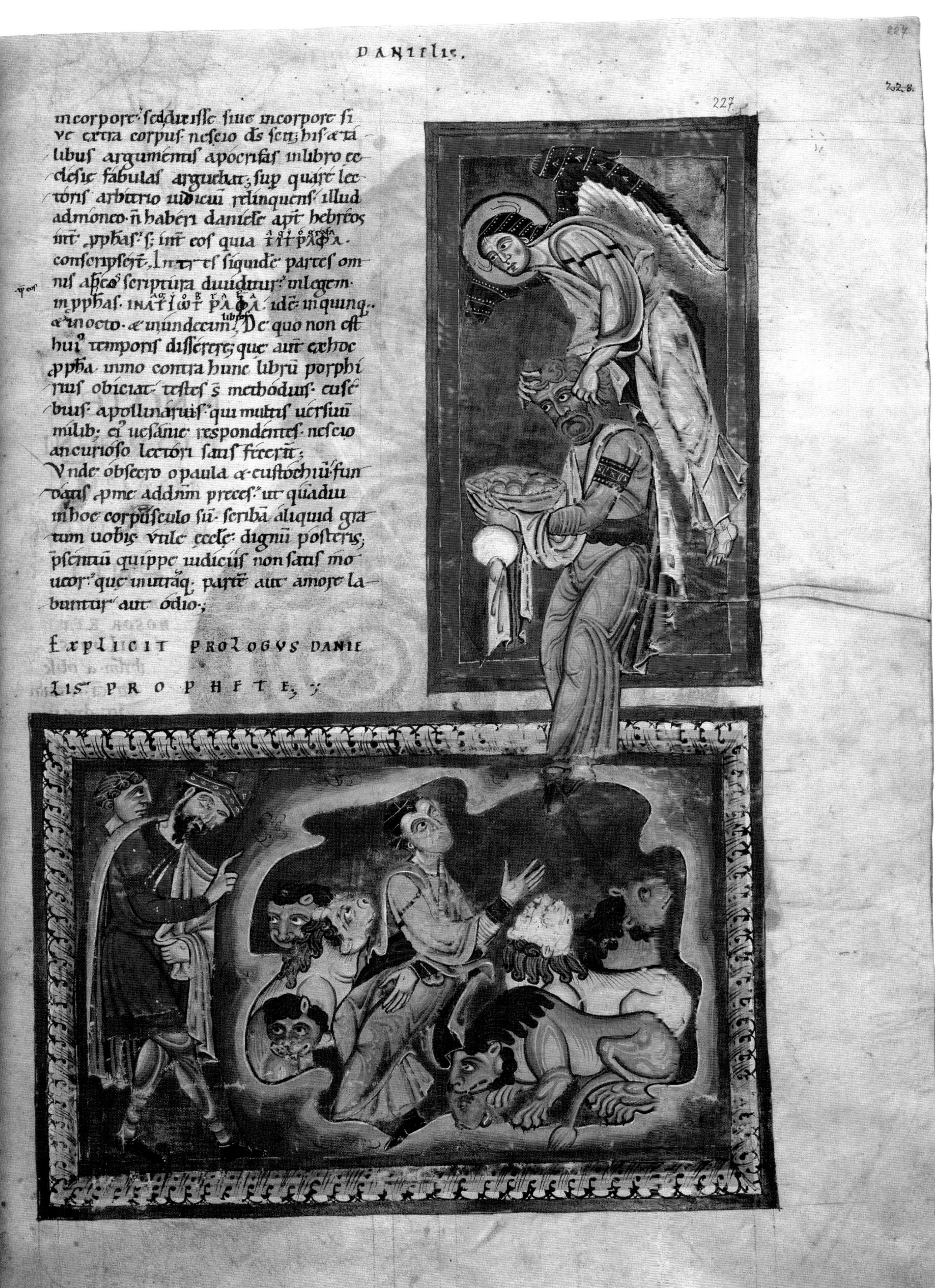

►► **Detail from fol. 109r (1 Samuel):** Scenes from the life of Hannah. Above: on the left, the childless Hannah is weeping; beside her stands Peninnah, Elkanah's second wife, cradling an infant in her arms. Within an architectural surround of towers and a gable, Hannah places a young bull on the altar as a sacrifice.

II.2 Lilienfeld Bible

Cistercian abbey of Lilienfeld (Lower Austria), 2nd quarter of the 13th century

In which library this first volume of the Bible, which was purchased by the Austrian National Library from the fine art trade, was originally housed was a question that remained for a long time unanswered. It was only with the identification of the rather unassuming library binding that light was finally shed on the production and provenance of the manuscript, which can now be confidently assigned to the Cistercian abbey of Lilienfeld in Lower Austria.

The form in which the manuscript has come down to us is symptomatic of the way in which luxury large-format Bibles were produced. The effort and co-ordination involved in obtaining the materials (parchment), copying out the text and adding the illustrations meant that the Bible "production line" frequently stopped and started. The decoration might be left unfinished (cf. the Wenceslas Bible: Cat. II.4), abandoned entirely or – as likely in the present case – resumed only after an interruption. In the library of Lilienfeld abbey, however, there survive two other large-format Bibles from the second half of the 13th century which were probably compiled to supplement the present volume.

Codex Ser. n. 2594 was produced in the early years of the abbey, which was founded in 1202. This was a period of fruitful growth, reflected in the consecration of the completed eastern section of the Gothic church in 1230. By this time, at the latest, the abbey had evidently established its own workshop of scribes and illuminators, one competent enough to embark on ambitious Bible manuscripts. The attribution of the present Bible to the Lilienfeld scriptorium is evidenced by the fact that the scribe and illuminators of the present Bible are known to have worked on other codices from the same abbey.

Detail from fol. 103v (Numbers): Foliate initial *L(ocutus)*. The lower part of the initial is formed by a dragon.

▸ **Fol. 8v (Genesis):** The Creation of Adam and Eve, the Fall, and the Expulsion from Paradise; beneath, Eve at the distaff and Adam toiling in the fields.

Incipit liber Genesis.

CREAVIT Deus celum
Terra autem erat inani
cua. Et tenebre erant sup
abissi. et sps di ferebatur
aquas. Dixitque ds. fiat l
ta est lux. Et uidit ds lu
esse bona. et diuisit lucem
bras. Appellauitque lucem
tenebras noctem. Factum
pere et mane dies unus.

Dixit quoque ds. fiat
tum in medio aqu
uidat aquas ab aquis. Et
firmamentum. diuisitque
que erant sub firmamen
his que erant sup firm
Et factum est ita. Voca
firmamentū celum. Et
uespe et mane. dies sec

Dixit uero ds. Cong
aque que sub celo
locum unum. et appare
Factumque est ita. Et uoc
aridam terram. congregat
aquarum appellauit maria
ds quod esse bonum. et ait
terra herbam uirentem e
semen. et lignum pomifer
fructum iuxta genus su
semen in semetipso sit su

EC • SUNT • 52

Nomina filiorum isrl̄. qui in
gressi sunt in egiptum cū iacob.
Singuli cum domib; suis in

EXTENT: 214 parchment folios
FORMAT: 410 x 290 mm
BINDING: Baroque library binding by Lilienfeld abbey
CONTENT: Bible (Old Testament: Genesis to Ruth [Octateuch])
LANGUAGE: Latin

ILLUSTRATION: one full-page ornamental initial at the beginning of the Book of Genesis; one figural initial drawn in pen (St Jerome); numerous foliate initials
PROVENANCE: Cistercian abbey of Lilienfeld (Lower Austria)
SHELFMARK: Vienna, ÖNB, Cod. Ser. n. 2594

The script and the illustrations place the work in the period of transition from the Romanesque to the Gothic. The "classical" foliate initials that were widespread in Romanesque art and were mostly executed in pen continue to make up the large part of the illustrations. Here, a dense network of scrolling, interweaving forms develop around the body of a letter, which at times becomes barely recognizable. This ornamental carpet of stylized, vegetal motifs is occasionally inhabited by mythical beasts (see ill. p. 70). These are predominantly small dragons, which are lent grotesque features by the hoods on their heads. In the majority of cases they are simply part of the decoration, since they are inserted into the initials without bearing any obvious relevance to the biblical text.

Only at the start of the manuscript does one such initial also contain a figure. Placed in front of the first book of the Old Testament (Genesis) is the letter of St Jerome (347–419) to Bishop Paulinus of Nola (c. 355–431). Jerome is depicted as a holy bishop and holds, as if they were the attributes of his authorship, a stylus and a writing tablet in the shape of a two-part diptych.

In line with a widespread tradition of Bible illumination, however, the decorative scheme concentrates upon the initial *I* at the beginning of the first book (ill. p. 71), Genesis (*In principio creavit Deus celum et terram ...* – "In the beginning God created the heavens and the earth ..."). Almost monumental in its effect, this *I* takes up the full height of the page and illustrates the story of Creation in an unusual choice of scenes. It depicts not the individual days of Creation, but the events that followed: the creation of Eve, the Fall, the Expulsion from Paradise and – as its consequence – Adam and Eve's atonement through their labour at the distaff and in the field. *A. F.*

Fol. 52r (Exodus): Foliate initial *H(ec sunt)*, containing a fabulous beast.

II.3 Krems Bible

Krems (Lower Austria) (?), last quarter of the 13th century and 1333/34

The first four volumes, containing the Old Testament, were executed in the last quarter of the 13th century, and were subsequently complemented by a fifth volume containing the New Testament. The colophon at the end of this volume states that copying was commenced in 1333 and work completed in 1334. The scribe gives his name as Chunradus Sweuus (Conrad the Swabian).

The last volume of the Old Testament contains a hastily-written inscription from the 15th century, identifying the manuscript as the property of the Dominican convent in Krems (Lower Austria), founded in 1236. It is probable that the Bible was also rebound at this time and furnished with heavy wooden boards covered with leather.

The illustration of the four earlier volumes embraces two types of decoration. Subordinate sections of text, such as prologues and chapters, are introduced by so-called *fleuronnée* initials. In this Gothic type of initial, the shape of the letter – which was often hard to decipher amidst the dense weave of scrolling, foliate forms that made up Romanesque initials – is once again emphasized and visually distinguished from the surrounding decoration. The body of the letter is divided by means of tiny gaps into two colours, usually red and blue, but remains easily legible. It thereby stands out clearly from the surrounding linear ornamentation, known as *fleuronnée*, which in contrast to Romanesque manuscript illumination contains almost no naturalistic motifs.

Higher up in the decorative hierarchy are the initials executed in body colour and gold which make up the second type of decoration chosen to illustrate the books of the Krems Bible. Some of these initials comprise purely decorative designs of exuberant foliage, while others also incorporate figures, sometimes grotesques. On fol. 251r of Codex 1171, for example, a dragon has clamped its jaws around the base of the initial *I*,

Detail from Cod. 1170, fol. 1r: Author portrait of St Jerome as a scribe, seated with a pen and a book.

▸ **Detail from Cod. 1171, fol. 3r (1 Samuel):** Samuel anoints King Saul.

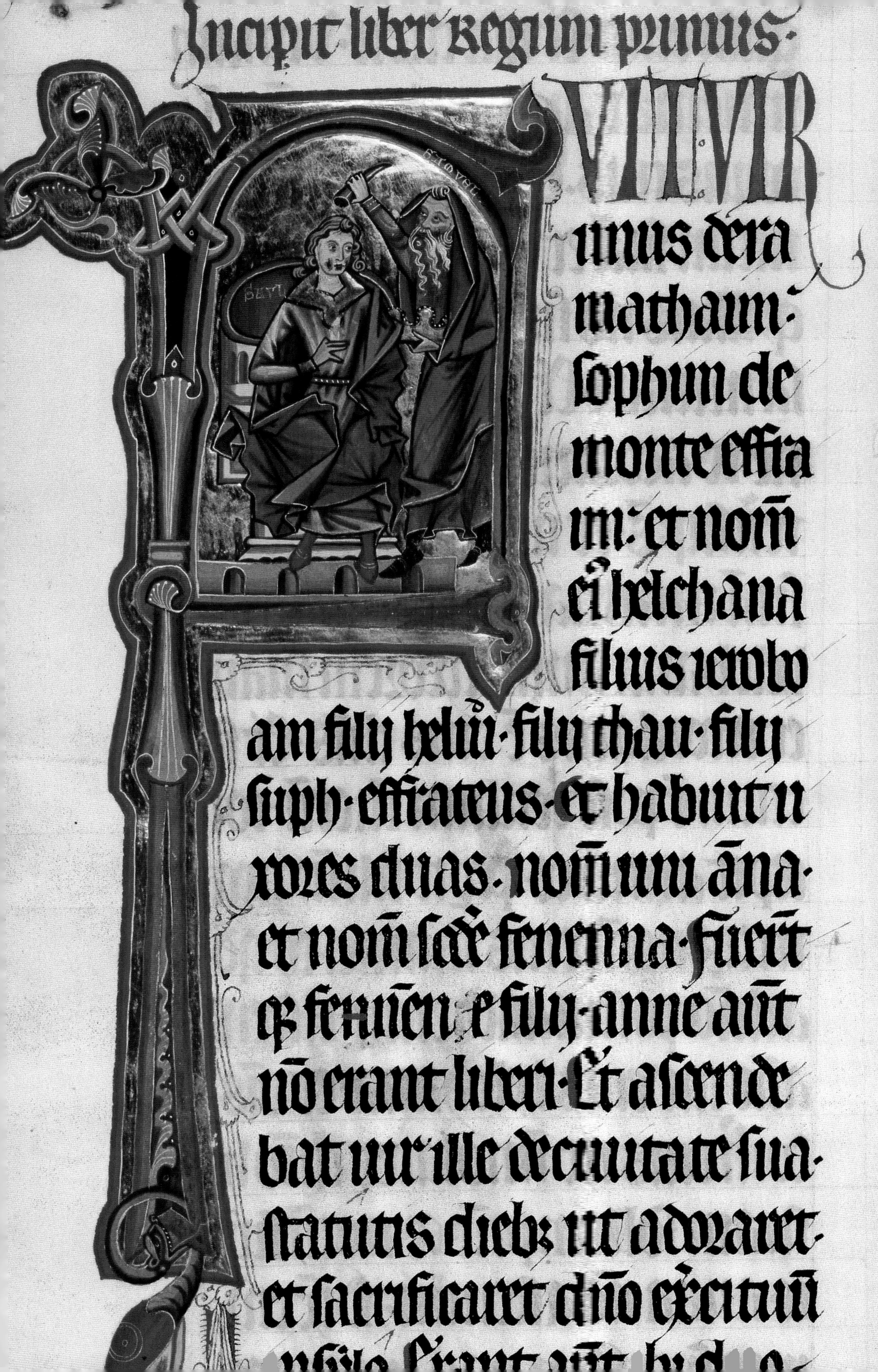

Incipit liber Regum primus.

FUIT VIR
unus de ra
mathaim
sophim de
monte effra
im: et nom
ei helchana
filius ierobo
am filii heliu. filii thau. filii
suph. effrateus. et habuit u
xores duas. nomen uni anna.
et nomen secunde fenenna. fuerunt
que fenenne filii. anne autem
non erant liberi. Et ascende
bat vir ille de civitate sua
statutis diebus ut adoraret
et sacrificaret domino exercituum
in silo. Erant autem ibi duo

Incipit bresyht .i. liber
Genesis. Rubrica.

IN PRINCIPIO

Creavit deus celum et terram.
Terra autem erat inanis et va
cua. Et tenebre super faciem
abyssi; et spiritus dei ferebatur super
aquas. Dixitque deus: fiat lux. Et fac
ta est lux. Et vidit deus lucem quod esset
bona et divisit lucem a tenebris.
Appellavitque lucem diem et
tenebras noctem. Factumque est
vespere et mane dies unus.
Dixit quoque deus: Fiat firma
mentum in medio aquarum et
dividat aquas ab aquis. Et
fecit deus firmamentum. divisit
que aquas que erant sub firma
mento ab hiis que erant super
firmamentum. Et factum est ita.
Vocavitque deus firmamentum
celum. et factum est vespere et mane
dies secundus. Dixit vero deus: Con
gregentur aque que sub celo sunt
in locum unum et appareat a
rida. Factumque est ita. Et voca
vit deus aridam terram. con
gregationesque aquarum appellavit ma
ria. Et vidit deus quod esset bonum et ait:
Germinet terra herbam virentem et faci
entem semen et lignum pomiferum faciens
fructum iuxta genus suum. cuius semen
in semetipso sit super terram. Et factum est
ita. Et protulit terra herbam virentem et
afferentem semen iuxta genus suum. lig
numque faciens fructum et habens unum
quodque sementem secundum speciem suam.
Et vidit deus quod esset bonum. Factumque est
vespere et mane dies tercius. Dixit autem
deus: fiant luminaria in firmamento celi
et dividant diem ac noctem et sint
in signa et tempora et dies et annos.
ut luceant in firmamento celi et illu
minent terram. Et factum est ita. Fecitque deus
duo magna luminaria. Luminare
maius ut preesset diei et luminare
minus ut preesset nocti. Et stellas. et po
suit eas in firmamento celi. ut luce
rent super terram. ut preessent diei ac no
cti et dividerent lucem ac tenebras. Et vi
dit deus quod esset bonum. et factum est vespere et
mane dies quartus. Dixit etiam deus:
Producant aque reptile anime vi

EXTENT: five volumes; 1226 parchment folios in total
FORMAT: *c.* 500 x 370 mm
BINDING: Late Gothic leather blind tooled binding over wooden boards; decoration with single tools, ornament rolls and panel printed ornaments; traces of former chain fastenings
CONTENT: Bible (Old and New Testament)
LANGUAGE: Latin
SCRIBE: Chunradus Sweuus

ILLUSTRATION: numerous *fleuronnée* and ornamental initials, including 15 figural initials
PROVENANCE: A 15th-century inscription in the manuscript records it as the property of the Dominican convent in Krems. From the 16th century onwards the codex is documented in the Vienna Hofbibliothek.
SHELFMARK: Vienna, ÖNB, Cod. 1170–1174

while a hedgehog takes a quiet walk across the top (ill. Cod. 1171, fol. 261r). In another instance, the figure of an Atlas is holding the full weight of an elaborate initial above his head. In other of the biblical books, however, the space inside the initial is filled with historiated miniatures, i. e. small-scale illustrations that relate directly to the neighbouring text. Owing to the cramped confines in which they have to "live", such miniatures are usually reduced to single figures or essential details, as in the case of the initial showing Judith cutting off the head of Holofernes (ill. p. 78). The sole exception is the initial at the beginning of Genesis, which occupies the full height of the page, and in which the upright of the *I* illustrates the story of Creation up to the Fall in eight distinct fields, seven of them medallions (ill. p. 76).

It is interesting to observe how these decorative forms have evolved in the New Testament volume which was added some 50 years later. The *fleuronnée* initials which, in the decorative hierarchy of the first four volumes, were employed in a subordinate role and in modest garb, are here the only type of initial employed. The illustrative emphasis of the first four volumes has also diminished, and the figural elements are reduced to motifs, some of them grotesque, bearing no relevance to the text. Examples include the hybrid form of a dragon with the head of a nun and a stag hunt (Cod. 1174, fol. 37v), a motif that also frequently appears on manuscript bindings. Through its rich use of body colour and gold, however, and through the monumentalization of its initials, this fifth volume also offers a sumptuous decorative programme. *A. F.*

Detail from Cod. 1170, fol. 9r (Genesis): Initial *I(n principio)* containing the story of Creation: (1) The Creator enthroned. (2) Separation of the light and the darkness. (3) Separation of the land and the seas. (4) Creation of the plants. (5) Creation of the sun, moon and stars. (6) Creation of the birds and beasts. (7) Creation of Adam; beneath, the Fall.

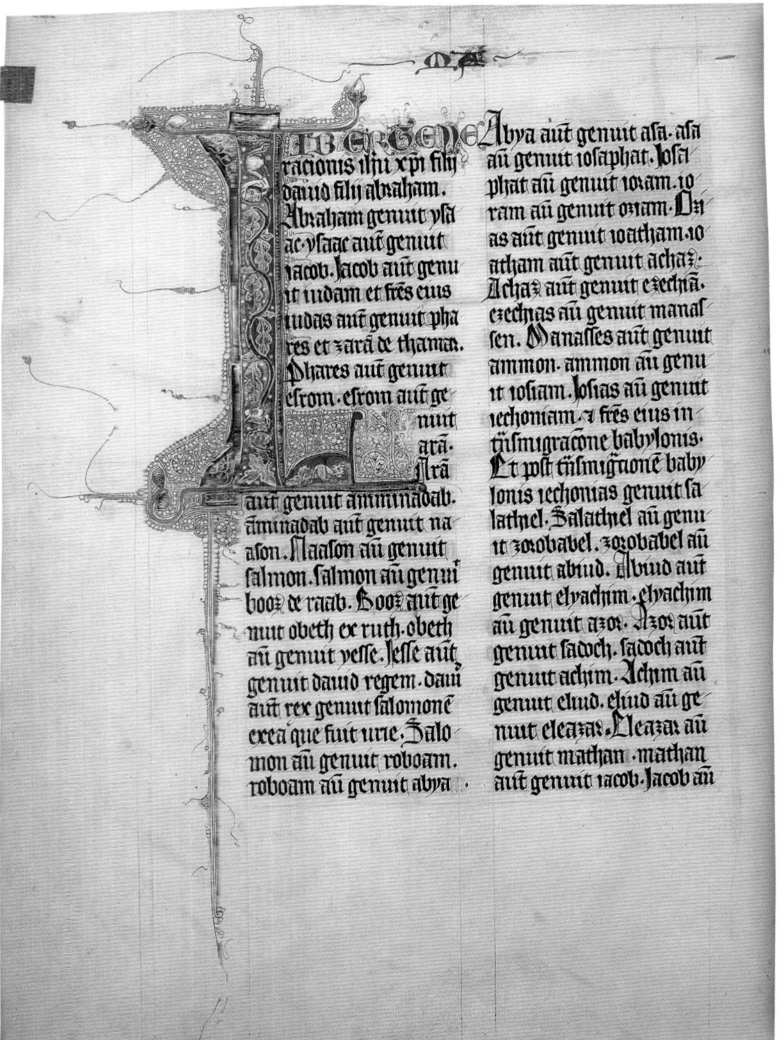

Cod. 1174, fol. 2v (St Matthew): Initial *L(iber generationis)*.

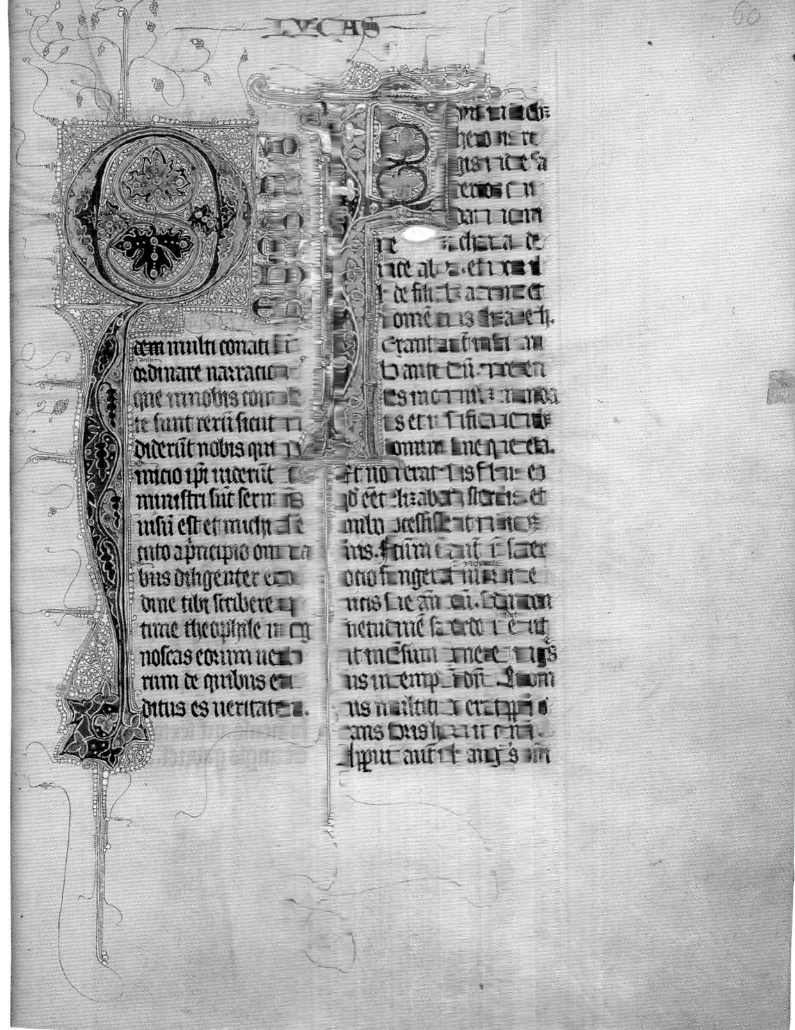

Cod. 1174, fol. 60r (St Luke): Initials *Quoniam quidem* and *Fuit*.

▸ Detail from Cod. 1174, fol. 189v (Thessalonians): Initial *A(d Thessalonicenses)* from the Prologue, initial *P(aulus et Silvanus)*

/ ut integer /

nos pomnia. // Ipse uir. et anima et corpus sine querela in aduentu dni seruet nri. Fidelis est deus qui uocat nos qui etiā faciet. Fratres orate p nobis. Salutate te omis in osculo sco. Adiuro uos p dominū ut legatur epla hec omnibz sanctis fratribz. Gra domini nri ihu xpi sit nobiscum. am E

AD THESSALONICENSES secundam eplam scribit apls et notū facit eis de tpribz nouissimis et aduersarii destructione. scribens hanc eplam ab athenis p tithicum dyaconē et honesimū acolitum.

gra uob et pax a deo pre nro et dno ihu xpo

PAULUS ET siluanus et thymotheus ecclie thessalonicensium in deo pre nro et dno ihu xpo. Gras agere debemus deo semp p uobis fres ita ut dignū est. qm supercrescit fides ura. et habundat caritas uniuscuiusqz urm in inuicem: ita ut et nos ipi in uobis gloriemur. in ecclesiis dei p paciencia ura et fide in omnibz persecucionibz uris et tribulationibz quas sustinetis in exemplum iusti iudicii dei ut

II.4

The Wenceslas Bible

Prague, around 1389/95

The first translations of the Bible into German were not sanctioned by the authorities of the Church, and in 1369 a proclamation issued by Emperor Charles IV even declared the distribution of German-language editions a heresy. This move admittedly failed to silence the ever more vociferous calls for a renewal of faith, and by time Wenceslas IV took over as head of the kingdom in 1378, the Church – and with it the Bohemian nobility – had been divided by the schism into two camps. Broad sections of the Bohemian populace had already embraced the *Devotio moderna* movement with all its reformational potential, and in this situation the young monarch saw himself as the personal guarantor of a renovation of Church and Empire. The copy he commissioned of the most modern and best German translation of the Bible is thus not simply an indication of his love of books – it is a statement of a marked change in imperial relations with the authorities of the Church.

The monarch's self-confident stance vis-à-vis the Church is reflected in an extraordinarily sumptuous decorative programme which made the Wenceslas Bible – despite being left unfinished after 2,428 pages – one of the most famous of all Bibles. Contributing not least to this programme are the monarch's own emblems, repeatedly used but difficult to interpret, which – as it now appears – marry genealogical heraldry with symbols of his personal ideals. Stated briefly, the cleansing properties of water as a symbol of renewal, and Wenceslas' ties to Bohemia and the Holy Roman Empire are recurrent concepts which lie at the heart of the pictorial programme (cf. ill. p. 81, 83).

In contrast to the script, which is written with perfect uniformity, the unfinished state of the illustrations offers us an insight into the enormous amount of planning and work that went into the project, which must have involved at least nine illuminators,

Detail from Cod. 2759, fol. 160r (Numbers): In the foliate medallion, a bathing maid. (Balaam Master)

▸ **Cod. 2759, fol. 2v (Genesis):** The initial letter of Genesis, containing seven medallions illustrating the Creation, together with apostles, prophets, Wenceslas trapped in a letter block and bathing maid. In the borders, the coats of arms of the Holy Roman Empire and Bohemia with helmets above, drapery knots with kingfishers. (Seven Days Master)

Nanegenge schepfte got himel
vnd erde. Di erde was aber vnnucz
vnd lere vnd vinsternusse waren
auf der gestalt der abegrund vn
gotes geist wart gefurt auf den
wassern. Vnd got sprache. Es
werde ein liecht. vnd es wart ein
liecht. Vnd got sach das liecht
das es gut was vnd schid das
liecht von der vinsternusse. vnd
nante das liecht tack vnd die vi
sternusse nacht. Vnd wart ge
macht abent vnd morgen ein
tag. Vnd got sprach. Es werde
ein vestenunge in der mitte der
wasser vnd teilte die wasser vō
den wassern. Vnd got machte
ein firmament. vnd schied die
wasser die da waren vnder dem
firmament von den die do wa
ren auf dem firmament. vnd
es geschach also. Vnd got nan
te das firmament himel. vnd
wart gemacht abent vnd mor
gen der ander tag. Got vorwar
sprach. Die wasser die vnder de
himel sint sammen sich an ein
stat vnd erscheine die trucken
Vnd es geschach also. Vñ got
nante die trucken erde vnd die
sammenunge der wasser nante
her die mer. vnd got sach das
es gut was. Vnd sprach. Ge
bere die erde grunende wurcze
vnd machende samen. Vnd
ein opfeltragendes holcz vnd

stifte das rippe das er hette ge-
numen aus adamen in ein wi
vnd furte sie czu adamen · vn

adam sprach · Das bein nv v
meinen beinen vnd vleisch v
meinem vleische · Die wirt ge
heissen ein menninne · wenne
sie ist aus dem manne genvme
Vmb dise dinck wirt der mensch
lasen vater vnd muter · vnd
wirt anhangen seiner haus-
vrowen · Vnd werden czwei sein
in einem vleische · Sie waren a
ber beide nackent · adam vnd
sein hausfrawe vnd schamten
sich nicht IIIC
Under auch die nater d

EXTENT: 1,214 parchment folios, unfinished
FORMAT: 530–535 x 365–370 mm
CONTENT: Old Testament (Isaiah and Jeremiah appear twice). Copy of the second-oldest German translation of the Vulgate, financed in around 1375 by Martin Rotlev, banker to Emperor Charles IV and former Kuttenberg mint master (his name is mentioned in the first prologue).
LANGUAGE: Middle High German
MINIATURISTS: Balaam Master, Seven Days Master, Frana, Ezra Master, Simson Master, Solomon Master, Morgan Master, Ruth Master, N. Kuthner
ILLUSTRATION: gold and blue *fleuronnée*, foliate borders with emblems, 654 miniatures, designs for a further 600 illustrations
PATRON: Wenceslas IV (1361–1419), King of Bohemia and Holy Roman Emperor
PROVENANCE: According to the second prologue, the Bible was created for King Wenceslas IV; after Wenceslas' death in 1419, the Bible became the property of Emperor Sigismund. In 1437 it was inherited by King Albert II, after whose death in 1439 it passed to Emperor Frederick III, guardian of Albert's posthumously-born son, Ladislaus Postumus; Frederick probably had the manuscript bound (in three volumes). After his death in 1493, the Bible was inherited by Emperor Maximilian, in the treasury of whose Innsbruck castle the Bible is recorded around 1500. Around 1574 it was moved to the new library in Ambras Castle, from where, in 1665, it was transferred to the Hofbibliothek in Vienna.
SHELFMARK: Vienna, ÖNB, Cod. 2759–2764

as well as florators and assistants. How these artists were organized – whether in a single royal workshop or in several workshops supplying the court – remains unclear, since some, although not all, of the quires are the products of close collaboration. A so-called praeceptor was responsible for the overall pictorial programme, which he relayed to the artists in the form of notes in the margins, written in Latin and revealing an extremely well-founded knowledge of theology (Cod. 2761, fol. 90r). Some of the illustrators must have had a command of the German language, since their miniatures occasionally reflect the mistakes in the German translation. As Josef Krása (1971) has pointed out, stylistic links lead onto miniatures in Chronicles produced in southern Germany in the period around 1380/90. Other masters probably came to the flourishing imperial capital from neighbouring regions such as Moravia and Silesia. Together, in Prague, these artists shaped the style of the so-called Wenceslas Workshops. Since the majority of them remain anonymous, they are named after their chief works: the Seven Days Master and Balaam Master (representing the older generation), together with the Solomon Master, Ezra Master, Ruth Master, Simson Master and Morgan Master. Only two actual names have come down to us – those of N. Kuthner and a certain Frana, both of whom signed their works, probably to be sure of getting paid. By good fortune, their names were not trimmed when the manuscript was bound. Frana can in all probability be identified as the court painter Frantisek, who is named in documents.

On the basis of the chivalric epic *Willehalm* (ÖNB, Cod. Ser. n. 2643), illuminated by the same masters in 1387, work on the undated Wenceslas Bible probably proceeded from the late 1380s to around 1395. *M. T.*

Detail from Cod. 2759, fol. 4r (Genesis): Creation of Eve. In the border, two prophets, drapery knot, *W* monogram. (Balaam Master)

Cod. 2759, fol. 174v (Deuteronomy): Two bathing maids attend to Wenceslas. In the foliate border, a kingfisher with the royal motto *toho bzde toho* ("This one here belongs to that one there"). (Balaam Master)

▸ **Detail from Cod. 2759, fol. 47v (Genesis):** Joseph and his brothers rejoice at being reunited. In the foreground, a horse-drawn carriage as a gift from the Pharaoh. In the foliate medallions, two bathing maids attend to Wenceslas. (Balaam Master)

…haben spise · Nicht
…rat sunder vō go
…hin ich her gesant
…at gemachet sam
…haraonis vnd e…
…alles seines house
…fürsten in aller egip
…n · Eilet vnd tzihet
…nem vater vnd e…
…m · Das enpeutet
…ioseph · Got hat
…icht einen herren
…isther erden · Kum
…mir vnd nicht pei
…ne in der erden ges
…i mir wirstu sein
…ne kinder · Deine
…eine rinder vnd al
…besitzest · Vnd also
…neren · Wenne
…ander iar werden
…er das du icht ver

weinte · Vnd ioseph der kuste
seine bruder alle · vnd weinte
vber ytlichen · Darnach wur
den sie kune zu reden mit im ·

Vnd gehort wart das · vnd
mit vreudenricher rede geof
fenbart in des kuniges hofe

was aber die erde einer
zungen und einer spra
id do sie wanderten von
o funden sie ein velt in
i sennaar und wonten
. Und der ander sprach
em nehsten. Komet hin
d mache wir tzigel und
e in dem fewer. Und sie
die tzigel fur steine und
n kalch. Und sprachen.
i und mache wir uns
und einen turme. des
iche bis an den himel.
er wir unsern namen
eteilet werden in alle er
steig aber unser herre
besehe die stat und den
en do bauten die kinder
s. Und sprach. Secht
volk ist es und habent
tzunge. Und tzu mach
n sie das angehaben.
lasen nicht von irn ge
n und bis sie das mit
rken volbrengen. Ku
n derumbe steige wir
und machen zu schan
tzungen also das ein y
nicht vorneme die tzunge
nehsten. Und also teilte
er herre von der stat in
en und horten auf zu
die stat. Und dorumb
heissen ir name babel
do zu schanden worde

ist die tzunge aller erden und
von danne zu strewte sie unser
herre auf die gestalt aller rei
che. Ditz sint die geperunge
sems. Sem was hundert iar
alt do er geperte arphaxat tzwei
iar noch der flute. Und sem
lebte dornach und er geperte
arphaxat funfhundert iar
und geperte sune und tochter
Dornach arphaxat lebte funf
und dreissig iar und geperte
sale. Und es lebte arphaxat
noch dem und her geperte sa
le dreihundert iar und gepe
te sune und tochter. Und sale
lebte dreissig iar und geper
te heber. Und sale noch dem
und her geperte heber lebte
vier hundert iar und geper
te sune und tochter. Und he

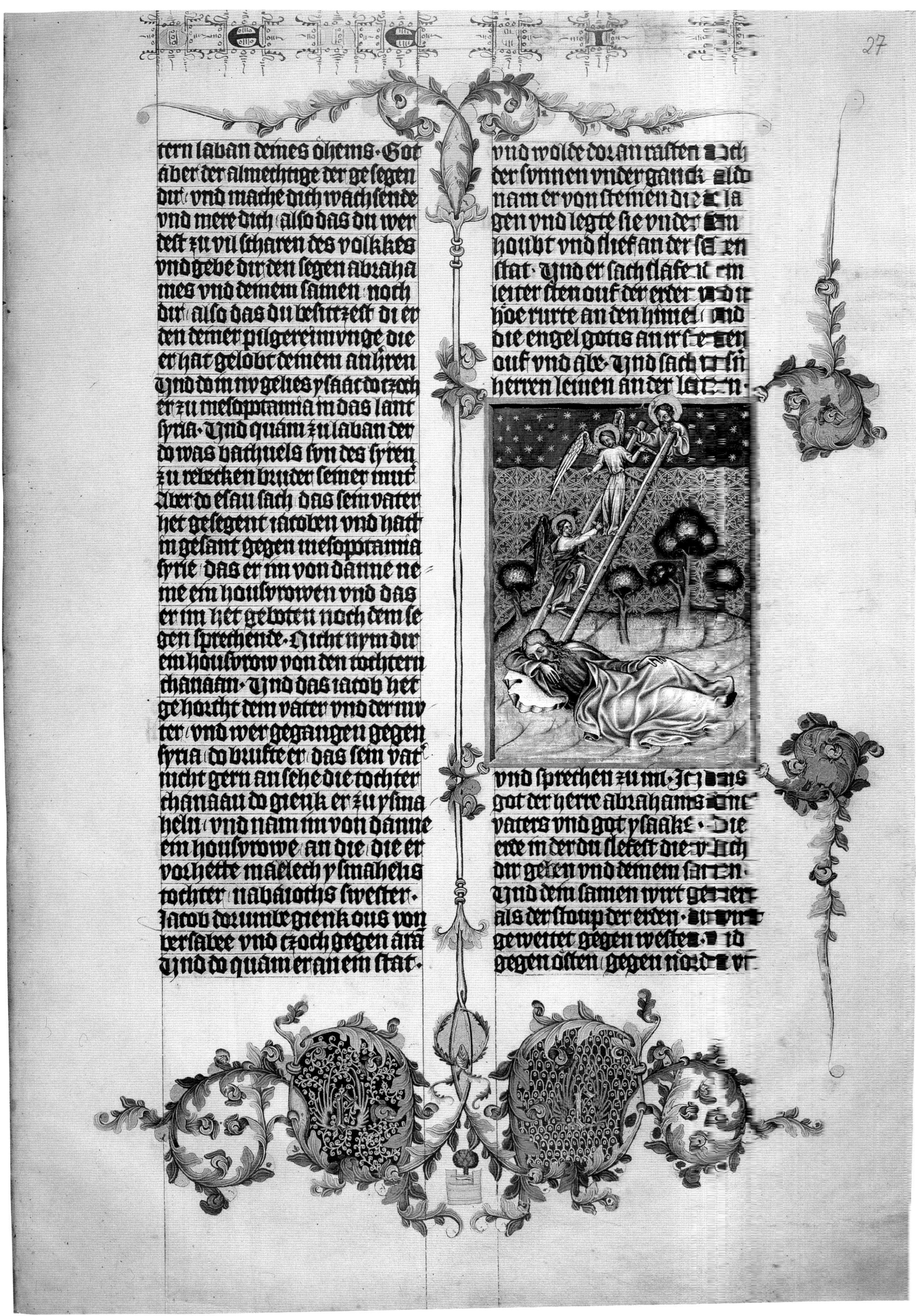

Cod. 2759, fol. 27r (Genesis): Jacob dreams of a ladder leading up to Heaven. In the foliate medallions, two winged *e* monograms, knots and a pail of water. (Balaam Master)

◂ **Detail from Cod. 2759, fol. 10v (Genesis):** The Tower of Babel. (Frana)

▸ **Detail from Cod. 2760, fol. 33r (1 Samuel):** Two winged men hold the royal jousting helmet over the head of King Wenceslas, seated on his throne. In the margins, a bathing maid with motto and Wenceslas in the letter block *W*. (Frana)

das buch ein ende das do ge
nant ist Ruth. Dornach so he
bit sich an das erste buch das
do genant ist zu latein regu
und heisset zu deutsche das
erste buch der kunige. i. ca.
s was ein man von ramatha
im sophim von dem perge ef
fraim und sein name was el
kana sun ieroham des sunes
helin des sunes than des sunes
suph ein effrateer. Und hatte

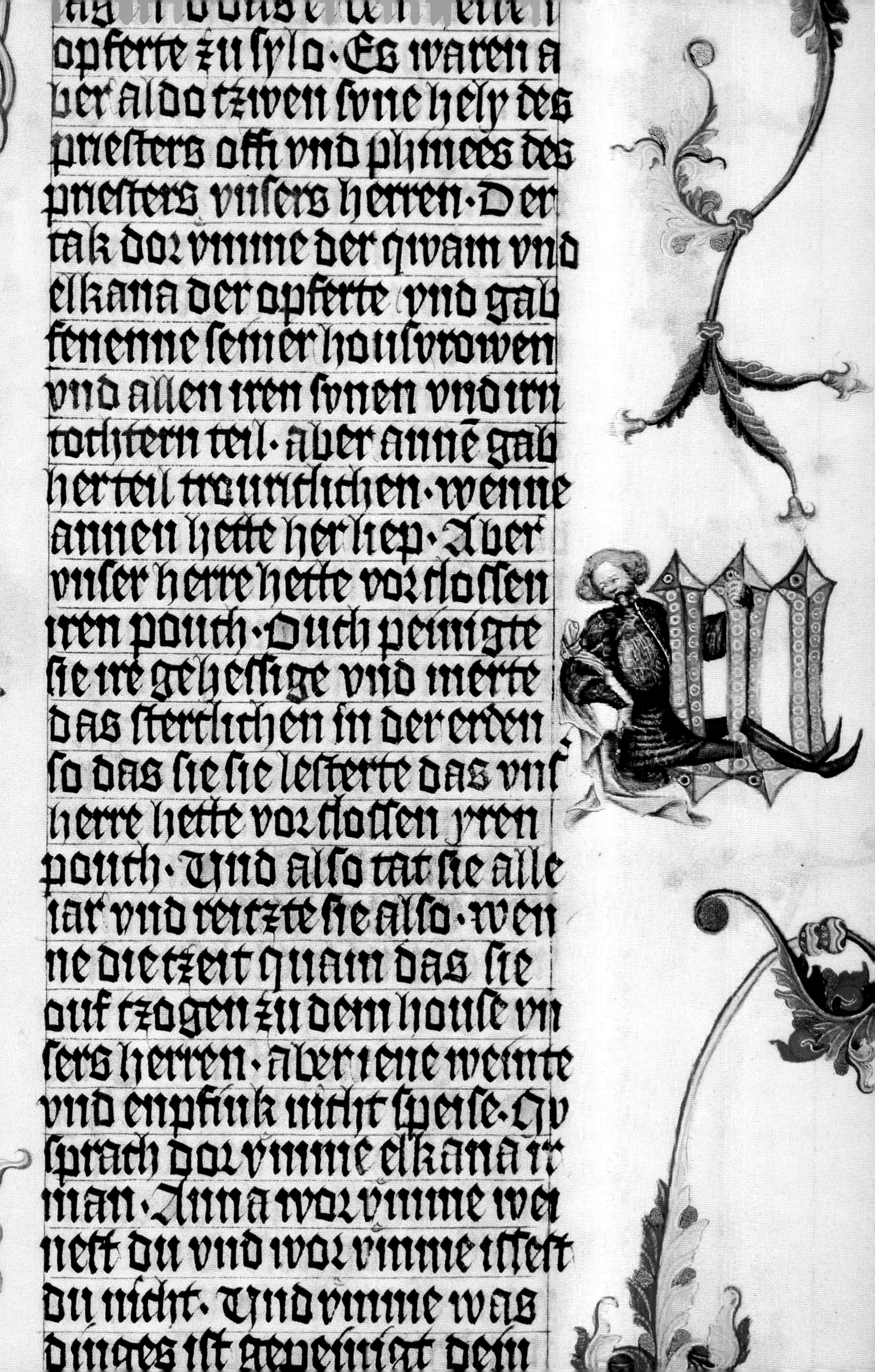

opferte zu sylo · Es waren aber aldo tzwen svne hely des priesters offi vnd phinees des priesters vnsers herren · Der tak dor vmme der qwam vnd elkana der opferte vnd gab fenenne seiner housvrowen vnd allen iren svnen vnd irn tochtern teil · aber anne gab her teil trourichlichen · wenne annen hette her liep · Aber vnser herre hette vorslossen iren pouch · Ouch peinigte sie ire gehessige vnd merte das sterclichen in der erden so das sie sie lesterte das vnser herre hette vorslossen iren pouch · Und also tat sie alle iar vnd reitzte sie also · wenne die tzeit quam das sie ouf tzogen zu dem house vnsers herren · aber ienne weinte vnd enpfink nicht speise · Nv sprach dor vmme elkana ir man · Anna wor vmme weinest du vnd wor vmme issest du nicht · Und vmme was dinges ist gepeiniget dein

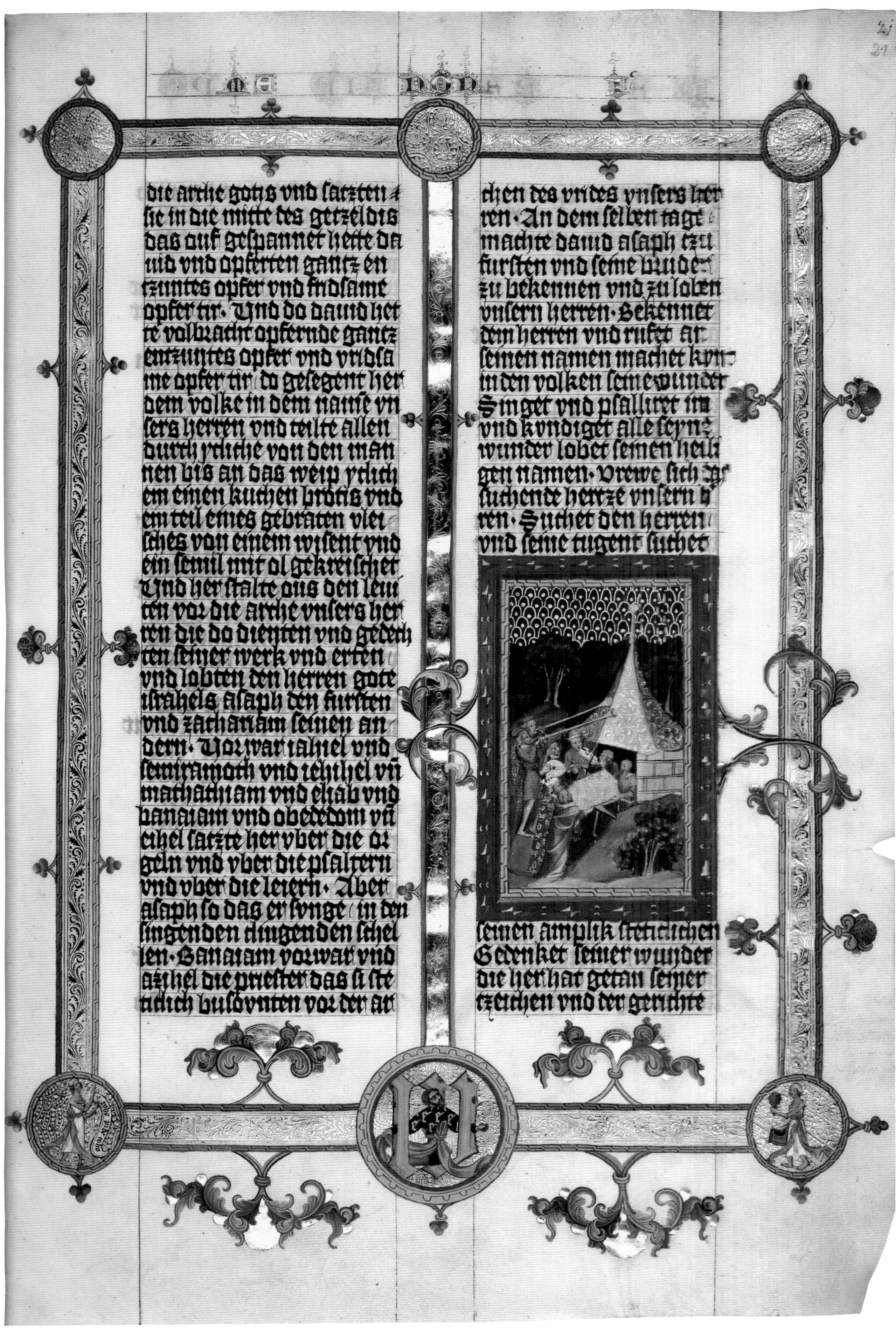

Cod. 2761, fol. 21r (1 Chronicles): King David places the Ark of the Covenant in the Tabernacle. In the borders, two bathing maids, Wenceslas in the letter block *W.* (Ezra Master)

▸ **Detail from Cod. 2760, fol. 116r (1 Kings):** The building of Solomon's Temple. In the borders, Wenceslas in the letter block *W.* (Frana)

peide mit e
ynd der kv
velte arbeiter
eistrahel vnd
dreissic tou
her sante sie
gen perk cze
ch die mened
lich also das
waren in irn
dor an was
tzal ditz ge
o hette salo
tousent man
n trugen vn
steynmetzen
n die probste
ytliche wer
vier tousent
ert gepitend

dem virden iare des mened
des meien der do ist der ander

man des kvnigs salomons
vber israel do hub er an czu

II.5 Korczek Bible

Prague, 1400–1410

Per manus Martini Kathedralis dicti Korczek is how the scribe signed the second volume of his Bible, today housed in the Badische Landesbibliothek in Karlsruhe (Cod. St. Blasien 2). Korczek completed the manuscript for Hanuš in 1400. Thanks to research by Karel Stejskal (1960), we know that Hanuš was cook to King Wenceslas IV and a wealthy Prague patrician. Whether Korczek was ever paid for his work, however, is doubtful, since Hanuš died in that same year of 1400. A question mark also hangs over the actual date of the Bible's magnificent illustrations. On the basis of the decoration of the opening pages, however, we may assume that Korczek's work was probably only illuminated towards 1410.

The majority of the miniatures stem from a Prague studio which evidently specialized in the production of Bibles and service books, and whose work is well documented from 1409/10 onwards. The Missal after which the master of this workshop is today called was commissioned in 1409 by Zbyněk Zajíc de Hasenburg, archbishop of Prague. Further works by the Hasenburg Master include a Bible (Prague) and a Gradual of *c.* 1410 (Lucerne), the Missal of Johann Strniště of 1410/15 (Prague) a Bible dated 1414 (Gnesen) and finally a Vesperal and Matutinal from around 1420 (Zittau). Throughout his œuvre, the artist shows himself to have been inspired by the International Gothic of the turn of the century, painting narrow-shouldered figures with doll-like heads enveloped in voluminous, cascading robes. Over the course of the ten or so years through which we can follow his work, he hardly varies his figural types at all, although a shift towards a cooler palette is noticeable. In their bright colours, the miniatures in the Korczek Bible correspond closely to those of the Hasenburg Missal of 1410. A further parallel can be seen in the filigree decoration of some

Detail from fol. 1r: Decorative border.

▸ **Fol. 1r:** St Jerome composing his prologue to Genesis. (Master of the Gerona Martyrologium?)

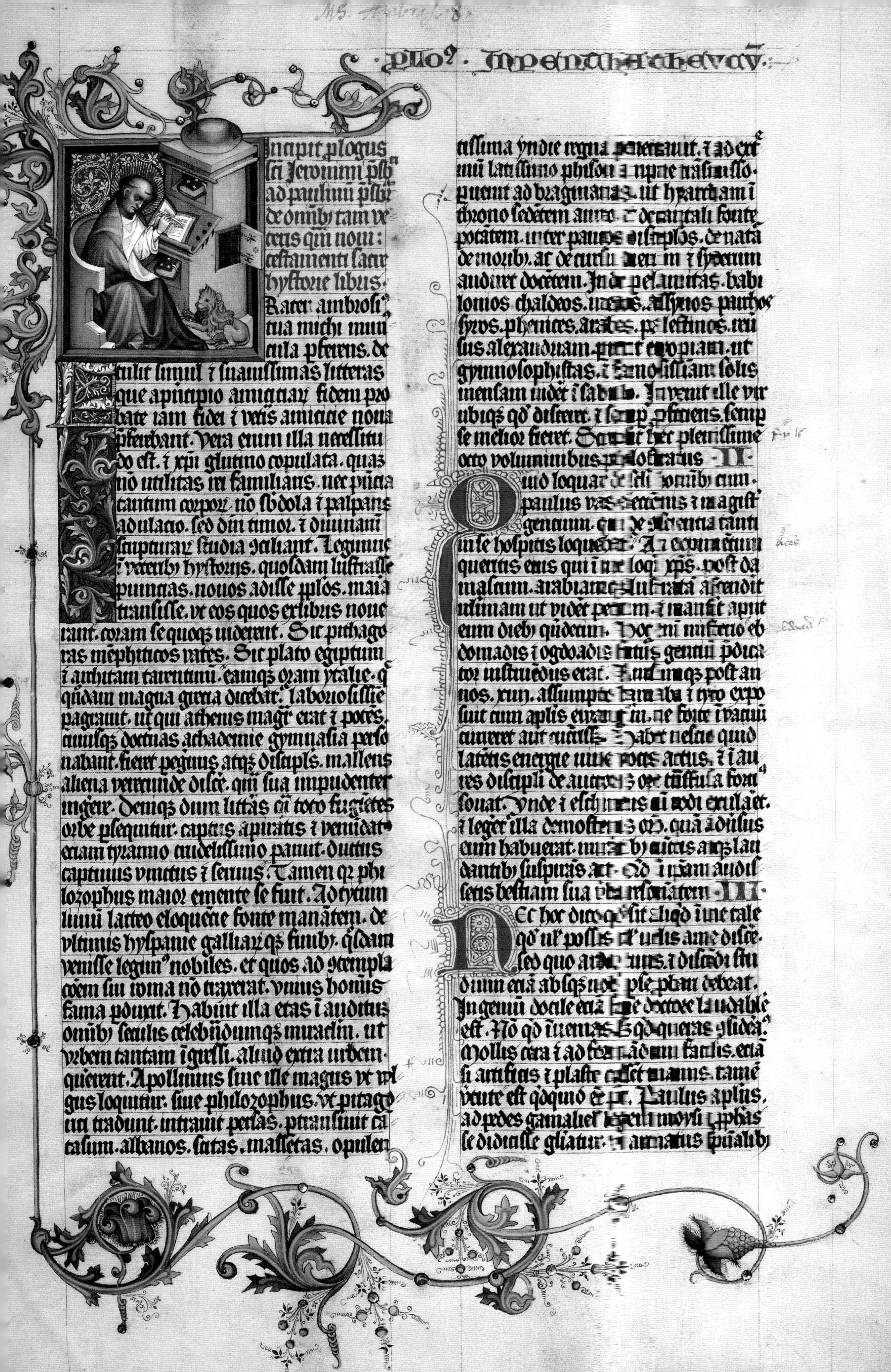

Incipit prologus sancti Jeronimi presbiteri ad paulinum presbiterum de omnibus tam veteris quam novi testamenti sacre hystorie libris.

Frater ambrosius tua michi munuscula perferens. detulit simul et suavissimas litteras que a principio amicitiarum fidem probate iam fidei et veteris amicitie nova preferebant. Vera enim illa necessitudo est. et xpi glutino copulata. quam non utilitas rei familiaris. non presencia tantum corporum. non subdola et palpans adulacio. sed dei timor. et divinarum scripturarum studia conciliant. Legimus in veteribus hystoriis. quosdam lustrasse provincias. novos adisse populos. maria transisse. ut eos quos ex libris noverant. coram se quoque viderent. Sic pithagoras memphiticos vates. Sic plato egiptum et architam tarentinum. eamque oram ytalie que quondam magna grecia dicebatur. laboriosissime peragravit. ut qui athenis magister erat et potens. cuiusque doctrinas achademie gymnasia personabant. fieret peregrinus atque discipulus. malens aliena verecunde discere. quam sua impudenter ingerere. Denique dum litteras quasi toto fugientes orbe persequitur. captus a piratis et venundatus. etiam tyranno crudelissimo paruit. ductus captivus vinctus et servus. Tamen quia philozophus maior emente se fuit. Ad tytum livium lacteo eloquencie fonte manantem. de ultimis hyspanie galliarumque finibus quosdam venisse legimus nobiles. et quos ad contemplacionem sui roma non traxerat. unius hominis fama perduxit. Habuit illa etas inauditum omnibus seculis celebrandumque miraculum. ut urbem tantam ingressi. aliud extra urbem quererent. Apollonius sive ille magus ut vulgus loquitur. sive philozophus ut pitagorici tradunt. intravit persas. pertransivit caucasum. albanos. scitas. massagetas. opulentissima yndie regna penetravit. et ad extremum latissimo phison amne transmisso pervenit ad bragmanas. ut hyarcham in throno sedentem aureo. et de tantali fonte potantem. inter paucos discipulos. de natura de moribus. ac de cursu dierum et syderum audiret docentem. Inde per elamitas. babilonios. chaldeos. medos. assyrios. parthos. syros. phenices. arabes. palestinos. reversus alexandriam. perrexit ethiopiam. ut gymnosophistas. et famosissimam solis mensam videret in sabulo. Invenit ille vir ubique quod disceret. et semper proficiens. semper se melior fieret. Scripsit super hoc plenissime octo voluminibus philostratus. II.

Quid loquar de seculi hominibus. cum apostolus paulus vas electionis et magister gentium. qui de consciencia tanti in se hospitis loquebatur. An experimentum queritis eius qui in me loquitur xpistus. Post damascum. arabiamque lustratam ascendit ierosolimam ut videret petrum. et mansit apud eum diebus quindecim. Hoc enim misterio ebdomadis et ogdoadis futurus gentium predicator instruendus erat. Rursumque post annos. xiiij. assumpto barnaba et tyto exposuit cum apostolis evangelium. ne forte in vacuum curreret aut cucurrisset. Habet nescio quid latentis energie vive vocis actus. et in aures discipuli de auctoris ore transfusa fortius sonat. Unde et eschines cum rodi exularet. et legeretur illa demostenis oratio. quam adversus eum habuerat. mirantibus cunctis atque laudantibus suspirans ait. Quid si ipsam audissetis bestiam sua verba resonantem. III.

Nec hoc dico quod sit aliquid in te tale quod vel possis vel velis a me discere. sed quo ardor tuus et discendi studium eciam absque nobis per se probari debeat. Ingenium docile eciam sine doctore laudabile est. Non quid invenias sed quid queras consideramus. Mollis cera et ad formandum facilis. eciam si artificis et plastes cessent manus. tamen virtute est quicquid esse potest. Paulus apostolus. ad pedes gamaliel legem moysi et prophetas se didicisse gloriatur. ut armatus spiritualibus

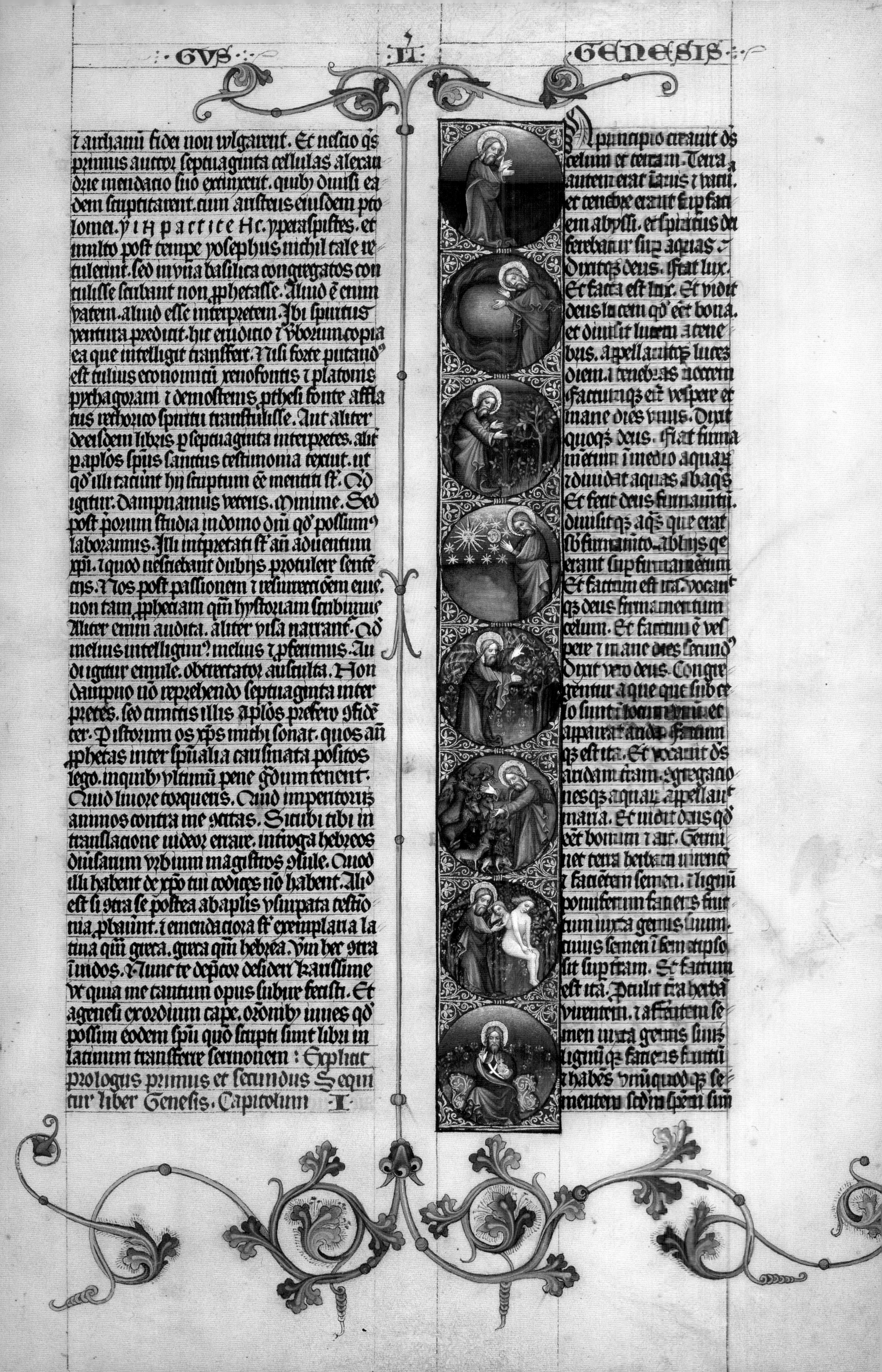

et archani fidei non vulgarent. Et nescio quis primus auctor septuaginta cellulas alexandrie mendacio suo extruxerit. quibus divisi eadem scriptitarent. cum aristeus eiusdem ptolomei ὑπερασπιστής et multo post tempore iosephus nichil tale retulerint. sed in una basilica congregatos contulisse scribant non prophetasse. Aliud est enim vatem. aliud esse interpretem. Ibi spiritus ventura predicit. hic eruditio et verborum copia ea que intelligit transfert. Nisi forte putandus est tullius economicum xenofontis et platonis pythagoram et demostenis prothesi fonte afflatus rethorico spiritu transtulisse. Aut aliter de eisdem libris per septuaginta interpretes. aliter per apostolos spiritus sanctus testimonia texuit. ut quod illi tacuerint hii scriptum esse mentiti sint. Quid igitur. dampnamus veteres. Minime. Sed post priorum studia in domo domini quod possumus laboramus. Illi interpretati sunt ante adventum christi. et quod nesciebant dubiis protulere sententiis. Nos post passionem et resurrectionem eius. non tam prophetiam quam hystoriam scribimus. Aliter enim audita. aliter visa narrantur. Quod melius intelligimus melius et proferimus. Audi igitur emule. obtrectator ausculta. Non dampno non reprehendo septuaginta interpretes. sed cunctis illis apostolos prefero confidenter. Per istorum os christus michi sonat. quos ante prophetas inter spiritualia carismata positos lego. in quibus ultimum pene gradum tenent. Quid livore torqueris. Quid imperitorum animos contra me concitas. Sicubi tibi in translatione videor errare. interroga hebreos diversarum urbium magistros consule. Quod illi habent de christo tui codices non habent. Aliud est si contra se postea ab apostolis usurpata testimonia probaverunt. et emendaciora sunt exemplaria latina quam greca. greca quam hebrea. Verum hec contra invidos. Nunc te deprecor desideri karissime ut quia me tantum opus subire fecisti. et a genesi exordium capere. orationibus iuves quod possim eodem spiritu quo scripti sunt libri in latinum transferre sermonem. Explicit prologus primus et secundus. Sequitur liber Genesis. Capitolum I

In principio creavit deus celum et terram. Terra autem erat inanis et vacua. et tenebre erant super faciem abyssi. et spiritus dei ferebatur super aquas. Dixitque deus. Fiat lux. Et facta est lux. Et vidit deus lucem quod esset bona. et divisit lucem a tenebris. appellavitque lucem diem. et tenebras noctem. Factumque est vespere et mane dies unus. Dixit quoque deus. Fiat firmamentum in medio aquarum. et dividat aquas ab aquis. Et fecit deus firmamentum. divisitque aquas que erant sub firmamento. ab hiis que erant super firmamentum. Et factum est ita. Vocavitque deus firmamentum celum. Et factum est vespere et mane dies secundus. Dixit vero deus. Congregentur aque que sub celo sunt in locum unum et appareat arida. Factumque est ita. Et vocavit deus aridam terram. congregationesque aquarum appellavit maria. Et vidit deus quod esset bonum et ait. Germinet terra herbam virentem et facientem semen. et lignum pomiferum faciens fructum iuxta genus suum. cuius semen in semetipso sit super terram. Et factum est ita. Protulit terra herbam virentem. et afferentem semen iuxta genus suum. lignumque faciens fructum et habens unumquodque sementem secundum speciem suam

EXTENT: 230 parchment folios
FORMAT: 505 x 355 mm
BINDING: original binding of tooled and painted leather; yellow head, fore and tail edges painted with foliate arabesques
CONTENT: Old Testament from Genesis to Psalms (Volume 1)
LANGUAGE: Latin
SCRIBE: Martin Korczek
MINIATURISTS: Master of the Gerona Martyrologium (?), Master of the Hasenburg Missal
ILLUSTRATION: red and blue *fleuronnée* initials, 30 initial miniatures at the start of each of the biblical books and Psalms
PATRON: Hanuš, King Wenceslas IV's cook and councillor in Hradčany castle in Prague
PROVENANCE: The codex appears in the inventory of the Innsbruck treasury in 1536; around 1574 it was moved to the new library in Ambras Castle and from there was transferred in 1665 to the Hofbibliothek in Vienna under the supervision of court praefect Peter Lambeck.
SHELFMARK: Vienna, ÖNB, Cod. 1169

initials (*fleuronnée*), which was executed by the same hand in both the Hasenburg Missal and the Korczek Bible.

A small number of illuminations in these two codices were executed by an artist working in the Franco-Flemish style. This illustrator is responsible for one page in the Hasenburg Missal and the first three miniatures in the Korczek Bible: St Jerome, the translator of the Vulgate, who was born in Dalmatia and was thus highly venerated in Bohemia as a Slavic saint (ill. p. 93), a prophet and the Genesis initial (fol. 4r; ill. p. 94). New here are the pastel shades, the clarification of outlines and the emphasis upon physical presence. The architecture, too, is no longer merely a backdrop, but a convincingly three-dimensional component of the whole.

This illuminator must undoubtedly be seen in conjunction with one of the key works of Bohemian manuscript illumination, the Martyrologium of Gerona which was produced around 1410/15. Probably commissioned by Waclav Krolik (King Wenceslas IV's chancellor, 1416), this magnificent codex marks the transition from the Late Gothic style of the royal workshops to the Prague manuscript illumination of the 1420s.

The St Jerome miniature is so close to the style of the Martyrologium Master that Josef Krása (1971) considered it to be the work of the same artist and proposed a slightly later dating for the Korczek Bible, originally put at 1400 as recorded by the scribe. In terms of palette and figural type, and also in their repertoire of background motifs, crisply-drawn foliate forms and long-stemmed arabesques adorned with spheres, filigree decor, flowers and pounced droplets of gold, the first three illuminated pages of this Bible clearly match the style of the Master of the Gerona Martyrologium and his circle, artists who around 1410 were injecting fresh ideas into manuscript illumination. *M. T.*

Fol. 4r (Genesis): Genesis initial with eight medallions illustrating scenes from the Creation. (Master of the Gerona Martyrologium?)

...ysque su
os mag
it: Sun
uilib; de
is ab eo
ta erit q
s usqz ad
stiqm at
ni suam
i icaitis
rtib; pu
odepnabi
is est sag
les ipsi
i urbes su
itacōnis
r: nec alit
qui alti9
ibi vestr
o eui su
XVI
iliaz ga
anasses
utiqz st
unt. Tibi
diuides
is ini da
altius tb
essio sua
editate
deist qui
ssimida
adalios

Ioseph i possessio que illis fuat attributa
mansit i tribu i familia pris eax. Hec st
mādata atqz iudicia q̄ p̄cepit dn̄s p manu
moysi ad filios isrl̄ i campestrib; moab
sup̄ yordanem 9tra yericho. Explicit liber
numeri. Incipit elleadabarim .i. deutronomi9

Hec st uba
que locutus ē
moyses ad oēz
isrl̄ trāsyordanē
i solitudie cā
pestri. 9t ma
re rubrū. inter
pharan i tofel
i laban i asse
roth ubi auri
ē plurimū. un
decim diebus
de oreb p viā mōtis seyr usqz cades barne. q
dragesimo anno. undecimo mēse. p̄ma die
mensis locutus ē moyses ad filios isrl̄ oia.
q̄ p̄cepat ei dn̄s ut diceret eis. Postq̄ p̄cussit
seon regē amoreox qui hitauit i esebon. et
og. regem basan qui māsit i asseroth i edrai.
trāsyordanē i tra moab. Cepitqz moyses ex
planare legē et dicē. Dn̄s ds nr locutus ē ad
nos i oreb dicēs. Sufficit vob' qd' i h' monte
māsistis. reuertimini i venite ad mōtes amoreox
i ad cetera que ei p̄xima st cāpestria atqz mō
tana i humiliora loca 9t meridiem i iuxta litt9
maris. tram chananeox i lybani usqz ad flu
men magnū eufraten. En iqt tradidi vobis.

◂ **Detail from fol. 63r (Deuteronomy):** Moses addresses the Israelites. (Master of the Hasenburg Missal)

Fol. 177v (Tobit): Tobit is blinded by [illegible]. (Master of the Hasenburg Missal)

II.6

Neapolitan Luxury Bible

Naples, around 1360

Lavishly illustrated with miniatures, the manuscript comprises the Latin text of the Vulgate and, added at the end, the Psalter and the *Interpretation of Hebrew Names.* It was produced around 1360 in Naples, where richly illuminated Bibles were in vogue at court, particularly during the reign of Joanna I. A total of six sumptuously illustrated Vulgate manuscripts have survived from the Naples workshop, of which the earliest (now Louvain University Library, Ms. 1) was executed for Nicola d'Alife and is signed by Naples' most important illuminator, Cristoforo Orimina. The wealth of illustrations accompanying the Vienna Bible – the coats of arms on fol. 291v and 349v and on the head, fore and tail edges have yet to be identified – were executed by altogether four miniaturists, whose hands can also be identified in other manuscripts in the group. For all their differences, three of the illuminators employ a similar style, depend more closely upon earlier French models and come close to Sienese art both in their types and their technical sophistication. The most important of them was responsible, among other things, for the initial at the start of Genesis. The illustrations by the fourth miniaturist – who carried out the lion's share of the decoration – recall, in their layout and palette, Florentine painting under the influence of Giotto. The illumination of the present Bible thus serves as a pointer to the chief sources of the new Neapolitan art of the early Trecento, a period during which artists from further afield, such as Cavallini, Giotto and Simone Martini, were recruited by King Robert of Anjou (reigned 1309–1343).

In its layout and decoration with foliate borders filled with drolleries, and also in its script and format, the present Bible is based on Bolognese luxury manuscripts of the late 13th and early 14th century. New, however, is its almost unsurpassable wealth of pictures. The text is lavishly illustrated by miniatures variously located inside initials, at

Detail from fol. 8v (Genesis): Border with Atlas figure.

▸ **Fol. 4r (Genesis):** Initial in Genesis showing the Creation of the heavens and the earth, the sun, moon and animals, and Adam and Eve. Two further pictorial fields show Adam and Eve being led through Paradise, and the Fall. An angel in the left-hand margin and Mary on the right together form an Annunciation, while at the top more angels, saints and drolleries surround the figure of God the Father in majesty.

scribant nō ꝓphasse. Aliud ē enim
uatem aliud ē interptem. Ibi spūs
uētura predicit. hic eruditio et uborū
copia ea que intelligit transfert. ni
si forte putandus ē tullius. ecco
nomicum xenofontis. ⁊ platonis
pythagoram. ⁊ demostenis ꝓ ctesi
fontem afflatus rethorico spū tran
stulisse. aut aliť de eisdem libris ꝑ sep
tuaginta interpretes. aliter ꝑ aplos
spūs scūs testimonia texuit: ut qđ illi
tacuerunt. hi scriptum ēē mentiti sint.
Quid igitur? Dampnamus ueteres?
Minime. Sʒ post priorum studia: in
domo domini qđ possumus laboramꝰ.
Illi interpretati sunt ante aduentum xpi.
⁊ quod nesciebant dubiis protulere
sententiis. Nos post passionem ⁊ resur
rectionem eius: nō tam ꝓphetiam q̄ hysto
riam scribimus. Aliť enim audita:
aliť uisa narrantur. Quod melius
intelligimus. melius ⁊ proferimus.
Audi igitur emule: obtrectator au
sculta. Non dampno. nō reprehendo
septuaginta: sʒ confidenter cunctis illis
aplos prefero. Per istorum os michi
xpc sonat. quos ante ꝓphetas inter
spiritualia karismata positos lego: in
quibus ultimum pene gradum inter
pretes tenent. Quid liuore torque
ris? Quid imperitorum animos
contra me concitas? Sicubi tibi in
translatione uideor errare. interroga
hebreos. diuersarum urbium ma
gistros consule. Quod illi habent
de xpo: tui codices nō hñt. Aliud est
si contra se post ab aplis usurpata te
stimonia probauerunt. ⁊ emendatio
ra sunt exemplaria latina quam
greca. greca quam hebrea. Verum
hec contra inuidos. Nunc te precor
desiderii karissime ut quia tantum
opus me subire fecisti. ⁊ a genesi ex
ordium capere: orationibus iuues
quod possim eodem spiritu quo
scripti sunt libri. in latinum eos
transferre sermonem.

In principio creauit deus celum et
terram. Terra autem erat inanis et ua
cua. Et tenebre erant super faciem abyssi.

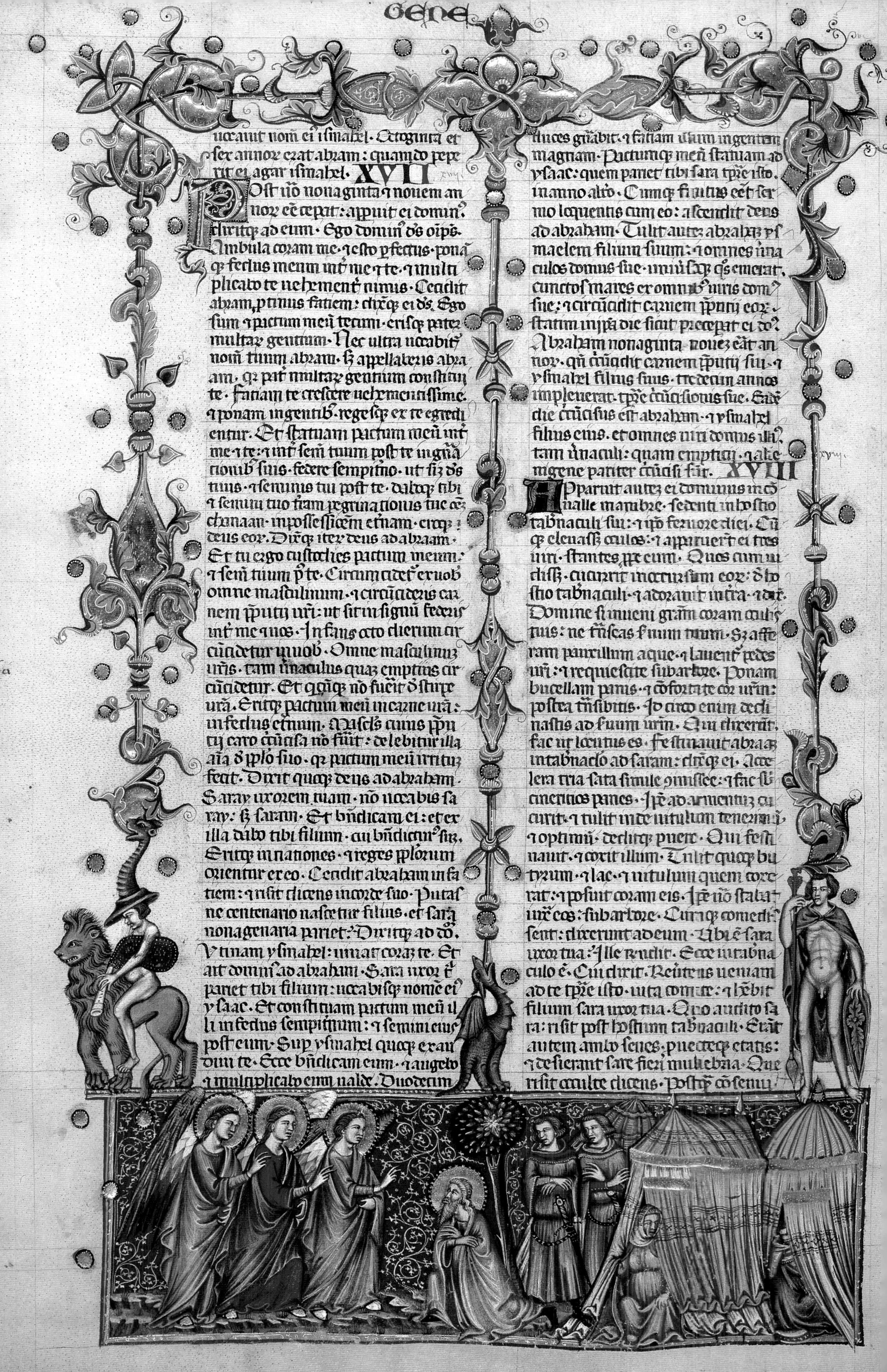

vocavit nomen eius ismahel. Octoginta et sex annorum erat abram: quando peperit ei agar ismahel. XVII

Postquam vero nonaginta et novem annorum esse cepit: apparuit ei dominus dixitque ad eum. Ego dominus deus omnipotens. Ambula coram me et esto perfectus. ponamque fedus meum inter me et te. et multiplicabo te vehementer nimis. Cecidit abram pronus in faciem: dixitque ei deus. Ego sum et pactum meum tecum. erisque pater multarum gentium. Nec ultra vocabitur nomen tuum abram. sed appellaberis abraham. quia patrem multarum gentium constitui te. Faciam te crescere vehementissime. et ponam in gentibus. regesque ex te egredientur. Et statuam pactum meum inter me et te: et inter semen tuum post te in generationibus suis. federe sempiterno. ut sim deus tuus. et seminis tui post te. daboque tibi et semini tuo terram peregrinationis tue omnem chanaan in possessionem eternam. eroque deus eorum. Dixit iterum deus ad abraam. Et tu ergo custodies pactum meum: et semen tuum post te. Circumcidetur ex vobis omne masculinum. et circumcidetis carnem preputii vestri: ut sit in signum federis inter me et vos. Infans octo dierum circumcidetur in vobis. Omne masculinum vestris. tam vernaculus quam emptitius circumcidetur. Et quicumque non fuerit de stirpe vestra. Eritque pactum meum in carne vestra: in fedus eternum. Masculus cuius preputii caro circumcisa non fuerit: delebitur illa anima de populo suo. quia pactum meum irritum fecit. Dixit quoque deus ad abraham. Sarai uxorem tuam. non vocabis sarai: sed saram. Et benedicam ei: et ex illa dabo tibi filium. cui benedicturus sum. Eritque in nationes. et reges populorum orientur ex eo. Cecidit abraham in faciem: et risit dicens in corde suo. Putasne centenario nascetur filius. et sara nonagenaria pariet? Dixitque ad deum. Utinam ysmahel vivat coram te. Et ait dominus ad abraham. Sara uxor tua pariet tibi filium: vocabisque nomen eius ysaac. Et constituam pactum meum illi in fedus sempiternum: et semini eius post eum. Super ysmahel quoque exaudivi te. Ecce benedicam eum. et augebo et multiplicabo eum valde. Duodecim duces generabit. et faciam illum in gentem magnam. Pactum vero meum statuam ad ysaac: quem pariet tibi sara tempore isto. in anno altero. Cumque finitus esset sermo loquentis cum eo: ascendit deus ab abraham. Tulit autem abraham ysmaelem filium suum: et omnes vernaculos domus sue. universosque quos emerat. cunctos mares ex omnibus viris domus sue: et circumcidit carnem preputii eorum statim in ipsa die sicut preceperat ei deus. Abraham nonaginta novem erat annorum. quando circumcidit carnem preputii sui. et ysmahel filius suus tredecim annos impleverat tempore circumcisionis sue. Eadem die circumcisus est abraham. et ysmahel filius eius. et omnes viri domus illius. tam vernaculi: quam emptitii. et alienigene pariter circumcisi sunt. XVIII

Apparuit autem ei dominus in convalle mambre. sedenti in hostio tabernaculi sui: in ipso fervore diei. Cumque elevasset oculos: et apparuerunt ei tres viri. stantes prope eum. Quos cum vidisset. cucurrit in occursum eorum de hostio tabernaculi. et adoravit in terram. et dixit. Domine si inveni gratiam coram oculis tuis: ne transeas servum tuum. sed afferam pauxillum aque. et laventur pedes vestri: et requiescite sub arbore. Ponam buccellam panis. et confortate cor vestrum: postea transibitis. Idcirco enim declinastis ad servum vestrum. Qui dixerunt. Fac ut locutus es. Festinavit abraam in tabernaculo ad saram: dixitque ei. Accelera tria sata simile commisce: et fac subcinericios panes. Ipse ad armentum cucurrit. et tulit inde vitulum tenerrimum et optimum. deditque puero. Qui festinavit. et coxit illum. Tulit quoque butyrum. et lac. et vitulum quem coxerat: et posuit coram eis. Ipse vero stabat iuxta eos: sub arbore. Cumque comedissent: dixerunt ad eum. Ubi est sara uxor tua? Ille respondit. Ecce in tabernaculo est. Cui dixit. Revertens veniam ad te tempore isto. vita comite: et habebit filium sara uxor tua. Quo audito sara: risit post hostium tabernaculi. Erant autem ambo senes. provecteque etatis: et desierant sare fieri muliebria. Que risit occulte dicens. Postquam consenui

EXTENT: 522 parchment folios
FORMAT: 360 x 253 mm
BINDING: Vienna library binding of 1752
CONTENT: Bible (Old and New Testament)
LANGUAGE: Latin
SCRIBE: Johannes (colophon on fol. 455v)
MINIATURISTS: four anonymous miniaturists from the workshop of Cristoforo Orimina (active around 1330–1365)
ILLUSTRATION: 39 large, historiated initials and 1,398 small initials, plus 184 square-framed miniatures

PROVENANCE: The manuscript was copied and illuminated for the circle of the Neapolitan court in around 1360. The coat of arms on fol. 291v and 349v and on the head, fore and tail edges has not yet been identified. The codex has been the property of the Vienna Hofbibliothek at the latest since 1576 (shelfmark inscriptions by the prefect Hugo Blotius).
SHELFMARK: Vienna, ÖNB, Cod. 1191

the start of the biblical books and chapters and along the bottom of the page. Elaborate series of illustrations are contained in particular in the Biblical narrative from Genesis to the end of the 2nd Book of Kings, then again in the 1st and 2nd Book of the Maccabees, Acts of the Apostles and the Apocalypse. The other books are sparsely illustrated, some only with historiated initials. Particularly striking is the complete absence, in the Gospels, of a cycle of the Life of Jesus, as found for example in the Hamilton Bible (Berlin, Kupferstichkabinett, Ms. 78 E 3) from the same Neapolitan workshop. Apart from portraits of the Evangelists with their respective symbols, the Gospels in the Vienna Bible are illustrated by only the Tree of Jesse in Matthew (fol. 362r), John the Baptist pointing to a bust of Christ in Mark, the Crucifixion in Luke (fol. 382r) and a Throne of Grace in John.

The selection of illustrations – which is similar to those in the other Bibles produced by this workshop – is based on the pictorial cycles which were ready to-hand in Naples. Thus the illustrations of the Apocalypse are based on the frescos in S. Maria di Donnaregina (executed after 1317) and on the so-called Erbach Panel painted in the 1330s (now Stuttgart, Staatsgalerie). The cycle of Old Testament scenes derives from the same sources as the wall paintings in the church of S. Maria Incoronata, which cannot be dated before 1368, however.

On fol. 455v the scribe gives his name as Johannes. He may possibly be identical with Magister Johannes of Ravenna, who wrote the Hamilton Bible in Berlin and a Breviary (Ms. a. III. 12) in the Escorial.

K.-G. P.

Fol. 9v (Genesis): Three angels appear to Abraham.

▸ **Fol. 23v–24r (Genesis, Exodus):** Jacob prophesies to his sons. Death of Jacob. On the right, the sons of Israel enter Egypt

▸▸ **Detail from fol. 19r (Genesis):** Joseph is sold to the Ishmaelites.

t̃dicit i manu ipi̅ uniu̾sos uinctos q
i custodia tenebant̃. ⁊ qcqd fiebat sub
ipo erat. nec nouat aliqd cunctis ei cre
ditis. Et dns enim erat cum illo. ⁊
oia opa ei9 dirigebat. XL xl

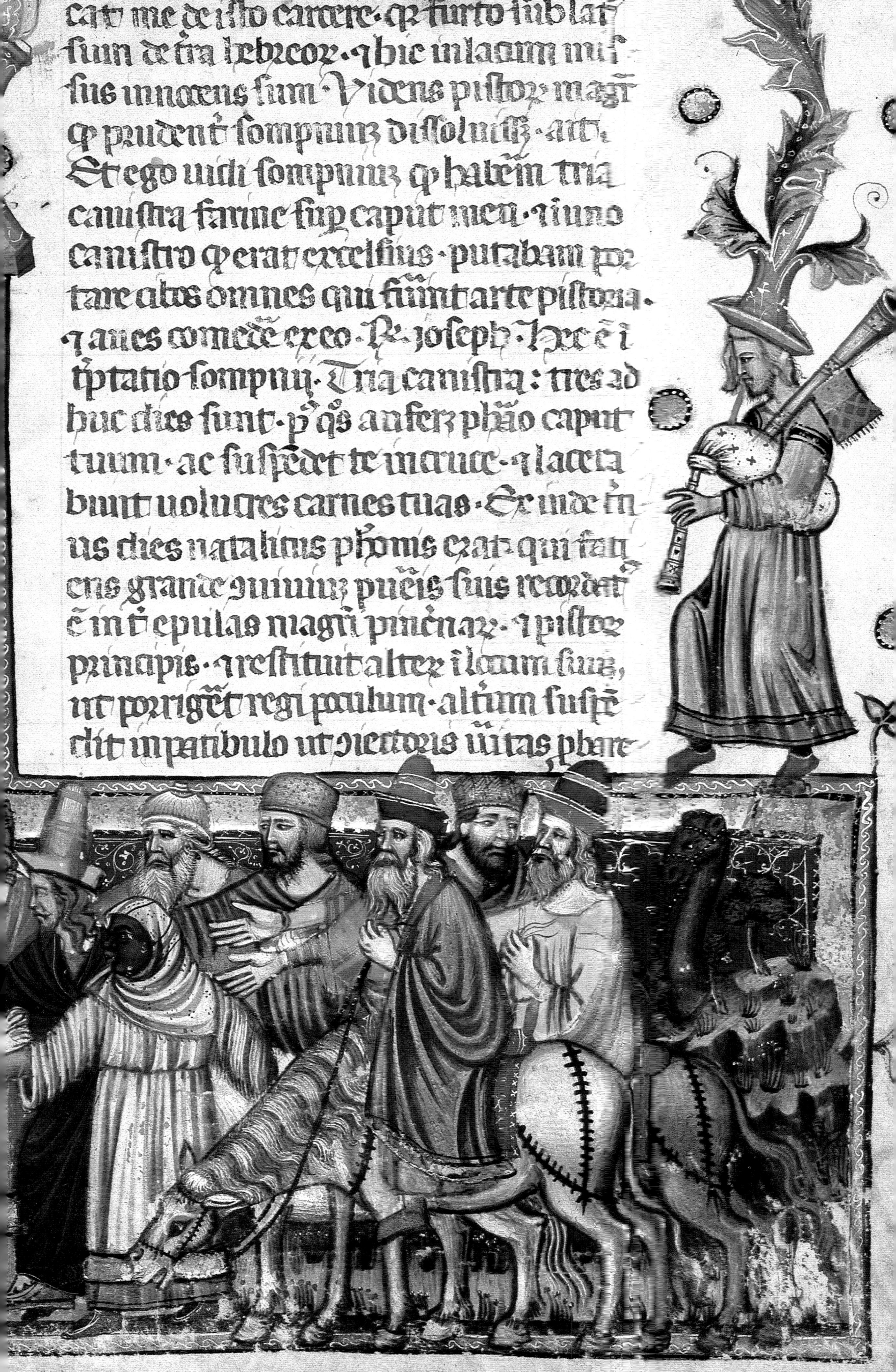

cat me de isto carcere. quia furto sublatus
sum de terra hebreorum. et hic in lacum mis
sus innocens sum. Videns pistorum magister
quod prudenter sompnium dissolvisset. ait.
Et ego vidi sompnium quod haberem tria
canistra farine super caput meum. et in uno
canistro quod erat excelsius. putabam por
tare cibos omnes qui fiunt arte pistoria.
et aves comedere ex eo. Respondit joseph. Hec est in
terpretatio sompnii. Tria canistra: tres ad
huc dies sunt. post quos auferet pharao caput
tuum. ac suspendet te in cruce. et lacera
bunt volucres carnes tuas. Exinde ter
us dies natalicius pharaonis erat. qui faci
ens grande convivium pueris suis recordatus
est inter epulas magistri pincernarum. et pistorum
principis. et restituit alterum in locum suum,
ut porrigeret regi poculum. alterum suspen
dit in patibulo ut coniectoris veritas probaretur

Detail from fol. 107r (1 Samuel): David and Goliath. In the background, the brothers try to keep David back.

Detail from fol. 197r (Ezra, Tobit): Tobias and his wife Hannah distribute alms to the brothers of his tribe. In the foreground he buries kinsmen murdered by Sanherib.

◂ **Fol. 457r (Psalms):** David with a psaltery accompanying Psalm 1.

Detail from fol. 444r (Acts of the Apostles): The storm at sea during Paul's journey to Rome as a prisoner (Acts 27:14–26).

II.7

Eberler Bible

Basle, 1464

Translations of scriptural texts belong amongst the very first instances of written German: the oldest surviving examples are the so-called Mondsee Fragments containing St Matthew's Gospel, dating from around 800 (Vienna, ÖNB, Cod. 3093*). Over the following centuries, further sections of the Bible were translated and began to be published as separate books, as in the case of the Psalter, which was used as a prayer book, and other books from the Old Testament.

The first complete Bibles in the German language only appeared in the 14th century and until the invention of printing and the dawn of the Reformation remained a somewhat rare phenomenon. The Eberler Bible belongs to a branch of these complete German-language Bibles which traces its descent from some of the better translations. One indication of the quality of its translation, for example, is the fact that the word order adheres relatively closely to German syntax rather than to the Latin of the original. In a striking number of places, the codex offers several possible translations or includes the original Latin word, leaving it up to the reader to decide how to interpret the text.

Matthias Eberler, who commissioned the two-volume Vienna codex, came from a wealthy Basle family. His grandfather converted from the Jewish to the Christian faith and obtained his Basle citizenship in 1393. His grandson, evidently eager to strengthen his social position, acquired himself a title and spent his inheritance on a lavish lifestyle. The reason for his decision to commission a complete German-language Bible is unknown, but was probably linked with his social ambitions and family history. The two volumes of the Eberler Bible contain illustrations by a number of illuminators, probably all based in Basle.

Detail from Cod. 2769, fol. 302v (The Wisdom of Solomon, Prologue): King Solomon, who was thought to be the author of the text, in front of an interior view of the Temple of Jerusalem.

▸ **Cod. 2769, fol. Iv:** Beneath the coat of arms unfurls a banderole, whose inscription gives 1464 as the year in which the Bible was produced and names Matthias Eberler as its patron.

In dem iar als man zalt m. cccc. und
lxiiij. hat Mathis Eberler dis bybly
lassen machen. Des sell ruwe in
dem friden gots. Am.

Prolo

Bruder Ambrosius brachte mir dine gabe
vnd ouch dine süssesten brieff / die mir die
trüwe der bewertter trüwe für getragen
hant von anbeginn die fründtschaffte
ouch furtreffender sind / die nüwen vnd
alten fründtschaffte. Wann das ist ge
ware notturfft vnd mit xpi eynung ge
füget / die nit gemachet ist mit nütze
eines dienstberen dinges / noch gegen
wertigs der personen / noch mit akustig
streichender gluchsinge / sunder die die
gotz forchte vnd die lere der heiligen
schriffte machent / Wir haben gelesen
in den historien der alten / das etlich die
lender durch füren / ze sehende ein nüwes
volke / vnd über das mer / durch daz si in
gegenwertigs gesehen / die die sie von den
büchern bekanten / also pitagoras die inem
phi ticos philosophos / vnd als Plato
Egiptum vnd Architentarentinum / vnd
daselbe lant Ytalie mit grosser arbeit

vnd die volcker

gebede

EXTENT: two volumes; Vol. I: II + 331 parchment folios; Vol. II: 263 parchment folios
FORMAT: Vol. I: 400 x 290 mm; Vol. II: 385 x 280 mm
BINDING: white parchment binding, dated 1756, with imperial *supralibros* and the initials of the Hofbibliothek and praefect Gerard van Swieten (1745–1772)
CONTENT: Bible (Old and New Testament). Vol. I: Genesis to Koheleth [Ecclesiastes]; Vol. II: Isaiah to Apocalypse (Revelation)
LANGUAGE: Middle High German
SCRIBE: Johann Liechtenstern of Munich
ILLUSTRATION: Vol. I: one coat-of-arms page, 24 historiated initials; Vol. II: one coat-of-arms page, 28 historiated initials
PATRON: Matthias Eberler, 1464
PROVENANCE: ex libris inscriptions place the Eberler Bible in the library of the Archdukes of Tyrol in Ambras Castle (Cod. 2769, fol. IIr: MS Ambras 20; Cod. 2770, fol. 1r: MS Ambras 21). In 1665, when the Tyrolean line of the house of Hapsburg died out, the collection was inherited by next-of-kin Emperor Leopold I, and the two volumes passed into the Vienna Hofbibliothek.
SHELFMARK: Vienna, ÖNB, Cod. 2769–2770

The prologues and biblical books all open with historiated initials. In Volume I, a single artist was responsible for the coat-of-arms page (ill. p. 111), the entire decoration of fol. 1r (ill. p. 112) and the internal fields of the initials from folio 2r to 237v (ill. p. 115). His figures, convincingly realistic in their poses and gestures, are set within landscapes that recede through successive planes into a bluish distance. For his border decoration, he employs green leaves of more or less the same shape, whose curling tips end in a different colour. By contrast, a second illuminator (aided by his workshop) uses a very varied repertoire of forms executed in bold colours, which has been convincingly traced back to earlier manuscripts preserved or illuminated in Basle (Escher [1923-25]). To this artist we can attribute the execution of the initials as from fol. 250v in the first volume and the entire decoration of the second volume. He or one of his assistants probably also completed the ornamentation of most of the initials by his colleague, plus the silver filigree on fol. Iv (ill. p. 111), since these all employ his formal repertoire.

The figures by the second artist differ strikingly from those of the first in their unusual poses, while the landscape in the distant background is rendered in paler, but not bluish, shades. A third painter was evidently responsible for the coat-of-arms page in the second volume, since the head of the donkey is shaped and modelled differently to that by the first artist (ill. p. 111). In its more limited palette and the greater uniformity of its ornament, the coat-of-arms page in the second volume also differs, however, from the style of the second artist, who executed the decoration on the opposite folio (ill. p. 112) and who would probably have aimed at a much better visual balance between the two pages. *C.B*

Detail from Cod. 2769, fol. 1r (Genesis, Prologue):
The Creation of Eve. The sun and moon look back to the earlier separation of the light and the darkness; the landscape in the background includes a castle, a city and a ship.

Nachdem todt Josue do rat fragetend die
süne israhel den hren vnd sprachen wer
vart vff vor vns wider chananeum
vnd wirt ein houbt vnsers striites/ der
herre sprach Judas fart vff Sehent
das lande han ich geben in sine gewalt
Vnd Judas sprach zu Symeon sinem
brüder far vff mit mir in myne lose
vnd strit mit mir wider chananeu
das ouch ich fare mit dir in dinem
teile Vnd Simeon für mit sme Vnd Ju
das für vff Vnd der hre gap chana
neum vnd pherezeum in sin hant vn
schlügen in bezech zehen tusent man
Vnd funden adonibezech in bezech vn
fachten wider in/ vnd schlügen cha
naneum vnd pherezeum Aber adoni
bezech vlohe Dem iageten sie nach
vnd betriffen in vnd gestümelten sin hen
de vnd füsse Vnd adonibezech sprach
Sibentzig künig samenoten aleiben
der spise/ vnder myne tisch mit abgeschla
gen henden vnd füssen Als ich getan
han/ also hat mir got wider gethan
Vnd fürten in in iherusalem/ vnd do
starp er/ Aber die süne Juda stürmete
an iherusalem/ vnd gewunnen sie vnd
schlugen sie mit dem swerte/ vnd vr
branten si miteinander/ Dornach
füren si aber vnd striten wider chana
neu/ der do wonte in dem gebirge/ vn
gegen dem mittellande vnd in velt
lande/ Vnd Judas für wider chananeu
der do wonte in Ebron/ des name von
alter was cariatharbe/ vnd schlüge
Sisai achiman vnd tholmai/ vnd für
darnach zu denen/ die do woneten
zu Dabir/ die nach dem alten na
men hiess/ Cariathsepher das ist ein
stat der büchstaben Vnd caleb sprach
wer schlahet cariath sepher/ vnd si zer
störet/ dem gib ich axam myne tochter
ze wibe Vnd do othoniel sun cenez ein
brüder calebs/ der der iungeste was/ die
stat gewinnt/ Do gab er im sine toch
ter ze wibe die mante ir man vff dem
wege das sie hieschte von irm vater eine
acker Vnd do sie rite vff einem esele
vnd ersufftzete Do sprach ir vater Ca
leb/ was ist dir Vnd si antwurte Gib
mir den segen/ wann du mir hast ge
ben ein dürre lande/ gip mir ouch das
füchte Vnd caleb gab ir ouch dz fücht
mit wasser vnden vnd oben Aber die
süne cynei magen moisen/ füren vff vo
der stat der palmen mit den sünen Jud
in die wüstin irs losses gegen dem mit
tellande arad/ vnd wonten mit ime
Vnd Judas für enweg mit Symeon
sinem brüder/ vnd erschlügen mitein
ander chananeu der do wonte in sepha
vnd der stat namen ward geheyssen
Horma/ das ist verdapnüsse Vnd Ju
das gewint gazam mit sinen landen
Vnd ascalon vnd accaron mit sinen lan
den/ Vnd der hre was mit Juda/ vnd
besass das gebirge/ noch mochte nit v
tilken die woner des tales/ wann si
vberflüssig waren mit gescharsache
ten wegenen/ Vnd si gaben Ebron ca
leb/ als moises gesprochen hate/ vnd
er tilkete us ir dry süne enach Aber
die süne Benyamyn vertilketen nit
Jebuseum der won zu iherusalem/ vnd
Jebuseus wonte mit sünen Benyamy
zu iherusalem bis vff disen tag Ouch
das huss Joseph für vff zu Bethel/ vn
der hre was mit inen/ wann do sie be
sessen hetten ein stat/ die vor lusa gehei
sen was/ do sahen si einen menschen vs
gan/ von der stat/ vnd si sprachen zu
im Zouge vns den ingang der stat
So wollen wir dich begnaden Vnd do
er in gezöugete/ do schlügen si die sta
mit dem swert/ Aber den menschen
liessen sie gan/ mit allem sinem gesch
lechte/ Vnd do er gelassen ward/ do fur
er in das lande ethim/ vnd buwete do
ein stat/ vnd nante die lusam vn heis
set also vntz vff disen tag Ouch
manasse tilkete nit bethsan vnd tha
nac/ mit sinen cleinen castellen Vnd
die woner der/ vn ieblaam vnd ma
gedde/ mit iren cleinen castellen/ Vnd
chananeus begonde wonen mit inen

Detail from Cod. 2769, fol. 60v (Numbers): The Lord commands Moses to take a census of Israelite men able to go to war.

Detail from Cod. 2769, fol. 310v (Ecclesiastes, Prologue): King David and his son Koheleth.

◂ **Cod. 2769, fol. 107v (Judges):** The Lord appoints Judah the new leader of the Israelites.

Detail from Cod. 2769, fol. 96r (Joshua, Prologue): The people of Israel about to cross the River Jordan, led by Joshua in full armour.

Detail from Cod. 2769, fol. 250v (Psalms, Prologue): King David with his harp (on a separate page to the Prologue text).

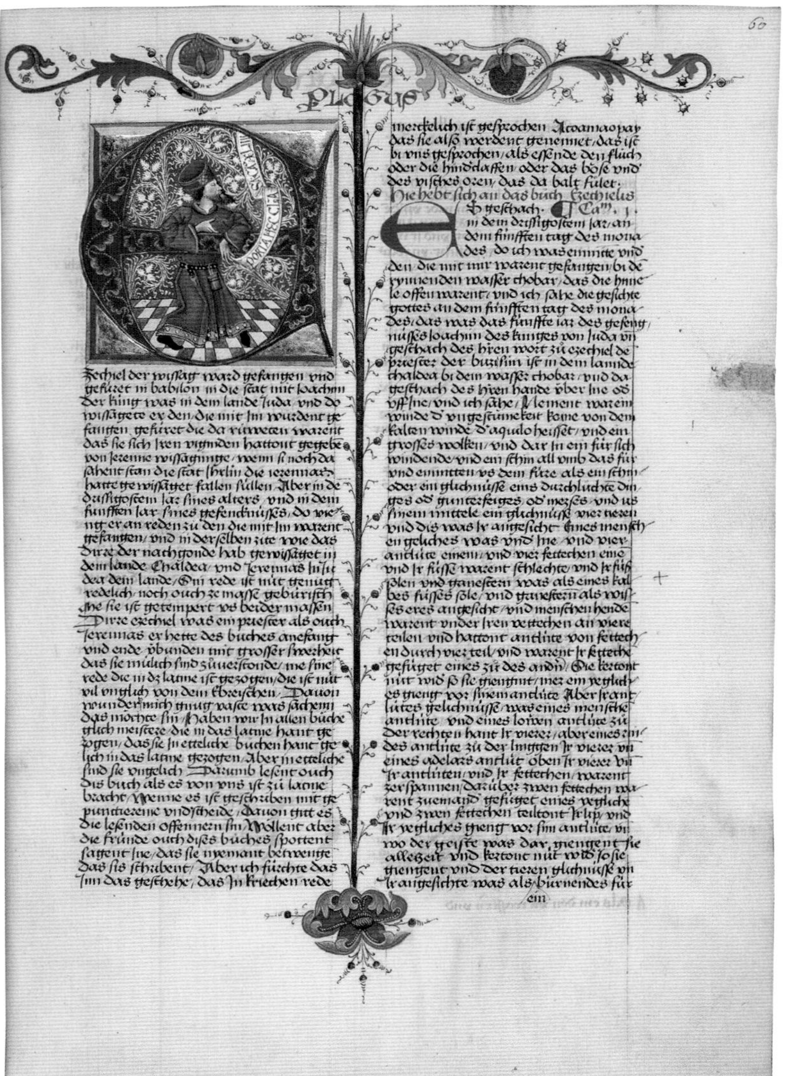

Cod. 2770, fol. 60r (Ezechiel, Prologue): The prophet Ezechiel with banderole inscribed: *PORTA HEC CLA(U)SA. CA(PITULUM) XLIIII.* ("This gate [shall] be shut, Chapter 44").

Cod. 2770, fol. 144v (St Matthew, Prologue): St Matthew the Evangelist with banderole inscribed: *(LI)BER GENERACIONIS. CA(PITULUM) I* ("Book of the generation of [Jesus Christ]. Chapter 1").

▸ **Detail from Cod. 2770, fol. 255r (Apocalypse, Prologue):** St John on Patmos.

ROLOGUS

Alle die in xpo wellent miltecliche lebē
als d' zwelffbott sprichet / die müssent
durchechtunge liden nach disem worte
Sun so du wilt zu gen zu gottes dienst
so sta in gerechtekeit und in forchte un
bereite din sele zu der bekorunge od zu
anfechtunge oder wann die bekorunge
od' anfechtunge ist des menschen le
ben uff dem ertrich Do aber die glou
bigen nüt gebresten an disen dingen
so tröstet sie d' herre und sterckert sie sprech
ende · Ich bin mit üch bis zu endunge
d' welte / und sollent üch nüt furchten
ir deine herte / darumb got der vatter
sehende die kestegunge die lidende wz
die cristenheit die von zwelffboten ge
fundieret ist · uff den xpm uff dz die be
trübde oder die kestegunge mynre we
dent gefurchtet so ist ez ze rate wor
den oder hat geordenot sament mit
dem sime / und mit dem heiligen geiste
ze offenbarende die kestegunge · Aber

II.8 Luxury Bible by Ulrich Schreier

Salzburg (?), 1472

Illuminated by Ulrich Schreier in 1472 and written for a member of the Prasch family in Hallein, the present Vulgate is one of many Bibles produced entirely by hand even after the appearance of the first printed editions. Contrary to widespread opinion, manuscript production continued to play an important role even after the publication of the 42-line Gutenberg Bible in around 1453/54. By 1472 no less than another nine Latin and two German editions of the Bible had rolled off the new presses, yet it was only towards 1480 that the manuscript industry truly began to decline. The reasons for this are various, with probably the most important being the high prices charged for the new printed books, and the fact that, for reasons of economy, they omitted decorative initials (the purchaser generally had to engage an illuminator to add them later). Ulrich Schreier himself illustrated several incunabula, including a Bible more or less contemporaneous with Codex 1194, which was printed in Strasburg around 1470 and is today housed in the Austrian National Library (ÖNB, Ink. I. A. 18).

Carefully but not excessively decorated with miniatures, Codex 1194 contains 63 *fleuronnée* and 21 mostly ornamental initials. Only four of them actually illustrate the text: St Jerome in the Prologue (ill. p. 120), the seven days of Creation in Genesis (ill. p. 119), a bust of St John accompanying the 1st Epistle of John and – most unusually – the depiction of a youth sitting in a flower accompanying the Song of Songs (probably Chapter 2:1). The busts contained in initials in Psalm 26, at the beginning of the books of Isaiah, Daniel, Obadiah and Jonah, and in Habakkuk, Malachi and Galatians are without attributes and are too unspecific to be able to identify them as portraits of David, the respective prophets or St Paul. They appear to have been chosen arbitrarily and do not correspond to the iconography conventionally used in Bibles, as seen in another Vulgate

Detail from fol. 271v (Baruch): Decorative border.

▸ **Detail from fol. 4r (Genesis):** The story of Creation.

Incipit liber bresith id est genesis

In principio creavit deus celum
et terram terra autem erat inanis
et vacua et tenebre erant super
faciem abyssi et spiritus dei ferebatur
super aquas Dixitque deus fiat
lux Et facta est lux Et vidit deus
lucem quod esset bona et divisit
lucem ac tenebras appellavitque
lucem diem et tenebras noctem
factumque est vespere et mane dies
unus Dixit quoque deus fiat fir
mamentum in medio aquarum et
dividat aquas ab aquis Et fecit
deus firmamentum divisitque aquas
que erant sub firmamento ab aquis
que erant super firmamentum Et factum
est ita Vocavitque deus firmamen
tum celum Et factum est vespere
et mane dies secundus Dixit
vero deus congregentur aque que
sub celo sunt in locum unum et
appareat arida Factumque est ita Et vocavit deus ari
dam terram congregationesque aquarum appel
lavit maria Et vidit deus quod esset bonum et ait Ger
minet terra herbam virentem et facientem semen
et lignum pomiferum faciens fructum iuxta genus
suum cuius semen in semetipso sit super terram Et
factum est ita Et protulit terra herbam virentem et

EXTENT: II + 419 parchment folios
FORMAT: 375 x 280 mm
BINDING: blind-tooled binding by Ulrich Schreier, Group I
CONTENT: Bible (Old and New Testament)
LANGUAGE: Latin
MINIATURIST: Ulrich Schreier (active *c.* 1450– *c.* 1490)
ILLUSTRATION: 21 decorated and illuminated initials, 63 *fleuronnée* initials

PROVENANCE: The manuscript was probably produced in Salzburg for a member of the Prasch family in Hallein (coat of arms on fol. 1r), and is documented at the latest around 1700 in the Salzburg archbishop's reference library. From there the codex passed to the Vienna Hofbibliothek in 1806.
SHELFMARK: Vienna, ÖNB, Cod. 1194

by Ulrich Schreier, illuminated in 1469 and today housed in the University Library in Graz (Cod. 48). The remaining, predominantly non-figural initials are opulently decorated with ornaments, flowers, grimacing faces and richly-varied tooling on a gold ground. The foliate arabesques that issue from them are populated by stylized flowers, a diversity of creatures such as ladybirds and birds, and also human masks and drolleries. The *fleuronnée* employed for the subordinate initials also features the human masks typical of Schreier.

The date of the manuscript is given both at the end of the text and in the initial on fol. 301v, which also includes the name of the artist in an illusionistically draped banderole: *die bibell hat illuminiert der schreier*. In total, more than 60 books and as many bindings can today be attributed to Ulrich Schreier, who worked as a bookbinder as well as a miniaturist and who not infrequently signed and dated his works. While the beginnings of his artistic activity remain shrouded in obscurity, we are well informed about his subsequent career. We meet him for the first time in 1459, in Codex 5038 in the Austrian National Library. Up till 1482, Schreier was active chiefly for the Salzburg archbishop Bernhard von Rohr (1466–1482) and for patrons in the Salzburg area. He then moved to Lower Austria, where he can be found working primarily in Vienna, Klosterneuburg and Preßburg. Towards the end of his life he is documented in Mondsee and Linz. His last known work is the lavishly illustrated Greiner Marktbuch (Upper Austria) from 1489/90.

K.-G. P.

Fol. 1r: St Jerome at his desk.

Detail from fol. 62v (Joshua): Ornamental initial.

Detail from fol. 210v (Song of Songs): Bust (of the bridegroom?) behind a rose, from the Song of Songs.

Detail from fol. 159v (Tobit): Initial from the Book of Tobit.

Detail from fol. 306r (Jonah): Bust of a scholar from the Book of Jonah.

▸ **Fol. 200v (Proverbs):** Ornamental initials from the Prologue and Book of Proverbs.

▸▸ **Fol. 304v–305r (Obadiah):** Ornamental initials and bust of a man in a hat from the Book of Obadiah.

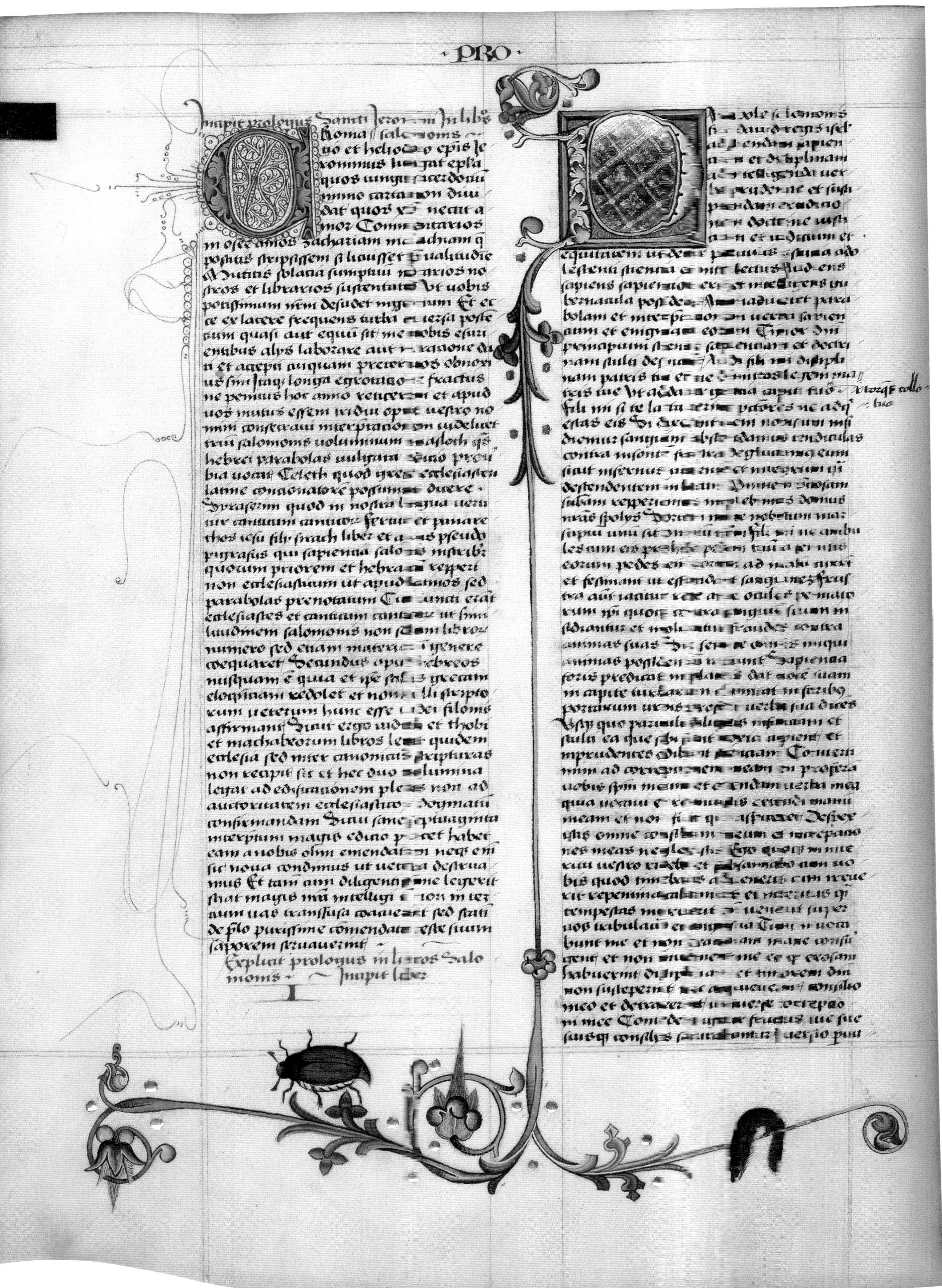

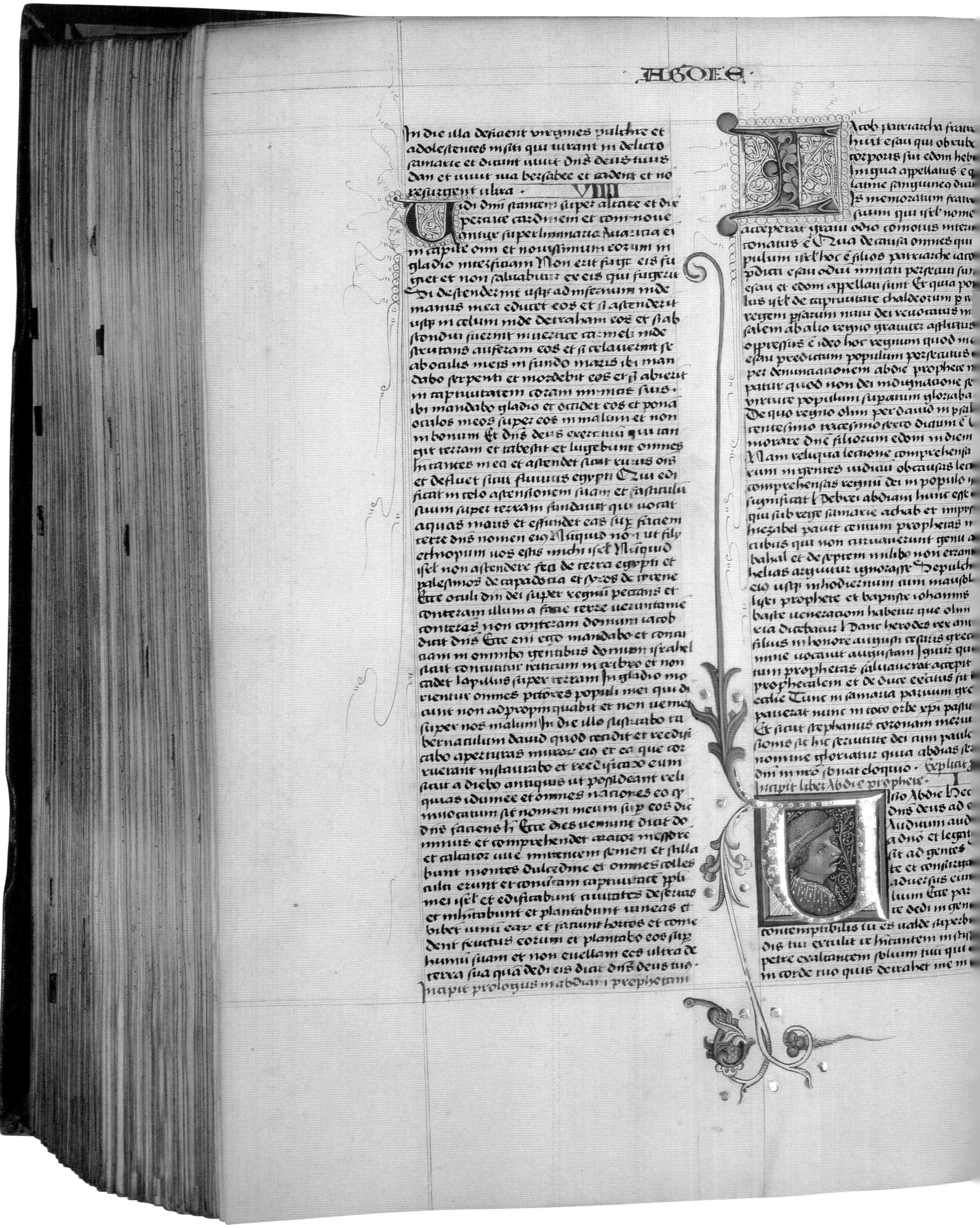

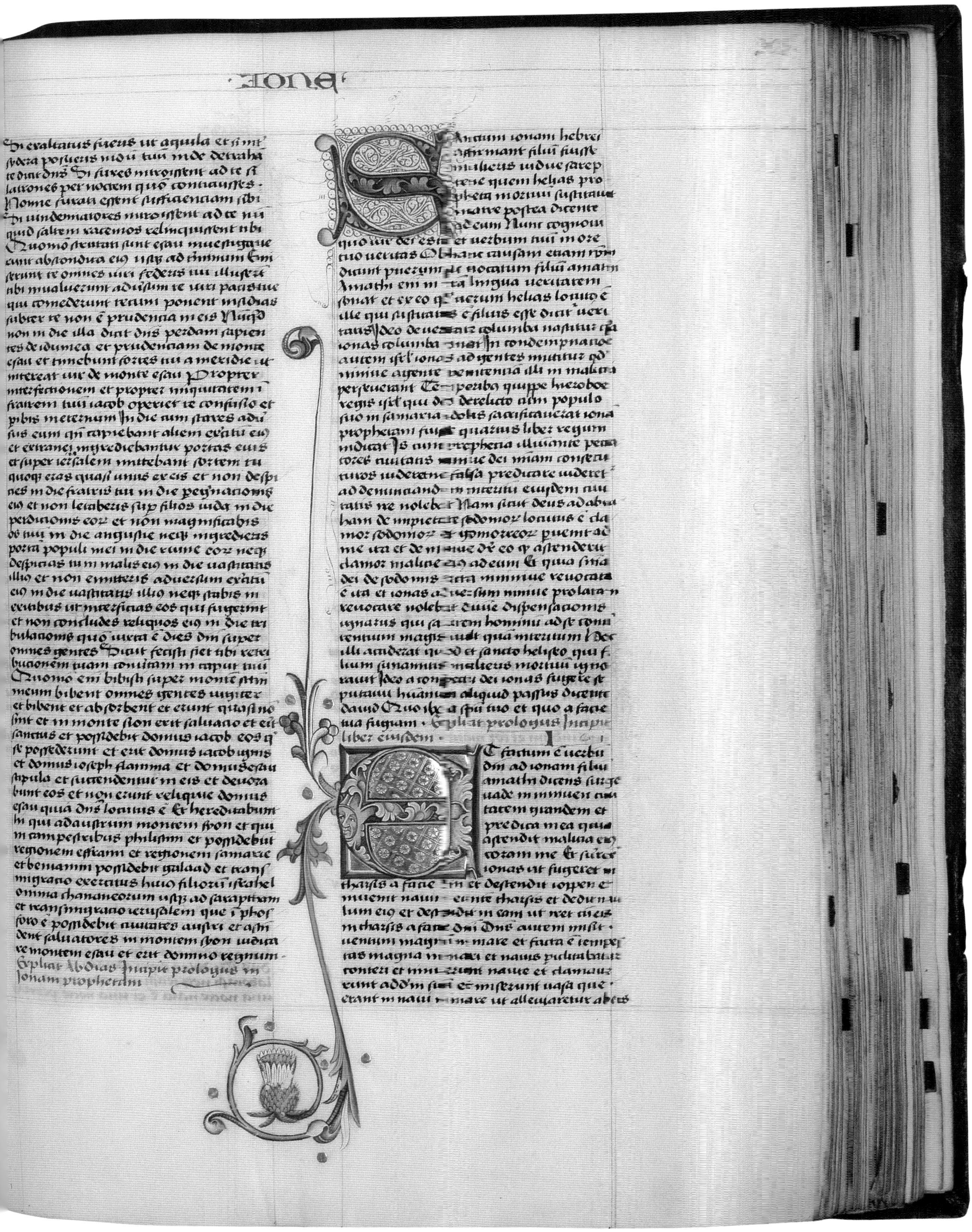

II.9

Utrecht Luxury Bible

Utrecht (Netherlands), around 1430

In the northern Netherlands towards the end of the 14th century, demand for illuminated manuscripts began to increase, first at the court of the Count of Holland, who from the second half of the 14th century resided in The Hague, and then in other towns and cities within the counties of the northern Netherlands and the bishopric of Utrecht. The increasing wealth of the inhabitants of these regions, coupled with the interest amongst the nobility, senior clergy and prosperous burghers in handsome manuscripts, provided the stimuli for the emergence of a local tradition of manuscript production and illustration.

Utrecht rapidly developed into an important centre of manuscript illumination, whose products were coveted far beyond the bishopric's bounds. Indeed, a document of 1426 from Bruges in Flanders reports of complaints by local artists about the import of illuminated manuscripts from "Utrecht and other towns" and upholds the ban on such trade. One of Utrecht's leading miniaturists during this same period – approximately 1415 to 1440 – was the illuminator of the first two volumes of the present Bible (Cod. 1199 and 1200). He is named after the Utrecht bishop Zweder van Culemborg, for whom he illuminated a Missal (Bressanone, Seminary, Ms. C. 20). This "Master of Zweder van Culemborg" frequently worked with other miniaturists; some of these were established artists in their own right, such as the Master of the Book of Hours of Catherine of Cleves (New York, Pierpont Morgan Library, Morgan 917 and 945), while others clearly worked in a derivative manner. How this collaboration was organized is a question yet to be answered, but it can be assumed that the Master of Zweder van Culemborg ran his own workshop.

Detail from Cod. 1199, fol. 120v (Joshua): God commands Joshua to cross the river Jordan with the people of Israel.

► **Detail from Cod. 1199, fol. 5r (Genesis):** The Fall. Illustrated in the marginal decoration are the Seven Days of Creation. The scribe has left space for a miniature cycle in the left-hand column (no rulings); why it was never used by the illuminator remains a mystery.

luce a tenebris Appellauitq3 luce die:
et tenebras nocte. Factuq3 est uespere
et mane: dies vnus. Dixit q3 deus.
Fiat firmamentu in medio aquaru:
et diuidat aquas ab aquis. Et fecit
deus firmamentu: diuisitq3 aqs que
erat sub firmameto ab hys que erat
sup firmametu. Et factu est ita. Vo
cauitq3 deus firmametu celu. Et fac
tu est uespe et mane: dies secudus.
Dixit uo deus. Congregetur aque
que sub celo sut in locu vnu: et appa
reat arida. Factuq3 est ita. Et uocauit
deus arida terram: congregatioesq3
aquaru appellauit maria. Et vidit
deus q eet bonu: et ait. Germinet tra
herba virente et faciente semen: et
lignu pomiferu faciens fructu iux
ta genus suu: cui seme sit in semet
ipso sit sup tiam. Et factu est ita. Et
protulit terra herbam virente et af
ferente seme iuxta genus suu: lig
q3 faciens fructu: et habens vnuqd
q3 semente scdm spe e sua. Et vidit
deus q eet bonu: factu q3 uespere et
mane dies tertius Dixit aute deus.
Fiant luminaria in firmameto celi. et
diuidat diem ac nocte: et sint i sig
na et tpa. et dies et anos: et luceant
in firmameto celi et illuminent terra.
Et factu est ita. Fecitq3 deus duo mag
na luminaria: luminare mai ut pre

Incipit epistola sancti iheronimi presbiteri
ad paulinum de omnibus diuine
historie libris Capitulum primum

Frater ambrosius tua mihi munuscula perferens
detulit simul et suauissimas litteras: que
a principio amicitiarum fidem probate
iam fidei et ueteris amicicie preferre-
bant. Vera enim illa necessitudo est et christi
glutino copulata: quam non utilitas
rei familiaris. non presentia tantum corporum.
non subdola et palpans adulatio:
sed dei timor. et diuinarum scripturarum
studia conciliant. Legimus in veteribus
hystoryis quosdam lustrasse prouincias.
nouos adisse populos. maria transisse: ut eos quos ex libris nouerant:
coram quoque viderent. Sic pitagoras
menphiticos uates. sic plato egiptum et architam tarentinum eandemque oram
ytalie que quondam magna grecia
dicebatur. laboriosissime peragrauit:
ut qui athenis magister erat et potens.
cuiusque doctrinas achademie gimna-
sia personabant. fieret peregrinus atque
discipulus: malens aliena uerecunde discere quam sua impudenter ingerere. Denique cum
litteras quasi toto orbe fugientes persequitur.
captus a pyratis et uenundatus etiam
tyranno crudelissimo paruit. ductus capti-
uus. vinctus et seruus: tamen quia philosophus maior emente se fuit. Ad titum liui-
um lacteo eloquentie fonte manantem. de
ultimis hispanie galliarumque finibus
quosdam uenisse nobiles legimus: et quos
ad contemplationem sui roma non traxerat: unius hominis fama perduxit. Habuit
illa etas inauditum omnibus seculis celebrandumque miraculum: ut urbem tantam ingressi aliud extra urbem quererent. Apollonius siue ille magus ut uulgus loquitur.
siue philosophus ut pytagorici tradunt. intrauit persas. pertransiuit caucasum.
albanos scithas massagetas. opulentissima indie regna penetrauit: et
ad extremum latissimo physon amne transmisso
peruenit ad bragmanas: ut hyar-
cam in throno sedentem aureo. et de tantali fonte potantem. inter paucos discipulos de natura de moribus. ac dierum syde-
rumque cursu audiret docentem. Inde per
elamitas babilonios chaldeos medos assirios. parthos syros. phenices.
arabes. palestinos. reuersus alexandriam. perrexit ethyopiam: ut gimnoso-
phistas et famosissimam solis mensam
videret in sabulo. Inuenit ille uir u-
bique quod disceret: et semper proficiens semper
se melior fieret. Scripsit super hoc plenissime octo uoluminibus phylostratus

Quid loquar de seculi hominibus cum
apostolus paulus uas electionis
et magister gentium. qui de consciencia tanti
in se hospitis loquebatur. an experimentum queritis eius qui in me loquitur
christus. post damascum arabiamque lustratam
ascendit iherosolimam. ut videret petrum
et mansit apud eum diebus quindecim.
hoc enim misterio ebdoadis et ogdoadis

EXTENT: four volumes; Vol. I: III + 159 parchment folios, Vol. II: II + 206 parchment folios, Vol. III: IV + 185 parchment folios, Vol. IV: III + 192 parchment folios
FORMAT: 350–360 x 255–265 mm
BINDING: Vols. I and IV: brown leather with blind-tooled lines over wooden boards (Netherlands, first half of the 15th century). Vols. II and III: 19th-century parchment binding over pasteboard covers.
CONTENT: Bible (Old and New Testament); Vol. I: St Jerome's letter to Paulinus, Genesis to Ruth; Vol. II: Samuel to Koheleth [Ecclesiastes]; Vol. III: Job to Ezechiel; Vol. IV: Daniel to Revelation
LANGUAGE: Latin
MINIATURISTS: Master of Zweder van Culemborg and two other illuminators
ILLUSTRATION: Vol. I: three historiated initials, eight *fleuronnée* initials; Vol. II: one historiated initial, four illuminated initials, 15 *fleuronnée* initials; Vol. III: two historiated initials, one illuminated initial, 18 *fleuronnée* initials; Vol. IV: one historiated initial, two illuminated initials, 59 *fleuronnée* initials
PROVENANCE: In 1665 the four-volume Bible was transferred from Ambras Castle (Innsbruck) to the Vienna Hofbibliothek (see inscriptions *MS. Ambras* [illegible] *3* and [illegible] in the top margin of the first text page in each volume, ill. p. 173)
SHELFMARK: Vienna, ÖNB, Cod. 1199–1202

The miniatures attributed to the Zweder Master in the Utrecht Bible are distinguished by a careful, highly precise manner of painting, apparent both in the fine cross-hatching used to differentiate areas of shade and in the painstakingly worked folds of the draperies and the detailed rendering of faces and writing utensils. The desire to create a realistic atmosphere which prompted the artist to portray Jerome's rejected drafts of text, surely written without the aid of the Holy Ghost, lying discarded on the floor (ill. p. 128), did not prevent him from considering and opting for a gold ground – already a somewhat dated device even in his own day – as the appropriate setting against which to present the authors of the biblical texts and biblical events themselves. With his marginal decoration of trifoliate and tear-shaped leaves, the artist found an alternative to the thorn-leaf tendrils still being used by the illuminator of the third volume of the Utrecht Bible. This artist employs an ornamental vocabulary which, in addition to a number of motifs borrowed from the Zweder Master, includes flower pistils underlaid with gold hexagons (Cod. 1200, fol. 86v). This unusual form is found in a number of earlier manuscripts (e. g. Liège, University Library, Ms. Wittert 35, fol. 23r) attributed to the Master of the Childhood Cycle in a Book of Hours in New York (Pierpont Morgan Library, M. 866). The animation of the figures and the loose modelling of the faces also seem to point to the school of the Master of the Childhood Cycle rather than to that of the Zweder Master. The illuminator of the fourth volume copies the ornament of the Master of Zweder van Culemborg, but his miniatures fail to attain the latter's quality (ill. Cod. 1202, fol. 40r).

CB

Cod. 1199, fol. 1r (Genesis, Prologue): St Jerome.

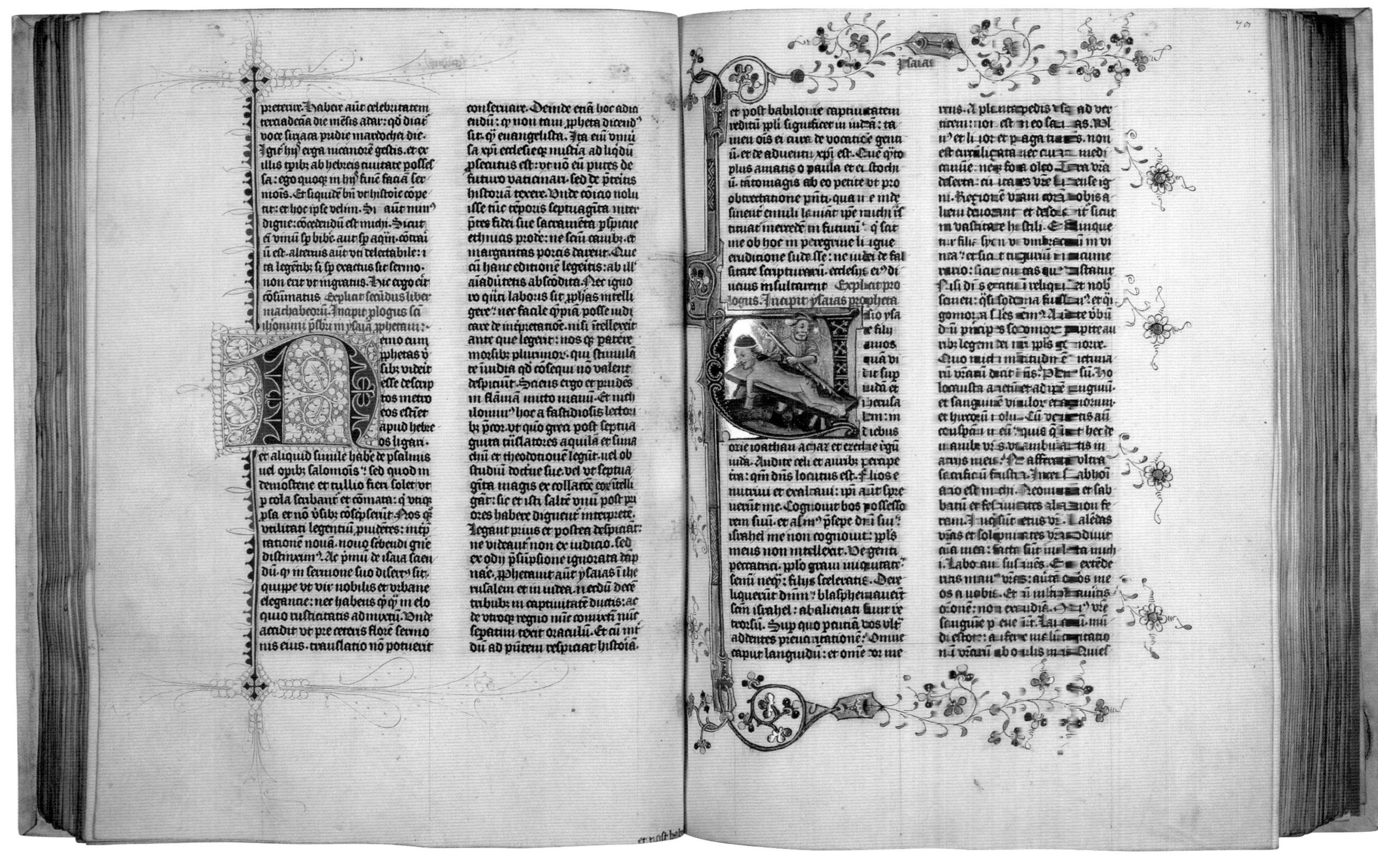

Cod. 1201, fol. 72v–73r (Isaiah, Prologue): *Fleuronnée* initial: *N(emo cum prophetas)*. Martyrdom of Isaiah.

► **Cod. 1200, fol. 1r (1 Samuel I Regum, Prologue):** St Jerome.

Incipit pfatio sci ierō[mi]. Uiginti

Uiginti
duas
esse
litte
ras
apud
hebre
os sy
rorūq;
lingua
et caldeorū testatur: que hebree in
magna ex parte cōfinis est. Nā
et ipsi viginti duo elemēta ha
bent: eodem sono sed diuersis ca
racterib;. Samaritani etiā pēta
teucū moysi totidē litteris scrip
titant: figuris tantū et apicib;
discrepantes. Certūq; est esdram
scribam legisq; doctorē post cap
tam iherosolimā et instauratio
nē templi sub zorobabel alias
litteras repperisse quib; nūc uti
mur: cū ad illud usq; tēpus idē
samaritanorū et hebreorū karac
teres fuerit. In libro quoq; nūo
rū hec eadem supputatio sub le
uitarū ac sacerdotū censu misti
ce ostendit: et nomē dnī tetra
grāmaton in quibusdā grecis
uolumīb; usq; hodie antiquis
expressū litteris inuenim9. Sed
et psalmi tricesim9 sextus et cen
tesimus decim9 et centesim9 un
decim9 et centesim9 octauus deci
mus et centesimus qdragesim9
quartus. q̄q̄ diuiso scribantur
metro: tamē eiusdem nūi tex

unt alphabeto: et ieremie lame
tationes et oratio eius. Salomo
nis quoq; in fine pūbia ab eo
loco in quo ait: mulierē fortem
quis inueniet. eisdē alphabetis
uel incisiōib; supputantur. Porro
qnq; littere duplices apud hebre
os sūt: caph. mem. nun. phe. sade.
Aliter enī p has scribūt pncipia
medietatesq; uborū: aliter fines.
Unde et qnq; a plerisq; libri du
plices estimantur: samuel. mala
chim. dabreiamin. esdras. iere
mias. cū cynoth id est lamentatiōib;
suis. Quomodo igit viginti du
o elemēta sūt p que scribimus
hebraice omē qd loquimur. et eo
initiis vox humana cōprehendit:
ita viginti duo volumina supputa
tur. quib; qsi litteris et exordiis
in dei doctrina tenera adhuc et
lactens uiri iusti erudit infantia.
Primus apud eos liber uocatur
bresith: quem nos genesim dici
mus. Secundus hellesmoth: qui
exodus appellatur. Tercius uaie
tra: id est leuiticus. Quartus uage
daber: quē numeri uocam9.
Qntus addabarim: qui deu
tronomiū prenotatur. Hy sūt
qnq; libri moysi: quos pprie tho
rath id est legem appellant. Scd'm
dū pphaꝝ ordine faciūt: et inci
piunt ab ihu filio naue. q apud
eos iosue bennun dicit. Deinde
subtexūt sophtim id est iudicum
librū: et in eūdē copingūt ruth:
quia in dieb; iudicū facta narrat

III. Biblical exegesis from the Church Fathers to Scholasticism

Commentaries on the Bible and biblical exegesis were perceived as a necessary response to Christianity's use of the Greek Septuagint as its "Old Testament". Why the holy scriptures should include the Septuagint – a translation of the Hebrew Bible – required particular explanation, one found in the doctrine of types. Thus individuals, facts and events in the Old Testament were understood to parallel and foreshadow their counterparts in the New Testament (cf. Luke 24:44; Acts 13:29; Romans 5:14 etc.). One such type was the Sacrifice of Isaac by Abraham, for example, which was seen to foreshadow the Crucifixion of Christ (antitype). The theory of types thereby provided one of the bases of Christian commentary and ensured that the Old Testament was a regular subject of Christian exegesis.

Information about the first Christian commentaries is sparse. Both in the East and West, these early works of exegesis were suppressed, in some cases almost completely, by the following, 4th-century generation of Church Fathers. Amongst the reasons for their suppression was the fact that, after lengthy high-level debates over dogma, many of them had since been declared heretical. One author whose writings suffered such a fate was the most important "Bible scholar" of early Christianity, Origen (*c.* 185–253). He was schooled in the best Hellenic tradition and was taught philosophy by Neoplatonists in Alexandria, where his education included the allegorical interpretation of ancient myths. In Caesarea he devoted himself to compiling a critical edition of the Septuagint, which he considered the prerequisite for any attempt at exegesis. Origen was opposed on a number of theological issues even during his lifetime, however, and in 542/543 was partially anathematized by Emperor Justinian, a move which probably contributed to the loss of many of his writings.

Ludolf of Saxony, Life of Christ, Cod. 1379, detail from fol. 121v: Half-length figure of a monk.

▸ Ludolf of Saxony, Life of Christ, Cod. 1379, detail from fol. 53v: The Flight to Egypt.

DE REDITU DOMINI EX EGIPTO.
ET INICIO PENITENTIE IOHANNIS
BAPTISTE. CAPITULUM QUATUORDECIMUM

Building upon Platonic philosophy, Origen developed in his work *De principiis* (IV 2) the system of the threefold levels of meaning that was subsequently employed by almost all commentators on the Bible (and made known to the West in 398 via the translation by Rufinus of Aquileia). These threefold levels of meaning are explained in anthropological terms as the tripartition of body, mind and spirit. According to this system, the Holy Scripture required not just a somatic (i. e. literal or grammatical; from the Greek *soma*, body) explanation, but also a psychic (moral) and pneumatic (allegorical) interpretation. Origen was thereby building upon the exegetical work of Philo (1st century AD), a Hellenized Jew also based in Alexandria, who in his Greek treatises on the Pentateuch attempted to reconcile Judaism with philosophical models. These writings were employed by Christian authors as the bases for their messianic interpretations.

As, in the 4th century, Christianity found itself tolerated, encouraged and finally the official religion, so Christian exegetic literature experienced a flowering both in the East and the West in the works of a number of theologians who had been educated in the classical tradition. Later canonized, these so-called Fathers of the Church were, in the West, Ambrose, Augustine, Pope Gregory the Great and Jerome. Also known as the Latin Doctors, these authors enjoyed an authority which equalled that of the four Evangelists.

The Church Fathers addressed their exegetic attention above all to the books of the Old Testament, which they interpreted in the standard threefold fashion. Ambrose commented on individual Psalms, Genesis and the Gospel of St Luke in ten volumes; Augustine's writings included treatises on Genesis (in three works), the Gospel of St John, and Psalms (in the Middle Ages, this *Enarrationes in Psalmos* would be his most influential commentary). Pope Gregory the Great moralized on the Book of Job, while Jerome (cf. Cat. III.1) was the Latin pendant to Origen. He, too, considered it vital to establish a reliable biblical text – something he was commissioned to do by Pope Damasus. This was all the more necessary in his own day as the Bible was available in a number of different translations, which made the text even harder to comprehend (cf. Chapter I, Introduction). At the same time, the existing threefold system was augmented by a fourth level of meaning, the anagogic (from the Greek *anagein*, to uplift or lead up); this was an eschatological interpretation of the Holy Scripture, an exegesis that pointed to the future fulfilment of God's promises. These four models of interpretation became the foundations of medieval biblical exegesis.

The exegetic writings of the following centuries were based on the many works by the Church Fathers, which they cited, compiled and expanded upon. Thus the Venerable Bede (*c.* 673–735), the most important English theologian of the $7^{th}/8^{th}$ century, compiled a commentary on the Epistles of St Paul from all the works by Augustine in which the latter comments on Paul. This tradition was continued during the Carolingian Renaissance ($8^{th}/9^{th}$ century), although this period also saw a number of important, independent exegetic writings such as the commentary on St Matthew by Radbert of Corbie (*c.* 790–860) and the commentary on St John by John Scot Eriugena (*c.* 810–877).

A new type of literary exegesis arose with the emergence of the cathedral schools and their teachings on the Bible in northern France (Chartres, Laon, Auxerres, Paris) from the late 11th century. Alongside these early Scholastic studies, there developed a compact method of incorporating commentary material into Bible manuscripts in the form of Glosses, which were written between the lines or in the margins. This development was part of a trend towards reducing the profusion of allegorical interpretations from the previous centuries to only the most essential annotations, in particular those pertaining to history. These annotations were once again drawn from the writings of the Church Fathers, but also from Carolingian exegetes. This type of commentary is called a *glossa* (often titled *Glossa ordinaria* or, synonymously, *Collectanea*, Peter Lombard, *Catena aurea*, St Thomas Aquinas and *Postilla*, Nicholas of Lyra. The first authors of such commentaries came from the schools of Laon (Anselm of Laon and his brother Radulf),

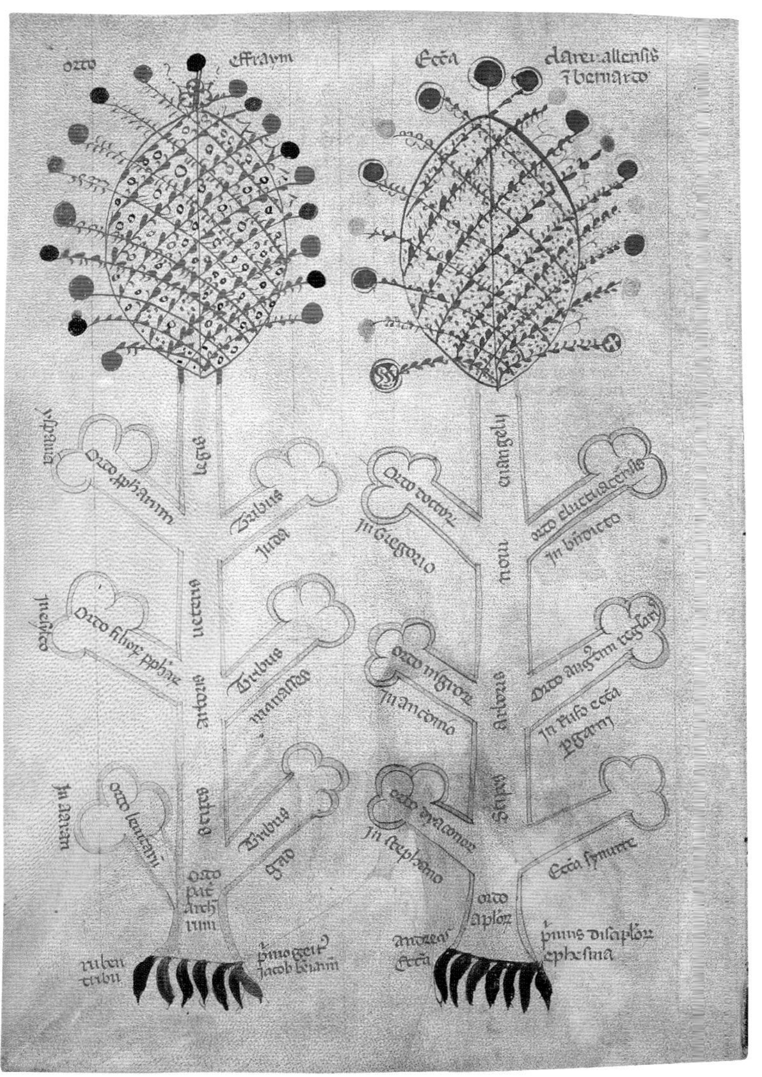

Auxerre (Gilbert of Auxerre) and Paris (Peter Lombard). The *glossa* was always presented separately to the Bible text, whereby in the East a similar type of gloss took the form of so-called catena commentaries (from the Latin *catena*, chain), in which quotations from the Church Fathers were noted around the text in closely-linked sequence.

Also during this period, the commencement of the Crusades (from 1095) brought a new awareness of the Holy Land, which in turn resulted in the Bible and its Hebrew sources being utilized as a supply of historical information (cf. Chapter IV, Introduction). Scholars embarked on histories of humankind from the Creation to the time of Jesus; we might mention here Peter Comestor and Peter of Poitiers, who wrote a genealogy of Christ (cf. Cat. IV.1). Commentaries on the Bible (with allegorical interpretations) conceived as books in their own right naturally continued to appear as evidenced in particular by Honorius Augustodunensis, Rupert of Deutz, who combines his commentaries with a theology of history, and Joachim of Fiore (cf. Cat. III.2). *CG*

Pseudo-Joachim of Fiore, Commentary on Isaiah, Cod. 1400, fol. 21v: Family trees of the Old and New Covenant.

St Thomas Aquinas, Catena aurea (on St Luke), Cod. 1[illegible]1, fol. 24r: Catena commentary on St Luke, Chapter 3.

III.1

St Jerome, Commentaries on the Bible

Florence, 1488

This magnificent manuscript, produced in Florence in 1488, contains St Jerome's commentaries on the Gospels of St Matthew and St Mark and on the Old Testament Book of Koheleth (Ecclesiastes). These are rounded off by shorter pseudoepigraphical and apocryphal writings: an address to bishops Heliodor and Chromatius wrongly attributed to St Jerome, the Life of the Virgin Mary and her correspondence with Bishop Ignatius of Antioch, the epistle of Prince Abgar of Edessa to Christ and the latter's reply, and an 11th-century disputation over the superiority of the Jewish, Christian or Moslem religion.

The codex formed part of the famous humanistic library created by Matthias Corvinus, King of Hungary, who made Vienna his residence between 1485 and 1490. During this period he commissioned a particular number of luxury manuscripts for his celebrated collection. Universal in its scope, his library embraced not only the Greek and Latin classics, but also the works of Church Fathers and Scholastics, as well as contemporary literature from the age of humanism.

According to an inscription by the scribe on fol. 238r, the present manuscript was completed on 19 October 1488 by one of the most important calligraphers of the Quattrocento, Sigismondo de' Sigismondi da Carpi, in a humanistic script (the so-called *Humanistica Formata*). It was probably illuminated immediately afterwards in Florence for King Matthias Corvinus, whose coat of arms and imprese (diamond ring, crowns, raven with ring) appear several times within the codex, together with a portrait of the King himself. In addition to its decorative title-page, frames and borders, the manuscript contains five large and 205 small gilt initials, and thereby represents a major work of Florentine miniature painting of the Quattrocento. Its illustrations are attributed to the

Detail from fol. 1r: Border with putto.

► **Fol. IIv:** Title-page vignette of a wreath of fruits containing the insignia of Matthias Corvinus (sphere and diamond ring).

EXTENT: II + 239 parchment folios
FORMAT: 355 x 240 mm
BINDING: Renaissance binding (from Ofen in Hungary, between 1488 and 1490); red morocco over wood with blind tooling, hand gilding and leather carving
AUTHOR: Jerome (347–419)
CONTENT: *Commentaria in sacram scripturam* (St Matthew, St Mark, Ecclesiastes)
LANGUAGE: Latin
SCRIBE: Sigismundus de Sigismundis, comes Palatinus Ferrariensis
MINIATURISTS: Gherardo (1446–1497) and Monte di Giovanni (1448–*c.* 1532/33)
ILLUSTRATION: five large and 205 small initials, one decorative title-page vignette, one decorative surround and one miniature, six decorative bars, one with a miniature
PROVENANCE: Written for Matthias Corvinus, King of Hungary (reigned 1458–1490) in 1488 in Florence, and illuminated immediately afterwards. By 15[illegible] the manuscript was already in the possession of the Vienna Hofbibliothek.
SHELFMARK: Vienna, ÖNB, Cod. 930

brothers Gherardo and Monte di Giovanni (del Fora), who are documented as both painters and mosaicists. This attribution is confirmed by a comparison with other manuscripts by these two miniaturists, such as a Missal completed between 1474 and 1476 for Sant' Egidio and today housed in Florence. Both artists also worked on the Psalter executed for King Matthias Corvinus in 1488 (Florence, Biblioteca Medicea Laurenziana, ms. Plut. 15, 17).

In comparison to works by other Italian contemporaries, the miniatures by the two brothers are distinguished by their technical mastery, their naturalism, the individualization of their figures and the vibrancy of their palette. The softness of the modelling and the use of transparent layers of glaze are taken from panel painting. The works by Gherardo have always been considered the more significant and are characterized by influences from Netherlandish painting – influences which can similarly be seen in the works of one of his temporary rivals, Domenico Ghirlandaio. Which parts of the illumination were painted by which brother is not easy to distinguish, but the figural miniatures are today generally attributed to Gherardo and the ornamental miniatures to his younger brother.

Significant, too, is the red morocco binding made for King Matthias Corvinus in Ofen between 1488 and 1490. Tooled with numerous decorative motifs – interlace, stamped palmettes and circles – and gilded by hand and richly painted, it is leather-carved on its front and back cover with the crowned coat of arms of King Matthias, presented in the centre of a quatrefoil which extends upwards and downwards like an ogee arch and is decorated with arabesques. Created by the so-called Corvinus Master, its design smoothly incorporates aesthetic impulses from both Italian and oriental bookbinding.

[illegible]-G. P.

Fol. 1r: Frontispiece to the introduction to the Commentary on St Matthew's Gospel, with a miniature of St Jerome surrounded, in the borders, by the four Evangelists, King Matthias Corvinus and Christ in majesty. In the centre of the lower border, the royal coat of arms.

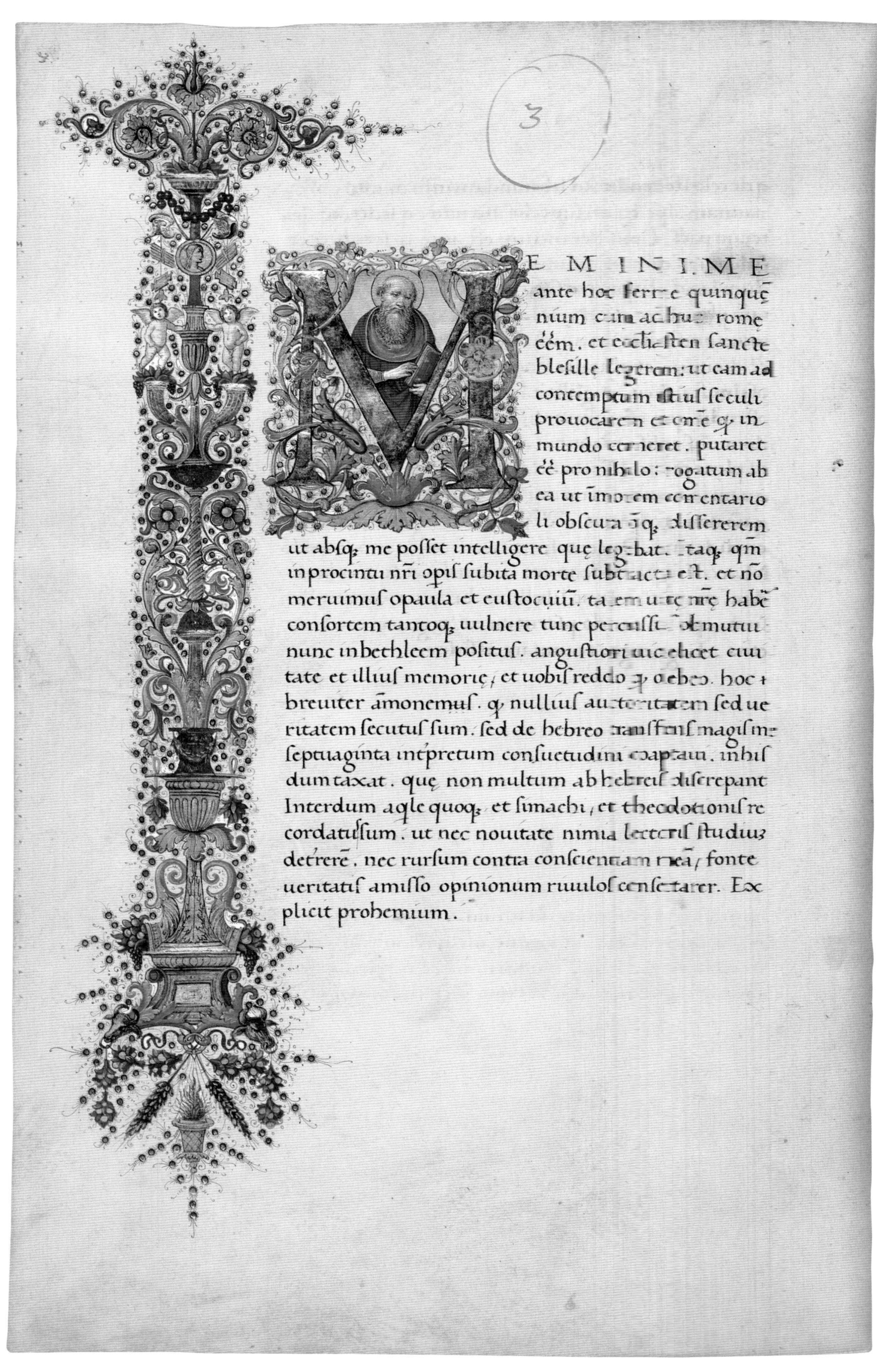

Fol. 147v: Preface to the Commentary on Koheleth (Ecclesiastes) with a portrait of St Jerome.

▸ **Detail from fol. 148r:** Ornamental initial *V (erba)* at the start of the Commentary on Koheleth (Ecclesiastes).

E R

eccliastes. f

gis ierlm. T

bus uocatu

monem scp

stissime ed

cum id. sal

idida hoc e

et q nunc c

eccliasten.

greco sermo

qui cetum.

get quem n

possumus concionatorem. eo q loquit

et sermo eius non specialiter ad unum.

sos gnaliter dirigat. Porro pacificus et c

ab eo q in regno eius pax fuit. et cum d

rit appellatus est. Nam et psalmus quac

et septuagesimus primus. dilecti et pacif

notantur. Q tametsi ad prophiam

III.2 Pseudo-Joachim of Fiore, Commentary on Isaiah

Southern Italy, 1st half of the 14th century

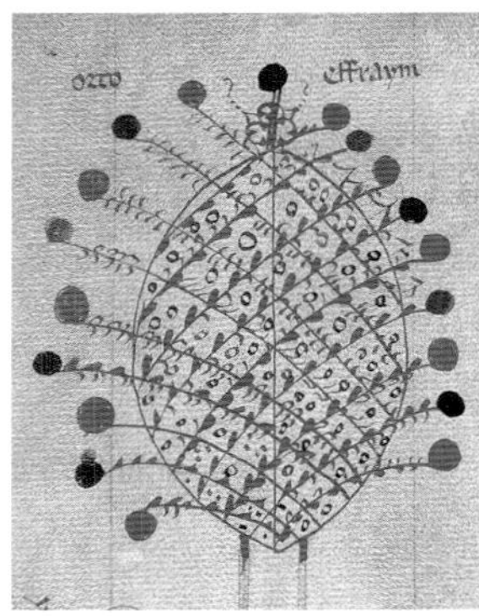

Joachim of Fiore was born in *c.* 1135 in Celico (Calabria) and began his career as a notary, like his father, at the court of the Norman kings in Palermo. He then decided to turn his back on the world and embarked on a pilgrimage to the Holy Land, after which he withdrew for a while to a cave in Sicily to fast and pray. Later he entered Corazzo monastery, where he was soon elected abbot. Through his offices, Corazzo was affiliated to the Cistercian abbey of Fossanova by Pope Clement III in 1188. In nearby Petralata, meanwhile, Joachim created for himself a place of solitude and quiet in which to pursue his exegeses of the Bible. He evidently refused to obey a summons from the Cistercian general chapter of 1192, but instead founded his own monastery (S. Giovanni in Fiore), which became the starting point for the Florensian order, which was eventually amalgamated with the Cistercian order by Pius V in 1570. Joachim died on 30 March 1202 in S. Martino di Giove.

Joachim was greatly admired for his prophecies. He represented a very pronounced form of typological exegesis: between the Old and New Testament, he believed, there existed a correlation so close that the events of the New Testament were not only already foreshadowed in the Old Testament (the doctrine of type and antitype), but that by projecting these parallels forward it was also possible to make predictions about the future. He divided history into three *status*, or periods: the age of the Father, that of the Son and that of the Holy Spirit. Joachim's exegetic works were primarily concerned with determining the nature of this third age, which would last until the end of time. He foresaw this age – whose dawn was imminent – as one of a new spiritual order characterized by a contemplative monastic life and by the recognition of the truth by all believers. First, however, the Antichrist, already present in the world, had to be overcome.

Detail from fol. 21v: Family tree of the Old Covenant.

▸ **Detail of fol. 21r:** Eagle – The number symbolism of 5 + 7 = 12, which Joachim originally linked with the eagle and which refers to the tribes of Israel, is reflected in the text above the eagle and in the number of divisions on his wings. Here, however, it applies to the Bible's different layers of meaning.

certorum in uno xpo conuenerunt. Dum quit es sacerdos i eter
nu3 secundum ordinem melchisedec qui fuit rex et sacerdos non
secundum ordinem aaron qui solus pontifex et umbratilis exti
tit non eternus.

Qui confidunt in domino mutabunt fortitudinem assumet
pennas ut aquile uolabunt et non deficient.

EXTENT: 36 parchment folios
FORMAT: 245 x 350 mm
BINDING: cerise paper binding over pasteboard (Vienna, 17th/18th century)
AUTHOR: Pseudo-Joachim of Fiore
CONTENT: Commentary on Isaiah (excerpts) with *Praemissiones* (?)

LANGUAGE: Latin
ILLUSTRATION: 41 text illustrations
PROVENANCE: The manuscript is documented in the possession of the Vienna Hofbibliothek from the 17th century onwards.
SHELFMARK: Vienna, ÖNB, Cod. 1400

Joachim's typological interpretations of Christian history were spread in particular through his *Concordia novi et veteris testamenti*, *Expositio in Apocalypsim* and his *Psalterium decem chordarum*, works whose influence on subsequent generations should not be underestimated. After Joachim's death, numerous authors – some of them writing under the pseudonym of Joachim himself, as in the case of the present commentaries on Isaiah and Jeremiah – sought to develop his ideas and adapt them to recent events and the present. Works by such pseudo-Joachims were particularly popular amongst the mendicant orders.

The present manuscript, whose text deserves closer analysis than it has yet received, contains excerpts – littered with corruptions – from the Commentary on Isaiah, plus a text known as the *Praemissiones*, so-called after the title given to it in another 14th-century manuscript. A sort of introduction (or "handbook") to the Commentary and indeed to Joachimite philosophy in general, it consists of pictures accompanied by brief commentaries and ultimately derives from the *Liber figurarum* (or preliminary studies for it) – a "book of figures" probably designed by Joachim himself in order to clarify his exegesis. The pictures are intended to make the text of the Commentary, which presupposes a familiarity with Joachim's ideas, more accessible to the reader. A number of grave misinterpretations of Joachim's drawings have found their way into the present illustrations (cf. ill. p. 145), however, which recent research suggests are likely to have been executed by artists working in Joachimite circles in the mid-13th century in southern Italy, rather than by artists from a Franciscan background. *M. W.*

▸ **Fol. 22v:** *Mysterium* (in this manuscript wrongly called *Ministerium*) *ecclesiae*. A misinterpretation of Joachim's *Liber figurarum*. The spiral, which in the latter symbolizes the liturgical year (seen as a parallel to the course of the history of salvation), is here misconstrued as a dragon.

▸▸ **Fol. 23v:** Dragon (cf. Revelation 12:3) with seven heads, symbolizing the seven persecutions of the Church.

▸▸▸ **Fol. 24r:** Babylon-Rome figure. This illustration, which derives from Joachim's *Liber figurarum* and whose appearance varies in the manuscripts and is difficult to interpret, symbolizes the history of the Old and the New Israel.

Hic liber numeri

Hic deuteronomius

Hic Josue regum

Hic liber judicum

Hic dominica ... usque in lamenti passionis

Hic legitur actus apostolorum et epistole canonice

Hic leguntur libri regum

Hic parabole salomonis ... libri eius

Hic liber job ...

Hic leguntur macabei

Hic legitur ezechiel

Hic leguntur prophete ab hinc usque ad xl

Dominica quarta in quadragesima.

Dominica quinta in xl. de passione domini

Dominica sexta in ramis palmarum ...

Dominica tercia in xl ...

Tempus ...

Hic inchoatur liber genesis

Hic leviticus

Dominica prima post ...

Dominica in kalendis augusti ...

Dominica in kalendis septembris ...

Kalendis octobris ...

A kalendis novembris ...

Dominica ...

Omnia tempora ... revolvuntur

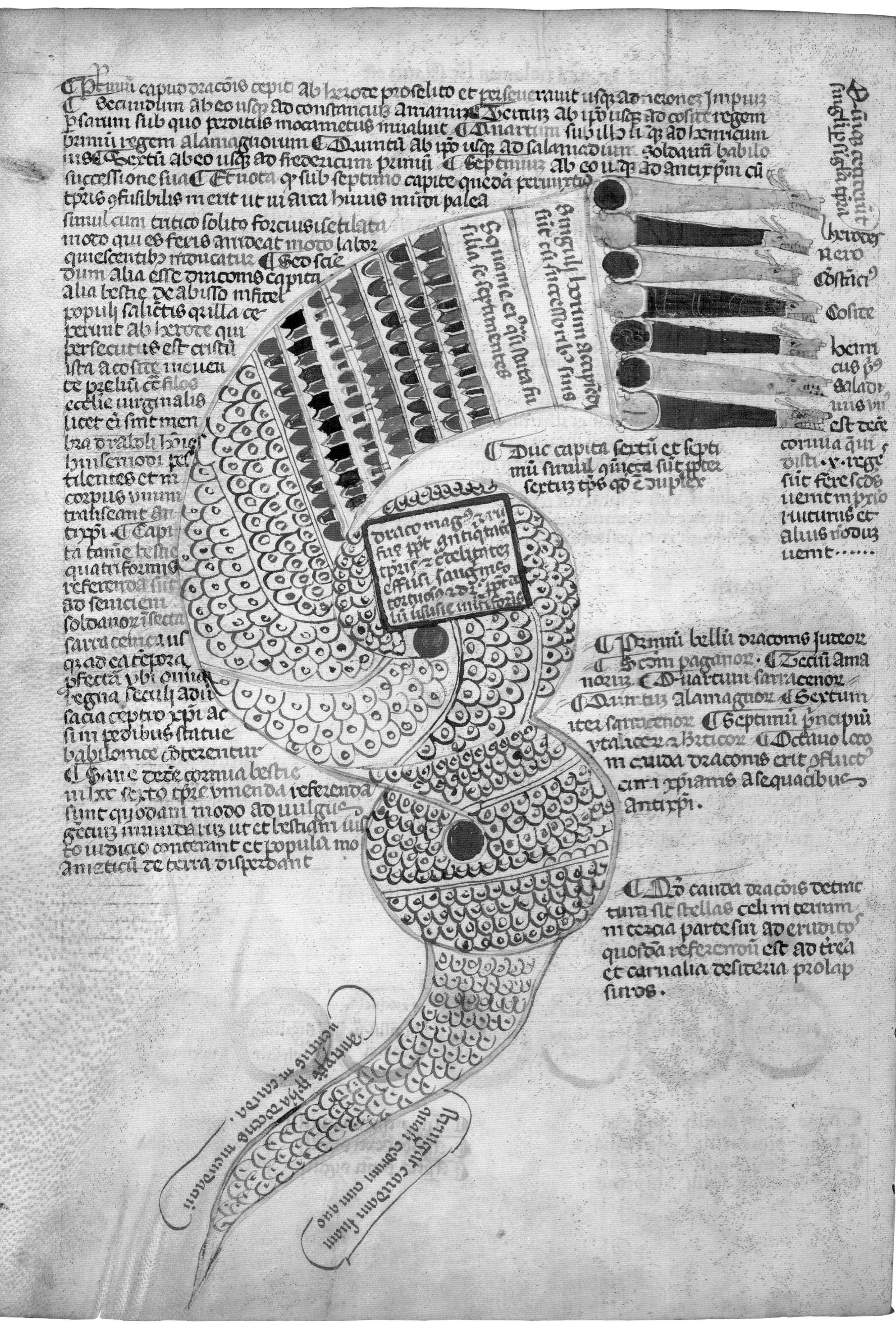

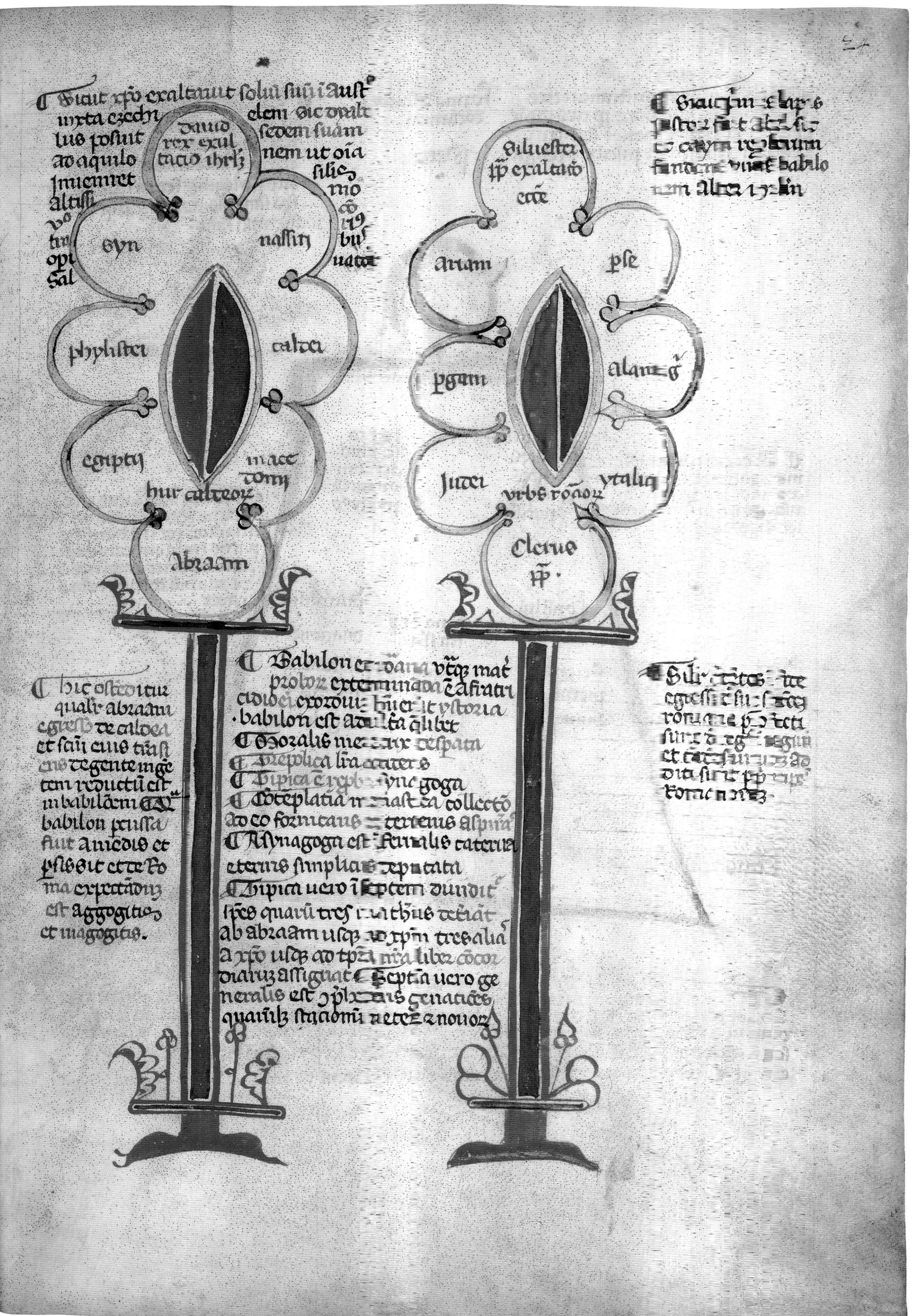

phylistei
caldei
egipty
Abraam
Iudei
ytalia
Clerus

III.3 Ludolf of Saxony, Life of Christ

Upper Italy (Venice?), between 1433 and 1445

The *Vita Christi* by Ludolf of Saxony is one of most successful works of German mysticism. In the late Middle Ages perhaps the most widely-owned of all prayer books, it was quickly translated into many languages and was available in print as from 1470.

The name of the author, who was born around 1300 in North Germany, survives in a number of variations. In addition to Ludolf, it appears as Landulfus, Leutolphus, Litoldus, Ludoldus and Rudolf. His epithets include Alemanus, Cartusianus, Cartusiensis, de Saxonia and Natione Teutonicus. A Dominican in his youth, in 1340 Ludolf – now a doctor of theology – joined the recently founded charterhouse in Strasburg. After spending lengthy periods in Koblenz and Mainz, he settled back in Strasburg, where he died in 1377 or 1378. His chief works are his *Enarratio in Psalmos* and his *Vita Christi*, which arose between 1348 and 1368.

The text, which is divided into two parts, is not a Life of Christ in the usual sense, but a series of contemplations on the mystery of Christian salvation as a whole. It is generally followed by the Harmony of the Gospels compiled by the 12th-century theologian Zacharias of Besançon (Chrysopolitanus), together with its commentary. The contemplations are divided into reading – exposition, understanding – application and conclude with a prayer. The *Vita Christi* unites exegetic form with the style of ascetic tracts and homilies, symbolic imagery with practical application. For Ludolf, Jesus is an image of God the Father, the model and mirror of all holiness. In the life of Jesus, the Christian can find new life and, by embracing it as his model, achieve communion and fellowship with Christ. One of the keys to the enduring success of Ludolf's *Vita Christi* are his sources, which include virtually all the major patristic writings of the early Middle Ages as well as works from his own day.

Detail from fol. 285v: Decorative border.

▸ **Detail from fol. 5v:** Jesus dictates the text to Ludolf of Saxony.

OC. DIVINA. ET. AETERNA. XPI
GENERATIONE. CAPITULUM. PRI

C. PLE
NITU
DINE.
EVAN
GELII.
VINI.
SCILICET
BONI.
QUOD.
USQ3.
AD HEC.
TEMPO
RA. G
TE. DO
MINUS. IHS. SERVAVIT. QUIDAM
haurire guttas cupientes. Summam eius circa
diuinam eius generatione de qua euangelista Iohannes
specialiter loquitur. quia omnia ad hoc inducit
ut diuinitas ubi manifestetur et maxime
contra quosdam hereticos dicentes xpm purum ho
minem esse. et per consequens temporalem necessitatem
non semper non ante originem fuisse. Et ideo de eius
tate ubi incipit ostendens diuinam et naturam
quam aliter possit operari. Et ponit quam
de diuinis personis quod per ordinem tanguntur
in sequentibus. Primo declarat in eius a
patre eternam generationem dicens. In principio
erat uerbum. i. In ipso deo qui ab omnibus
supponitur primum principium necessario esse
uerbum esse dicitur tamquam in ipso eius est acsi di
ceret filius erat in patre patri .s. aeternus
non in maria cepit esse. sed in principio .i. in patre
qui est principium sine principio. est filius. qui est
principium de principio. Dicitur autem ue
rbum dei filium quia ihesus xps dominus noster quemadmodum
modum dicitur filius dei sicut dicitur uerbum dei sic et

PRIMO.

q filiu
dictu
nomi
mentu
quantum
illud
Ita illu
hoc au
uocel
in am
amq p
Cum q
uocal
menta
recedn
Secund
ut p p
patre
eo et i
cogitat
nata e
dicere u
ipse et
tione di
sic con
et filiu
filij a p
tem po
q sb n
parato
ratoen
qd pu
et ad c
atur.
non in
cedit s
quam
grissi
de schu

EXTENT: III + 300 parchment folios
FORMAT: 385 x 270 mm
BINDING: black leather binding over wooden boards (Italian, 2nd half of the 16th century); in the centre of the front cover, in gold letters, *ALB. CAPR.*, on the back cover *DEC. MANT.*, standing for *Albertus Caprianus, Decanus Mantuanus* (see Provenance)
AUTHOR: Ludolf of Saxony (*c.* 1300–1377/78)
CONTENT: *Vita Jesu Christi quatuor evangeliis et scriptoribus orthodoxis concinnata, Part 1*
LANGUAGE: Latin
MINIATURIST: Cristoforo Cortese (*fl.* 1409–*c.* 1445)
ILLUSTRATION: 94 decorative bar borders, 93 major and 95 minor historiated initials
PROVENANCE: Executed for a member of the Gonzaga family, probably Marquis Lodovico III (1414–1478). In the 2nd half of the 16th century the manuscript was in Piedmont, in the possession of Alberto Capriano, Bishop of Alba (1593–1595), previously *commendatar* of San Marco in Mantua. In the library of Salzburg cathedral around 1700, the manuscript passed to the Vienna Hofbibliothek in 1806.
SHELFMARK: Vienna, ÖNB, Cod. 1379

The present manuscript is one of the great line of descendants from Ludolf's original text, whereby its sumptuous decoration makes it unique. It includes no less than 94 decorative bar borders, together with 93 major and 95 minor decorated initials. The pages are in part framed by ornate foliate borders incorporating exotic flowers and inhabited by birds, naturalistic hares, roe deer, etc., as well as putti. On fol. 1r (ill. p. 150), the decoration also includes individual pictorial fields set within a pseudo-Cufic gold border and – across the top – two stylized braids. The coat of arms contained on the same page suggests that the manuscript was commissioned by the Gonzaga in Mantua some time after 1433, the year in which Emperor Sigismund awarded the family the one-headed black eagle in its arms.

The lavish illustration continues with the historiated initials which, on fol. 1r and 5v at the beginning of the manuscript, show the author at his desk in front of Christ (ill. p. 149, 150). Subsequent initials are primarily devoted to scenes from Jesus's youth and his public ministry, supplemented by figures of monks and prophets. A companion volume to the present manuscript containing the second part of the text, has not yet come to light and is probably lost, if indeed ever executed at all.

The illumination is the work of Cristoforo Cortese (*fl.* 1409–*c.* 1445), who was active in the first half of the 15th century chiefly in Venice, and whose only signed work is a manuscript in the Wildenstein Collection in the Musée Marmottan in Paris. Probably the most important Venetian miniaturist of his day, he absorbed influences from Bolognese, Venetian and Lombard art and fused them into a decorative programme of overwhelming, almost unsurpassable magnificence. *K.-G. P.*

Fol. 1r: Ludolf of Saxony's vision of Christ, accompanied by angels making music. In the pictorial fields in the margins, beside the Gonzaga coat of arms, the virtues of Love, Justice, Wisdom and Moderation.

uncta sunt opitur ... ca et patrem per
unigenitum filium suu omnia legimus fu
isse opatum. Hec Aug. In eundem
Aug. hoc inicium sci euangelij quidaz
platonicus aureis lris pscribendum et p
omnes ecclias in locis eminentissimis po
nendum ee dicebat.

Domine ds pr omnipotens q
coeternum et coeqlem et cosba
lem t ante omnia secla ineffabilr
filium genuisti cum quo atqz spu
sco omnia uisibilia et inuisibilia ac me im
sum peccorem int omnia creasti te adoro
te laudo te glifico esto ppitius mihi peccori
& ne despicias me opus manuu tuaru
sz salua et adiuua me pp nomen sanctuz
tuum opi manuu tuarum dexteram
porrige carnali fragilitati succurre qui
me fecisti respice infectum uicijs qui me
formasti reforma corruptum peccatis ut
secundum miam salues animam mea. Am.

In principio cum lucifer
creatus esset erexit se cont
deum creatorem suum et
i ictu oculi proiectus e de
excelso celorum in infer
num et ob hanc causam
decreuit deus humanuz
genus creare ut p ipm
post casum luciferi
et sotiorum eius restau
rare. Quapp diabolus
homini inuidens s insidiabatur. &
ad pcepti transgressionem ipm inducere
nitebatur. Et qddam genus spentis
s elegebat qui tunc erectus gradiebatur
& cap uirgineum hebat que h fraudu
lentus deceptor intrauit et p os eius lo

qui sus uerba deceptoria mulieri narrauit
ac eam decipiens sup omne genus
narum mortem induxit. Et opor
bat nos omnes carcerem inferni in
de quo non poteramus alicuius adi
torio eripi. Sz tandem pr miarum
deus totius consolationis clementer
spexit statum nre dampnationis et
p eum eripere liberare decreuit sup q
signum p oliuam dedit quam col
ba inclusis in archa afferebat. q m
di futuram inclusis in limbo pretend
bat non solum enim ijs qui in arc
erant nra pmittebatur sz & tot
co lignum salutis i oliua dabatur.
hoc idem deus pfigurauit nob i multi
alijs figuris. A principio autem c
ditionis nre. Adam in agro damas
no iuxta ebron de terra formato
domino in paradisum uoluptatis t
latato ac Eua in paradiso de cost
dormientis fca et pro consorte ei dat
ipsisqz pmis parentibus in paradiso ad
ancum et custodiendum collocat
de hinc pp ligni ueti esum p diuin
creti seueritatem expulsis supna mis
no destitit homines incitare ad bo
p occultos instinctus nec distulit ho
errabundum ad penitentiam reu
re spem uenie dando prepmissum
uatois. Et ne forte ignotam et
titudinem tanta di dignatio nre sa
foret inefficax i quinqz h secli etat
p patriarchas iudices sacerdotes
& pphas ab Abel iusto usqz ad ioh
baptistam filij sui aduentum pnu
repromittere et prefigurare no desti
ut p multa milia tempora & annor
magnis et uarijs multiplicans oracul
intelligentias nras ad fidem erig
et affectu spmia et uiua desideria
flammare. Gn leo pp. Cessent
tum qrele q de dominice natiuita

◂ **Fol. 7v:** Christ and Satan.

Fol. 35v: The Virgin and Child and two other women accompanying the chapter on the Circumcision

IV.

Medieval versions of history in world chronicles and history Bibles

Although the subject of history was not expressly anchored in the academic systems of the Middle Ages, the discussion of historical concepts was encouraged by a growing awareness of the problems of chronology in liturgical practice (with regards to calculating the date of Easter, for example).

It is in this connection that we may also see the roots of manuscripts devoted to a chronological ordering of the events of the past. History in the Middle Ages was understood not as a cyclical development, but as a purposeful (teleological) series of events unfolding in linear succession, divided into ages and subdivided into epochs. Amongst the sources of inspiration for this system of chronology was the Bible. The biblical method of plotting the course of history in terms of generations (*generationes*), for example, is taken up in world chronicles and paralleled with the rules (*regna*) of heathen kings (cf. Cat. IV.1). Another means of calculating time was the division of history into world years, starting from the Creation: according to the Vulgate, for example, the birth of Christ thus occurred in the year 3952.

Yet another, frequently adopted chronological device was the division of the history of the world into six ages (*aetates*); this system was still in use in the late 15th century and can be found in the famous Nuremberg Chronicle of 1493 by Hartmann Schedel (1440–1514). Another commonly encountered system, finally, employs a model inspired by the prophecies of Daniel and recounts the history of the world in terms of four heathen kingdoms (Babylonian, Medo-Persian, Greek and Roman). Accents are thereby also placed by decisive events such as the foundation, re-foundation and destruction of the Temple in Jerusalem and the Babylonian Captivity (deportation of the Jews; Cat. IV.1).

Histoire ancienne jusqu'à César, Cod. 2576, detail from fol. 4r (Genesis): God curses Adam and Eve after the Fall.

▸ **History Bible, Cod. 2823, detail from fol. 236r (1 Kings):** The Judgement of Solomon: King Solomon orders a servant to cut in half the child being claimed by two women, but the real mother begs him to spare the infant's life.

Medieval chronicles took as their starting point the chronological tables (*chronicorum canones*) compiled by Eusebius of Caesarea (before 264/265–*c.* 339/340), which were translated into Latin and extended by St Jerome (*c.* 347–419) and which represented a synchronism of biblical history and ancient dynasties. Medieval chronicles generally embraced a time span that commenced from the events of Creation and ended at the author's day. Depending on their type, such chronicles were either universal in their chronological and geographic scope (so-called world chronicles) or more concise; their sequence was dictated by the historical framework of the Bible, although sometimes also by events from pagan history (cf. Cat. IV.2).

Chronicle codices have been grouped into three different textual traditions, each with its own narrative focus (von den Brincken [1969]). Although the manuscripts still extant today mostly represent a mixture of these traditions their identification can nevertheless provide an insight into the structure and emphasis of the text. Chronicles of the *series temporum* type, for example, are primarily laid out in an annalistic fashion and concentrate upon the chronological sequence of historical events; they are particularly suited to the common practice of adding to the manuscript at a later date. They thereby differ from the *mare historiarum* type, in which narrative diversity stands in the foreground and which also incorporates reflective observations upon history. The third, *imago mundi* type is characterized by its encyclopaedic scope and embraces other spheres of knowledge such as geography.

These various types of manuscript are all linked by the underlying assumption that the events of history are determined not by humankind but by God, for the benefit and salvation of the world. All factual events were also seen and evaluated from this point of view. This eschatological dimension was always present, above all when the divinely-steered nature of history was underlined by the inclusion, at the end of such chronicles, of the Last Judgement and end of the world.

The medieval understanding of history briefly sketched here finds its most condensed expression in the genealogical tree. The example discussed in the following section (Cat. IV.1) demonstrates – with the maximum of concision and in the appropriate form of a scroll – the chief characteristics of such overviews of world chronology: a synchronistic presentation of history subdivided according to kings, dynasties and ages. While many genealogies are simply laid out as names in a series of medallions, the present example is animated by miniatures that bring vividly to life the different epochs of the past and the concept of the history of salvation that runs through the whole.

A narrative alternative to this pithy form of historical presentation is offered by the *Bible historiale*, or history Bible, of which two examples are discussed here (cf. Cat. IV.3–5). Written in German prose and supplemented with apocryphal material and events from secular history, these retellings of biblical history are accompanied by illustrations relating directly to the text. Their chief sources include, alongside the Latin Vulgate, Peter Comestor's *Historia scholastica* of around 1169–1173, Vincent of Beauvais' *Speculum historiale* of around 1250 and the rhyming German world chronicles of the 13th and 14th centuries. Over 100 history Bibles still survive today, the majority of them illuminated. They vary widely as regarding their extent, text and relationship to earlier copies, and on the basis of their contents were divided by Vollmer (1912–1929) into ten groups, some of these containing further subdivisions. History Bibles were found across the entire German-speaking realm, whereby the majority of surviving examples stem from the Alsace, Swabia and the Bavaria/Austria region. Already documented in the 1300s, the history Bible saw its greatest flowering between *c.* 1440 and 1470/80.

These prose history Bibles do not contain the same volume of text as the sources on which they were based. They concentrate upon the narration of biblical events; edifying commentaries and theological excursions are omitted. Their language is also simpler: the elaborate descriptions found, for example, in rhyming chronicles are

pared down to only pertinent details. Their content is thus presented in a manner that can be understood by all. In this respect, history Bibles were responding to the needs of a wider readership, one consisting increasingly of members of the laity – albeit still only the wealthy and the educated. History Bibles offered these readers the opportunity to inform themselves about the Bible and "world history".

History Bibles gradually had to cede their role as purveyors of biblical knowledge to the laity to the printed editions of the Vulgate which appeared in German translation as of the 1460s. As a paraphrasing compilation of diverse, partially non-biblical texts, and with the Reformation about to dawn, the history Bible could no longer compete with the Bible itself. For this reason, too, it was issued in print only rarely, and only in excerpts. "The rejection of apocryphal material by humanism and the Reformation contributed to the final disappearance of the history Bible in the 16th century." (Gerhardt [1983], p. 73)

A.F./K.H.

History Bible of Evert van Soudenbalch, Cod. 2771, detail from fol. 257v: The rebuilding of Jerusalem. (Master of the Cirrus Clouds)

History Bible, Cod. 2766, detail from fol. 68v (Numbers): The scouts Joshua and Caleb tear their clothing because the Israelites are refusing to go on to the Promised Land.

IV.1

Genealogy of Christ

Upper Italy, 3rd quarter of the 15th century

The scroll, which is made up of six sheets of parchment glued together, measures almost six metres in length. It narrows at both ends into a sort of tongue which, at the top end, is pricked with holes, providing a possible clue to the manner in which the scroll was used: perhaps it was pinned up on the wall as a "teaching aid", allowing it to be studied if not at full length, then at least in sections.

The present genealogy derives its basic form from the *Compendium historiae in genealogia Christi* by Petrus Pictaviensis (*c.* 1130–1205), who was active in Paris as master and chancellor of the cathedral school. At the heart of the *Compendium* lies the so-called *Linea Christi,* an overview of biblical history from the Creation to the martyrdom of the apostles Peter and Mark. Even the earliest copies of this text began paralleling the genealogy of Christ with other genealogies, ultimately expanding the overview into a chronicle of the world. In the present example, the kings of the Babylonians, Persians and Romans on the left and the Assyrians, Egyptians, Shechemites, Syrians and Greeks on the right are named as collateral branches of the family of Christ.

The names given in the medallions are accompanied by explanatory captions, which vary greatly in their content and length from manuscript to manuscript. They draw upon various "historical" sources, the most important of which is Peter Comestor's *Historia scholastica*, completed around 1170.

The captions to the names are complemented by an ambitious pictorial programme, which opens with a schematic representation of the world and the story of Creation, told in six medallions (ill. p. 159). Adam and Eve, the primogenitors from whom the genealogy of Christ descends, are portrayed after their Fall and Expulsion from

Detail from segment 3: King David enthroned (start of the fourth age of the world).

▸ **Segment 1:** The Creator with a representation of the world composed of concentric circles: earth, water, air, fire, planets, zodiac, firmament of fixed stars. Below left and right: Adam and Eve. The story of Creation: (1) The creation of light: the four elements arranged in bands, and above them the rays of the light. (2) God divides the waters. (3) God separates the land and the seas. (4) Creation of the stars and the vegetation. (5) Creation of the animals and birds. (6) Creation of Eve out of Adam's side. Noah building the Ark (start of the second age of the world); below right, the city of Salem (ancient name of Jerusalem).

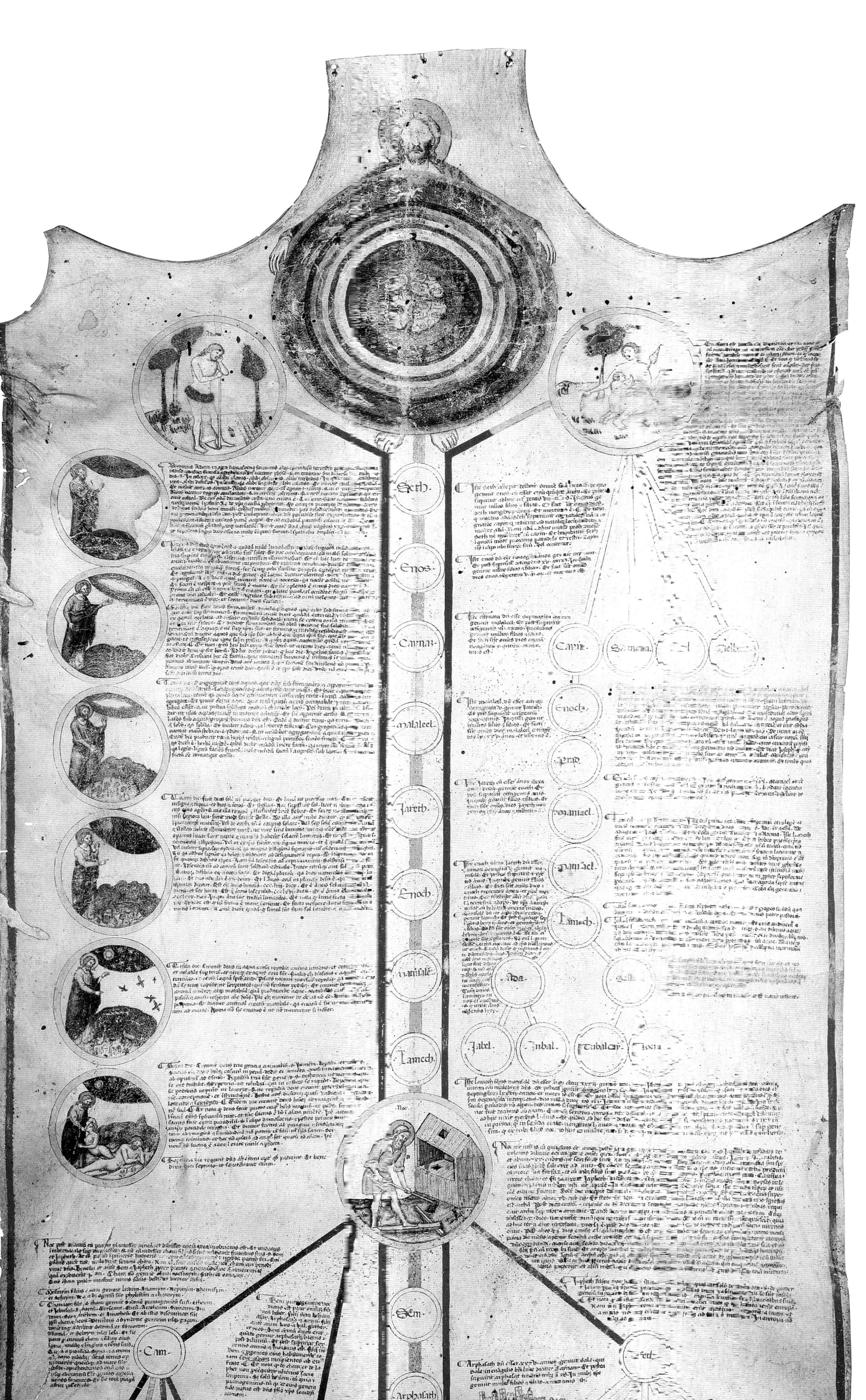
Seth
Enos
Caynan
Malaleel
Iareth
Enoch
Matusale
Lamech
Sem
Arphaxath
Cam
Cayn
Enoch
Irad
Maviael
Matusael
Lamech
Ada
Sella
Iabel
Iubal
Tubalcain

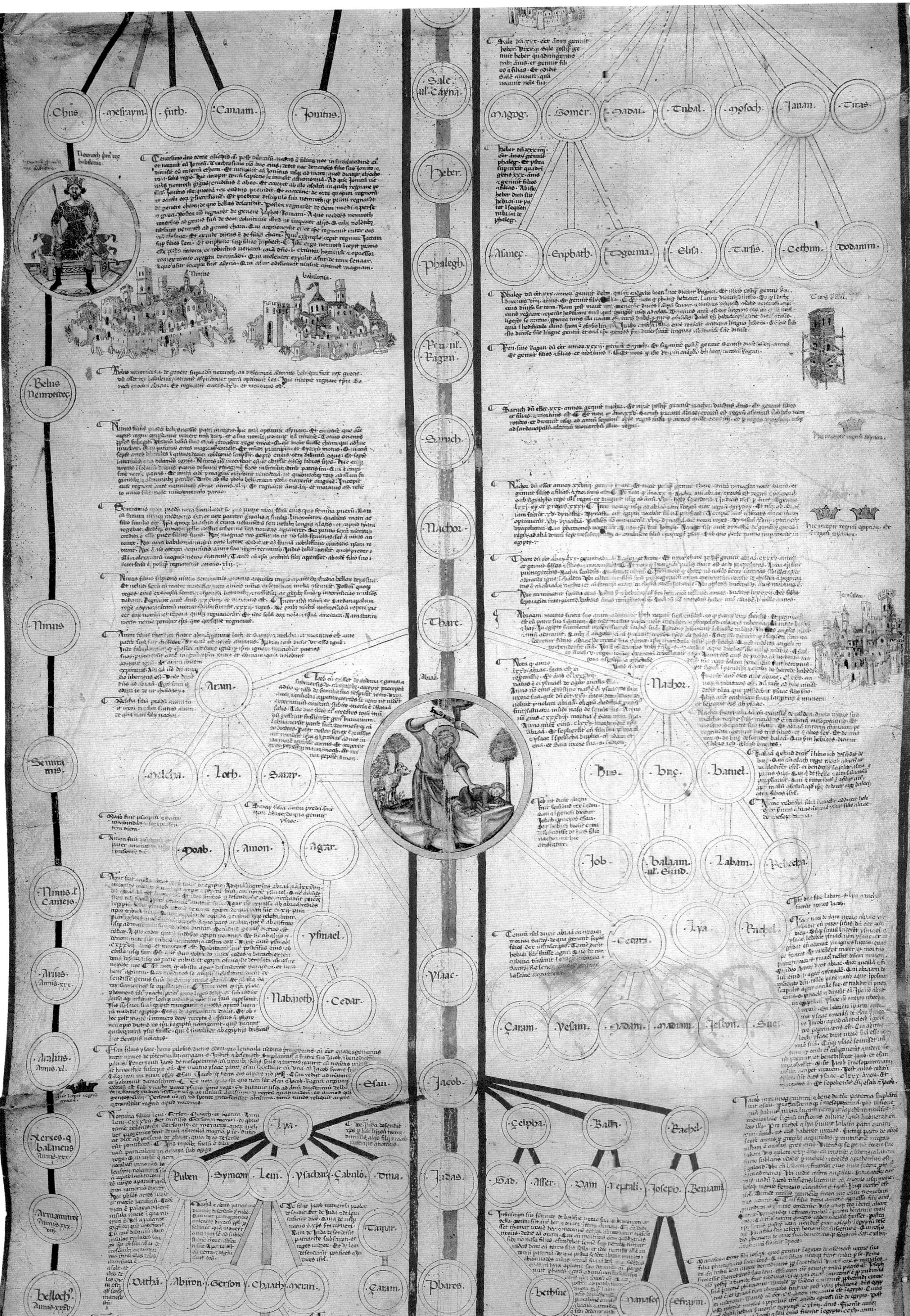
Chus
Mesraym
Futh
Canaam
Jonitus
Sale ul. Cayna
Heber
Phalegh
Saruch
Nachor
Thare
Ysaac
Jacob
Judas
Phares
Magog
Gomer
Madai
Tubal
Mosoch
Iauan
Tiras
Elisa
Tarsis
Cethim
Dodanim
Aram
Loth
Moab
Amon
Ysmael
Nabaioth
Cedar
Job
Labam
Rebecha
Lya
Rachel
Esau
Ruben
Symeon
Levi
Ysachar
Zabulo
Dina
Gad
Asser
Dam
Neptali
Joseph
Beniami
Manases
Effraym
Thamar
Zaram

EXTENT: parchment scroll
FORMAT: 5860 x 620 mm
CONTENT: Genealogy of Christ
LANGUAGE: Latin
ILLUSTRATION: historiated medallions containing scenes from the Creation and biblical figures; numerous city views and schematic illustrations

PROVENANCE: The scroll was purchased from a private collector in 1913.
SHELFMARK: Vienna, ÖNB, Cod. Ser. n. 3394

Paradise. Thus they appear in the medallions beneath the circle of the world accompanied by a hoe and a distaff as the "attributes" of human toil. The genealogy of Christ unfolds in the following medallions with illustrations of Noah building the Ark, the Sacrifice of Isaac, King David on his throne and the high priest Salathiel. It concludes with three medallions depicting the Birth of Christ, the Crucifixion and the Resurrection. These scenes are not selected at random, but mark the boundaries of the six ages of the world, divided into the periods lasting from the birth of Adam to the Flood (1), from Noah to Abraham (2, ill. p. 160), from Abraham to David (3), from David to the Babylonian Captivity (4), from the Babylonian Captivity to the birth of Christ (5) and from Christ's birth to his Resurrection (ill. p. 162–163).

In the collateral branches arranged parallel to the direct lineage of Christ, we find the proverbial hunter Nimrod, in his capacity as the ancient, legendary king of Babylon, and Alexander the Great as the "progenitor" of the rulers and empires born of his legacy.

In addition to these historiated medallions, the scroll contains more than twenty city views. Although seeming to vary individually in their shape and setting, they are all composed of more or less interchangeable elements. In keeping with the realism of the artist's day, these ancient cities have been transported into the 15th-century present; only occasionally do meaningful details such as the minaret in the view of Babylon (ill. p. 160) find their way into them. In line with their significance in the Bible, illustrations are also devoted to the Tower of Babel and to a ground plan of Jerusalem as it looked after the return from the Babylonian Exiles.

A. F.

Segment 2: Nimrod, legendary ancient king of Babylon; beside him, views of Nineveh (capital of the Assyrian Empire) and Babylon. Abraham and the Sacrifice of Isaac (start of the third age of the world); below left, a crown marks the start of the genealogy of the Greeks: on the right, the city of Jerusalem and three crowns, signifying the genealogies of the Assyrians, the Egyptians and the Shechemites.

Detail from segment 6: Birth of Christ (start of the sixth age of the world); Crucifixion with the Virgin and St John; the Resurrection of Christ.

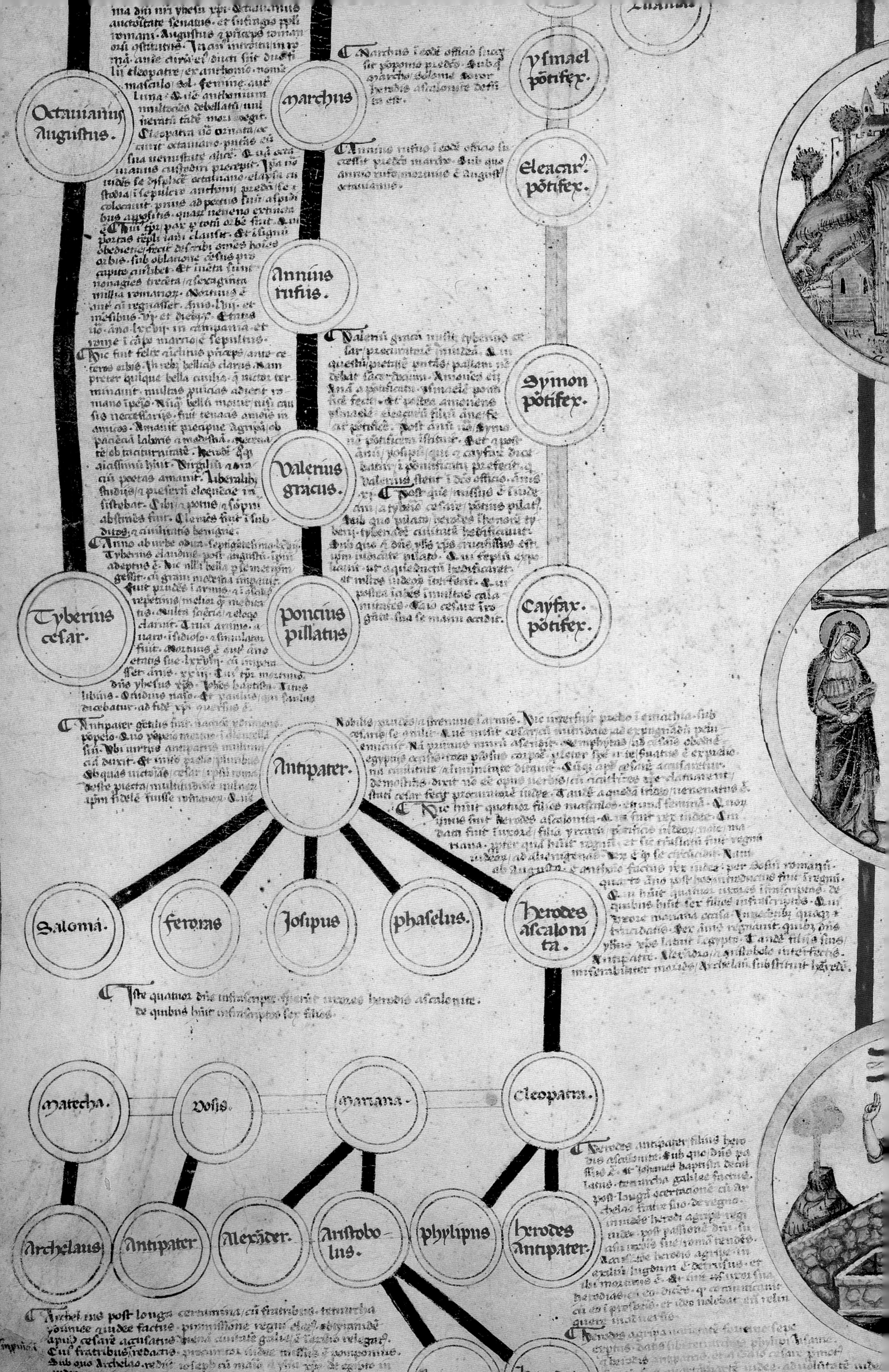

Octauianus augustus.
marchus
Annius rufus.
Valerius gracus.
Poncius pillatus
Tyberius cesar.
ysmael pōtifex.
Eleacar pōtifex.
Symon pōtifex.
Cayfax pōtifex.
Antipater.
Saloma.
Feroras
Josipus
phaselus.
herodes ascalonita.
Matecha.
Dosis.
Mariana.
Cleopatra.
Archelaus
Antipater
Alexāder.
Aristobolus.
phylipus
herodes Antipater.

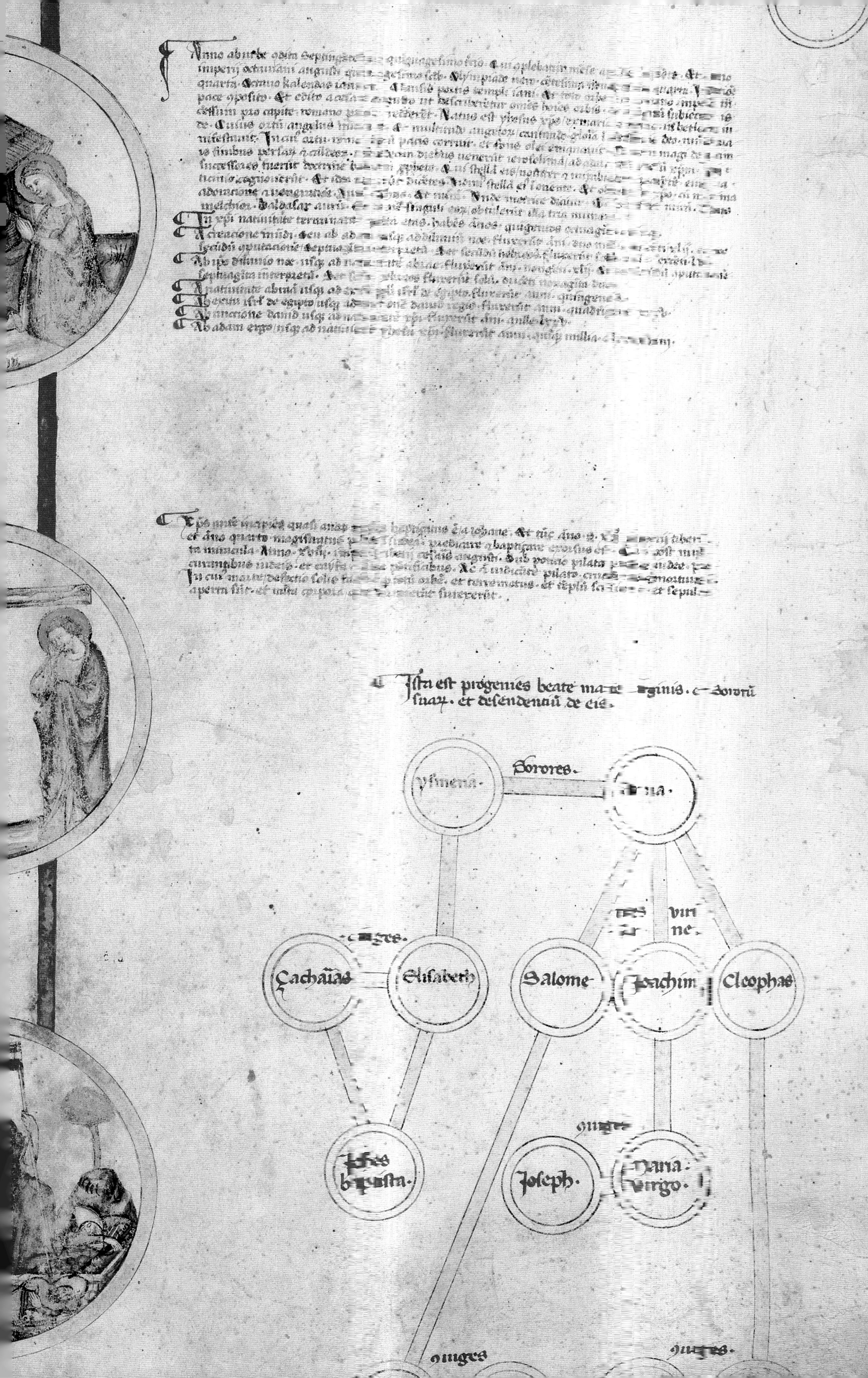

Salome
Cleophas
Joseph

IV.2

Histoire ancienne jusqu'à César (Histoire universelle)

Venetia, 2nd quarter of the 14th century

Medieval world chronicles offer a "universal" view of history that perceives biblical stories in the same overall context as secular events, myths and legends. Often lavishly decorated and written in the vernacular, such chronicles were aimed at a lay public and were both educational and entertaining. The *Histoire ancienne jusqu'à César*, which originated within court circles in northern France, was one of the most popular works of this genre. It was written in the early 13th century for a châtelain of Lille by the name of Roger (IV) and represents the earliest surviving world chronicle in French. It was widely distributed in the Middle Ages, as evidenced by more than 70 copies from France, Acre (Palestine) and Italy, together with two revised versions in French and several Italian translations.

The text contains Genesis and other Old Testament stories about Judith and Esther, together with pagan tales from the Orient and Greek and Roman antiquity. Its rich collection of prose texts, some of them furnished with a prologue and moralizing interpolations in verse form, is influenced not just by major theological treatises such as the *Historia adversum paganos* by Orosius (*c.* 418) and Peter Comestor's *Historia scholastica*, but also by various classical epics and more recent vernacular romances.

The present codex represents one of the copies of the *Histoire ancienne* produced in Italy in the late Dugento and Trecento in response to a widespread interest in French literature. Dante described the *langue d'oïl*, the old language of northern France, as the language of vulgar prose, citing as an example a Bible compiled with the deeds of the Trojans and Romans (*De vulgari eloquentia* I,X,2). He was undoubtedly referring to an *Histoire ancienne*.

Detail from fol. 32v (Genesis): Jacob visits his aged father Isaac in Mamre.

▸ **Detail from fol. 9v (Genesis):** Building of the Tower of Babel. The figure of God borne by angels appears in front of the tower, probably as an abbreviated illustration of the Babylonian confusion of tongues.

seroient
r feroiet
fondue
ntesse si
r paine
et la seign
a faire
parfaire

uenil q
.vii. as
re de tes
ofont et
costes e
or nos ne
lautese
casum
e et bie sa
de la tour

sploitoient dure mt porce q la tor fust tant
poraene q ele fust .m. cel pointe de poies
savoir et entendre q ces iens estoiet de mult fo
lle sience q cotre dieu cuidoient estriuer et con
tendre. Encore adonqz nestoit parle par toz
le mõde cuns sols lengage. Deignors cestoit
ebrieus q li uif parolent encore que deuant
cene adonqz quant cele tour fu comẽcees na
noit encore este ois nec troues q un sol lẽgage
o.nis par celle tour furet les [illegible] e le dui
se parole primes troues et parlees si porés savoir
coment et en quel maniere. Coment li lengaige
Quant nostre sire dieu qui furent troues
toute creature. a moult ordenee et faite a si
nolente uit le grant orgoil et le grant outrage
de celle ient q ne recreioient mie il abaissa
lor orgoil et lor folles cuidances ẽ mult petit de
termine. Car quant la tour fu si a mont menee
com ie le uos ai deseure nostre sire i enuoia .ii.

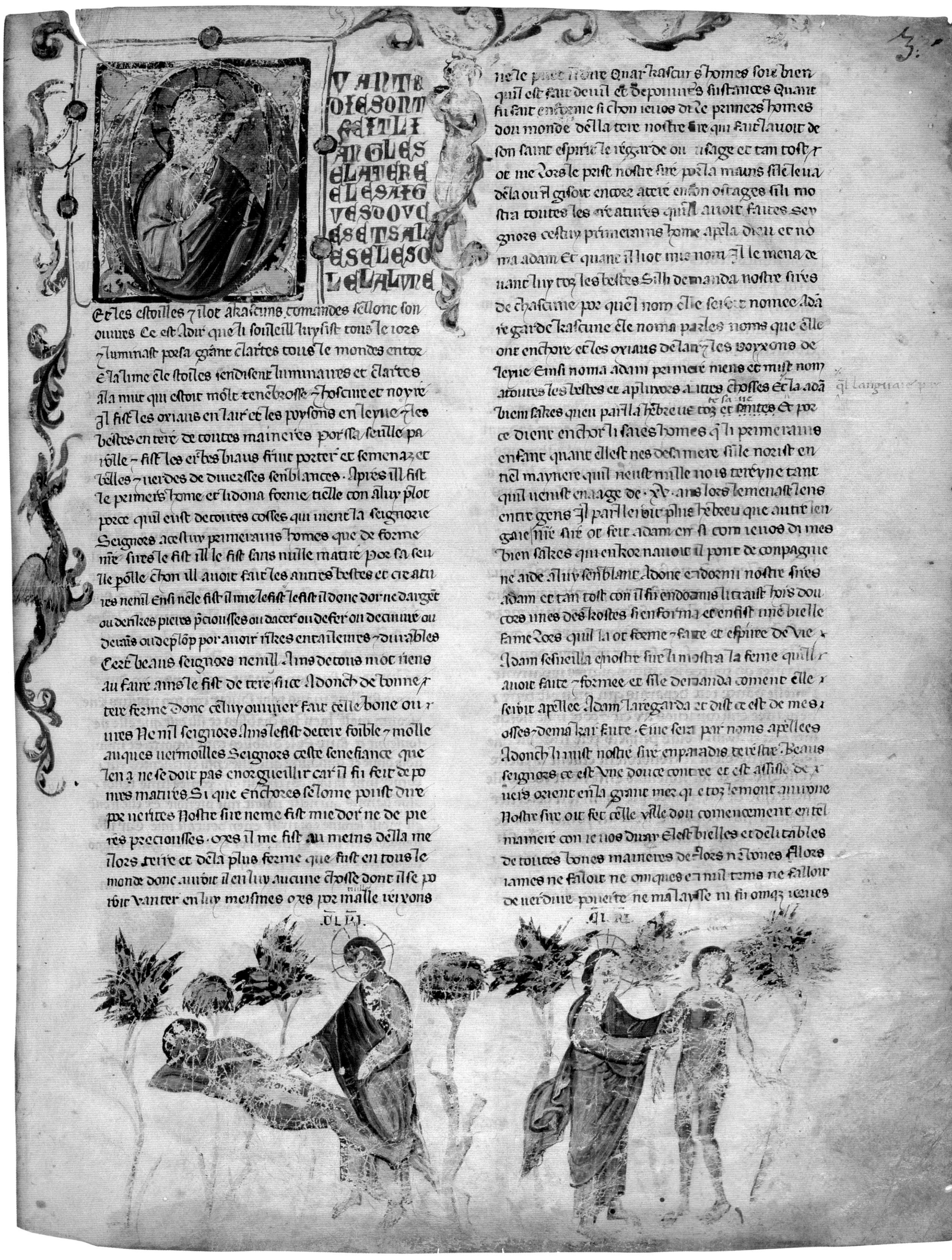

EXTENT: 155 leaves of parchment
FORMAT: approx. 335 x 255 mm
BINDING: ornamental roll binding of Johann Benedikt Gentilotti, prefect of the Vienna Hofbibliothek (1705–1723), dated 1720
CONTENT: *Histoire ancienne jusqu'à César* (also known as *Histoire universelle*)
LANGUAGE: French
ILLUSTRATION: 46 miniatures; eight historiated and nine non-historiated initials; *fleuronnée* lombard initials. The initials from fol. 111v onwards frequently include decorative bar borders incorporating animals and figures drawn in pen.
PROVENANCE: In 1665 the codex passed to the Vienna Hofbibliothek from Ambras Castle, near Innsbruck.
SHELFMARK: Vienna, ÖNB, Cod. 2576

Codex 2576 contains a number of linguistic peculiarities which seem to point to the fact that the manuscript was produced in Venetia. This argument is supported by the illustrations, which were initially thought to be Provençal but which are now generally considered to be Venetian dating from the mid-14th century (or slightly earlier). The numerous miniatures, which unfold across the lower margin of the page and are not framed, illustrate a variety of subjects in an unequal series of scenes. More than half of the entire pictorial programme is devoted to Genesis, which is accompanied by a cycle of 24 miniatures. These are followed by secular illustrations, such as "chivalrous" scenes of knights in battle in accordance with the conventions of medieval epics. Codex 2576 thereby exhibits almost no connection with the iconography of other copies of the *Histoire ancienne*. Its distinctive illustrations are based instead on different sources, which in the case of the Genesis cycle can be traced specifically to Venice. Many of its scenes are indebted to the pictorial vocabulary of the Cotton Genesis of late antiquity, and to the 13th-century mosaics on the porch of San Marco depending on it directly. This intensive assimilation of the pictorial sources of late antiquity can be seen, for example, in the inclusion of small, moving figures in rear view, which appear closely related to the illusionistic style of the *Vienna Genesis* (Cat. I.2). There is nothing rare about such borrowings in Venetian manuscript illumination of the Trecento (see, for example, the *Roman de Troie* in Madrid, Bibl. Nac., Ms. 17805; *c.* 1340/50). Early Bibles were evidently available in Venice and, as the present codex makes clear, continued to exert a powerful influence upon Venetian art centuries after their origin. *V.P.-A.*

Fol. 3r (Genesis): Initial with the Creator giving a gesture of blessing. In the lower margin, two scenes from the Creation of Eve: God removes one of Adam's ribs while he sleeps and then breathes life into Eve.

par le dieu q goūne le ciel 7 la terre q tu me donras
le ay sa ac mō fil se ie muir feme dou lignaye de
iens en contre cay iem aȳ 7 habite ains en yras a
lignaie ē mesopotamie 7 la li q̄ras feme 7 se aug
ne te neue sur de ma gñation a luy oes dou sairem
sems tu toz deliures. Eliezer iura tout ē si le sairē
mt com li demanda abraam sō sire. Lors sapareil
eliezer sans nule demorance por luy tost mettre
la uoye 7 biē sakies ql mena .x. kameaus ē sa cō
gnie 7 aueuc les sergens ql les casoyent 7 bien es
pent li sergēs kargies 7 li kameaus de riches auo
7 de nobles tels 9 ō q̄z adonc sauoit p̄ser ens en cel
cōtree argent 7 or 7 dras de soye 7 se pyseon ē asse
ēcore 7 de ces coses meisme mt porta il a ses aue
luy. Car il sauoit que poy auoit ē celle terre manc
7 autre rikeses. Car bien sakies q̄ .x. cameaus pe
porter mist grāt fais 7 grāt somes. Et bien sakies s
uoir estoit ou que eliezer uenist ql fu amout prei

Re becha

Eliezer

◂ Detail from fol. 23v (Genesis): Eliezer and Rebekah at the well rendered in Venetian style with an acanthus capital

Fol. 37r (Genesis): Pharoah's cup-bearer dreams of the vine whose grapes he squeezes into a cup. Pharoah's baker dreams of the three bread baskets which are emptied by birds.

IV.3 History Bible

Urach (Swabia), 1463

The present German-language history Bible represents the only surviving copy of what Vollmer has identified as version Ic of the text (see Introduction). It relates the history of the world from the Creation to the destruction of Jerusalem (70 AD), incorporating along the way events from secular history, in particular from the life of Alexander the Great. It is thereby based on version Ia of the original text, here expanded and modified in structure, using as a chief source a 14th-century world chronicle by one Henry of Munich.

Codex 2823 differs from the second history Bible discussed in this chapter, Codex 2766 (Cat. IV.4), in its format, which measures only about half the size, in its use of paper instead of parchment as a material, and in its "modest" illumination with pen drawings in just a few different colours rather than with miniatures and initials in body colour and gold. Its illustrations also reflect an entirely different artistic concept. This manuscript conforms, in fact, to a type of book which was not only faster and cheaper to produce and which could therefore be afforded by a broader section of the population, but which also took into account the requirements of its readers, most of whom were members of the laity.

The illustrations in the present codex reveal the same reduction to essentials that characterizes the text of history Bibles in general (see Introduction). The portrayal of events is pared down to only what is absolutely necessary; narrative details that do not directly serve to convey the meaning of the scene are omitted, and no attempt is made to describe the setting in any depth: nothing is to distract the viewer from the central message of the picture. Hence there is also no attempt at dramatic staging or colouristic "effects". Instead, those individuals and objects important to the scene are

Detail from fol. 37r (Genesis): Abraham's servant, who has returned to his master's homeland to seek a wife for Abraham's son, Isaac, meets Rebekah at the well outside the town.

▸ **Detail from fol. 65v (Genesis):** Joseph is pulled by his brothers out of the well into which they had thrown him naked, and is sold to Midianite merchants.

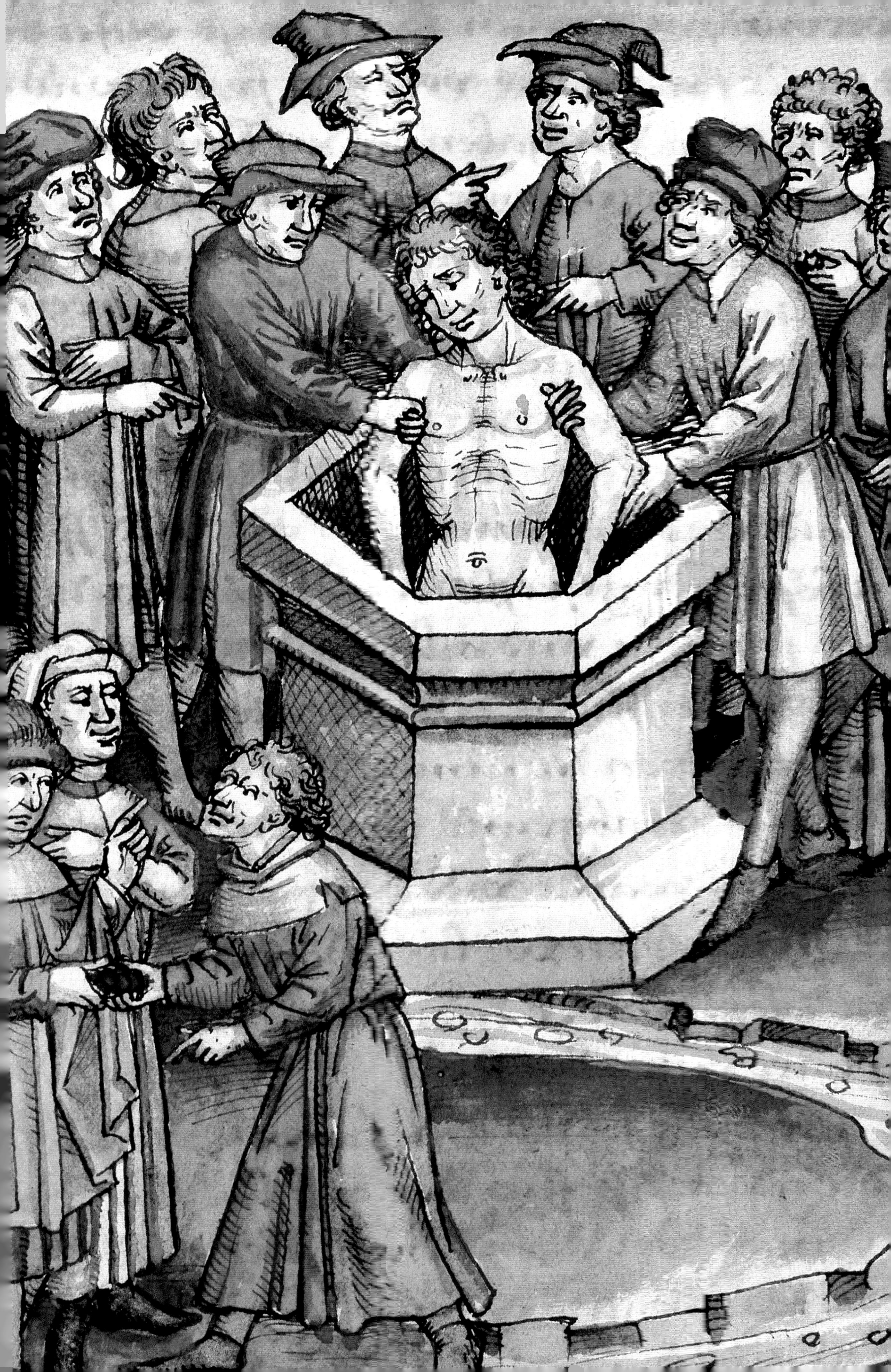

1 figur

Hie schaft got himel vnd Erde

EXTENT: III + 417 sheets of paper
FORMAT: approx. 290 x 205–210 mm
BINDING: red leather over wooden boards, blind lines on the front and back cover, traces of two clasps; original binding, 1463 or shortly afterwards, made by Renbold, a bookbinder in Urach
CONTENT: history Bible
LANGUAGE: German (Swabian dialect)
SCRIBE: On the grounds that the manuscript originated from the collection of the Zimmern family, the scribe, who has signed his initials on fol. 412v, has been identified with Gabriel Sattler-Lindenast from Pfullendorf, who copied several books for Johann Werner von Zimmern the Elder. Since the scribe's initials should probably be read as *E. S.* and not as *G. S.*, however, this identification is likely to be incorrect.
ILLUSTRATION: lombard initials and rubrication by one Stefan Sesselschreiber (perhaps the same as "Stephan Schreiber" from Urach); 116 mostly full-page coloured pen drawings by an artist from Urach, with captions in red ink
PROVENANCE: The manuscript was probably produced for Johann Werner von Zimmern the Elder (1454–1495) or for his father Werner (c. 1423–1483); whichever the case, in 1576 it was presented to Archduke Ferdinand II (1529–1595) by Wilhelm von Zimmern (1549–1594) and passed from the Zimmern collection to the library at Ambras Castle. In 1665 it was transferred to the Vienna Hofbibliothek by praefect Peter Lambeck.
SHELFMARK: Vienna, ÖNB, Cod. 2823

brought together in simple compositions that are easy to understand and remember. They are clearly characterized so that their respective roles within the scene can be immediately discerned. It is the artist's intention that the entire composition should be grasped quickly and easily. This is encouraged by the repetition of individual elements and compositions that the reader can soon learn to recognize, and by pictures which summarize a story in a single, condensed image rather than in a series of separate scenes as employed in world chronicles.

The captions written above or below the illustrations play an essential role when it comes to recognizing the scenes portrayed. Thus clearly identified, the pictures take on a new autonomy vis-à-vis the text. This allows them to be extracted from their traditional location within the column of text and placed on a separate page – in some cases at a considerable distance from the passage they accompany. The illustrations are quite clearly intended to be contemplated "for themselves". In this way they provided the educated lay reader with easy access to the history of salvation. It should thereby be noted that, both in the individual drawings and the choice of scenes illustrated, there emerge certain thematic emphases that remain to be defined.

The production of this history Bible is unusually well documented: it is dated 1463 on fol. 412v, and its copyist can perhaps be identified by his initials (regarding his previous, probably inaccurate identification, see Scribe above). Furthermore an account drawn up on fol. 417v also provides details of the names and/or place of work of the other individuals involved in the production of the codex (see Binding, Illustration). At the same time, this list of expenses provides information about the cost of the materials and the respective wages of the artists and craftsmen. E. E.

Fol. 1r (Genesis): A summary of the story of Creation up to the creation of man, including the creation of the angels.

▸ **Fol. 1v–2r:** Lucifer and his supporters are flung into the jaws of Hell by other angels. The two pictures on fol. 1r and 1v appear in front of the text, which begins on fol. 2r with a plain lombard initial instead of the usual decorative initial.

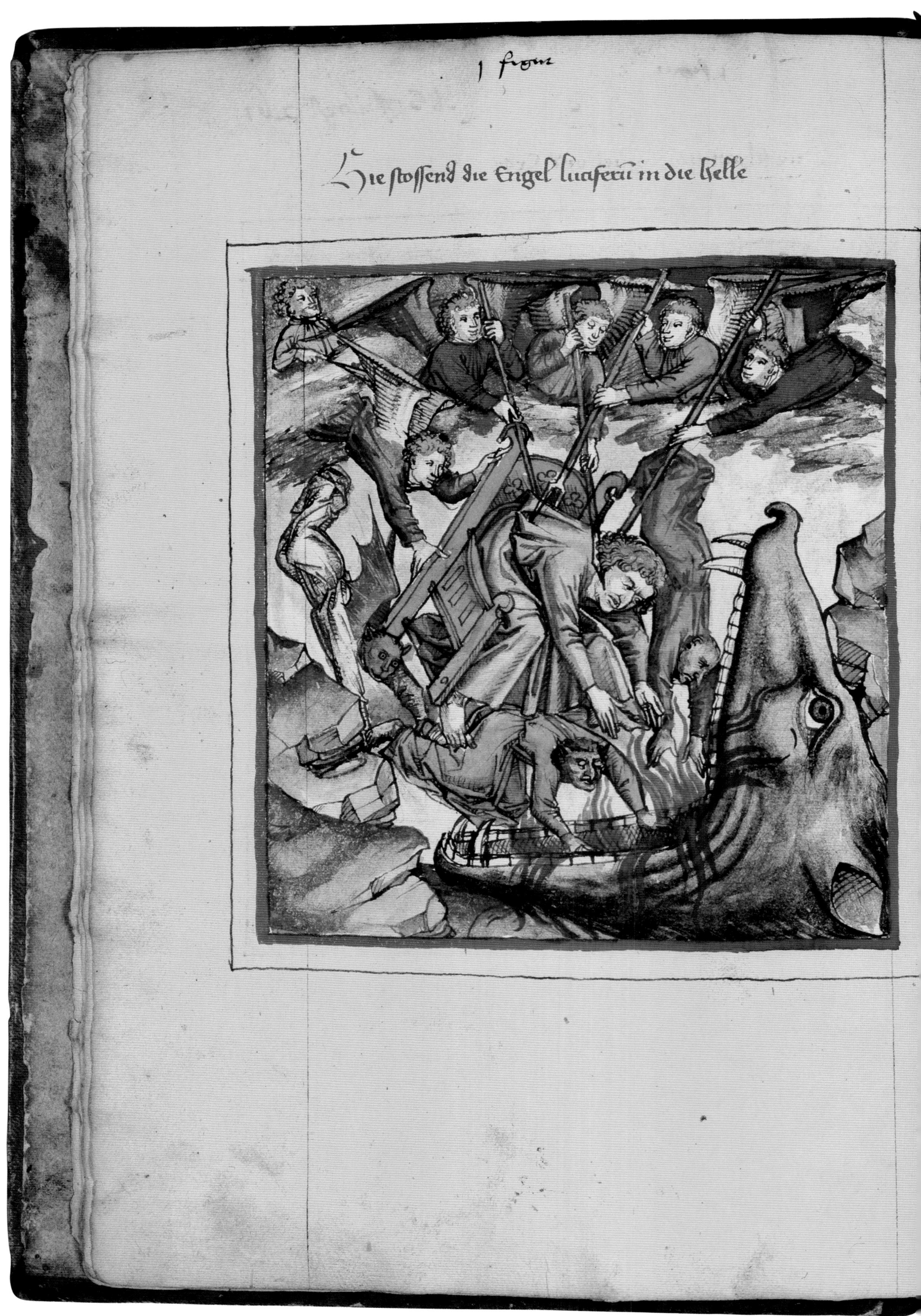
Hie stossend die engel lucifern in die helle

Do got in siner maiestat und kraft schwe
bet und alle ding in siner wißhait hette
und bracht sie in liechtem schin zů gnauden un
beschůff den himel wunneglichen mit sonne mo
nen und sterne Da mit zieret er sie In hocher ere
und beschůff dar In nün kör die engel dienet got
und wonen by Im und sind betten und etlich engel
sind Im näher die senden die andern in botschafft
wise So sind etlich gewaltiger dan die andern
und wie vil die engel zů dem mentschen botschaft
werben so schaiden sie sich doch nit von got und sen
hen mit fröden und sie her wider und lobend In alle
zitte Es wissend och die engel zů künfftige ding
die sehen sie In gottes ougen und verkünden sie den
mentschen nauch gottes gebott Und hätt öch ain
etlicher mentsch ain engel der sin hüttet und bring
et sin gebett und allmůsen und was er güttes tůt
für gott Die hösten ertzengel das ist gabriel raph
ahel und michahel Sant gabriel haisset gottes
sterckin So ist raphahel gottes ertzny Sant micha
hel ist by got nahe und haut in got zů probst ge
macht in hocher kraft über das paradis So sind
sust vil tusent engel vor got der namen wir nit
wissent

Do got die engeln beschůff In den himeln wun
nenglich gar schön und lieht do waz lucifer über
alle engel schar der aller schönst und clarest dess

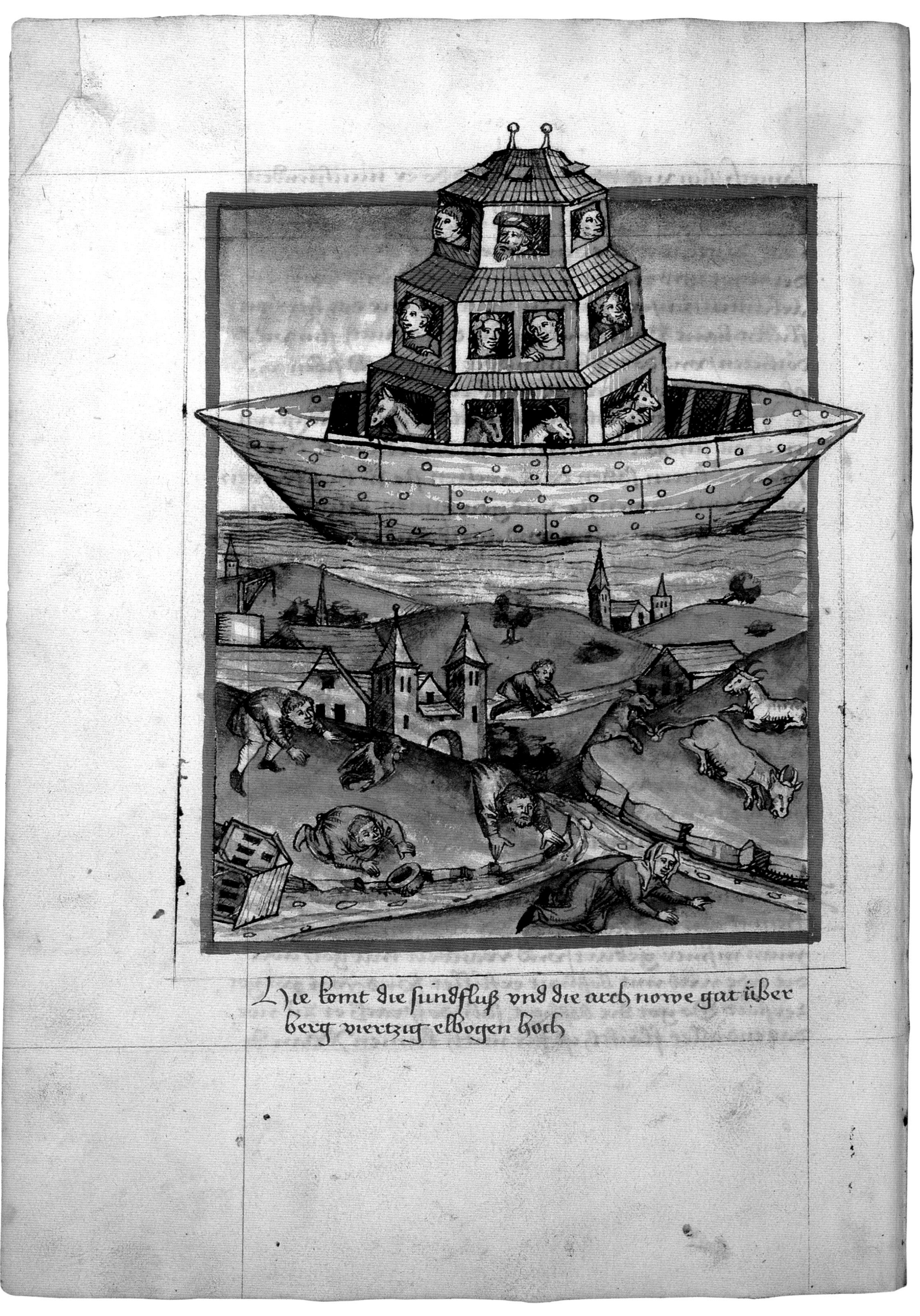

Hie komt die sundfluß vnd die arch nowe gat über
berg viertzig elbogen hoch

Fol. 18v (Genesis): The waters of the Flood cover the earth, drowning people and animals; Noah's Ark floats over the hilltops.

▸ **Detail from fol. 31v (Genesis):** The Destruction of Sodom and Gomorrah and the Saving of Lot: as Lot and his family flee from the burning city, his wife looks back, against divine instructions, and turns into a pillar; Lot and his two daughters carry on.

◂ **Detail from fol. 97v (Exodus):** The Crossing of the Red Sea. While the Israelites, who have passed through the Red Sea without getting their feet wet, continue on their way, the Egyptians pursuing them are drowned as the waters flood back.

Detail from fol. 181r (1 Samuel): David and Goliath: David swings his catapult in the direction of the enormous Philistine who is here equipped with a staff, the usual attribute of giants.

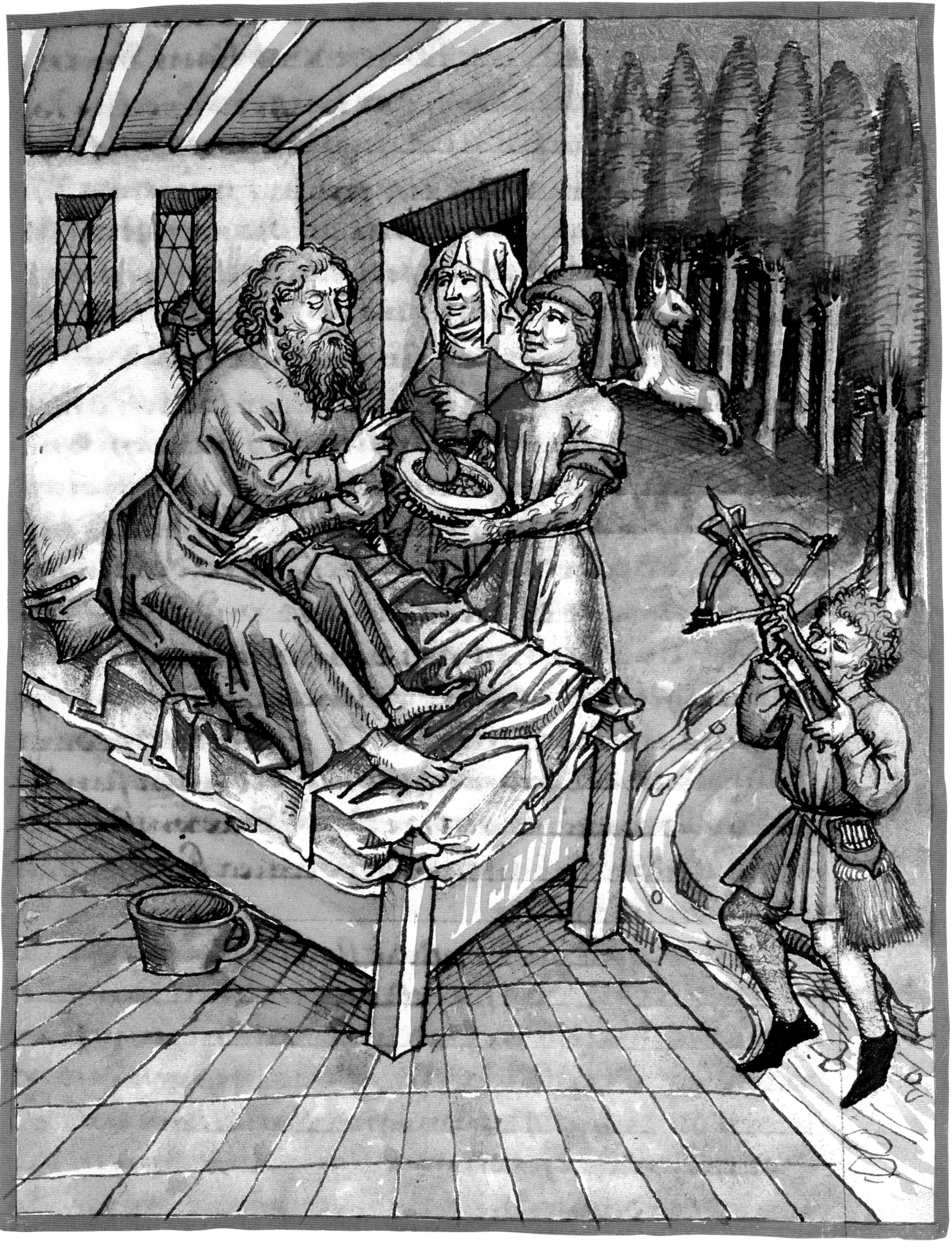

Fol. 42r (Genesis): The blind Isaac gives his younger son Jacob the blessing due to the first-born, while the elder Esau is out hunting game for his father.

▸ **Detail from fol. 341r (Judith):** Holding the severed head of Holofernes, Judith arrives at the gate of her native town of Bethulia, whose inhabitants greet her with astonishment.

IV.4 History Bible

Vienna (?), *c.* 1470 (?)

The text of Codex 2766 preserves what Vollmer (see Introduction) has classified as version IIIb of the German-language history Bible, which starts from the Creation and continues up to just before the life of Charlemagne (747–814). The author has thereby reworked the Old Testament version IIIa, a German extract from Peter Comestor's *Historia scholastica*, by expanding or replacing the biblical stories, by introducing episodes from secular history such as the founding of Rome, and – most significantly – by adding a New Testament section focusing primarily on the history of the emperors and popes. The primary source for these additions was a 14th-century world chronicle by Henry of Munich, from whom the division of history into six ages is also derived. The present version IIIb also survives in six other manuscripts, all produced in Austria in the 3rd quarter of the 15th century.

Both in its technique and choice of material, and in the form taken by its illustrations, the present history Bible bears little relation to the "modern" editions of the same text which were being produced with simpler, more economic means and aimed at a much broader lay public, as represented by the history Bible discussed earlier in this section (Cat. IV.3). Like other codices in group IIIb – some of which boast an even greater number of illustrations, even if few surpass the dimensions of the present manuscript, whose format and use of parchment clearly identify it as a de luxe edition – it takes up the tradition of chronicles written in rhyme. This deliberate revival of an "old-fashioned" style of manuscript undoubtedly reflected the wishes of the patron.

In line with tradition, the text in Codex 2766 is subdivided by decorative initials and illustrated with relatively small, framed miniatures. These are dotted about within the columns of text, always near the passages to which they relate. This form of

Detail from fol. 54v (Exodus): God delivers his Commandments to Moses on Mount Sinai.

▸ **Detail from fol. 5v (Genesis):** God creates the sun and the moon (4th day of Creation).

EXTENT: 258 sheets of parchment
FORMAT: 475 x 340–345 mm
BINDING: Vienna, after 1713, Étienne Boyet the Younger; dark blue leather over pasteboard with a linear frame and the arms of Prince Eugene of Savoy (1663–1736) in gold tooling on the front and back cover; also on the back cover, an entwined double *E*
CONTENT: history Bible
LANGUAGE: German (Bavarian-Austrian dialect)

SCRIBE: The text was copied by the notary Kuntz Kwermrewter, who placed his signet and name in the lower margin of fol. 52v.
ILLUSTRATION: 58 decorated initials, two of them historiated, at the beginning of the six ages of the world, the books of the Bible and their subdivisions; the majority terminate in foliate arabesques occasionally inhabited by animals; 222 framed miniatures illustrate the text.

PROVENANCE: The manuscript's first owner has yet to be traced; the two coats of arms on fol. 1r may help to establish his identity. In 1738 the manuscript passed to the Hofbibliothek from the collection of Prince Eugene of Savoy.
SHELFMARK: Vienna, ÖNB, Cod. 2766

illustration guarantees that words and image are grasped at the same time, with the role of the picture being to express the content of the text in another "language". Thus we are dealing here with narrative representations in which the episodes in the text are staged in clear and lively scenes, even infused with a certain drama, whereby colour is also used as a means of expression.

To what extent the illustrations in this manuscript are dependent upon the iconography typically employed in earlier world chronicles, and to what extent they adopt the abbreviated manner characteristic of the history Bible as a genre (cf. Cat. IV.3), are questions that have yet to be addressed. Quite different aims, however, inspired the exquisite distant landscapes which form the background to many of the present miniatures, and which can sometimes contain secondary scenes and even genre-like motifs painted on a truly miniature scale (e.g. ill. p. 186). The illumination of Codex 2766 has also yet to be examined more closely from a stylistic point of view. It was evidently executed by at least five different artists, some of whom can be grouped in the vicinity of the Lehrbüchermeister (Master of the Textbooks) active in Vienna in the 1450s–60s. It is on the basis of this link that the manuscript has been provisionally classified; in order to confirm its origins, however, it would be helpful not only to identify the first owner and scribe, but also to undertake an in-depth analysis of the various individual styles represented within the illuminations.

K. H.

Fol. 1r: Opening page with a decorative foliate border inhabited by animals and vegetal masks; in the right-hand margin, the arms of the first owner, yet to be identified. At the start of the text, an ornamental initial depicting the Holy Trinity in the image of the Throne of Grace.

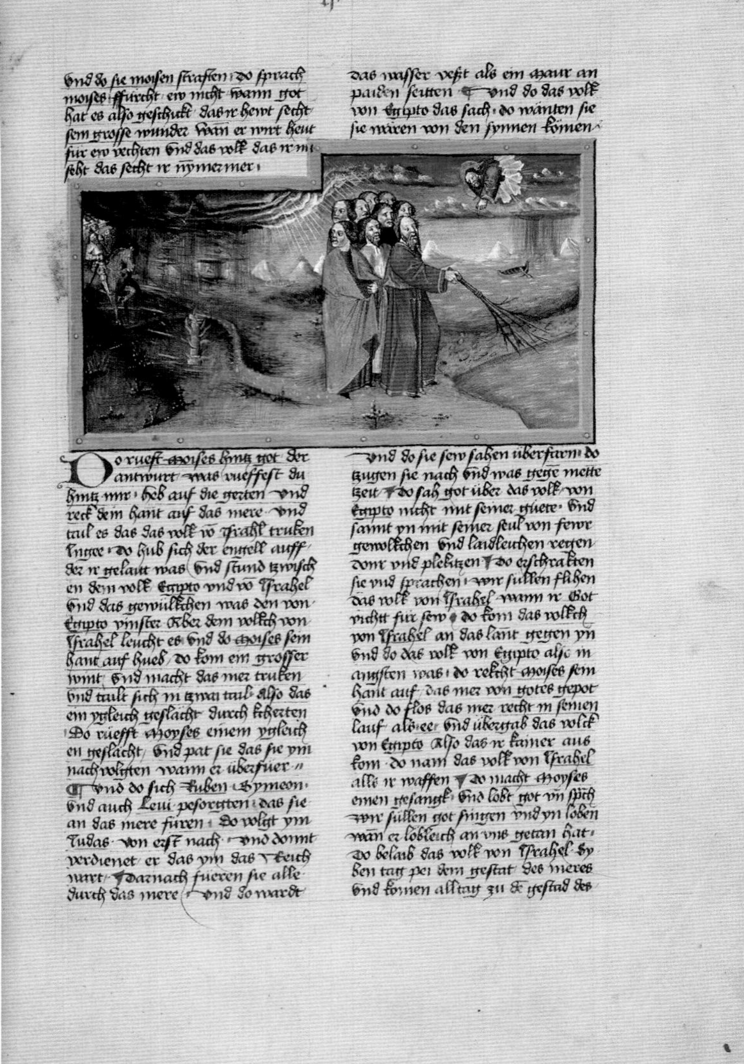

Fol. 39v (Genesis): Joseph orders his brothers to be arrested. He instructs his brothers' sacks to be filled with grain. Joseph's brothers return with their grain to their father, Jacob.

Fol. 51r (Exodus): The Crossing of the Red Sea: God shows his people the way – by means of clouds in the daytime, and at night with a pillar of fire.

▸ **Detail from fol. 59v (Exodus):** The dance around the Golden Calf; Moses raises up the stone tablets in order to smash them.

er die tauelen vor tzorn das sie tze
prachen vnd verprant das kalbel

vnd das tzold das do von kchom
prant er tzepuluer vnd strewte
es in das wasser vnd gab es dem
volk ze trinken Vnd do moyses

Details from fol. 70r (Numbers): Aaron and the princes of the tribes of Israel discover that Aaron's staff has sprouted and blossomed. When Moses strikes the rock with his staff, water flows out of it.

Details from fol. 113r (2 Samuel): Ahithophel hangs himself because his advice, which would have brought ruin upon King David, was ignored. Below: Absalom, David's son, remains hanging from a tree, his hair caught in its branches, and is killed by Joab.

▸ **Detail from fol. 143r (Isaiah):** The prophet Isaiah is sawn in two.

durch des weissagen gepet willen
¶ Epiphanius schreibt do d' kunig
Sennacherib von Egipto tzoch do er
sich fuer Jerusalem legte · Do legt
er sich zu dem weier · Siloe darumb
das das her da wasser hiet · wann
der weier was also gelegen das die
veint vnd die frewnt da mochten
wasser gehaben · Do pat d' weissag
hintz got / wenn man vo der stat
cham das dem wasser da wär ·
wenn aber die veint chamen das

aus dem
wider in
Jerusalem
götter vn
got getan
pracht g
das volk d
pechert er
Vnd nam
Vnd pesser
Jerusalem
wart pet
seinem h
funf vnd
Amon pe
Von Amo
vo Josia d
Do
re
got als s
tan het
huet vnd
haws · d
verderbten
vnd petr
grab ¶ d
gewesen
ten ward

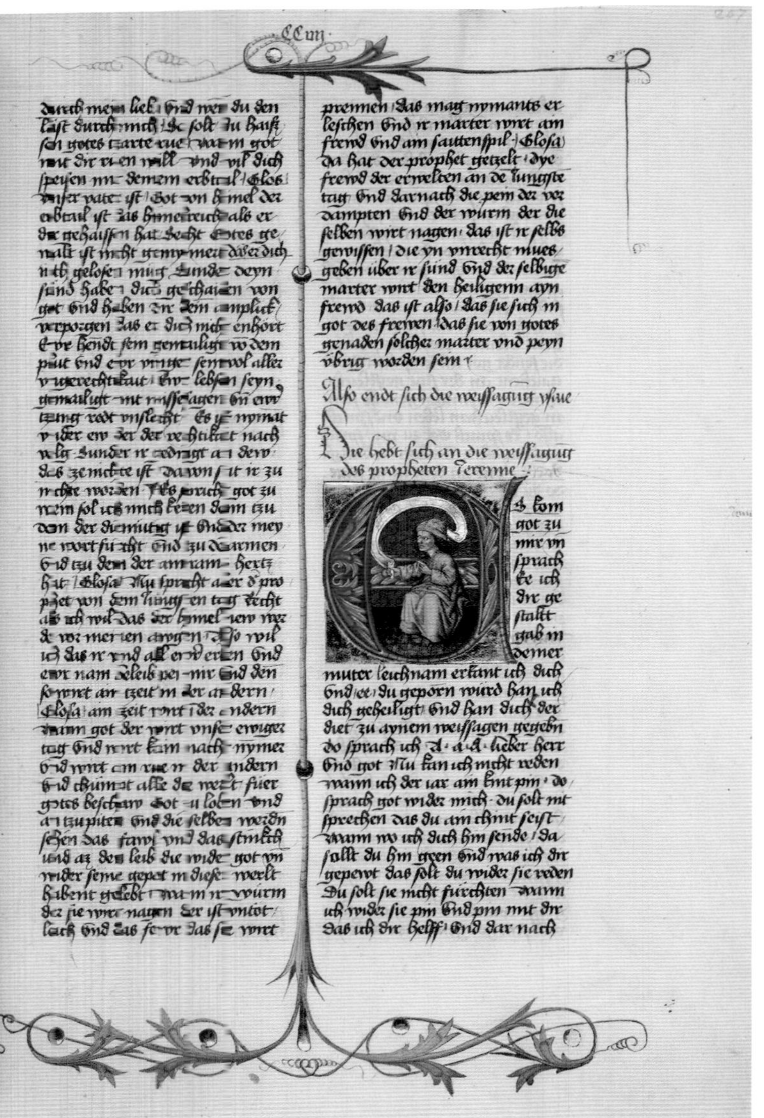

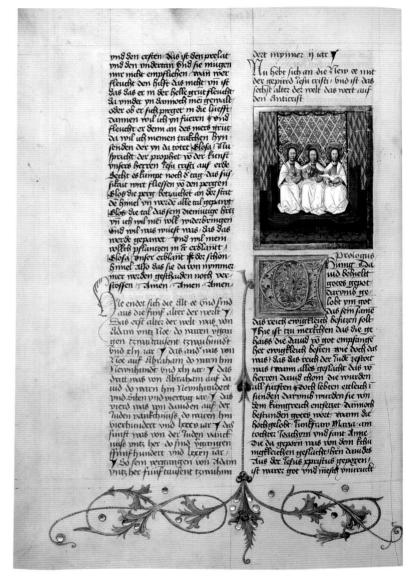

Fol. 207r (Jeremiah): Ornamental initial at the start of the Book of Jeremiah with a portrait of the seated prophet, holding a banderole in his right hand as a symbol of his prophecies.

Fol. 231v: Ornamental initial marking the start of the sixth age of the world, which dawns with the birth of Christ; above, a representation of the Holy Trinity in the shape of three identical enthroned figures.

▸ **Detail from fol. 228r (Jonah):** Jonah is thrown out of the boat by the oarsmen and is swallowed by a big fish.

IV.5

History Bible of Evert van Soudenbalch

Utrecht (northern Netherlands), *c.* 1460

In terms of the scope, lavishness and meticulousness of its artistic decoration and the quality and originality of its miniatures and decoration, the Soudenbalch Bible is undoubtedly the most outstanding of all the Middle-Netherlandish history Bibles still surviving today. It represents a copy of the first Netherlandish translation of the Bible, which was made in the southern Netherlands probably around 1360/61 (Deschamps [1972]). A masterpiece of Dutch manuscript illumination, its inclusion of the arms of the Utrecht canon Evert van Soudenbalch allows it to be confidently localized to Utrecht. The pictorial cycles in this Bible signify a turning-point in the history of Bible illumination insofar as they show the artists beginning to emancipate themselves from the traditional conventions of biblical illustration. Instead, they take the inspiration for their pictures directly from the biblical text in its vernacular form. These first attempts to establish a direct, personal relationship with the material of the Bible pave the way for the emergence of a "freely inventive" narrative style which would reach its high point in Rembrandt's unremitting, unorthodox interpretations of biblical events. The illuminators are often concerned less with portraying the external scene than – for the first time – with conveying the psychological dimension of the events taking place. This is something specifically Dutch. In one example in the present Bible, Daniel is seen being led into the lion's den on King Darius' orders. Darius is portrayed not giving a gesture of command, but rather as a passive ruler being coerced by two villains. In this way the Master of Evert van Soudenbalch illustrates Darius' unwillingness, as described in the Bible, to throw Daniel to the lions (fol. 247v).

Part of the explanation for the divergence in the present Bible from canonic iconography lies in the fact that the illustrations are inspired not by the Vulgate but by

Detail from Cod. 2772, fol. 189v: Decorative border.

▸ **Cod. 2771, fol. 9r:** Right-hand side of the double-page diptych: The celestial sphere with the planets and signs of the zodiac; above, God the Father enthroned in the choir of a church; around the choir and the sphere, worshipping angels. (Master of Evert van Soudenbalch)

Sol
Luna

EXTENT: 343 and 261 parchment folios
FORMAT: 395 x 293 (Cod. 2771) and 395 x 288 mm (Cod. 2772)
BINDING: bindings of blue morocco by Etienne Boyet the Younger, Vienna, after 1713.
CONTENT: copy of the "first history Bible in Middle Netherlandish"; in addition to the books of the Bible, also secular texts (e. g. the history of Alexander, excerpts from Flavius Josephus' *De Cyro* and *The Jewish War*, including the description of the destruction of Jerusalem); extracts from Peter Comestor's *Historia scholastica* as a commentary on the biblical texts; own prologues to the individual books of the Bible.
LANGUAGE: Middle Netherlandish
MINIATURISTS: The hands of altogether six illuminators have been identified in the two volumes: Master A (represented by one full-page miniature, Cod. 2771, fol. 8v), Master of Evert van Soudenbalch (chief master of the 1st volume), Master of the Cirrus Clouds (represented in both volumes), Master of Gysbrecht de Brederode (one miniature in Cod. 2771, f. 243v; mostly represented in Cod. 2772), Master E and Master F (a small part of Cod. 2772)
ILLUSTRATIONS: Cod. 2771: 134 miniatures; 27 decorated initials; numerous *fleuronnée* initials. Cod. 2772: 110 column-width miniatures; 23 historiated and 33 ornamental initials; eight smaller historiated initials; numerous *fleuronnée* initials.
PATRON: The Bible was commissioned by Evert van Soudenbalch, canon of Utrecht cathedral from 1445–1503 (donor portrait in the block of Creation miniatures.)
PROVENANCE: The manuscript passed into the possession of Prince Eugene of Savoy (1663–1736) and was acquired by the Hofbibliothek in 1738.
SHELFMARK: Vienna, ÖNB, Cod. 2771–2772

the commentaries of the *Historia scholastica* and by the prologues to the biblical books written specifically for this Bible. In the first volume, a number of the pictures are inspired by passages of text that had never before been selected for illustration, with the result that the illustrations include a series of iconographically unique compositions, such as the Burial of Cambyses (Cod. 2771, fol. 265r). Furthermore, there is no clear division between the books of the Old Testament and those of the New Testament (in Codex 2772 the New Testament is followed by the books of the Maccabees and the Book of Psalms).

In seeking to explain the emergence of this new approach to biblical illumination, we must also consider the religious climate prevailing in the northern Netherlands, which was strongly influenced by the *Devotio moderna* movement and its calls for religious renewal. This movement had begun in the Netherlands and by the end of the 14th century had spread across the whole of Europe, finding a particular reception in Germany and Bohemia. The new kind of narrative style and the departure from traditional iconography are encountered in the work of all six illuminators engaged on the present Bible, and most clearly of all in the miniatures by the Master of Evert van Soudenbalch. Colour also plays a particular role for all the artists, be it in the vibrant palette employed by the Master of Evert van Soudenbalch in his figures and settings, or in the gloomy, matt palette adopted by the Master of the Cirrus Clouds.

It is probable that the six illuminators were all employed in the same workshop, as they also collaborated on other codices (on a Book of Hours in Brussels, Bibl. Royale, ms. II 7619, for example, and another in Liège, Univ. Bibl., ms. Wittert 13). A single editor was in charge of the overall pictorial programme of the Bible. Some of his instructions to the artists have survived in the lower margin, and have clearly been closely adhered to by the illuminators. The present history Bible is undated, but can be assigned together with other works by the Soudenbalch Master – one of them dated 1460 (the Brussels Book of Hours) – to around 1460. *U. J.*

Cod. 2771, fol. 10r (Genesis): The seven Creation scenes and the dedication scene with patron Evert van Soudenbalch, the canon of Utrecht cathedral, who commissioned the manuscript. Historiated initial depicting the Fall. (Master of Evert van Soudenbalch)

In den begin sciep god
hemel ende eerde. mer
die eerde was onnut
eñ ydel eñ donckerhei
den waren op dat aen
sichte des afgronts.
Eñ gods geest wart
gedragen bouen den
wateren Scolastica

In den begin was
tswoert eñ dat
woert was int beginne
Inden welken eñ by
den welken die vader
die werlt sciepe. dat
woert was sijn ewige soen. men hept
die werelt in vier manieren. Eerst so
heytmen den geesteliken hemel die wer
relt om sijn suuerheyt. en te sulke tijt
dese begripelike werelt. eñ die grieste
heten die werelt pan. Eñ die latijnsce
hetense omen dat is al. Wāt die philo
sophi en kenden den geesteliken hemel
niet. eñ sulke tijt heetmen die werelt
dat lantscap alleen dat onder der ma
nen loep is. Want dese werelt het et
alleen in die dietē die wi kennen eñ
hier of is geseit. die prīce der werelt
dats die duuel en sal daer niet werden
verdreuen. Eñ sulke tijt so heetmen die
menschen die werlt. want hi heeft in
hem alle die gelikenisse der werelt eñ
daer om is hi vandē heer indē ewange
lio geheten alle. eñ die grieken heten den
mensche microcosmū dat is die mynre
werelt. Die geestelike werelt eñ die begri
pelike werelt eñ dat lantscap onder dye
mane dat sciep god
ypperlick. dat is hy
maecter van niete.
Mer den mensche
niet properlicken
want hi blasfame
reden. Eñ daer in
is beteykent sijn
hoge wesen. om
dat hi mit voirsie
nicheiden gemaket was. Ende vander
sceppinge vanden eersten drien werelde
seyt moyses. Inden begin sciep god he
mel eñ eerde. hi sciep den hemel dats
te verstaen eñ dat daer in was sculdich
te sijn dats den geesteliken hemel eñ

Die geestelike wer
relt of die geestelike
hemel dat heetmen
in latijn empyriū
dats die hemel daer
god eñ sijn lieue
moeder in sitte. Eñ
daer die neghē cho
ren der heiligen en
gelen in sitten.

Ende het gescie
de na dien
dat saul doot
was dat da
uid weder ke
rede va ame
lechs geslech
te en dat hi
twe dage ge
duerde in sy
celech En ten
derden dage
openbaerde een man comende wt sauls
getelde mit gescoerden cleederen en mit
gemul op thoeft gespreyt En doe hi tot
dauid comen was so viel hi op syn aen
sichte en aenbeden. En dauid seide tot hem
waen coemstu. En hi seide hem. Ic byn ge
vlogen wten getelden van ysrl. Ende da
uid seide tot hem wat woerde datter ge
sciet is segt my. Hi seide tvolc vloech va
den stride en hoe veel vanden volke syn
daer geuallen en doot gebleuen. mer
saul en yonathas syn daer doot gebleuen
En dauid seide totten iongelinc die daer
boetscapte. waer bi weetstu dat saul ende
syn sonen doot syn. En die iongelinc die
hem boetscapte seide bi auontueren quam
ic inden berge gelboe en saul lach en loene
de op syn spere en die wagene en die ge
redene quamen hem aen. Ende hi keerde hem
om doe hi my sach en so hi my sach so riep
hi my. En doe ic hem antwoert had ...

hoeft was en die a...
en ic hebse gebrach...
Dye yoden seg...
ghen dat dese...
sone van ydumea. ...
so gaf hem syn vad...
teykene die hi plac...
dragen soude tot d...
de dauids vriensc...
daer na viel hi oec...
reden en is niet to...
hiete van ydumea...
lech. want die van...
ydumea. want am...
soen die ezaus zone...
Ende dauid ...
cledere en s...
manne die...
weenden en sy scre...
auonde op saul en ...
op sheren volc en o...
datsi mitten zweerde...
dauid seide totten io...
scapt hadde. waen ...
bin eens toecomeli...
amelechs soen. En ...
om en ontsaechstu ...
steken om sheren co...
En dauid riep ene...
seide coempt voert...
en die sloechen en ...
de tot hem. want d...
di seluen gesproken...
consacreerde conic ...
nede dit geween op...
syn soen. En hi gebo...
van ysrl ten boghe ...
rechter boec gescreue...
Als dauid ver...
bleuen was...
hi datme die kinder...
als inder rechter bo...
boeck so en heeftme...
nen dat hy inder ge...
lonien verloren wa...
daer men af verma...
te. Enige waren die...
boeck der gerechtige...

Cod. 2771, fol. 49v (Genesis and Exodus): Jacob's Blessing. The burial of Joseph. The Israelites working in bondage to the Egyptians (making mud bricks). (Master of Evert van Soudenbalch)

Cod. 2771, fol. 129v (Deuteronomy): God shows Moses the Promised Land from the top of Mount Nebo. The burial of Moses (two scenes in one miniature). (Master of Evert van Soudenbalch)

◂ **Detail from Cod. 2771, fol. 174v (2 Samuel):** David learns of Saul's death. (Master of Evert van Soudenbalch)

Detail from Cod. 2771, fol. 165r (1 Samuel): Samuel cuts Agag into pieces before the Lord. (Master of Evert van Soudenbalch)

Detail from Cod. 2771, fol. 166v (1 Samuel): David kills Goliath. (Master of Evert van Soudenbalch)

Detail from Cod. 2771, fol. 173r (1 Samuel): Saul visits the medium of Endor; the prophet Samuel appears and prophesies that Saul and his sons will die the next day. (Master of Evert van Soudenbalch)

Detail from Cod. 2771, fol. 218v (2 Kings): Queen Jezebel is torn apart by two dogs and trampled by two horses. (Master of Evert van Soudenbalch)

▸ **Cod. 2772, fol. 10r:** The symbols of the four Evangelists as the title-page to the concordance of the four Gospels; below, bridal couple. (Master of Gysbrecht de Brederode)

Hier beghint dat prologus optie ewangelie

Nu sijn wi come
totten nywe
testament en
hier na volgẽ
die ewange
lien · Maer om
dat wij dye
neesten van
den hystorie
volgẽ willen
so sullen wy
hier bescriue
die ewangelien diemen heet concordan
cien dats vten vier ewangelisten een
ewangelie ghemaket bi orconde En so
waer dat elc ewangelist yet seit son

Cod. 2772, fol. 231r (Psalms): David and Goliath: title-page to the Book of Psalms. Historiated initial underneath: King David kneeling before an altar. (Master of the Cirrus Clouds)

▸ **Detail from Cod. 2772, fol. 198v (Josephus Flavius, Jewish Antiquities XIII–XVI):** The queen gives a command to a messenger (left-hand foreground). Aristobulus' mother in prison (right-hand background). (Master of the Cirrus Clouds)

seide wilke tijt hi moste [illegible] daer om
si souden hare doot beter achten dan o
licheit. Hier om lach daer Jan te lange
Maer dat zevende Jaer dattie Joeden v
an quam En̄ Jan toech vandē poertek
ptolomeus doode sijn moeder en̄ sijn br
en̄ hi vloech tot senonen den conīc ph
phien diemen heet cotilia en̄ toenaen
Hier na beleyde antyochus ponticus
En̄ om dese zake dede Jan hyrcaen op
vandē acht coffers die omtrint dauids
stonden. En̄ hi nam daer wt meer dan
talente. En̄ hi gaf antyocho. iijᶜ. talen
hi van yerosolima trecken soude. En̄ o
hi die murmuracie vanden volke vre
woude dat hi dat graft ondien hadde so
kede hi mittē anderen gelde binnē yero
teerste hospitale vā armen. Dese Jan v
samarien en̄ slechtet. Maer daer na vm
herodes en̄ hietse sebasten. En̄ doe Jan.
iaer die dingen alte wel geregiert had
sterf hi en̄ hi liet vijf sonen na hem da
aristobolū den eerst geboren en antigo
mit drien minderen broeders. En̄ om a
ment van hē ludē tamelic en was om
te regeeren so sette hi boue iudea hē en
en̄ sijn wijf die alte wijs was. Hoe der

moechstu aldus proeuē· Beuele hē dat hi tot v
come en̄ coemt hi ghewapēt so wes zeker dat wi
segghē· Hier om leyde aristobole ghewapēde mān
ī een duwiere die ond' die eerde was diemē hiet
purghastroton daer ātigonus om lydē soude dat h
en doot slaen soudē waert dat hi ghewapēt q̄me
En̄ aristobel riep den bode tot hē en̄ beual hē dat
hi sine broed' seide dat hi niet ghewapēt en quame
ay die coniginne verwan den bode mit ghiftē dat
hi hem segghē soude dat hi ghewapēt quame·
wāt die conīc begheerdē te zien ī sin̄ scoen wapen

V.

The juxtaposition of the Old and New Testaments in typological picture Bibles

Typology is the name given to a method of biblical interpretation which sees a meaningful connection between specific events or figures in the Old Testament and similar events or the figure of Christ in the New Testament. The Old Testament element is thereby understood as the prefiguration, or type, of its New Testament counterpart, which represents its fulfilment, or antitype (Schrenk [1995]). This typological "method" was necessitated by the (Christian) view that the Old Testament occupied a firm place in the history of salvation through its references to the New Testament.

The foundations of typological exegesis in literature and the arts were first laid down in the early years of Christianity. Typology subsequently saw a significant flowering in the picture Bibles of the late Middle Ages: in addition to the manuscripts discussed here, further important codices of this kind include Ulrich von Lilienfeld's *Concordantia caritatis* (arose after 1350) and the Marian-oriented *Defensorium inviolatae virginitatis beatae Mariae* by Franz von Retz (1427).

In Codices 2554 (Cat. V.1) and 1179 (Cat. V.2), the Österreichische Nationalbibliothek owns the oldest surviving examples of a type of Bible known as a *Bible moralisée*, a luxury manuscript in which scenes from the Bible are paired, in large-scale pictorial programmes, with an interpretation of their meaning. To assist the reader in understanding the connection between the pictures, brief captions identify the individuals and events portrayed. The connection between biblical passage and interpretation is generally established by the phrase "signifies that". For example, in Codex 2554, the fact that Saul forbids his people to eat or drink until the end of the battle signifies that the good princes and prelates forbid the Christians to turn to worldly things before they have defeated the devil (ill. p. 205; lower left-hand pair of medallions). Since most commen-

Biblia pauperum, Cod. 1198, detail from fol. 9v: 33rd picture group (above): Moses receives the Tablets of the Law from God.

▸ Bible moralisée, Cod. 2554, detail from fol. 37r (1 Samuel): (1) Samuel rebukes the sons of Israel; below: Christ rebukes the Jews. (2) The Israelites bring iron into the country and make weapons; below: the wicked students go to Bologna to study law. (3) Saul forbids his people to eat or drink until the battle is over; below: the good princes and prelates forbid the Christians to turn to worldly things before they have conquered the devil. (4) Saul is victorious over the Saracens, but his son licks a stick with honey on it; below: the good Christians are victorious over God's enemies, but the wicked turn to worldly things.

taries in these books adopted the same or a similar moral slant, they became known as *Bibles moralisées*, "moralizing Bibles" – a term which appears in a 15th-century copy of the text of one such Bible. Other methods of exegesis are also employed, however, including typology, and the miniatures permit associations that go beyond the explanations in the captions.

A total of seven fully-illustrated *Bibles moralisées* have survived into the present, six of which arose between *c.* 1220 and 1480 in Paris; the seventh, produced in England, is a copy of one of these other six. It is very probable that these manuscripts (with the exception of the English copy) were executed for members of the French royal family: a number of invoices relating to the *Bible moralisée* ms. fr. 167 in the Bibliothèque Nationale de France, Paris, name the French king John the Good (1319–1364) as patron. Housed in the Pierpont Morgan Library in New York is the final sheet of the copy belonging to Toledo cathedral, showing a queen and king enthroned above a monk and an illuminator who are both working on a *Bible moralisée*. The clearest evidence that these Bibles were produced for royalty is provided by the final sheet of Codex 1179 in Vienna, which shows a king holding up an open *Bible moralisée* (ill. p. 25).

Another typological work highlighting the unity of the Old and New Testaments, this time in a condensed form following the life of Christ, is the *Biblia pauperum*. The term is misleading: this intellectually sophisticated "Bible of the Poor" was certainly not intended for an uneducated class of *pauperes* (poor) or *illitterati* (illiterate), but for an educated, clerical circle of users. The oldest surviving manuscripts of the genre, dating from the first half of the 14th century, originate from the Bavaria/Austria region and probably arose within a Benedictine or Augustinian context; their prototype is thought to have appeared at the latest around the middle of the 13th century. More than eighty examples of the *Biblia pauperum* are still extant, not just as – in the majority of cases – illustrated manuscripts, but also as block books and later printed versions. Together they testify to the enduring popularity of the so-called "Bibles of the Poor" and document the longevity of typology well past the Middle Ages. The typological comparisons they offer may arise out of biblical events or be symbolic or theological in nature. The fact that such comparisons are frequently only superficial reflects an intellectual watering-down that is characteristic of the late phase of typological picture cycles. In the case of the *Biblia pauperum*, it can be explained to a certain degree by the systematic layout, in which Old Testament types and prophesies are always arranged in the same fashion around a central New Testament scene. An insight into the comprehensive scope of the themes is offered by the present Codex 1198 (Cat. V.4), here reproduced almost in its entirety. An early example of a *Biblia pauperum*, it adheres to a strict visual programme comprising 34 uniformly structured picture groups laid out over 17 pages (Cat. V.4, ill. p. 222–227). If we compare this to the *Biblia pauperum* housed in the Österreichische Nationalbibliothek as Codex 370, it becomes clear how the linear arrangement of the pictures there leads to a considerable vagueness in the typological relations (Cat. V.3, ill. p. 216–221).

Surviving, lastly, in at least 350 to 400 Latin and vernacular manuscripts as well as numerous printed copies, is the most widely distributed typological work of the late Middle Ages, the *Speculum humanae salvationis*. Although fewer than half of these manuscripts are illuminated, the "Mirror of Salvation" must have been conceived with illustrations right from the beginnung, probably in the long, 45-chapter version represented here by Codex Series nova 2612, an early example of the genre (Cat. V.5; ill. p. 228–237). Its simple, memorable pictures and detailed texts address themselves to a broad public drawn from both the clergy and the laity. The origins of the *Speculum* remain obscure. Initially thought to be a work by the Strasburg-based Dominican Ludolf of Saxony (cf. Cat. III.3) dating from 1324, it is now increasingly assumed to be an Italian work of the late 13th or early 14th century. Astonishingly, the first examples emerge more or less simultaneously from about 1320/30 in Italy (Bologna) and southern Germany,

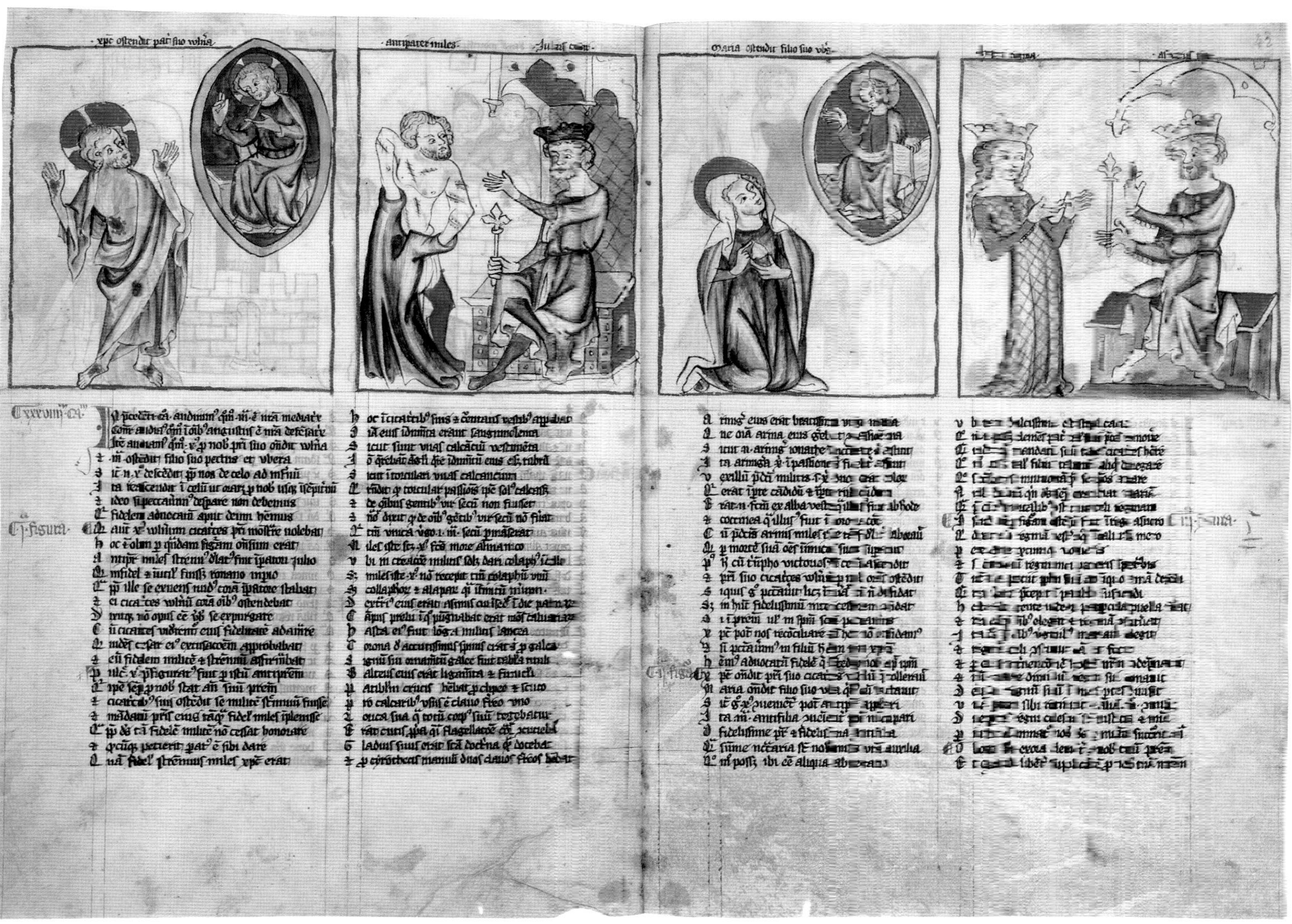

whereby certain details establish a link with the Dominican order – the vision of a Dominican, for example (ill. p. 236).

Typology in the *Speculum* becomes the starting-point for a broader contemplation of the mystery of the Divine Plan from the beginning to the end of the world. As suggested by its title, it seeks to hold up to man a mirror that will reveal the connections running through the history of salvation in order to save his soul. In addition to Christ, the Virgin Mary now also plays a prominent role: as the counterpart to the Man of Sorrows, who is showing his wounds to his Father, we find the Mother of God baring her bosom to her Son – both symbolic images of *intercessio*, the intercession with God on behalf of humankind (ill. p. 207). Strikingly, the Dominican receiving the stigmata in the vision mentioned above is also shown with the Virgin's sword in his heart, symbolizing her pain at the loss of her son (cf. ill. p. 236). The underlying concept here is that of *compassio*, the compassion aroused by contemplating the Passion. Such devotional images which in the *Speculum* accompany the traditional scenes from the New Testament, announce a new quality in typology, one inconceivable without the influence of contemporary mysticism.

A. F. / C. B. / V. P.-A.

Speculum humanae salvationis, Cod. Ser. n. 2612, fol. 41v–42r: 39th chapter: *Christ shows God the Father his wounds* (symbolic image of intercession). Antipater shows Julius Caesar his scars to refute the accusation that he is a disloyal and ineffective soldier (after Peter Comestor, *Historia scholastica*). *The Virgin Mary bares her bosom to her Son* (and thereby intercedes, like Christ, for humanity). Esther intercedes with Ahasuerus for her people.

V.1-2 Bibles moralisées

Paris, 1st half of the 13th century

Codices 2554 and 1179 in the Austrian National Library are the oldest surviving examples of a type of commentary on the Old and New Testaments known as the *Bible moralisée*. Not a very common genre, the *Bible moralisée* offers interpretations of the Christian scriptures, conveyed in a particularly sumptuous and attractive format. Neither manuscript gives the name of its first owner, but the circle of possible patrons for such lavish manuscripts, whose concept, text and iconography were entirely new and whose design was modified and expanded upon in every subsequent copy, was surely very limited. The commission for codices 2554 and 1179 is most likely to have come from a member of the French royal family in the 1st half of the 13th century. Support for this argument is offered, in the case of Codex 1179, by the penultimate medallion on the right-hand side of fol. 246r (ill. p. 19): it shows a king on his throne, holding a sceptre with fleur-de-lys in his left hand and the open *Bible moralisée* in his right. The inscription accompanying this medallion in the right-hand margin was erased by a later hand, and it is no longer possible to make out a name. Since the manuscript can be dated, on grounds of its style and content, to the period between 1220 and 1230, the king in question might be Philippe Auguste II († 1223) or his son Louis VIII († 1226). Louis IX was still a minor when his father died and it is more likely that he would have been portrayed without a beard. The original owner of Codex 2554, which unlike Codex 1179 is written in French, not Latin, is popularly imagined to have been Blanche of Castile, who married Louis VIII in 1200. After her husband's death, she took over the running of government for a few years on behalf of her son, Louis IX, and died in 1252. Unfortunately, the end of the manuscript, which might originally have contained a reference to the owner, is today missing, as are a number of other pages.

Detail from Cod. 2554, fol. 10r (Genesis): Christ's arrival in Hell.

▸ **Cod. 2554, fol. 1v (Genesis):** God as the Creator of the world.

I : CRIE : DEX : CIEL : ET : TERRE : SOLEIL

Ci rauist
dex Enoch
la nue.

Ce qe dame
dex rauist
och en la
e senefie re
crist qi en
ane les su
z rauist
la celestial
npagnie.

ci enuoie Noe
colon fors por
voir s'il trovast
re ferme. z al
reuint puis z
s'enuoia un au
z al reuint leg
z emboez z pu
nuoia un cor
z cil s'asist sor
e charvigne.
s enuoia un
on z il troua
re ferme. et
rta un raim
ue en sa bo
...

Ce qi enuoia fors
oiseaus senefie
en prelat q'en
fors les deciples
preechier li p
ans colons sen
e boen doctrine
uert en doist
lons qi reuin
boez emboez se
ie le boen moi
qi ne trueue
e non z il trueue
erez. li corbeau
e fle le mauue
me qi sa reste
a charvigne
onde.

Ci
en
le co
dame
trois f
me..

Ce
sa
de z
nes
crist
o sa r
les s
te egl

Ci
cel
eu
Noe s
o to
z re
deu d
geta

Ce
celu
toz
deu c
peril
ente
mer
giet

EXTENT: 130 parchment folios
FORMAT: 344 x 260 mm
CONTENT: *Bible moralisée* (commentaries on the books of Genesis, Exodus, Leviticus, Numbers, Deuteronomy, Joshua, Judges, Ruth, 1 and 2 Samuel, 1 and 2 Kings); the page order was altered by mistake when the binding was replaced
LANGUAGE: French
ILLUSTRATION: one full-page miniature, 129 pages each containing eight miniatures in medallions
PATRON: Blanche of Castille (?)
PROVENANCE: Codex 2554 arose in the first half of the 13th century in Paris and was probably commissioned by a member of the French royal family. In the 1[illegible]th century, an additional page was inserted, bearing the arms of the Mercy, Luxembourg, Beaupart, Beauvau Craon, Lenoncourt and La Marck families, all of whom were based in the Lotharingian Luxemburg area. To which particular member of these families the manuscript might have belonged has yet to be determined. The codex later reached the Damenstift in Hall (Tyrol), following whose closure it passed to the Hofbibliothek in 1783, together with the convent's other holdings.
SHELFMARK: Vienna, ÖNB, Cod. 2554

The manuscripts arose just a few years apart and were each illuminated by a team of artists, some of whom contributed to both Bibles. Which of the two can lay claim to the title of first *Bible moralisée* remains a matter of dispute. Those who argue that Codex 1179 came after Codex 2554 point out, by way of supporting evidence, that its page layout is easier for the viewer or reader to follow and was adopted by later *Bibles moralisées*. The medallions are grouped in vertical pairs: a scene from the Old Testament on top, and below it a second scene interpreting its meaning. In Codex 2554, the second pair of medallions does not follow beneath the first but beside it so that the direction in which the page is read is different. In Codex 1179 and in later *Bibles moralisées*, the captions inserted between the two columns of medallions ensure that the viewer's eye is guided from the top to the bottom. The second pair of medallions is now found beneath the first one and not beside it (ill. p. 210).

Who designed the impressive pictorial programme is unknown. A theologian who understood something of the methods of biblical exegesis was undoubtedly involved. In most cases, the texts beside the medallions are closely related to the scenes portrayed, although less so in Revelation, where the medallions are accompanied by lengthy passages from the scriptures (on fol. 246r., for example, (1) is accompanied by Rev Apc 22:6–15, (2) by Apc 22:16–17 and (3) by Apc 22:18–21). These extracts from the Bible combine with the illustrations to weave an even more complex web of inter-relationships. In the following section we shall confine ourselves simply to identifying the figures and symbols in the medallions; for a proposed interpretation of their meaning, see Tammen (2002). There are nevertheless inconsistencies within the programme for which no other source demonstrating the same flawed knowledge of the Bible has yet been found.

There is still a great deal of research to be done into the thought underpinning *Bibles moralisées*. Relatively easy to understand, on the other hand, is the typological

Cod. 2554, detail from fol. 3r (Genesis): (1) God gathers up Enoch; below: Christ gathers his own into the company of heaven. (2) Noah saves himself and his family in the Ark; below: Christ saves his own in the holy Church. (3) Noah sends out birds to look for dry land; below: the good prelate sends his disciples out to preach. (4) God has saved Noah from danger; below: God saves the faithful from dangers.

EXTENT: 246 parchment folios
FORMAT: 430 x 300 mm
BINDING: dark blue morocco over pasteboard, hand gilded, bearing the arms of Prince Eugene of Savoy (Vienna, Étienne Boyet the Younger, after 1713).
CONTENT: *Bible moralisée* (commentaries on the books of Genesis, Exodus, Leviticus, Numbers, Deuteronomy, Joshua, Judges, Ruth, 1 and 2 Samuel, 1 and 2 Kings, Nehemiah, Job, Daniel, Tobias, Judith, Esther, 1 and 2 Maccabees, Apocalypse)
LANGUAGE: Latin
ILLUSTRATION: one full-page miniature, 242 pages each containing eight miniatures in medallions, on fol. 42r and 52r one ornamental initial and four medallions, on fol. 162r one ornamental initial and two medallions
PATRON: King Philippe Auguste II († 1223) or his son Louis VIII († 1226)
PROVENANCE: It is fairly certain that the Bible was produced for a member of the French royal family in the 1st half of the 13th century in Paris. A coat of arms incorporating a double-headed eagle and a heart-shaped shield divided into red and white fields on fol. 1r and 246v have not yet been identified with certainty. The manuscript was later owned by Prince Eugene of Savoy (1663–1736). In 1738 Emperor Charles VI acquired parts of the Prince's collection, including the present *Bible moralisée*, from his heiress Victoria of Savoy, Duchess of Sachsen-Hildburghausen (oder Saxe-Hilburghausen). In 1809 the manuscript was taken to Paris. Since 1914/15 it has been housed in the Vienna Hofbibliothek.
SHELFMARK: Vienna, ÖNB, Cod. 1179

relationship between the two medallions making up each pair, whereby the Old Testament scene in the first medallion serves to prefigure the second, New Testament scene. An example of this is illustrated in the pair of medallions in the lower right-hand corner of fol. 5r in Codex 2554: in the upper of the two medallions, we see Abraham approaching an altar in the mountains, where he is to sacrifice his son Isaac at God's command. Isaac is carrying on his back the wood needed for the sacrificial fire. The artist has portrayed the bundle of wood in the shape of a cross, in order to make clear the parallels between the Sacrifice of Isaac and the Crucifixion of Christ in the medallion underneath. The caption to the lower medallion explains: "That Isaac is carrying the wood for the sacrifice signifies Jesus Christ, who is carrying his Cross for his Crucifixion".

In addition to such typological illustrations, there are many which attempt to infer from the stories in the Old Testament lessons about the right way to behave, and thus to unlock the moral message of the holy scriptures. Relatively frequently, these take the form of instructions about correct learning and teaching, and about problems such as usury, greed and the threat posed to the Church by unbelievers. In the top left-hand medallion on fol. 22*v of Codex 2554, for example, the Israelites have gone against Moses' instructions and have kept some of their manna overnight. The terse observation in the Bible that "it bred worms and stank" (Exodus 16:20) has been dramatized in the *Bible moralisée* into a scene of worms and snakes slithering out of the chests of manna and attacking the Israelites, as revealed by the caption beside it. The text next to the medallion underneath explains: "That the sons of Israel want to take out the manna they had put aside, and worms come out, signifies the bad students who open their desks too late, and devils come out and bite their tongues; and the usurers, who watch over their money so well, will be defeated by the earthly lords."

▸ **Detail from Cod. 2554, fol. 10r (Genesis):** (1) The synagogue makes accusations about Christ to the philosophers. (2) Pilate commands Christ to be beaten and nailed to the Cross. (3) Joseph is thrown into jail and venerated by the other prisoners; below: Christ descends into Hell and is venerated by men of honour and good prophets. (4) Joseph in prison between Pharoah's cup-bearer and baker; below: Christ between those who do good works and those who commit wicked deeds.

HIC · ORBIS · FIGVLVS · DISPONIT SINGVLA SOLVS

Clues to the approximate date of these two early *Bibles moralisées* are provided by a number of more specific references to contemporary life. On fol. 57r in Codex 2554, in the second medallion from the top on the right-hand side, we can identify students who are leaving their teachers in Paris to go and study law in Bologna – something which confuses and muddles them, as the accompanying text admonishes (ill. p. 205). The study of civil law in Paris was forbidden in 1219 by a bull of Pope Honorius III; the problem described here must thus have arisen in the years following this date. An approximate *terminus ante quem* can also be deduced from the lack of references to the two mendicant orders who were gaining in importance and who had established houses in Paris by 1229. By contrast, several references to these mendicant monks appear in another *Bible moralisée* commenced by the illuminators of the Vienna codices, and today housed in Toledo cathedral.

Little is known about the illuminators themselves. The bottom right-hand medallion on fol. 246r in Cod. 1179 shows a painter working on a *Bible moralisée* (ill. p. 19). His clothes are those of a layman, from which we can deduce that this picture Bible was not produced in a monastic scriptorium. Both Vienna codices open with a full-page miniature of the Creator (ill. p. 209 and 214). These miniatures rank amongst the masterpieces of 13th-century painting and are attributed to the main master of these early *Bibles moralisées*, who was probably also in overall charge of the illumination and contributed several pages of medallions. Whether the other artists were members of his workshop or were engaged specifically for the project has yet to be determined. *C. B.*

Cod. 1179, fol. 1v (Genesis): God as the Creator of the world.

V.3

Biblia pauperum Krumau Picture Bible

Southern Bohemia, in the region of Krumau (Český Krumlov), shortly before 1350

The most striking feature of the present *Biblia pauperum* is the fact that the elements within each picture group are arranged in a line and extend without a break across both pages of the open book. At the beginning and end of the codex they are laid out in two rows and in the middle section in three rows per page. Captions relating to the figures and scenes immediately below are written in the narrow gaps at the top of the page and separating each row The *Biblia pauperum* preserved in Codex 370 is the only one of its kind whose layout is not centred around a New Testament antitype. Through their arrangement in succession, all the components of a picture group are lent equal value in formal terms. The usual sequence of Prophet – 1st type (Old Testament scene) – Prophet – Antitype (New Testament scene; titled in italics in the captions to ill. p. 217–221 below) – Prophet – 2nd type (Old Testament scene) – Prophet is interrupted in a number of groups, either by the omission of prophets or even scenes. The Latin inscriptions appearing above the pictures also follow the linear layout of the illustrations. They give the names of the prophets and brief captions to the pictures. Banderoles accompanying the prophets contain quotations from their prophecies, although from fol. 14v onwards they have not been filled in. The lengthier captions and commentaries that usually form part of the repertoire of a *Biblia pauperum* are entirely absent.

Whereas all other "Bibles of the Poor" focus on just one or two picture groups on each page (cf. Cat. V.4), the illustrators of Codex 370 have made no attempt to keep each page a self-contained whole. Thus it is often necessary to turn the page while reading a picture group, and even halfway through a scene. The typological correlations that are established by the formal layout are thereby confused in Codex 370 by the linear arrangement, and it becomes evident that this sequential method of composition is irreconcilable

Detail from fol. 15r: Part of the 17th picture group: Salomon. Absalom conspires against David. (Hand II)

▸ **Fol. 9r:** Part of the 10th picture group: Prophet. Temptation in Paradise. Isaiah. Part of the 11th picture group: David. *Transfiguration of Christ.* (Hand I)

Ada et eva decepti sut a serpente
ysaias
Perversa est cogitacio
david
Transfiguracio xpi
Specios⁹ forma p̄ filius homiū

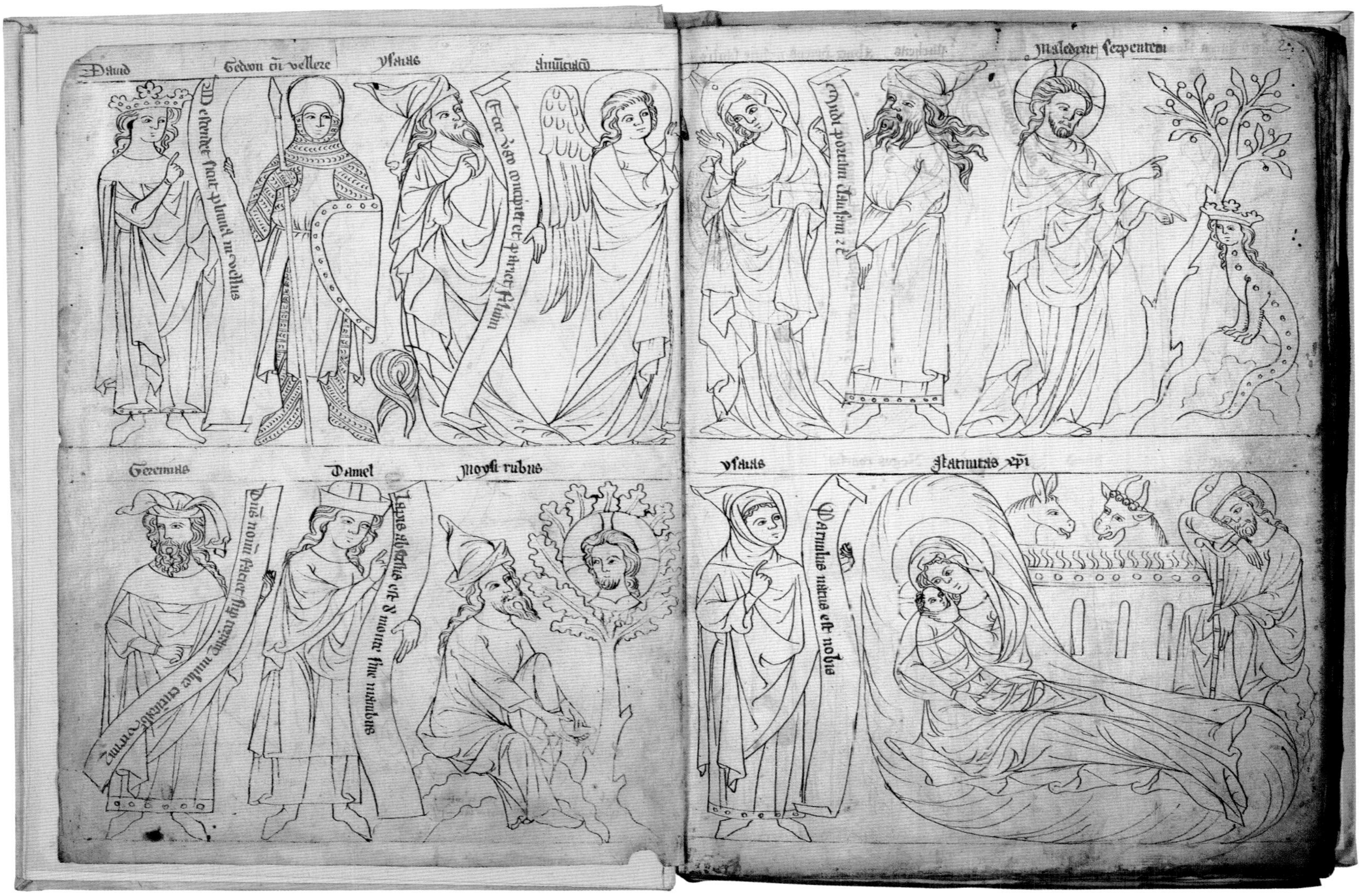

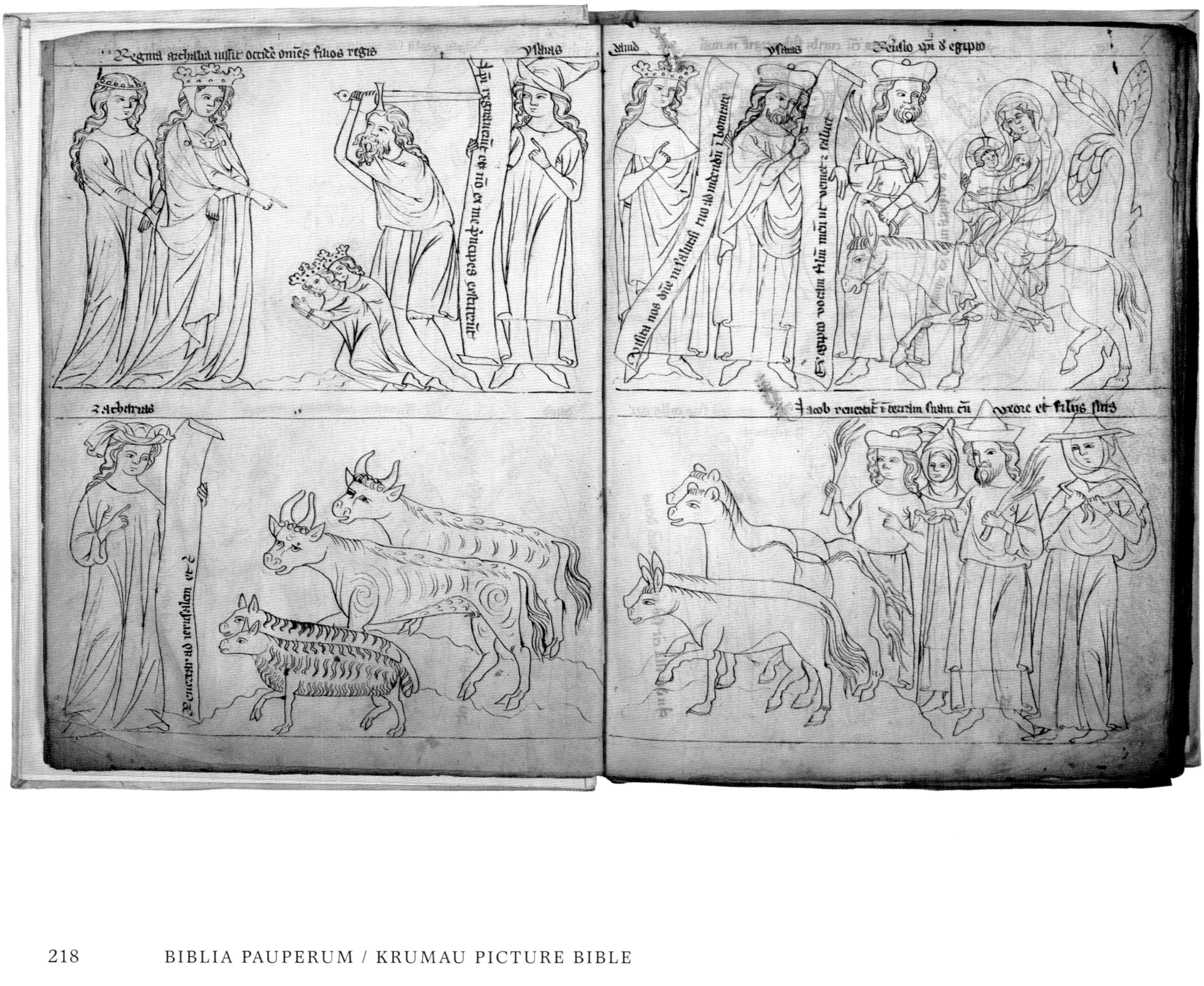

EXTENT: 172 parchment folios
FORMAT: 350 x 250 mm
BINDING: modern parchment binding over thick cardboard, made in 1966 when the facsimile edition was prepared (prior to this, 18th-century parchment binding)
CONTENT: *Biblia pauperum*, two parables, 30 legends, 21 of them legends of saints (with an emphasis on Bohemian saints such as Wenceslas, Ludmilla, Vitus and Procopius) and nine of the Virgin
LANGUAGE: Latin
MINIATURISTS: three artists (Hands I, II, III) from a mural workshop in the Krumau region
ILLUSTRATION: The present manuscript is a true picture book; in other words the illustrations – drawings in brown and black ink – entirely dominate every page. The codex thereby consists of individual scenes in continuous succession, in most cases across a double-page spread; three full-page drawings.
PROVENANCE: The manuscript was in all probability intended for one of the Rosenberg family (members of the Bohemian aristocracy whose estates lay predominantly in southern Bohemia, where Krumau formed the political and cultural centre from the 14th century onwards). When Catherine of Rosenberg founded the Minorite monastery in 1350, the already completed picture codex was presented to its new library. Following the closure of the monastery under Joseph II in 1782, the codex passed from the Krumau Jesuit convent to the Hofbibliothek.
SHELFMARK: Vienna, ÖNB, Cod. 370

with the concept of typology. The originally centrally-weighted pictorial system, which arose at the latest in the middle of the 13th century and reflected Scholastic ideas, has now been overtaken by a more modern, contemporary style of pictorial narrative.

The manuscript was illustrated by three artists (Hands I, II and III) who probably came from a mural workshop in the vicinity of Krumau. The relationship between Hand I – an older master – and Hand II – a younger artist – was probably that of teacher– pupil/assistant. They illustrated the *Biblia pauperum* together. (The somewhat weaker Hand III is stylistically similar to Hand II, but only worked on the captions.) Both the elder Master I and the younger Master II reveal extremely close stylistic links with the wall paintings in the former Hospitallers' church in Strakonice, where figures and scenes (for example, the paintings of the Passion) are laid out in rows one above the other.

The best drawings were executed by the elder master. His illustrations are based on an early style of 1320/1330: his figures appear to have no joints and to be inscribed within a sweeping flow of movement. They fill the entire height of the elongated pictorial plane in which they appear. Their solidity is emphasized by the wide sweep of their long draperies (cf. the line of apostles in Strakonice).

About half of the *Biblia pauperum* illustrations and many of the captions to the saints were executed by the younger master, Hand II, who is anchored in the contemporary style of around 1350. The neutrality typical of the scenes by the first master is here lost as the setting is rendered more concrete through the inclusion of architectural and landscape details. This striving towards a greater realism contributes substantially towards bringing the illustrations to life, in particular the various scenes from the lives of the saints. Trends of this kind can be identified in Bohemian painting as a whole around the middle of the 14th century and are a valuable source of information about the medieval world.

[illegible].J.

Fol. 1v–2r: 1st picture group: David. Gideon dressed as a knight, the fleece beside him on the ground. Isaiah. *The Annunciation.* Ezekiel. Cursing of the serpent. Jeremiah. Part of the 2nd picture group: Daniel. Moses before the Burning Bush. Isaiah. *The Nativity.* (Hand I)

Fol. 6v–7r: Part of the 7th picture group: Queen Athaliah orders the royal children to be killed. Isaiah. 8th picture group: David. (1st type is missing). Isaiah. *The Holy Family Returns from Egypt.* Zechariah. The return of Jacob with his family and herds. (Hand I)

Fol. 7v–8r: Part of the 8th picture group: Hosea. 9th picture group: Isaiah. The passage through the Red Sea. David. *Baptism of Christ.* Ezekiel. Prophet. The spies bring back the bunch of grapes from the Promised Land. Zechariah. 1st part of the 10th picture group: Job. David. *Temptation of Christ.* Jeremiah. (Hand I)

V.4

Biblia pauperum

Klosterneuburg, *c.* 1330/31

Codex 1198 ranks amongst the oldest and finest examples of an illustrated *Biblia pauperum* – a typological work which holds up, in captioned illustrations, the parallels between the Old and New Testament and thereby serves as a sort of "teaching aid". The present manuscript dates from the early years of the genre and adheres, characteristically, to a strict visual programme, whose layout is especially fitted for books, comprising 34 uniformly structured picture groups with accompanying captions. Starting on a verso page, four self-contained but thematically related picture groups are laid out per double-page. At the centre of each picture group is a scene from the New Testament (the so-called antitype; titled in italics in the captions to ill. p. 222–227), extending from the Annunciation to the Life of Christ and ending with the Death of the Virgin. Assigned to these are two prefigurations from the Old Testament (the so-called types) and the busts of four half-length figures of prophets. Two extended prose lessons, tituli in verse, prophecies on banderoles held by prophets and additional titles accompanying the figures and scenes help to illustrate the typological significance of the whole. Text and image in combination propose parallels, on various levels, between Old and New Testament events and between their symbolic and theological meanings, most frequently in the memorable form of "rhyming" situations.

Within the manuscripts of the so-called "Austrian family", Codex 1198 is closely linked to the *Biblia pauperum* produced in St Florian's abbey (Stiftsbibliothek, Cod. III, 207) around 1310, when manuscript illumination at this Augustinian abbey in Upper Austria was at its height. Both manuscripts probably derive from the same St Florian prototype. The illuminator demonstrates a masterly ability to translate, within the pre-set framework, the eurhythmic style of the original influenced by western

Detail from fol. 1v: 1st picture group (above): Cursing of the serpent (a virgin in the treetop treads on the serpent's head). Prophets Isaiah and Ezekiel.

▸ **Fol. 2r:** 3rd picture group (above): Abner guides the Israelites to David. *Adoration of the Magi.* The Queen of Sheba pays homage to Solomon. 4th picture group (below): purification sacrifice (Leviticus). *Presentation of Christ.* Hannah brings Samuel to Eli the priest.

dauid
Epyphania dni
Regina saba
Micheas
Balaam
Purificacio
hely sacerdos
ysaias

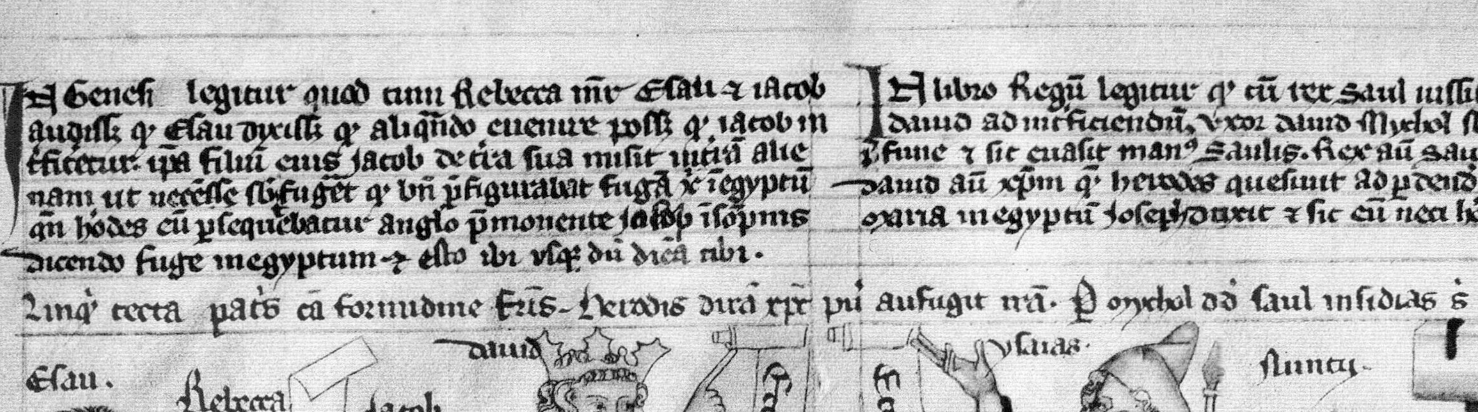

In Genesi legitur quod cum Rebecca mr Esau et Jacob audisset quod Esau dixisset quod aliquando eveniret posset quod Jacob interficeretur. ipsa filium eius Jacob de terra sua misit in terram alienam ut necesse sibi fugeret quod bene prefigurabat fugam Christi in egyptum quando herodes eum persequebatur angelo premonente Joseph in sompnis dicendo Fuge in egyptum et esto ibi usque dum dicam tibi.

In libro Regum legitur quod cum rex Saul misisset ut quererentur david ad interficiendum, uxor david Mychol sub misit per fenestram per funem et sic evasit manus Saulis. Rex autem Saul significat herodem david autem Christum quem herodes quesivit ad perdendum quando ihesum Christum cum maria in egyptum Joseph duxit et sic eum nece herodis subtraxit.

Linquit terram patris cum formidine fratris. Herodis diram Christus pueri aufugit iram. Per Mychol dd Saul insidias evasit.

Legitur in Exodo quod moyses cum venisset ad radicem montis et eo descendente de monte vidit vitulum quem in manu fecerat de auro. ipse enim moyses tabulis confractis vitulum destruxit quod significabat Christum intrantem in Egyptum ydola egypti corruerunt

In primo libro Regum legitur quod cum phylistim archam domini que capta in bello posuissent iuxta dagon deum suum, de mane intrantes templum invenerunt dagon iacentem in terra et caput fractum et manus que figura completa est quando archa domini in egyptum beata missa est [illegible] ydola et errores infidelium

Per moysen sentitur vituli simulacrum. ydola pro te Christe cecidere repente. Archa repentine dagon fit causa ruine. corruerunt

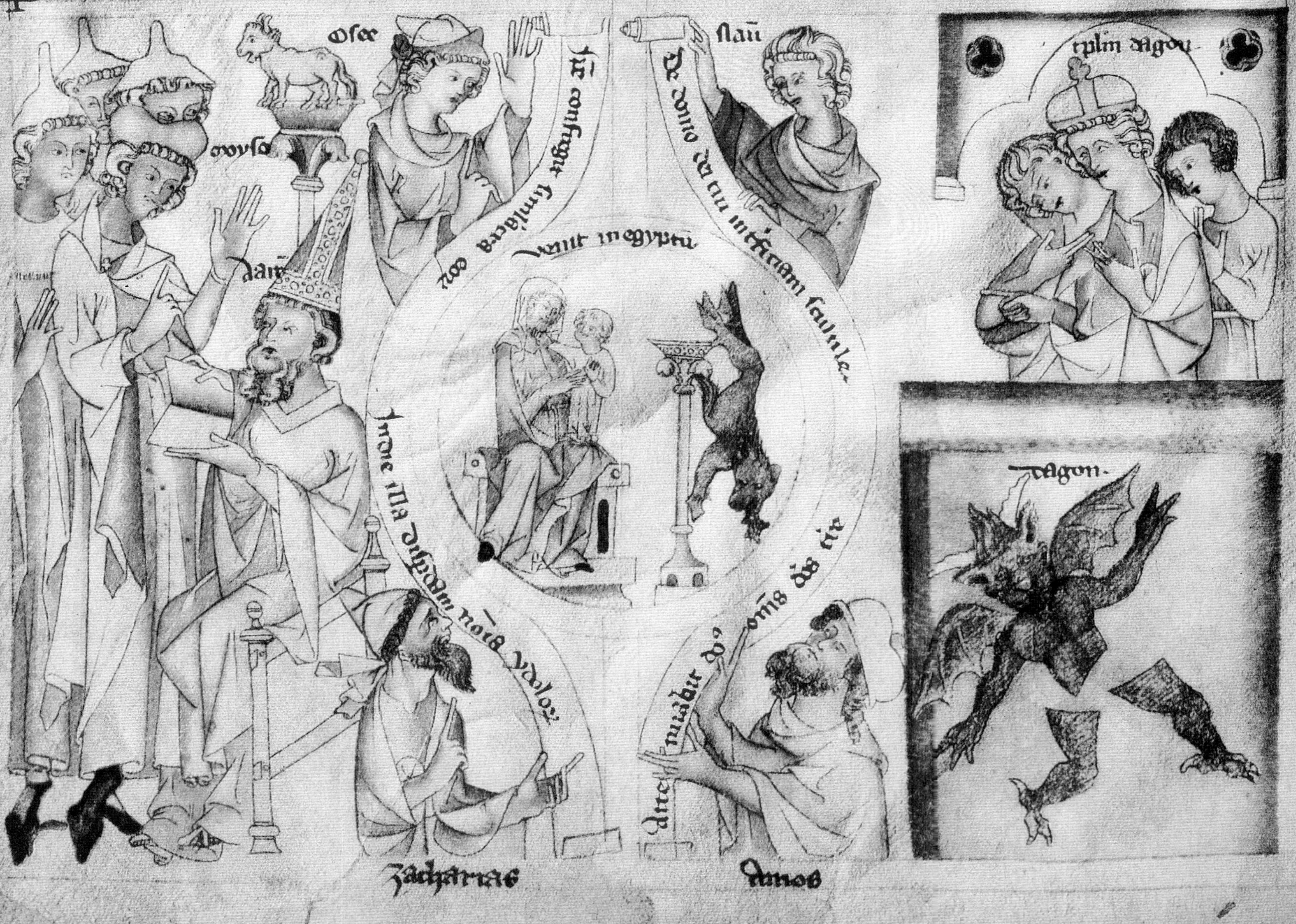

Osee
moyses
Aaron
Et confringet simulacra eorum
ysaias
De domo domini tui interficiam sculptile.
Venit in egyptum
Tablum dagon
Dagon
In die illa disperdam nomina ydolorum
Attenuabit dominus omnes deos terre
Zacharias
Amos

EXTENT: nine parchment folios
FORMAT: approx. 365 x 255 mm
BINDING: parchment binding of Gerard van Swieten, prefect of the Vienna Hofbibliothek (1745–1772), dated 1753
CONTENT: *Biblia pauperum*
LANGUAGE: Latin
ILLUSTRATION: 17 pages with ink drawings incompletely coloured
PROVENANCE: The manuscript is documented in the Vienna Hofbibliothek probably under the prefect Hugo Blotius (1576) and certainly under his follower Sebastian Tengnagel (1608–1636).
SHELFMARK: Vienna, ÖNB, Cod. 1198

Gothic into a more individual and progressive language. Characteristic of his achievement are faces wearing at times forceful expressions, and items of furniture drawn in perspective (fol. 6r). Unusually, the finely shaded, pastel colouring was only added after the manuscript had been bound and just extends to the first few pages.

Art-historical research has convincingly localized the illuminator to the region of Lower Austria. It is even possible to narrow this down to the Augustinian abbey at Klosterneuburg, near Vienna, since the present codex not only shows stylistic links with the local manuscript illumination, but must have been made during the redesign of the "Verdun Altar" in 1330/31, when the ambo of Nicholas of Verdun was modified into a winged altarpiece with six additional enamel plaques and four large tempera paintings. The innovative style of these important Klosterneuburg panels, with their specific mixture of elements from the art of north-western Europe and Trecento Italy, leads to the progressive "realism" of the illuminator of the *Biblia pauperum*. On the other hand it appears that pictures from a *Biblia pauperum* of the same type as Codex 1198 (if not from this very codex itself) were used as models for part of the new enamels. Such correlations seem to prove the fact that both works were produced in the same place and at the same time. The iconography of the present *Biblia pauperum* is also reflected in a somewhat later fragmentary typological cycle in the stained glass of St Stephen's in Vienna. Even these few remaining examples from the Vienna region can give an impression of the importance the *Biblia pauperum* assumed in the late Middle Ages as a vehicle of typological instruction.

V. P.-A.

Fol. 2r: 5th picture group (above): Rebekah advises Jacob to flee from Esau. *The Flight to Egypt.* David flees from Saul's soldiers. 6th picture group (below): Moses before Aaron and the Golden Calf. *An idol falls in the presence of the Christ Child.* Fall of the idol of Dagon in the temple.

[illegible]-4r: 9th picture group (above): Passage through the Red Sea. *Baptism of Christ.* The spies with the bunch of grapes from the Promised Land. 10th picture group (below): Esau sells his birthright to Jacob. *Temptation of Christ.* The temptation of Adam and Eve by the serpent. 11th picture group (above): Abraham and the three angels. *Transfiguration of Christ.* Nebuchadnezzar and the three young men in the fiery furnace. 12th picture group (below): Nathan rebukes David. *The Penitence of Mary Magdalene (Supper at Simeon's house).* Moses hears the [illegible] Miriam.

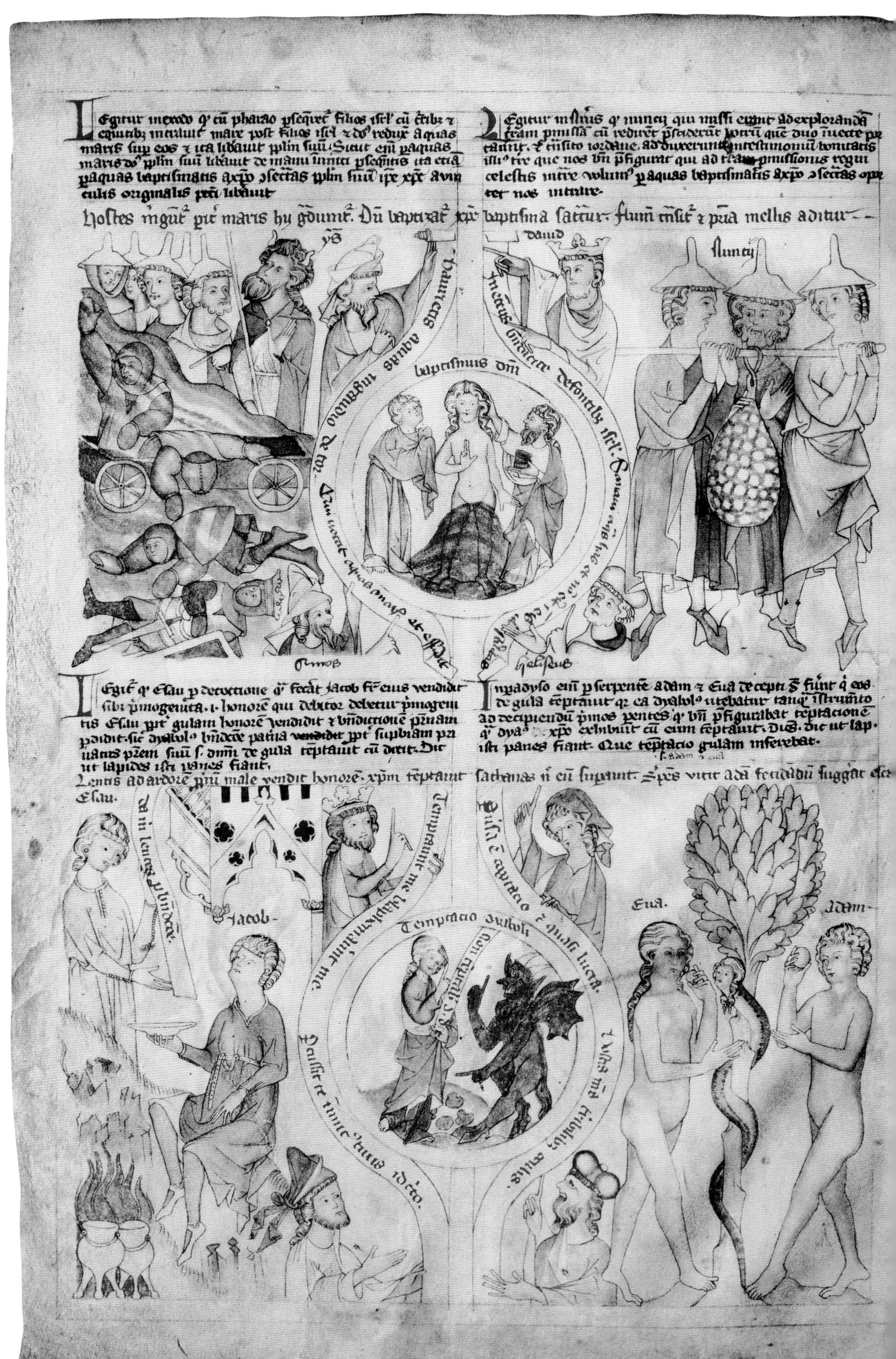
baptismus dñi
Temptacio dyaboli
Dauid
Jacob
Esau
Eua
Adam

Dauid
Malachias.
Abacuk.

Dauid
Johel.

V.5

Speculum humanae salvationis

Lake Constance region (?), 1330s (probably 1336)

Sacra Scriptura est tamquam mollis cera ... – "The Holy Scripture is like soft wax that assumes the form of the seal pressed upon it"; thus runs the preface to the *Speculum humanae salvationis*. The chief subject of this "mirror of human salvation" are the redemptive works of Christ, which are interpreted with a host of typological-allegorical references. The reader is called upon to immerse himself in the mystery of the history of salvation "with the eyes of the heart" (*oculis cordis*). The codex addresses itself both to the clergy and the laity: it aims to instruct the educated (*litterati*) through its texts and the illiterate (*rudes*) through its pictures.

The *Speculum humanae salvationis* was a very popular type of devotional book in the late Middle Ages and the present Codex Series nova 2612 belongs to the earliest examples of the genre. Extending to exactly 100 pages, comprising 45 illustrated chapters and a preface without illustrations, it adheres in its careful layout to a rigorous overall system. The first 42 chapters each occupy one double-page spread and contain 100 rhyming lines, divided into four columns and illustrated by four pictures. Chapters 1 and 2 trace the divine plan of salvation from the Fall of Lucifer to Noah's Ark. Chapters 3 to 42 are structured typologically and show, on the left, scenes from the lives of Christ and the Virgin (titled in italics in the captions to ill. p. 229–237) and symbolic images (of the Passion, intercession etc.), spanning the period from the Annunciation of the Birth of Mary to the last things. These are followed on the right by three types taken either from the Old Testament or from heathen secular or natural history. The manuscript concludes with three devotions, twice the length of the earlier chapters, on the seven stations of the Cross and the seven sorrows and seven joys of the Virgin Mary, each devotion illustrated by a picture of a vision and seven "stations of salvation". Overall, the *Speculum* has al-

Detail from fol. 31r: The ostrich frees its young from the glass jar with the blood of the worm (after Peter Comestor, *Historia scholastica*, referring to Christ, who burst open Hell with his blood; 28th chapter).

Detail from fol. 20v: 18th chapter: *Judas betrays Jesus with a kiss.*

xpc tradebat a iuda

Cxviij Capitulum

In precedenti cap̄ audiuimus q̄m xpc hostes suos prostrauit
Nunc audiamus q̄m iudas ĩ dolo eū salutauit
Iudas tradicor saluatoris nr̄i dedit iudeis osculi signum
Nunquā fuit p̄ modū iniquus et malignum
Osculum n. q̄ ꝯsueuit ee signū dilectionis
hoc nunquā iudas ꝑmutauit ĩ signū tradicionis
Ista nunquā salutacio q̄m xpc tā dolose fuit ꝑpetrata
Olim fuit ĩ Joab ⁊ ĩ Amasa ꝑfigurata
Joab Amasā salutās dolose iuxte fratrē vocabat
Iudas xpm salutās ꝑ itencōne magistrū appellabat

C. j. figura

Nec ignis n̄ estus solis eum obussissent
Nulla bestia nulla auis ipm̄ ifestaret
Nullꝰ aer nulla aura eū molestaret
Nūqͣ hoīes iter se lites habuissent
Tamqͣ frēs mutuo se dilexissent
Subiecta eēt hoī omnis creatura terena
Sēp ī gaudio viuet sine cura
Et cum dō creatori suo placuisset

EXTENT: 51 parchment folios, paper flyleaf at front and back
FORMAT: approx. 280 x 200 mm (irregular)
BINDING: half leather binding with blind lines and blind stamping from the 1st half of the 16th century
CONTENT: *Speculum humanae salvationis*
LANGUAGE: Latin

ILLUSTRATION: 192 coloured pen drawings – four per double-page spread – within 48 folios; three later penwork sketches
PROVENANCE: Documented in Ambras Castle near Innsbruck in an inventory of 1613, the manuscript passed to the Kunsthistorisches Museum and in 1936 passed to the National Library.
SHELFMARK: Vienna, ÖNB, Cod. Ser. n. 2612

ready shifted away from the rigid form of typology still found, for example, in the *Biblia pauperum* (cf. Cat. V.3, V.4). The method is not longer employed primarily to prove the unity of the Old and New Testament, but has become part of a larger whole serving spiritual edification.

The manuscript was previously thought to be an example of Upper or Lower Austrian work from the year 1336, but this has recently been called into question (Roland [1997]). Its dubious dating – deduced from the number *XXXVI* in an erased inscription by the scribe on fol. 51r – is nevertheless plausible and marries well with the drawings whose style points to the 1330s and bears, for example, comparison with the Passion altarpiece in Klosterneuburg and the commentary on the Gospels in Schaffhausen (Stadtbibliothek, Codex 8; Schmidt [1962]). Despite these Austrian connections, other evidence suggests that the manuscript may have been produced in south-west Germany: the text *Von den 15 Wundern in der Geburtsnacht Christi* ("Of the 15 miracles on the night of Christ's birth") added at a later date on fol. 1r, is written in an Alemannic dialect and points westwards, also regarding its content (probably to the circle around the so-called Engelberg Preacher). The pictorial programme, meanwhile, reveals clear parallels with the *Speculum humanae salvationis* of approximately the same date from the Premonstratensian monastery of Weissenau in Upper Swabia (Kremsmünster, Stiftsbibliothek, CC 243). Moreover, there are stylistic arguments in favour of southern Germany: in addition to examples cited in the literature (such as the Biel panels in the Schweizerisches Landesmuseum in Zurich), mention should be made of a Psalter from the diocese of Constance, whose figural style approaches the present drawings in its soft and powerful modelling (Manchester, John Rylands Lib. Ms. 95). This all suggests that the present codex may be an import from the Lake Constance region. Its points of comparison with Austrian works are thereby not self-contradictory, but testify to the many western influences also in this region. *V. B.-A.*

Detail from fol. 4r: 1st chapter: The serpent (in the shape of a siren) tempts Eve. First part of the eight-scene pictorial cycle illustrating Genesis

▸ **Fols. 17v–18r:** 15th chapter: *Christ's entry into Jerusalem.* Jeremiah laments the destruction of Jerusalem. David, with the decapitated head of Goliath, is greeted by the rejoicing Israelites (King Saul amongst them). Heliodorus is trampled and beaten.

C·xv^m cap^m

In p̄cedenti cā audiuī' q̄m ꝯuſio mūdi ē fc̄a
Cont' audia' q̄ ōc·x̄^m· ī die palmar ſūt pacta
I n illa·n·die cā p̄ncipi nobilia ꝯtigerunt
Q ue olim p̄ trēs figuraſ p̄moſtra fuerūt
v idēſ n·ihc ciuitatē ihrlm fleuit
C ū laudib' ſuſcept' fuit, mcātes d' tēplo eiecit
P ̄notādū ē q̄ ihc uidēs ciuitatē flebat
D̄ paciēſ ciuitati d' miſia que illi īmminebat

C·i·figa

I ſte fletus dn̄i nr̄i ſaluatoris iā p̄trayat'
f uit olim ī lamtacōib' ꝯemie p̄figurat'
Q̄ d'flebat d'ſolacōem ihrlm fcām p̄ babylōios
I ta ihc deflebat d'ſolacōem ei' futam p̄ rōanos
S ic & noſ exēplo x̄· ex ꝯpaſſioē flere debem'
Q̄ n̄ p̄ximoſ nr̄os afflictoſ & affligendos videm'
P lus ē ꝯpati afflicto q̄ bō tpalia erogare
Q̄ ꝯpaciēſ afflicto videt' ald de ſe ip̄o s' dare
D̄ pati debem' etiā malefcōrib' nr̄iſ q̄ ātis
E xēplo x̄· qui ꝯpaſſ' ē ſuiſ īimicis
I mpoſſibile ē ullū mīam dī & grām n̄ mereri
Q̄ ſcit afflictiſ ꝯpati ex corde & miſeri

C·ij·figa

S ecūdo notādum ē q̄ x̄· p̄pl's laudib' obuiauit
& hoc olim ē p̄figuratū p̄ regem dauid
C ui p̄pl's p̄' morte golie cū laudib' obuiauit
& cāticū laudis ī honore ip̄ius decātauit
I n q̄ cāntico ip̄m dauid regi ſauli p̄ferebāt
& ſauli mille & dauid ·xmilia attribuebant
D auid dn̄m nr̄m ihm xp̄m p̄figurauit
Q̄ goliam ·i· dyabolū aduſariū nr̄m ſupauit
I ſte verus dauid ·i· x̄· m die palmar
h onorat' fuit mltiplr̄ ī occſu turbar
Q̄ dam oſāna filio dauid acclamabāt
Q̄ dam bn̄dc̄s q̄ venit ī noīe dn̄i p̄ſonabāt
Q̄ dam regē iſrl' eum aſſerebant
Q̄ dam cū ſaluatorē mūdi ꝯtinebāt
Q̄ dam cū florib' q̄dā cū palmiſ occurerūt
Q̄ dam veſtimēta ſua ī uia p̄ſternauerūt
M iſtice ihrlm viſio pacis ītp̄tatur
P q̄ fidelis aīa ſpūali deſignatur
A d hāc ſaluator nr̄ oī hora parat' ē venire
& noſ ei ī occurſum p̄ ꝯtcōem d'bem' ire
L audeſ dn̄o clamoſis vocib' decantam'
Q̄ n̄ ī ꝯfeſſione pccā nr̄a cū gemitib' recitam'
R amoſ palmar ad laudē dī manib' p̄ferimus
Q̄ n̄ cor nr̄a in ſatiſfcōne diſcipline caſtigam'
v eſtimēta nr̄a ī via ad honorē dī p̄ſternim'
Q̄ n̄ tpalia nr̄a erogam' xp̄i pauꝑibus
Q̄ n̄ florib' dn̄o occurrim' & honoramus
Q̄ n̄ m̄r oꝑib' & diuſis v'tutib' noſ ornam'
x p̄m ihm q̄ venit ī noīe dn̄i bn̄dicim'
Q̄ n̄ p bn̄ficiiſ nob' deuote g̃ſes dicim'

Legem eius et domini nostri esse protestamur
Et omnia opera cum timore dei et reverencia operamur
Tercio notandum quod ihesus flagellum de funiculis fecit
Et ementes et vendentes flagellando de templo eiecit
Mensas subvertit nummulariorum et effudit es eorum
Nam et ipsi erant usurarii et collibiste phariseorum
Hec autem flagellacio domini iam recitata
Olim fuit in Eliodoro prefigurata
Rex enim Seleucus misit principem suum Eliodorum
Ut iret in iherusalem et spoliaret ibi domini templum
Cumque audacter intrasset in templum manu armata
Statim contra eum vindicta dei est provocata
Ex improviso enim ei fuit quidam equus horribilis
Et qui sedebat super eum armatus erat et terribilis
Qui autem Eliodoro priores calces immisit
Et ipsum deiciens fremebundus ad terram collisit
Apparuerunt insuper alii duo robustissimi adolescentes
Eliodorum flagellis usque ad mortem percucientes
Ad secundo predictus eques et duo adolescentes disparuerunt
Et eliodorum tamquam mortuum flagellatum reliquerunt
Orante pro eo summo pontifice Onias revixit
Et rediens ad dominum suum scientum dixit
Si habet rex aliquem hostem cuius mortem affectat
Illum ad spoliandum templum ierosolimis mittat
Eliodorus flagellatus fuit propter templi dei spoliacionem

Quia ei spoliata fuit propter usure palliacionem
Pharisei enim posuerunt in templo collibistas et nummularios
Qui volentibus offerre mutuo dabant denarios
Et quia per legem usuras accipere non debebant
Collibia tamen id est munuscula pro usura recipiebant
Ciceres uvas nuces poma quod vocabant collibia
Amigdala pullos anseres columbas et similia
Sicque usuram fraudulenter sub pallio tegebant
Hec verba domini in ezechiele scripta non attendebant
Usuram et omnem habundanciam non accipiatis
Fratres carissimi hoc verbum domini cum memoria recordetis
Pro dolor multi christiani hodie in ecclesia sunt
Qui fraudulenter similem usure palliacionem faciunt
Mutuum non dant pure propter dei dilectionem
Sed propter munera vel servicia favorem vel promocionem
Hii peccant contra verbum illud domini non ponderantes
Mutuum date nichil inde sperantes
Tales dominus de templo suo celesti expellet
Et radicem eorum de terra viventium evellet
Studeamus ergo templum dei et sanctuarium domini venerari
Si nolumus a domino flagello perpetuo flagellari
Caveamus nos ab usuris et omni specie usure
Ne expellamur a domino de templo glorie future
O bone ihesu doce nos hec omnia totaliter custodire
Ut mereamur in templo glorie tue eternaliter introire amen

· Maria superavit dyabolum per mirnam compassionem ·

· Judith · · holofernes ·

CXXX.^m Cap^m

Iam precedenti capitulo audivimus quomodo xpistus vicit dyabolum per passionem
Consequenter audiamus quomodo Maria vicit eundem per compassionem
Omnia que xpistus in sua passione tollerabat
Hec eciam Maria per mirnam compassionem portabat
Clavi qui transfixerunt pedes filii sui et manus
Per compassionem transfixerunt sanctissime matris pectus
Lancea que latus filii sui mortui perforavit
Per compassionem cor matris vivencius penetravit
Aculei spinarum qui caput xpisti pupugerunt
Per compassionem cor genitricis eius vulneraverunt
Gladius acutissimarum linguarum quas xpistus audivit
Per compassionem intimam Marie animam pertransivit
Et sicut xpistus superavit dyabolum per suam passionem
Ita est superavit eum Maria per mirnam compassionem
Armis passionis xpisti ipsa se armavit
Quando contra dyabolum ad pugnam se preparavit

C.j. figura. Que prefiguratur per iudith que restitit olofirni
Quia ipsa se opposuit dyabolo principi inferni
Iudith induit se vestibus iocunditatis
Et ornavit caput suum mitra et pedes scandaliis
Maria vestivit se tunica filii sui inconsutili
Et super induit se pallio derisionis eius duplici
Unum erat album in quo xpistus ab herode deridebatur
Aliud coccineum vel rubicundum in quo a militibus illudebatur
Et bis ergo pallio albo et rubicundo induebatur
Quia dilectus eius filius candidus et rubicundus decantatur
Tota eius passio comparatur fasciculo mirre
Quam comparari debet mater ubera diligentis anime
Omnes autem penalitates xpisti ergo diligenter collegit
Et compassione et fasciculum mirre ex ipsis compegit
Hunc fasciculum pro clypeo mater ubera sua collocavit
Et cum tali armatura contra hostem nostrum dimicavit
In vasculo mirre erant simul omnia colligata
Que dulcissimo filio suo in passione fuerant illata
Gladii fustes lanterne et arma quibus capiebatur
Lucerne ardentes et fascicule quibus in orto querebatur
Tristicia pavor tremor et trina oracio
Sudor sanguineus et angeli confortacio
Quod turbis occurrit et uno verbo omnes prostravit
Et restituens eis vires se capiendum presentavit
Cognicionis signum et osculum malignum
Dolosa salutacio et responsum xpisti benignum
Crudelis xpisti captivacio et victoris ligacio
Auricule restauracio et discipulorum fugacio
Sindoma relicto adolescento suo iohe
Exultacio iudeorum et interrogacio anne
Alapa servi pontificis et maliuce xpisti contusio
Trina negacio petri et eiusdem contusio
Omnia iudicium coram quibus ductus est et accusatus
Annas / Cayphas / herodes / pontius pylatus

Jahel uxor · Cysara princeps · Regina thamar · Cyrus occisus

Columpna virge flagella sputa harundo et funiculi
Crux claui lancea mallei corona et tabula tituli
Alape colaphi obprobria blasphemia et derisio
Velamen oculorum apphe. x. et vestimentorum diuisio
Sors super tunicam et vestis album indumentum
Tribunal iudicis [.]cio meritum et purpureum vestimentum
Sompnium uxoris pylati et lauacio uartab herod
Tumultus et clamor iudeorum et geratum crucifige
Sitis x. acetabulum et acetum felle amaritatum
Oracio x. clamor lacrime et latronis acceptacio
Arido cum sponsa propius et vinum mirratum
Ora verba x. iudee et discipuli ihesus commendacio
Expiracio x. lancea longini cum ipsius illuminacione
Effluxio sanguinis et aque centurio cum sua protestacione
Obscuracio solis terre motus scissio veli et petrarum (scissure)
Ruina partis templi apercio sepulcrum fetor et mors caluaria
Triginta argentei quibus x. erat venditus et emptus
Desperacio iude qui non est sanguine x. redemptus
Hiis et aliis x. penalitatibus o. i. virgo se armauit
Et tamquam pugnatrix contra nostrum hostem dicere conculcauit
Tunc impleta sunt tria prenosticate olim figure
Et quedam prophecia tam sacre scripture
Super aspidem et basiliscum tu o virgo ambulabis
Leonem et draconem i. sathanam conculcabis
Et tu sathane insidiaberis calcaneo eius homines impugnando

Ipsa conteret caput tuum per passionem te superando
Hic est olim iahel uxor aber cinei prefigurauit — C. x. figura.
Que cysaram aute per tympora clauo fixo perforauit
Cysara erat princeps milicie iabin regis
Et vexauit israel filios violentiam inferens eis
Tandem a iahel clauo per tympora est perforatus
Et populus israeliticus ab eius infestacionibus est liberatus
Sic x. clauis sancte crucis hostem nostrum superauit
Et nos a potestate quam super nos habuit liberauit
Regina thamari eciam mariam prefigurauit — C. xi. figura.
Que tyrannum crudelissimum hominem cirum decollauit
Qui tantum aspirabat ad hominum occisionem
Qui non potuit saciari per humanam sanguinis effusionem
Dominus iste dicebat et omnia regna inuadebat
Nulli parcebat omnem quem poterat sanguinem fundebat
Tandem regina thamari eius caput decollauit
Et caput in urnam proiciens pleno sanguine humano [..]
Saciare nunc te sanguine humano quem semper sitisti
Quia tua numquam saciari potuisti
Sic dyabolus qui ab inicio homicida erat
Nunc hominum dampnacione saciari poterat
Regina celi ipsum per passionem filii superauit
Et eius dampnacione quam nobis ... ipsum saciauit
O bone ihesu fac nos tuo adiutorio dyabolum superare
Et eternam mecum tecum in tua gloria habitare.

◂ **Fol. 32v–33r:** 30th chapter: *The Virgin Mary conquers the devil with the weapons of Christ (the instruments of the Passion).* Judith cuts off Holofernes' head. Jael kills Sisera. Tamar kills Cyrus and throws his head into a bucket full of human blood (after Peter Comestor, *Historia scholastica*, referring to Mary's victory over the murderer of men).

Detail from fol. 47v–48r: 44th (here 45th) chapter: Devotion on the seven sorrows of the Virgin Mary. Part 1: Vision of a Dominican receiving the stigmata and the Virgin's sword (the same figure is here shown twice). First sorrow: Presentation of Christ in the Temple. Second sorrow: the Flight to Egypt. Third sorrow: the twelve-year-old Jesus in the Temple.

▸ **Detail from fol. 35r:** Jonah is spat out by the whale (symbol for the Resurrection of Christ; 32nd chapter).

· Jonas exiuit de vētre ceti p⁹ triduū ·

a nō est putandū q̄ in parasceue eoꝝ surrexerit
s; illa die sepultra solūmo apta fuerint
r sicut primogenitus mortuorum surrexit primo

VI. Bible manuscripts of the Jewish and Eastern Orthodox faiths

When, in around 281/280 BC under King Ptolemy II of Egypt, the Hebrew Bible was translated into Greek – much to the displeasure of the Jews, as recent research has shown (Collins [2000]) – the foundation was laid for the spread of the text that the Christians would soon claim as their "Old Testament". As the Greek Septuagint, the Old Testament was now available to a readership that went beyond Jewish circles. In the early days of Christianity, the Jews also continued to use the Septuagint, until a rabbinical initiative in around AD 100 resulted in the laying down of a definitive Hebrew canon, after which all further distribution of the Greek translation amongst Jews was prohibited. The earliest extant Hebrew Bibles preserved in complete parchment codices, however, date only from the 9th/10th century. The first fragments of the Septuagint from the first decades of the Christian era may therefore be of both Jewish and Christian provenance.

It may be a reflection of the general distaste amongst the early Christians for pagan ostentation, and also of the danger inherent in owning a Bible in an era of continuing persecution, that luxury Bible manuscripts are only documented from the 4th century onwards (John Chrysostom, *In Ioannem* 32 [31], p. 3) and that the first surviving fragments of such a Greek Bible – the Cotton Genesis – date from the 5th/6th century. The *Vienna Genesis* from the 6th century has survived almost in its entirety (Cat. I.2). Further luxury codices with biblical illuminations issued from the workshops that flourished in the major centres of the Byzantine East, such as Constantinople and Antioch. As, over the course of the 7th century, the Byzantine Empire lost its Syrian-Palestinian and Egyptian territories to the Persians and the Arabs, the parting of the ways that had already taken place theologically some time ago finally became an actual split. National (Coptic and

Mahmûd ibn Ramadân, Rosary of Tidings, Cod. A. F. 50, detail from fol. 8r: Solomon.

▸ Slavonic Liturgical Apostolos, Cod. slav. 6, detail from fol. 215v: Paul the Apostle seated, above him Jesus Christ, to the right and left a crowd of people.

АПОСТО · ПАВЕ

Syriac) versions of the Bible now established themselves increasingly firmly in these areas. The number of artists calculated to have worked on the *Vienna Genesis*, for example, is indirect evidence that treasures of this kind must have been produced in relatively large numbers. Yet few traces remain of the manuscript tradition of this era. An impression of these magnificent codices can be gleaned from the works of the Macedonian Renaissance of the 9th and 10th century, which consciously look back to earlier codices from late antiquity. Examples include the Joshua Roll preserved in the Vatican Library and the Niketas Bible, named after its patron (cf. also Cat. VI.2).

According to the Acts of the Apostles (11:26), it was in Antioch (in Syria) that the disciples of Christ were first called Christians (*Christianoi*). Antioch subsequently became a centre for some of the most important theologians of the day, and also developed a leading school of biblical exegesis (which regularly ran into conflict with Alexandria). Tatian (2nd century AD) is recorded as having completed the first Syriac translation of the Bible, the *Diatessaron*, a compilation of Gospel texts presented in the chronological order of the life of Christ. The four Gospels (as well as Acts and the Epistles of Paul) were also translated in the conventional, "separate" order the (*Vetus Syra*). In the 5th century (at the latest), a new translation was then undertaken which became known as the Peshitta (the "simple"). The production of lavish Bible manuscripts began very early on: the Rabbula Codex, a Gospel book, was completed by the scribe Rabbula in St John's monastery in Zagba, Mesopotamia, in AD 586, and contains the canon tables devised by Eusebius, accompanied by numerous miniatures in the margins, and seven full-page biblical illustrations. The first illuminated complete Bible (today surviving only in fragments), the so-called Syriac Bible of Paris (6th/7th century), contains title miniatures and author portraits.

After King Tiridates IV adopted Christianity as Armenia's state religion in around 313, the need for a vernacular Bible quickly became apparent. The foundations were laid by Mesrop Mashtots in 406 with the creation of the Armenian alphabet; only now could the Holy Scripture be translated into Armenian (a project completed in 435). The oldest illustrations from an Armenian (?) Bible have survived almost by chance, on sheets bound within one of the most beautiful of all Armenian manuscripts, the Echmiadzin Gospel Book of 989, to which a five-part ivory diptych, probably from the 6th century, was later also added. Themselves dated to around the 6th century, parallel to illustrations in early Greek and Syriac Bibles, these sheets contain four full-page illustrations relating to Luke (fol. 228r/v) and Matthew (fol. 229r/v). The colophon in the Echmiadzin Gospel Book notes that the codex is a copy of a very old original.

The conversion of the Ethiopian kingdom of Aksum to Christianity was begun in the 4th century by the prisoners Frumentius and Aedesius, who were employed at court amongst other things as tutors to the royal princes. In the 5th century, Syrian Christians continued the missionary work. Theologically, the Ethiopian Church was oriented towards the Coptic Church in the north, where its bishops were also ordained. The Bible was translated into Ge'ez (later the liturgical language) soon after Christianization, but its text is today difficult to reconstruct: the earliest extant (Gospel book) codices date from the 10th/11th century (and the majority only from the 13th/14th century), and between these and the first Ge'ez translation undoubtedly lie various revisions and alterations. Ethiopia's geographical and political isolation led to the development of an independent iconography (cf. Cat. VI.8).

Christian missionary activity amongst the Slavs began immediately after their arrival in the Balkans (6th/7th century). Following initial missions arriving primarily from the West, the brothers Constantine (better known under his monastic name of Cyril) and Methodios made a lasting impact, at first in Moravia, where they were invited to teach by King Ratislav towards the end of 862 (or 863). In order to spread their message, they invented the Glagolitic alphabet, based on Greek (and soon replaced by a modified Cyril-

lic , and thereby laid the foundations for the production of Slavonic manuscripts, of which the earliest extant examples date from the 10th/11th century (initially Gospel books and Psalters). These codices reflect the influence of Byzantine manuscripts as well as other sources in their artistic design.

Muslim conquests in the Near East and Egypt from the 7th century onwards steadily weakened the link between Christianity and the Byzantine Empire. Alongside national languages, Arabic – as the language of communication and soon the vernacular – now assumed a central role in the transmission of the Holy Scripture, as evidenced by numerous bilingual and even trilingual Bible manuscripts. Recent research suggests that the Gospels were translated into Arabic from the middle of the 7th century; the oldest fragments of Arabic Bible manuscripts date from the 9th–11th century (the majority from St Catherine's monastery on Mount Sinai). *C. G.*

Slavonic Liturgical Apostolos, fol. 189v (St John): St John the Evangelist seated with a scroll in his left hand and a stylus in his right; desk with writing utensils and a piece of writing.

Greek Gospel Book, Cod. theol. gr. 240, fol. 235v (St John): St John the Evangelist standing with open book in hand; imaginary symbols are visible in the codex. The miniature has been bound as a separate sheet, and is drawn on a thin gilded sheet, glued onto the page.

VI.1

Hebrew Pentateuch with Haphtaroth

North-eastern Spain (?), final third of the 15th century

This small-format parchment Bible codex contains the Torah (the five books of Moses) and the Haphtaroth, i. e. the passages from the Prophets which are read out after the Torah reading in the synagogue. The Haphtaroth are usually thematically related to the passage from the Torah that they follow. The use of readings from the Prophets probably arose in the wake of the religious edict issued by King Antiochus I (168–165 BC), under which reading the Torah was forbidden. In order to get round this ban, a passage from the Prophets was read out during prayers instead – a practice that continued even after the edict had been lifted. The present codex thus contains only the texts used in the synagogue service, and is not a full Bible. Since, in the Jewish liturgy, such texts always had to be read from the Torah scroll, this handy codex is most likely to have served as a private "prayer book" in which the readings could be followed during the service.

The book, like many Hebrew manuscripts, has not survived intact. It is missing the beginning of Genesis, for example, which only starts from Chapter 10:25, and the end of the Haphtaroth is also incomplete. For a long time, the codex probably had no binding. Its illustration and script (vocalized square Sephardic script) indicate that the manuscript was produced in Spain in the final third of the 15th century, when Jewish culture on the Iberian peninsula was flourishing. It was probably in the wake of the expulsion of the Jews from Spain in 1492 that – as later inscriptions suggest – the codex travelled, via several owners, to Moravia. It eventually reached the Vienna Hofbibliothek in 1877, as part of a group of Hebrew manuscripts purchased for the library from Hirsch Lipschütz.

The illustration in the manuscript is purely ornamental and features none of the display scripts otherwise typical within this cultural sphere. This omission may point to the involvement of non-Jewish artists, who were frequently employed to illustrate Hebrew codices. At the start of the individual pericopes, the parashah symbols are in most

Fol. 187v (Deuteronomy): End of Deuteronomy (Debarim), with ornamental panel in front of the Haphtaroth.

בְמֹתוֹ לֹא כָהֲתָה עֵינוֹ וְלֹא נָס לֵחֹה׃ וַיִּבְכּוּ בְנֵי יִשְׂרָאֵל אֶת
מֹשֶׁה בְּעַרְבֹת מוֹאָב שְׁלֹשִׁים יוֹם וַיִּתְּמוּ יְמֵי בְכִי אֵבֶל
מֹשֶׁה׃ וִיהוֹשֻׁעַ בִּן נוּן מָלֵא רוּחַ חָכְמָה כִּי סָמַךְ מֹשֶׁה אֶת
יָדָיו עָלָיו וַיִּשְׁמְעוּ אֵלָיו בְּנֵי יִשְׂרָאֵל וַיַּעֲשׂוּ כַּאֲשֶׁר צִוָּה
יְהוָה אֶת מֹשֶׁה׃ וְלֹא קָם נָבִיא עוֹד בְּיִשְׂרָאֵל כְּמֹשֶׁה אֲשֶׁר
יְדָעוֹ יְהוָה פָּנִים אֶל פָּנִים׃ לְכָל הָאֹתֹת וְהַמּוֹפְתִים אֲשֶׁר
שְׁלָחוֹ יְהוָה לַעֲשׂוֹת בְּאֶרֶץ מִצְרַיִם לְפַרְעֹה וּלְכָל עֲבָדָיו
וּלְכָל אַרְצוֹ׃ וּלְכֹל הַיָּד הַחֲזָקָה וּלְכֹל הַמּוֹרָא הַגָּדוֹל
אֲשֶׁר עָשָׂה מֹשֶׁה לְעֵינֵי כָּל יִשְׂרָאֵל׃

חזק

וימת יוסף בן מאה ועשר שנים ויחנטו אתו ויישם
בארון במצרים: חזק

ואלה שמות בני ישראל הבאים מצרימה את יעקב
איש וביתו באו: ראובן שמעון לוי ויהודה: יששכר
זבולן ובנימן: דן ונפתלי גד ואשר: ויהי כל נפש
יצאי ירך יעקב שבעים נפש ויוסף היה במצרים:
וימת יוסף וכל אחיו וכל הדור ההוא: ובני ישראל
פרו וישרצו וירבו ויעצמו במאד מאד ותמלא הארץ
אתם: ויקם מלך חדש על מצרים
אשר לא ידע את יוסף: ויאמר אל עמו הנה עם בני

EXTENT: 247 parchment folios
FORMAT: 173 x 120 mm
BINDING: 19th-century half-leather binding with green marbled pasteboard
CONTENT: Pentateuch, Haphtaroth
LANGUAGE: Hebrew
ILLUSTRATION: five decorative fields, *fleuronnée* accompanying the parashah symbols

PROVENANCE: Several undated ownership inscriptions by a Meir Ben Isaac, Josef bar Isaak of Trest (= Třešť in south-west Moravia) and a Meir bar Neriah in Prerau (= Přerov in Moravia); later in the possession of Hirsch Lipschütz, from whom the manuscript was purchased on 25 February 1877 for the Vienna Hofbibliothek.
SHELFMARK: Vienna, ÖNB, Cod. hebr. 211

cases highlighted by means of lozenge-shaped decorative frames incorporating quatrefoils and *fleuronnée* forms in red ink. The chief illustrations in the manuscript, however, are the five decorative panels placed in front of the individual books of the Bible and at the start of the Haphtaroth (ill. p. 243, 244). Presented within an outer and in some cases elaborate frame, most of these panels centre upon a symmetrical floral motif, around which scrolling foliate tendrils, interspersed with semi-stylized, ornamental flowers and leaves, unfold in a gentle, flowing arrangement. The flowers are often executed in a wash style which frequently allows the whitish parchment ground to shine through. The pistils are always emphasized with a dot of burnished gold leaf. The floral motifs are occasionally joined by acanthus shoots. The ornamentation also continues partly beyond the edges of the frame in a sort of border, usually only employing a more abbreviated manner of decoration.

The illustration of Codex hebr. 211 cites developments in Flemish manuscript illumination which were taken up in Spain at the latest around 1430. Among the first to embrace these new trends were the Hebrew Bible in the Pierpont Morgan Library, Ms. Glazier 48, executed between 1422 and 1458, and the so-called Duke of Alba Bible (Ms. 399, Duke of Alba Library, Madrid), which was written in Toledo between 1422 and 1430. Whereas the assimilation of Flemish influence in the Duke of Alba Bible is still in its early stages, the forms of Cod. hebr. 211 reflect a later stage of development, as also found in the illustration of the *Compendi Historial* by Domenech Jaume, written between 1454–1455 in Catalonia (auctioned as Lot 38 by H. P. Kraus in 1974). *K. G. P.*

Fol. 45r (Genesis, Exodus): End of Genesis (Bereshith), with ornamental panel in front of the Book of Exodus (Shemoth)

VI.2

Greek Gospel Book

Constantinople (?), *c.* 1000

The patronage of the arts by the Macedonian dynasty of Eastern Roman Emperors (867–1056) contributed to a cultural flowering which has become known as the Macedonian Renaissance. For manuscript illumination, it spelled the end of the woeful iconoclasm of the 8th and early 9th century, when the illustration of codices with images of God and the saints was forbidden and illuminated manuscripts were destroyed, as the records of the Second Council of Nicaea of 787 testify. The era from which the present manuscript dates is also one that saw the introduction of minuscule as a codex script (it makes its earliest dated appearance in 835). Over the following years, majuscule was increasingly suppressed and only survived as a display script, as seen here in the headings at the start of each Gospel, which are designed in a particularly artificial manner with foliate and decorative elements within ornamental "arches" (cf. ill. p. 251).

The fact that manuscripts of the 9th and 10th century look back in their illumination to earlier sources is evidence that defenders of icons must have managed to keep safe at least some of their most magnificent codices containing images of God and the saints. These include the Joshua Roll, the only luxury manuscript of the Book of Joshua surviving in the form of a scroll (Cod. Vat. Pal. gr. 431), the Niketas Bible (today divided between Turin, Copenhagen and Florence), and the present manuscript – all dating from the 10th century.

The miniatures in Codex theologicus graecus 240 perpetuate the illusionistic tradition of late antiquity, in particular in the clearly-defined anatomy of the figures, who adopt poses from classical statuary (their arms draped in the manner of rhetoricians) and whose robes clearly reveal the proportions of their limbs (cf. ill. p. 247). The illustrations

Detail from fol. 256r (St John): Beginning of St John's Gospel with a decorative arch; the title ("Gospel according to John") written in display majuscule.

▸ **Fol. 97v (St Mark):** St Mark the Evangelist standing with codex in hand. The miniature has been bound as a separate sheet, and is drawn on a thin gilded sheet, glued onto the page.

ΜΆΡΚΟϹ

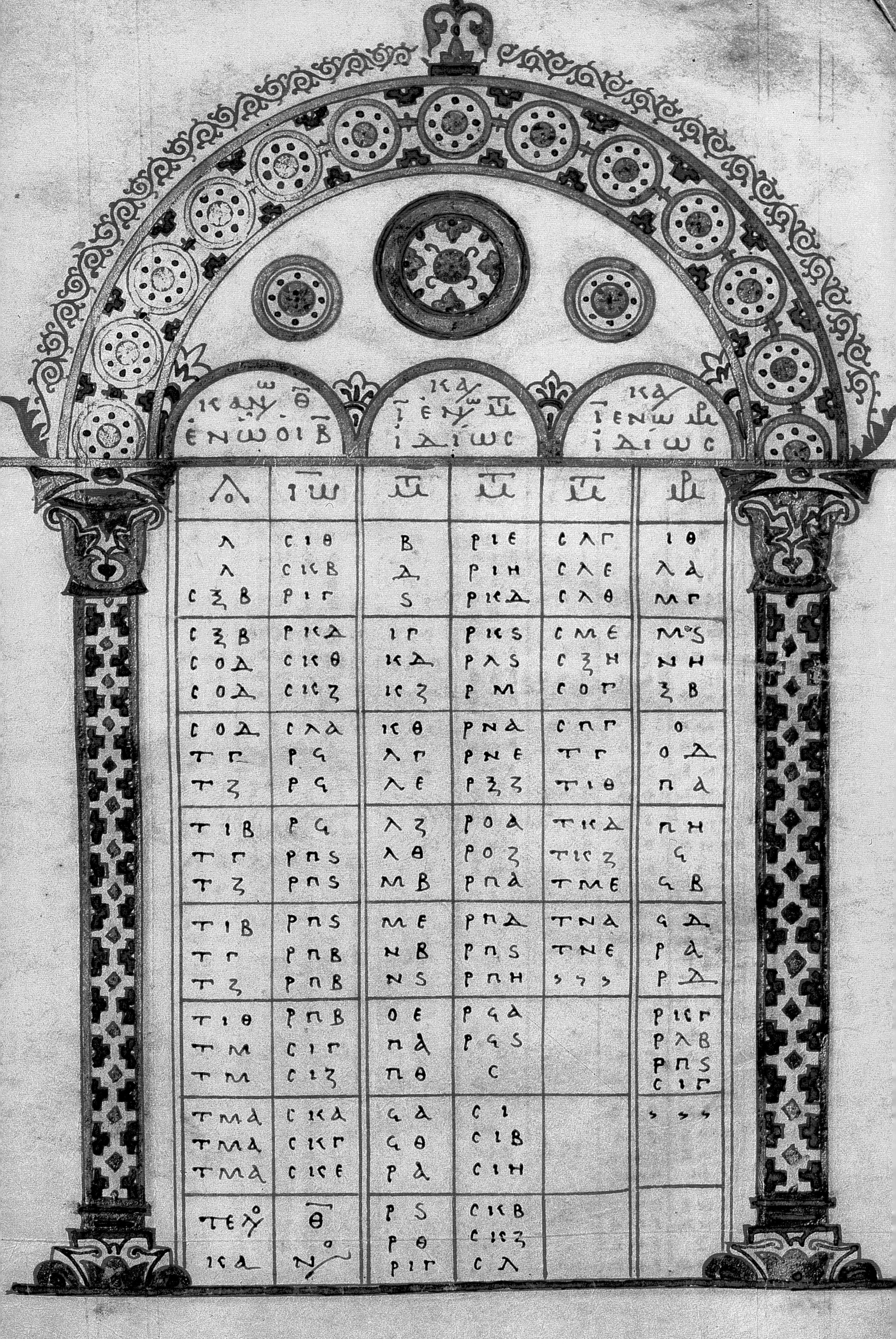

κανὼν θ̄ ἐν ᾧ οἱ β̄
κα(νὼν) ῑ ἐν ᾧ Μθ ἰδίως
κα(νὼν) ῑ ἐν ᾧ Μρ ἰδίως

Λο	Ιω	Μθ	Μθ	Μθ	Μρ
λ λ σξβ	σιθ σκβ ριγ	β δ ϛ	ριε ριη ρκα	σλγ σλε σλθ	ιθ λα μγ
σξβ σοδ σοδ	ρκδ σκθ σκζ	ιγ κδ κζ	ρκϛ ρλϛ ρμ	σμε σξη σογ	μϛ νη ξβ
σοδ τγ τζ	σλα ρϙ ρϙ	κθ λγ λε	ρνα ρνε ρξζ	σπγ τγ τιθ	ο οδ πα
τιβ τγ τζ	ρϙ ρπϛ ρπϛ	λζ λθ μβ	ροα ροζ ρπα	τκδ τκζ τμε	πη ϙ ϙβ
τιβ τγ τζ	ρπϛ ρπβ ρπβ	με νβ νϛ	ρπδ ρπϛ ρπη	τνα τνε ⸱ ⸱ ⸱	ϙδ ρα ρδ
τιθ τμ τμ	ρπβ σιγ σιζ	οε πα πθ	ρϙα ρϙϛ σ		ρκγ ρλβ ρπϛ σιγ
τμα τμα τμα	σκα σκγ σκε	ϙα ϙθ ρα	σι σιβ σιη		⸱ ⸱ ⸱
τελ(ος) κα(νόνος)	θ̄ ν(ος)	ρϛ ρθ ριγ	σκβ σκζ σλ		

EXTENT: 331 parchment folios
FORMAT: 203–212 x 150–158 mm
BINDING: Vienna Hofbibliothek leather binding of 1755 (re-bound under praefect Gerard van Swieten)
CONTENT: four Gospels (with Eusebius' letter to Karpianos and canon tables)
LANGUAGE: Greek
ILLUSTRATION: four full-page miniatures on a gilded ground

PROVENANCE: The codex was acquired in Constantinople between 1555 and 1562 from the imperial ambassador Ogier Ghislain de Busbecq. It is first documented in the Vienna Hofbibliothek under its second praefect, Sebastian Tengnagel (1608–1636)
SHELFMARK: Vienna, ÖNB, Cod. theol. gr. 240

are thereby the products of a first-class workshop, as evidenced, too, by the care with which they have been executed. The miniatures of the Evangelists were each executed separate from the main manuscript in a production stage that may have taken place in parallel to the work of the copyist, but was nevertheless entirely distinct from it. The artist began by drawing the Evangelists – not seated in the usual manner, but standing – on a wafer-thin sheet of metal foil, which was probably a more suitable ground for paint. He also managed to achieve a subtle differentiation between the foreground and background by employing two shades of gold. The entire sheet was then glued into the frame created for it on the parchment folio. This painted frame was then extended to overlap the edges of the wafer-thin sheet by a few millimetres, so that the sheet could no longer be recognized as such and the miniature appeared as if it had been executed within the frame. In creating his designs, the artist not only introduced spatial depth via the colour of the gold, but also used scoring (to depict the architecture) and shaving (for the trees). A luxury object such as Codex theologicus graecus 240 is, as might be expected, just one of many products from a single workshop in Constantinople (?). It has been assigned on stylistic grounds to a group of other manuscripts which are characterized by their inclusion of a gold ciborium as a decorative arch, for example at the start of the Gospels.

When the imperial legate Ogier Ghislain de Busbecq came to Constantinople between 1555 and 1562, he purchased a large number of manuscripts, including the present example, which today makes up one of the two mainstays of the Hofbibliothek's collection of Greek manuscripts. Codices such as these were probably plundered by the Turks from parts of the newly conquered Byzantine Empire, with a view to selling them in Constantinople to western visitors. *C. G*

Fol. 6v: 9th canon table and first half of the 10th canon table.

▸ **Fol. 8v–9r (St Matthew):** St Matthew the Evangelist standing with book in hand. The miniature has been found as a separate sheet and executed on a thin gilded sheet, glued onto the page. Beginning of St Matthew's Gospel with a decorative arch; the title ("Gospel according to Matthew") written in display majuscule.

ΜΑΤΘΑΙΟϹ

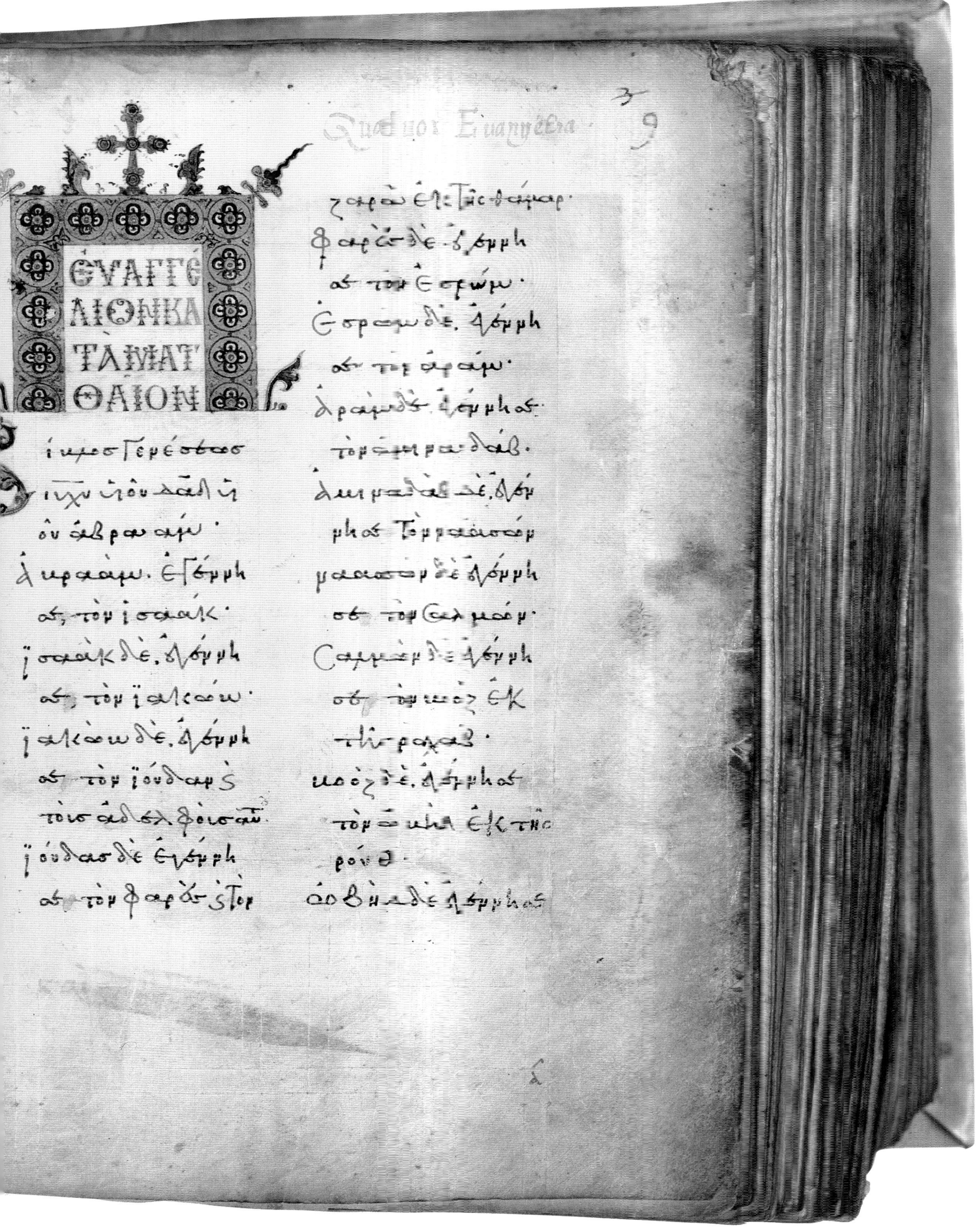

VI.3

Greek Gospels and Praxapostolos

Constantinople, middle to 2nd half of the 12th century

After a constant succession of emperors and fresh (and in part continuing) threats from the Normans, Seljuk Turks and Petchenegs, the 12th century under the rule of the Comnenian (1081–1185) and Angelos dynasties (1185–1204) was a period of cultural flowering in the Byzantine Empire. It was also a period of confrontation with the West, precipitated by the Crusades which led, on 13 April 1204, to the conquest of Constantinople by the Latins. The aesthetic minuscule script had by now passed its peak, and even though biblical and liturgical manuscripts continued to look back to "classical forms", a decline in standards became increasingly apparent.

It is against this backdrop that we must view the production of the present manuscript, which probably arose not in Grottaferrata in northern Italy, as was previously thought, but in a Constantinople workshop (Spatharakis [1999], p. 279). This luxury codex is distinguished by an unusual preface: a representation of the Trinity accompanied underneath by a text setting out, in two columns, pairs of Trinitarian opposites (*one* God – *three* persons, *one* nature – *three* hypostases etc.; ill. p. 253). This representation finds a parallel in a fresco based on orthodox rites in the monastery of Grottaferrata, although this fresco, which dates from around 1200, is probably not directly connected with the manuscript.

Facing this so-called *Paternitas* type of Trinity picture (God with Christ on his lap and the dove as a symbol of the Holy Ghost in Christ's hand, after St John 1:18; ill. p. 253) is the Nicene Creed as it was affirmed at the Council of Constantinople (fol. 1*r; ill. p. 252), containing the sentence that split the Eastern and Western Churches: namely, that the Holy Ghost proceeds (only) from the Father (and not also from the Son). Its prominent position at the beginning of the manuscript – in front of the magnificent

Detail from fol. 1*r: Nicene Creed as it was affirmed at the Council of Constantinople, with the depiction of a man raising his arms towards the Trinity on the opposite page.

▸ **Detail from fol. 1v:** Representation of the Trinity (God the Father with Christ on his lap and the dove in Christ's hand), surrounded by an angelic host (cf. Daniel 7:9).

Πατὴρ · Υἱός · Πνεῦμα ἅγιον

θεὸς εἷς,	πρόσωπα τρία·
οὐσία μία.	ὑποστάσεις τρεῖς·
φύσις μία·	ἰδιότητες τρεῖς·
μορφὴ μία.	χαρακτῆρες τρεῖς·
βασιλεία μία	ἀρχαὶ τρεῖς
δόξα μία·	λαμπρότητες τρεῖς·
δύναμις μία	κυριότητες τρεῖς·
βούλησις μία·	ἐνέργειαι τρεῖς

ΜΑΤΘΑΙΟϹ

EXTENT: 434 parchment folios
FORMAT: 245–250 x 175 mm
BINDING: 17th-century black leather binding over wooden boards with blind lines and gold tooling on the back (probably made for the Dominican Martin Harney, a previous owner), gilt edges
CONTENT: Gospels and Praxapostolos
LANGUAGE: Greek
ILLUSTRATION: half-page representation of the Trinity surrounded by a choir of angels; Creed miniature; canon tables; full-page miniatures of the four Evangelists; decorative bars and decorative initials at the beginning of the texts (decorative bar cut out on fol. 183r)
PROVENANCE: The first owner is named as Radulphus or Rolandus de Rivo († 1401/1403 Rome), who came from Belgium. The manuscript subsequently had a number of different Belgian owners (St Mary's abbey in Corsendonck, near Turnhout; Erasmus of Rotterdam 1519; financial commissioner van den Wouvere). After belonging to another owner named in an inscription as Martin Harney, a Dominican monk, the codex reached the Dominican abbey in Brussels. From there it passed into the possession of Prince Eugene of Savoy (1663–1736); it has formed part of the Vienna Hofbibliothek collection since 1738.
SHELFMARK: Vienna, ÖNB, Cod. suppl. gr. 52

canon tables (ill. p. 256) – lends it a programmatic emphasis which, in view of the constant conflict with the West, particularly in the 12th century, may perhaps be understood as a deliberate statement. As indicated by God's description as "The Ancient of days", the miniature itself is based on Daniel 7:9, where in the account of Daniel's dream the white-haired "Ancient of days" is also described, seated on a throne surrounded by countless beings. Fittingly for Christian exegesis, the Old Testament passage goes on to speak of a Son of man, who approaches the Ancient of days on the clouds of heaven.

The manuscript belongs to a group of codices containing a characteristic illustration of an Evangelist with a "whispering dove" (here in front of St Luke's Gospel; fol. 117v) and which can now be localized to Constantinople. A division of labour within the workshop is clearly apparent: the miniaturist worked independently of the copyist and executed his Evangelist portraits on thicker sheets of parchment, which were then bound at the start of the Gospels they accompanied.

Noteworthy is the fact that this manuscript passed into Western hands early on. Latin notes in the margin relating to the Trinitarian opposites can be dated to the 13th century; in the 14th century, the codex was used by Radulphus de Rivo, deacon of Tongeren church in Belgium, who had been taught in Greek by the Greek archbishop Simeon of Thebes while in Rome around 1380. The codex subsequently had a number of owners in Belgium. Erasmus of Rotterdam, who records at the start of the manuscript (fol. 1r, and again in Greek on fol. 181v) that he consulted the codex for his second edition of the New Testament on 1 July 1519, offers the following verdict on the text: "This exemplar ... I used ... alongside many others. For although the codex is beautifully written, it is not, as I have observed, well corrected, which shows that no one has consulted it."

C. G.

Fol. 13v: St Matthew beside a desk copying (!) the beginning of his Gospel from another open manuscript ("Book of the Lineage of Jesus Christ, the Son of David").

Fol. 8r: 5th canon table (end of the 5th canon, 6th and 7th canon).

▸ **Fol. 182v:** St John, his head inclined towards God's hand, dictates the opening of his Gospel to his scribe Prochoros ("In the beginning was the Word, and the [Word] …").

182v

VI.4

Slavonic Liturgical Apostolos

Dragomirna abbey (Romania, Moldavia region), 1610

Codex slavicus 6, a sumptuous and richly illuminated manuscript from the year 1610, originates from the Moldavian abbey of Dragomirna, which lies some seven miles north of Suceava in present-day Romania and was founded at the beginning of the 17th century by Archbishop Anastasie Crimca († 1627?), Metropolitan of Suceava. It was in fact the same Anastasie Crimca who donated the codex to the abbey, in memory of his parents Ion and Cîrstina Crimca, as can be deduced from a note (fol. 311v) and a dedication (fol. 314v). The manuscript was housed in the Church of the Holy Ghost attached to the abbey and probably completed around 1609. The subsequent history of the manuscript can be traced with the help of another inscription (fol. 11v–15r): following the destruction of Dragomirna by the Zaporog Cossacks in 1653, the codex was stolen and was only returned to the abbey after a ransom had been paid with money put up by the boyar Toma Cantacuzino. It is highly probable that the codex entered the Vienna Hofbibliothek at the beginning of the 18th century. Today it numbers amongst the oldest holdings in the library's Slavica collection.

A leading role in the story of this manuscript is played by the figure of Archbishop Anastasie Crimca, as he was not only the founder of Dragomirna abbey and the donor of the codex, but also its scribe and illuminator. The lower miniature on fol. 75r shows him kneeling in prayer and holding in his hand a scroll bearing a prayer to Jesus Christ. Opposite him in the right-hand half of the scene is a representation (according to the caption) of Dragomirna abbey with the figure of a nun, possibly his mother Cîrstina. The text on the left, beside the donor's self-portrait, gives his name and position.

Codex slavicus 6 is written in semi-uncial (*Poluustav*) on very soft and smooth parchment, and contains a wealth of miniatures and miniature-like illustrations which follow the tradition of Byzantine manuscript illumination. Particular mention should be

Detail from fol. 110v (Jude): Jude the Apostle seated.

▸ **Detail from fol. 172r:** St Michael the Archangel as horseman of the Apocalypse, above him to the right a youthful Jesus Christ.

въ раи же и въ третїе нбо въсхыщенїе ·
таже заповѣдавь не съгрѣшати ·
н жїкалати сѧ съгрѣшающїи наль ·
съ блгодаренїе аль
сїе онтаблѥ
посла
нїе

+ грозныи сканїи
страшныи нбны
силь воевода прѣ
стате прта у вели
чьствїа славы твоеа

кг

СИХЖЕАПЛЪ ЗНАМЕ
НІАНЧЮДЕСАІАЖЕСЪ
ТВѠРИШѦСѦСІНА

EXTENT: 317 parchment folios
FORMAT: 355 x 235 mm
BINDING: Byzantine leather binding with elaborate blind tooling over wooden boards
CONTENT: Acts of the Apostles, Epistles of the Apostles (both divided into pericopes), prefaced by an essay by Epiphanius of Salamis (*c.* 310/320–403) on the lives, deaths and acts of the Apostles and concluding with a liturgical appendix
LANGUAGE: Church-Slavonic Bulgarian edition
SCRIBE: Archbishop Anastasie Crimca, Metropolitan of Suceava (1627?)
MINIATURIST: see Scribe
ILLUSTRATION: Titles in gold script; initials decorative borders, decorative fields filled with interlace patterning, numerous small and full-page miniatures against an architectural and landscape background.
PROVENANCE: The Apostolos was written and illuminated by Archbishop Anastasie Crimca in 1610 and donated to Dragomirna abbey (16.3.1610). Housed in Vienna probably since the beginning of the 18th century, it is one of the oldest Slavonic codices in the Austrian National Library collection.
SHELFMARK: Vienna, ÖNB, Cod. slav. 6

made of the icon-like full-page miniatures of St Luke the Evangelist and the Apostles (St Luke: ill. p. 10; fol. 75v; St John: ill. p. 264; fol. 215v; fol 262v) and scenes from the New Testament, including for example the Annunciation (fol. 270r), Christ's entry into Jerusalem (ill. p. 265) and the Crucifixion group (fol. 292v).

Especially magnificent is a miniature portraying Archangel Michael mounted on horseback (ill. p. 259). The crowned commander of the heavenly hosts is riding a white horse towards the left and at the same time blowing a horn. Conquering a demon at his feet with his lance, he holds up in his left hand a Gospel book and a censer. Above him to the right appears the young Jesus Christ, and beside him to the left a number of lines of text naming his attributes in prayer form.

The starts of the Acts of the Apostles and the various Epistles (fol. 5r 76r 100r, ill. p. 264; 144r) are announced by decorative fields filled with interlace patterning and executed chiefly in gold, red, blue, green and orange. The elaborate titles are written almost exclusively in gold.

Recent research (Costea [1992]) has shown that the present manuscript, together with two others dating from 1609 (Codex slavicus 22 and 436, which today are both in Bucharest), forms part of a group of codices which issued from the scriptorium at Dragomirna abbey between 1609 and 1616, and which arose on the initiative or within the circle of Archbishop Anastasie Crimca. *M. P.*

Fol. 4r: Golden tree, based on genealogical trees, with portraits of Jesus Christ (top centre), the four Evangelists and the Apostles.

▸ **Detail from fol. 75r:** Representation of the Old-Testament Holy Trinity, served by Abraham (left) and Sarah (right), against an architectural and landscape background.

АВЛЕТЪ
Л

Fol. 99v–100r (1 John): John the Apostle seated in a cave, above him the Holy Ghost as a white dove, in front of him an open book containing the first sentence of his 1st Epistle. Start of the 1st Epistle of John.

▸ **Fol. 292r:** Entry into Jerusalem: Jesus on a donkey in the centre of the picture, riding towards the right; behind him the apostles, on the right a crowd of people bearing palms. Landscape background and representation of the city of Jerusalem.

ЦВѢТОСНЕ·ГНЕ
ІС ХС

ноученїоу. вѣдѧщабытиврѣмена.
вънихжеѿстѫпѧтьнѣціинѿвѣры.
наоутивжениїстобытибрашно·
ивъзвѣстивьѥллоулюбопернааи
стѫѕанїаиакосиѥвръннасѫща, оу
ѥланѣтисѧ. онихжейнѣціинхва
лѧщесѧ, прѣстѫпишѧвѣрѫ· и
ѥонецъ, ѥакоквьпотрѣбленаѧлѣ

тиобразъ, наѧла
ствоватиже
ноутинѣти.
сѥонѧа
влеть
посл
нїе·

◂ **Detail from fol. 246r:** The prophets Jonah and Gideon

Fol. 143v (1 Corinthians): Paul the Apostle seated in the lower left-hand corner of the picture and preaching to a crowd, above him the Holy Ghost as a white dove, in the background a city and landscape.

VI.5 Slavonic Liturgical Gospel Book

Bistrita abbey (Romania, Moldavia region), 1502

The present Gospel book ranks amongst the finest manuscripts in the Slavica collection of the Austrian National Library in Vienna. It was commissioned by Prince Stephen III, the Great, of Moldavia, who presented it to the Bulgarian monastery of Zographou on Mount Athos in 1502 – for the salvation of his soul and of those of his wife Maria and son Bogdan, as a dedication on fol. 245r informs us (ill. p. 273).

The manuscript arose during an era of great political change in south-eastern Europe. The Ottoman Turks had been pursuing their relentless expansion since the middle of the 14th century, conquering the Bulgarian Kingdom (1393), the Byzantine Empire (1453) and the Despotate of Serbia (1459), and were in the process of seizing the territories of the Hungarian throne.

Within this situation, only the principality of Moldavia, under the rule of Stephen III, succeeded in repulsing Ottoman invaders in the period between 1474 and 1501. In recognition of this achievement, the Pope awarded Stephen the epithet *Athleta Christi* ("fighter for Christ").

The Moldavian dynasty of princes had in the past founded and funded churches and monasteries both at home and abroad, and from the middle of the 15th century onwards, in emulation of the rulers of Bulgaria, Serbia and Byzantium, gave particular support to the monastery of Zographou. Stephen III followed this example: as well as building numerous churches and abbeys, he also donated generous sums of money to Zographou monastery, paid for new buildings to be erected and presented it with at least four manuscripts, three dating from 1463, 1475, 1492 (which today are all in Moscow) and the present codex.

Detail from fol. 190r (St John): Decorated page with interlace patterning and animal motifs (white doves).

▸ **Detail from fol. 120v (St Luke):** St Luke the Evangelist seated and writing on a scroll with writing utensils.

EXTENT: 258 parchment folios
FORMAT: 335 x 235 mm
BINDING: 19th-century half-leather binding
CONTENT: four Gospels (divided into pericopes) with preface by Theophylaktos of Ohrid (*c.* 1050–after 1126) and an appendix on the liturgical readings
LANGUAGE: Church-Slavonic Bulgarian edition
SCRIBE: Philippos the monk

ILLUSTRATION: gold sub-titles, decorative bars, decorative fields containing interlace patterning and animal motifs, four full-page miniatures of the Evangelists, dedication with decorative frame and representations of the moon, heraldic animal, coat of arms and sun
PATRON: Stephen III, the Great (Ştefan cel Mare), Prince of Moldavia 1457–1504

PROVENANCE: The Gospels were dedicated by Stephen III to Zographou monastery on Mount Athos. In 1827 they were purchased by Bartholomäus Kopitar for the manuscript collection of the Hofbibliothek in Vienna.
SHELFMARK: Vienna, ÖNB, Cod. slav. 7

At the instigation of Bartholomäus Kopitar (1780–1844), curator of the Hofbibliothek in Vienna, and with the agreement of the abbots, the present Gospel book and eleven other Slavonic codices from the monasteries of Hilandar and Zographou on holy Mount Athos were brought to Vienna in December 1826 for closer study. Having established their artistic and historical value, they were subsequently purchased for the library with the benevolent assistance of Emperor Franz I (1768–1835) and State Chancellor Klemens von Metternich (1773–1859).

This luxury manuscript is written in semi-uncial (*Poluustav*) on very fine parchment. Its captivating illustrations stand clearly in the tradition of Byzantine manuscript illumination (cf. the full-page miniatures of the four Evangelists). While the portraits of St Mark (ill. p. 272) and St Luke (ill. p. 269) correspond to probably the most common compositional type of the "writing Evangelist", the portrait of St John uses the type of the "meditating Evangelist" (ill. p. 241) and that of St Matthew "the Evangelist sharpening his stylus" (ill. p. 270). All four are depicted like icons against a gold ground.

The portraits of the Evangelists in each case precede the start of their respective Gospels. The opening of the Gospel texts themselves are announced by large decorative fields filled with interlace patterning. The palette they employ is in three cases chiefly blue, green, red and gold (fol. 6r; fol. 73r; fol. 190r) and in one case (fol. 121r) only gold. The dedication at the end of the manuscript is also worthy of attention (fol. 245r, ill. p. 273). It is written in gold ink and shows, clockwise from the right, the moon, an aurochs (the Moldavian heraldic animal), the prince's coat of arms and the sun.

On the basis of its illustration and calligraphy, Codex slavicus 7 has been assigned to a group of Gospels which can be dated to the 15th century and localized to the region of Serbia/Romania. *M. P.*

Fol. 5v (St Matthew): St Matthew the Evangelist seated and sharpening his stylus, with desk and writing utensils.

Fol. 72v–73r (St Mark): St Mark the Evangelist seated and writing at a desk with writing utensils. Decorated page at the start of St Mark's Gospel.

▸ **Fol. 245r:** Dedication in gold ink; moon, aurochs and sun in gold, family coat of arms in blue, green and gold.

Іѡ
СТЕФАНЬ ВОЕВО
ДА БЖІЕЮ МЛТІЮ
ГПДРЬ ЗЕМЛИ МОЛДАВС
КОИ СНЬ БОГДАНА ВОЕВО
И ВЪ ХА СЛОВЕСЬ РАЧИТЕЛИИ
ЕГОЖЕ РАДИ И ЛЮБВЕ ВЪЖДЕ
ЛѢ. И ПОТЪЩА СЕ И НО
ДАДЕ И НАПИСА СЕ
СИИ ТЕТРОЕУЛЬ. И ОКОВ
И ДАДЕ ЕГО НА МЛБѪ СЕБѢ И ГЖДИ
СВОЕИ МАРІИ И СНУ ИХЪ БОГДАН
ВЪ СТОИ ГОРѢ ВЪ СВОЕИ ЖЕ ЦРКВИ ВЪ МОН
СТИРЬ ИЗОУГРАФЬ. ИДЕЖЕ Е ХРАМЬ СТГО
И СЛАВНАГО ВЕЛИКОМѪЧЕНИКА И ПОБѢДОНО
СЦА ГЕОРГІА. В ЛѢТ
ОТ СЪЗДАНІА МИРОУ
А ГВА СВОЕГО ЛѢТА. М. И НАШЕСТОЕ
ТЕКѪЩЕЕ. МЦА АПРИЛІА. КГ
ПИСА ЖЕ СЕ РѪКОЮ ГРѢШ
НЕИШАГО ВЪ ИНОЦѢХЪ
ФИЛИППА СИМОНАХА
И СЪПРОСВЕЩАЕМ И АЩЕ И
НЕПОДОБАНІЮ. ОБАЧЕ
КЪ ВЪПОВѢЗМОЕ
НОМОУ

Syriac Gospel Book

Vienna, 1554

Within the Syriac-speaking sphere in the 2nd century, the four Gospels were read chiefly in the form of the *Diatessaron*, the concordance of the Gospels compiled by Tatian (2nd half of the 2nd century) and today surviving only in quotations. It was not long, however, before Syriac translations of each of the four Gospels were also prepared, themselves drawing upon the *Diatessaron*. In the process of transcription over the course of time, these translations underwent revision and alteration. The translation preserved in the present Gospel book became known in the 10th century as the Peshitta (i. e. the "simple" translation, in contrast to others much harder to read), and was originally prepared in the 5th century, again on the basis of earlier versions. It spread rapidly, supplanted the *Diatessaron* and was soon adopted by all Syrian churches. It remains today the standard New Testament text for Syrian Christians and is read in the liturgy. The present codex contains the Peshitta translation of the Gospels.

The manuscript is written in *Serto*, one of the three Syriac styles of script, which evolved from the 6th century onwards in the West-Syrian (Syrian Orthodox) Church and was employed in manuscripts from the 8th century onwards. Since only the consonants are written, systems of indicating the vowels were developed as from the early Middle Ages. The present codex employs the old system of diacritical points and in addition is almost completely vocalized with vowel signs of both the western and eastern Syrian systems, written somewhat thinner and almost always in black.

When Codex syriacus 1 was bound, three sheets of paper were included at the front and back of the manuscript to protect the inner book. On the first two parchment folios and one third of one paper page are a dedication to Emperor Ferdinand I included in a lengthy Latin colophon, in which the scribe, Moses of Mardin, sets out the

Detail from fol. 159v (St John): End of St John's Gospel.

▸ **Fol. 1v (St Matthew):** "With the power of our Lord Jesus Christ we start to write the text of the ho(ly) Gospels; first the Gospel according to St Matthew, which he recited in Hebrew in the land of Palestine." Beginning of St Matthew's Gospel.

EXTENT: 160 + II parchment folios, 6 sheets of paper
FORMAT: 92 x 75 mm
BINDING: brown leather binding over thin wooden boards with roller-stamped and plate-stamped decoration (Vienna [?], 16th century), pounced gold edges, clasps lost, on the front cover plate-stamped representation of an allegory of FIDES surrounded by foliate decor, on the back cover Crucifixion with the Virgin and St John, *SATISFACTI* beneath

CONTENT: Gospel book
LANGUAGE: Syriac (and Latin)
SCRIBE: Moses of Mardin, son of Isaac the priest, from the village of Qaliq near Mardin (documented in Rome in 1549 as the scribe of a Roman Missal in Syriac lettering [British Library, Harl. 5512]; 1592 or shortly afterwards)
ILLUSTRATION: ornamental design given to the beginnings of sections within the text; beginning and end of each Gospel written in outlined gold script; beginning of each Gospel also announced by three-sided ornamental border with interlace patterning; decorative page at the very front featuring a cross in interlace patterning with inscription (see below).
PROVENANCE: According to the dedication on fol. III–Vr, the manuscript was intended for Emperor Ferdinand I (1503–1564).
SHELFMARK: Vienna, ÖNB, Cod. syr. 1

aim of the undertaking and the transcription. The Bible text is introduced on fol. Ir by an ornamental page (ill. p. 276), which contains the following sentence in gold ink in the shape of a cross: "Through you we defeat our enemies and in your name we crush those who hate us." This is followed by the four Gospels. In line with earlier editions of the Peshitta, the pericope about the woman caught in adultery (John 7:53 – 8:11; fol. 137v) is absent. On fol. 39r the scribe notes in the margin that, in the context of Matthew 24:40, the text of Luke 17:34 "is missing". The codex otherwise contains no observations on the texts of the Synoptic Gospels. The Gospels are divided into the usual chapters and into the sections traditional in Syrian Bibles and are only sparsely illustrated (ornament on fol. 75v; 96r).

The Gospels are followed by two Syriac colophons bordered in red, and one in Latin (fol. 160r). In Syriac, the scribe introduces himself as Moses of Mardin, son of the priest Isaac, and as a "Jacobite" from the village of Qaliq, and asks the reader to pray for him and his family. He goes on to record that he wrote the text "in Vienna" (*b-byʼnʼ*) in the time of "Ferdinandus, the Roman King". He includes wishes of prosperity and victory for Ferdinand "and his brother Karolus, the King of Spain". He completed the manuscript on 28 Tammuz 1554 (in Latin on fol. IIIr, 10 August 1554). The scribe's name, year and dedication are repeated in the Latin colophon. The codex probably served as the basis for a first printed edition and as such for the first book to be printed in Syriac script in Vienna (1555, Johann Albert Widmanstad). *C. L.*

Fol. Iv: Ornamental page, sentence in the shape of a cross: "Through you we defeat our enemies and in your name we crush those who hate us."

VI.7 Armenian Gospel Book

Village of K'arahat in the region of Ganjak (Azerbaijan), *c.* 1680

Armenia was the first kingdom to declare Christianity its official state religion (in around AD 313), and the Bible played a correspondingly central role in its manuscript production and illumination. The emergence of Armenian manuscripts as an independent genre only became possible, however, following the creation of a new alphabet under Mesrop Mashtots in 406. The subsequent translation of the Holy Scripture was completed in 435. The Erkat'agir ("iron script") majuscule employed in early manuscripts gave way, from the 10th century onwards (until about the 16th century) to a Bolorgir minuscule ("round script"), which is also employed as a traditionalism in Codex armenicus 29.

For the Armenians, their Bible enjoyed the status of a holy relic, and they devoted particular care not just to its production, but also to its protection and preservation. Should a manuscript fall into foreign hands in the wake of military conquest, every effort would be made to pay the costly ransom demanded for its return. The great importance attached to the Bible is also indicated by the communal storage of medieval manuscripts in the Matenadaran book-depository in Yerevan – a literary horde which was severely depleted as a result of pillaging by the Seljuk Turks, Mongols, Persians and Ottomans, so that today only some 28,000 manuscripts survive.

Armenia's vicissitudinous position as a buffer state between Byzantium and Persia, and subsequently between Arab, Seljuk and Ottoman territory and Persia, also left its mark upon manuscript illumination, amongst other things in its assimilation of foreign styles, such as the Byzantine influence which is clearly apparent in Armenian codices of the 11th century.

Detail from P. 213 [fol. 107r, St Luke]: Beginning of St Luke's Gospel with lavish majuscule (Erkat'agir) in the shape of an animal.

▸ **P. 287* [fol. 194r, St John]:** Beginning of St John's Gospel with decorative arch, decorative element in the margin and lavish majuscule (Erkat'agir), initial in the shape of a bird.

Ըստ
Մարկոսի·

EXTENT: 264 sheets of oriental paper
FORMAT: 180 x 118 mm
BINDING: dark-brown leather binding over wooden boards, with additional flap to protect the fore edge; probably decorated in two phases: the blind stamping with quatrefoil flowers and plaitwork forming a cross on the front cover were executed first; later, the front and back covers were densely studded with metal (?) bosses, of which only circular imprints and the holes still remain. Patterned fabric is glued to the inside covers.
CONTENT: four Gospels with Gospel concordance and introductions to the Gospels.
LANGUAGE: Armenian (Grabar)
SCRIBE: Grigor, a priest, and Paleson, a deacon
ILLUSTRATION: decorative arch at the start of the Gospels, numerous calligraphic initials, some assuming the bird shape typical of Armenian manuscripts; decorations in light blue, orange, green, red, pink and gold in the margins dividing the chapters
PROVENANCE: According to the colophon, the manuscript was written in the time of Shah Suleiman I (1667–1694, of the Persian Safavid dynasty) and Katholikos Simēon of Aghwan (Caucasian Albania, today Azerbaijan); numerous dated entries from the 1st half of the 19th century (1813–1851) on the blank pages at the end of the manuscript (fol. 262r–264v) mention, amongst others, a Nersēs, Movsēs (son of Nersēs), a Menas, a Łukas and a Karapet (?) as owners. The codex was purchased for the National Library in 1927.
SHELFMARK: Vienna, ÖNB, Cod. arm. 29

The constant repression under which they lived prompted many Armenians to emigrate – to Cilicia, for example, where they founded the Kingdom of Little Armenia (1199–1375) with its own admirable tradition of manuscript illumination – and to establish a diaspora of communities, chiefly in eastern Europe. New cultural centres of Armenian manuscript production (and printing) were thereby established (amongst them, from 1717, the Armenian-Catholic Mechitharist congregation of San Lazzaro in Venice). Even within Armenia itself, however, the production of sumptuous Bible manuscripts did not entirely cease, as the present codex from the 2nd half of the 17th century clearly demonstrates. The manuscript employs a range of traditional elements of Armenian Gospel-book illumination: these include the decorative arches at the start of each Gospel, which are in each case followed by a title line in ornamental Erkat' agir, whose opening initial is given a zoomorphic shape (cf. ill. p. 280). At the beginning of St Luke's Gospel (fol. 106r–107r), the title line is also written in a "bird script", insofar as each letter presents itself in the form of a bird.

The circumstances in which the codex was produced are recorded – as is common in Armenian manuscripts – in the (in places highly detailed) colophon at the back, generally called the Hišatakaran (memorial). In the present case, it names Shah Suleiman I of Persia and Katholikos Simēon of Albania (today Azerbaijan). It should be noted in this context that the date of the manuscript coincides with efforts by the Armenians to free themselves from Ottoman sovereignty: from around 1678 until 1711, the Armenian diplomat Israel Ori travelled throughout Europe and Russia seeking the backing of Emperor Leopold I, Tsar Peter the Great and Pope Clemens XI for Armenia's campaign against Turkish and Persian rule.

M. K. K. / G. P. / C. G.

P. 105 [fol. 53r, St Mark]: Beginning of St Mark's Gospel with decorative arch, decorative elements in the margin and lavish majuscule (Erkat'agir), initial in a zoomorphic shape.

▸ **P. 148–149 [fol. 74v–75r, St Matthew]:** Part of St Mark's Gospel with decorative initials and marginal decorations (with numerals) to subdivide the text; Gospel concordance in the lower margin.

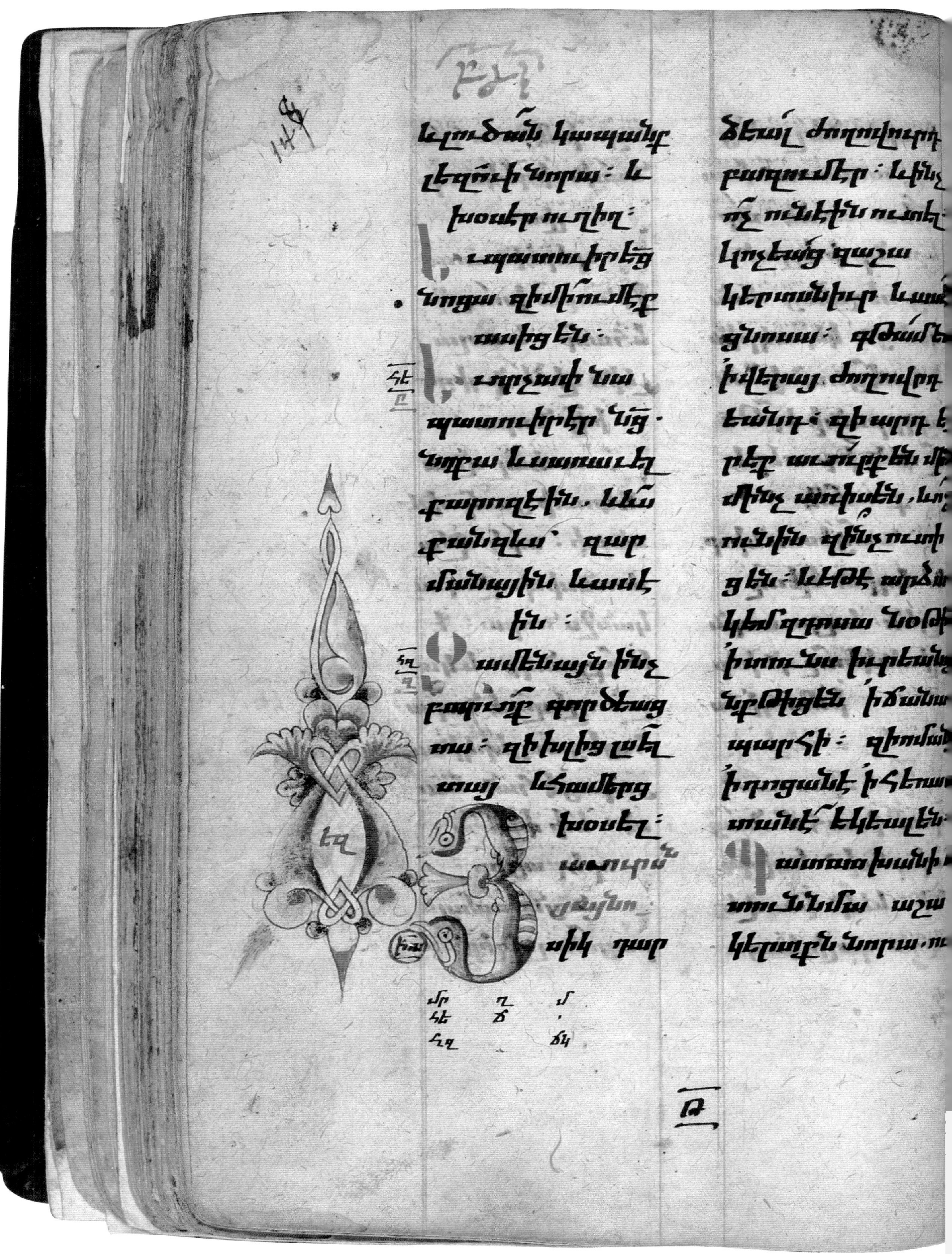

VI.8

Ethiopic Gospel Book

Ethiopia, around 1700

This luxury Ethiopic manuscript can be confidently dated to the end of the 17th or beginning of the 18th century, on the evidence of its fully-developed Gwelḥ script, the style of its miniatures and the royal names mentioned in later notes, which indicate that the manuscript must have been completed by 1755.

The codex is written in Ge'ez, which remains even today the liturgical language of the Ethiopian Church, which became independent of Alexandria in 1959. In contrast to almost all other Semitic languages, Ethiopic is written from left to right and uses no cursive characters.

Christianity reached Ethiopia in the middle of the 4th century with the baptism of King 'Ezānā. Through the influence of nine monks driven out of Syria, Ethiopia quickly embraced the doctrine of Miaphysitism; the translation of Christian texts into Ge'ez probably began soon afterwards. Although none of the Ethiopic codices still extant today dates from earlier than the 10th century, it can be assumed that the Gospels were the first to be translated, probably from the Greek, in around 500. Surviving texts also reveal strong Syrian and in particular Arabic influences, brought to Ethiopia via Coptic manuscripts and incorporated over the course of time.

The manuscript was commissioned by one Adarā Krəstos (fol. 15r); according to the dedication on fol. 22v, he and his father presented the Gospel book to the monastery of Anṭonyos, whose precise location has yet to be established.

The opening pages of the manuscript contain ten full-page miniatures, two of which portray scenes from the Old Testament that held particular significance for the Ethiopian Church. The first picture (ill. p. 288) shows King Solomon on his throne beneath an Ethiopian ceremonial parasol. Through the person of King Solomon, Ethiopia

Detail from fol. 23r (St Matthew): Beginning of St Matthew's Gospel.

▸ **Fol. 3v:** Moses receives the two Tablets of the Law from the hand of God reaching down from a cloud; the inscription in Ethiopic reads "Moses the Prophet".

ሙሲ፡ነቢይ፡

EXTENT: 138 parchment folios; fols. 123–132 are bound upside down and in the wrong order.
FORMAT: 320 x 365 mm
BINDING: probably the original, dark-brown leather binding over wooden boards; blind-tooled decoration with a cross in the centre; multiple rectangular frames with plaitwork and lozenge patterning; fabric covering glued onto inside covers
CONTENT: Gospel book with prefaces
LANGUAGE: Ge'ez (Ethiopic)
ILLUSTRATION: ten full-page miniatures
PATRON: Adarā Krəstos
PROVENANCE: Adarā Krəstos donated the manuscript to Anṭonyos monastery; it then passed into the possession of Sir Robert Napier (1810–1890), victor in the Battle of Maqdalā in 1868, who brought many Ethiopic manuscripts back with him to Europe. The codex entered the Hofbibliothek in 1868 (?).
SHELFMARK: Vienna, ÖNB, Cod. aeth. 25

could also lay claim to its part in Old Testament history, since Solomon's union with the Queen of Sheba produced a son, Menelek. He in turn became the first King of Ethiopia, from whom the Solomonean dynasty which ruled, with interruptions, until 1974, claimed its descent. The next scene (ill. p. 285) – Moses receiving the two Tablets of the Law – is also very closely connected with Ethiopia, because according to tradition the Ark of the Covenant (*tābot*) was brought out of Jerusalem by the companions of King Menelek. It continues to be housed even today in the city of Aksum, the former royal residence, and bears the six additions to the Ten Commandments from Matthew 25 scored into its reverse side by Jesus himself. Every Ethiopian church possesses a copy of this *tābot*, which is carried on the priest's head in a ceremonial procession around the church during Mass.

It is rare in Ethiopia to find the whole New Testament in a single codex; the Gospels usually stand alone. Typical of many Ethiopic Gospel books are prefacing texts, which are here visually distinguished by their smaller script and greater number of lines. An introduction into the nature, use and order of the Gospels is followed by the letter written by Eusebius of Caesarea to Carpianos, the Eusebian canon tables here highlighted with graphic means but not set within a decorative framework, as otherwise often commonly found, and finally the Gospels themselves.

In the Ethiopic liturgy, after the prayers and Scripture readings the Gospel is presented to all the faithful to be kissed; Codex aethiopicus 25, however, shows almost no traces of use and appears to have only been employed in the monastery. The only inscriptions added to its pages are notes at the front and back relating to inventories of church utensils.

S. P.

Detail from fol. 10r: The Virgin and Child; above, two angels holding a curtain

Fol. 2v: King Solomon seated on his throne with a cloth in his right hand and a sword in his left; beside him, a servant with a ceremonial parasol and sword; the inscription in Ethiopic reads "King Solomon".

▸ **Detail from fol. 9r:** St John the Evangelist with an eagle. In his hands, pen and paper; above him, a cloud with the hand of God; in front of him, writing utensils.

VI.9 Arabic Gospel Book

Egypt (?), 14th/15th century (?)

As several extant manuscripts from the 8th and 9th century (by Christian reckoning) demonstrate, translations of the Bible into Arabic go back a very long way. Although no translations survive from the pre-Islamic era, some (non-Islamic) historians of religion have raised the question of whether such translations might have been known to Muhammad and his contemporaries, in view of the fact that a whole series of "biblical" figures are encountered in the Koran. According to Islamic belief, these figures are prophets and those guided on the right path, and both books, Bible and Koran, were revealed by the same God: "Who revealed the Book which Musa [Moses] brought, a light and guidance to men?" (The Cattle, 6.91) Hence parallels between the two revelations pose no problem for Muslim believers and thus also do not represent proof that Arabic translations of the Bible may already have existed in Muhammad's lifetime. There is no doubt, however, that the pre-Islamic Arabs were familiar, through their daily contact with neighbouring Christian and Jewish communities, with the beliefs and legends of their religions.

With the spread of Islam, Arabic became the language of everyday speech in many parts of the Near East and suppressed the vernacular languages that had previously been spoken. This gave rise to a growing need for an Arabic version of the Holy Scripture, as many people could no longer read or understand it in their "old" language. In a number of these Near-Eastern countries, including Egypt, the written tradition went back considerably further than that of the Arab peninsula, so the conditions required to meet this need were already in place. There thus arose a whole series of complete and partial translations of biblical texts from the Hebrew, Greek, Coptic and Syriac, and later also from the Latin.

The Arabic Gospel book from the estate of Sebastian Tengnagel contains, in addition to the four Gospels, an anonymous preface on the spiritual benefits of the text,

Fol. 10v: 6th and 7th canon tables.

القانون السادس ثمنيه واربعون جدولا

متى	مرقس	متى	مرقس	متى	مرقس	متى	مرقس
[illegible]	[illegible]	[illegible]	[illegible]	[illegible]	[illegible]	[illegible]	[illegible]
[illegible]	[illegible]	[illegible]	[illegible]	[illegible]	[illegible]	[illegible]	[illegible]
[illegible]	[illegible]	[illegible]	[illegible]	[illegible]	[illegible]	[illegible]	[illegible]
[illegible]	[illegible]	[illegible]	[illegible]	[illegible]	[illegible]	[illegible]	[illegible]
[illegible]	[illegible]	[illegible]	[illegible]	[illegible]	[illegible]	[illegible]	[illegible]
[illegible]	[illegible]	[illegible]	[illegible]	[illegible]	[illegible]	[illegible]	[illegible]
[illegible]	[illegible]	[illegible]	[illegible]	[illegible]	[illegible]	[illegible]	[illegible]
[illegible]	[illegible]	[illegible]	[illegible]	[illegible]	[illegible]	[illegible]	[illegible]
[illegible]	[illegible]	[illegible]	[illegible]	[illegible]	[illegible]	[illegible]	[illegible]
[illegible]	[illegible]	[illegible]	[illegible]	[illegible]	[illegible]	[illegible]	[illegible]
[illegible]	[illegible]	[illegible]	[illegible]	[illegible]	[illegible]	[illegible]	[illegible]
[illegible]	[illegible]	[illegible]	[illegible]	[illegible]	[illegible]	[illegible]	[illegible]

كمل القانون السادس ويتلوه القانون السابع بسلام الرب

القانون السابع سبعه جداول

متى	يوحنا	متى	يوحنا	متى	يوحنا	متى	يوحنا
[illegible]	[illegible]	[illegible]	[illegible]	[illegible]	[illegible]	[illegible]	[illegible]
[illegible]	[illegible]	[illegible]	[illegible]	[illegible]	[illegible]	كمل القانون السابع	

اكثر خطا من كل الجليليين اذ اصابتهم هذه الاوجاع
لا اقول لكم ان لم تتوبوا كلكم فانتم تهلكون كلكم هكذا
واوليك الثمانيه عشر الذين سقط عليهم البرج
في سيلوحا وقتلهم. اتظنون انهم اكثر جرما من
جميع الناس الذين يسكنون بيروشليم كلا. واقول
لكم انكم ان لم تتوبوا فجميعكم تهلكون هكذا
وقال لهم هذا المثل شجرة تين كانت لواحد مغروسه
في كرمه جا يطلب فيها ثمرة. فلما لم يجد قال
للكرام هذه ثلث سنين اتي واطلب ثمرة في هذه
الشجره ولا اجد اقطعها ليلا تبطل الارض فاجابه
وقال له يا سيد دعها في هذه السنه لاقلحها واصلحها
لعلها تثمر في السنه الاتيه. فان هي اثمرت والا
اقطعها:

الفصل الحادي والخمسون

وفيما هو يعلم في احد المجامع في السبت واذا امراه
معها روح مرض منذ ثمان عشرة سنة. وكانت
منحنية لا تقدر ان تستقيم البته فنظر اليها يسوع

EXTENT: 217 sheets of oriental (cotton) paper
FORMAT: 260 x 175 mm
BINDING: Late medieval limp parchment binding
CONTENT: *Al-arba'a al-anâgii al-muqad-dasa* ("The four holy Gospels")
LANGUAGE: Arabic
PROVENANCE: The manuscript was purchased by prefect Sebastian Tengnagel (1608–1636) for 10 florins for his private library and bequeathed to the Hofbibliothek in his will.
SHELFMARK: Vienna, ÖNB, Cod. A. F. 97

its authors and its divisions. This is followed by the canon tables first drawn up by Eusebius of Caesarea (ill. p. 291), in which corresponding passages in the various Gospels are cross-referenced. As in the Byzantine tradition, each Gospel is accompanied by a brief introduction about its content and author. References to the Coptic, Syriac and Greek versions of the text are included in (red) Arabic glosses in the margins. Tengnagel also added the Latin Bible chapter numbers in the margin.

Sebastian Tengnagel, head of the Hofbibliothek from 1608 until his death in 1636, was a passionate Orientalist. His extensive private library, which he bequeathed to the Hofbibliothek and which he personally inventoried in two catalogues, included alongside 80 Hebrew manuscripts 100 "oriental" codices. Like many of the books in his collection, they served as a learning aid and as subject matter for his primarily lexical study of oriental languages: "I am fired with an incredible enthusiasm for the Arabic, Persian and Turkish languages and I am trying to procure the means to further my education in them from every quarter," he writes in a letter to a fellow librarian. Many of the manuscripts from his collection bear glosses in his characteristic handwriting, including the present Gospel book, which he probably read in tandem with a Latin version, writing the corresponding Latin phrase above any Arabic words that were unfamiliar to him (cf. ill. p. 292). *S. R.-D.*

Detail from fol. 141r (St Luke): Page from St Luke's Gospel (Luke 13:2–13:11) with marginal glosses in Arabic and interlinear glosses (Latin translation of Arabic words) in Sebastian Tengnagel's hand.

VI.10 Mahmûd ibn Ramadân, Rosary of Tidings

Istanbul (Turkey), around 1674

The Ottomans, like so many other European potentates of antiquity, the Middle Ages and the Renaissance, sought to underpin (and legitimize) their claims to power through genealogies which traced their descent from famous rulers or even gods. The fabled prince Oghuz, ancestor of the Oghuz people, was descended in a direct line – so legend had it – from Noah's son, Japhet; and so Ertugrul, the father of the first Ottoman sultan and head of a Turkish line, also belonged to this same people of Oghuz. This was seen as clear proof that the Ottoman dynasty was at least the equal of other ruling families, such as the descendants of Genghis Khan.

There thus arose a whole series of genealogical tables, some of them in codex form, others in the form of scrolls (cf. Cat. IV.1), which – starting from Adam and Eve – illustrate not only the lineage of the Turkish sultans, but also numerous other Arab, Persian and Turkish dynasties. Some of these genealogical tables are without illustrations and consist "only" of medallions containing names (albeit usually in a beautiful calligraphy); others are richly decorated with miniatures of the "main characters", as in the case of the present luxury manuscript from the 17th century.

The protagonists include the patriarchs and prophets of the Old Testament and figures from the New Testament, who are also mentioned in the Koran: "And We gave to him [Abraham] Ishaq [Isaac] and Yaquob [Jacob]; each did We guide, and Nuh [Noah] did We guide before, and of his descendants, Dawood [David] and Sulaiman [Solomon] and Ayub [Job] and Yusuf [Joseph] and Musa [Moses] and Haroun [Aaron]; ... And Zakiriya [Zechariah] and Yahya [John] and Isa [Jesus] and Ilyas [Elijah]; every one was of the good ... This is Allah's guidance, He guides thereby whom He pleases of His servants" (The Cattle, 6.84–88). Medallions containing miniatures and the names of all

Detail from fol. 5r: Enoch and his son.

▸ **Detail from fol. 1v:** Vignette in blue and gold with vegetal and floral ornament and the title *Subhat al-ahbâr* ("Rosary of Tidings").

سپاس علی الاطلاق و ستایش باستحقاق اول باری خلایق حکیم قدیم حضرتنه
اولسونکه وجود عالم بل عالم وجود انک بحر جودندن بر قطره در و شهود نور ظهور
انک ظهور نور شهودندن بر لمحه در بر مبدعدر که بر کلمهٔ کن ایله بو نسخهٔ بیک کلمات حقایق ذات
ام الکتابدن لوح فطرت اوزره تصویر بیوردی و وجود انسانی کلمهٔ جامعه و هم صحیفهٔ کامله
قلوب عالم نسخه سندن انتخاب ایدوب لطیف دوزدیکه ایچنده صور جمله معانی و کلمات
سبع المثانی تجرید بیوردی بر مختردر که محض اصطفا و خلوص اجتبا ایله حضرت آدم صفی
علیه السلام مجموعه سندن گزین قلوب خمرت طینة آدم سدا اربعین صباحا موجبی اوزره دست
قدرت و کار ... ت برله دایره وجود صفحه شهود عالم اوزره رعنا ایدی

شيث نبي عليه السلام
شيث اوغلی انوش
انوش اوغلی قينان
قينان اوغلی مهلائيل
مهلائيل اوغلی برد
كيومرث اوغلی سيامك
هابيل مقتول

EXTENT: 17 sheets of oriental paper
FORMAT: 300 x 185 mm
BINDING: 17th-century Turkish binding, brown kidskin with gold-tooled medallion
AUTHOR: Mahmûd ibn Ramadân (16th century)
CONTENT: *Subhat al-ahbâr* ("Rosary of Tidings")
LANGUAGE: Turkish
MINIATURIST: Hasan al-Istanbûlî (17th century)
ILLUSTRATION: title-page vignette, 102 portrait miniatures, name medallions, page backgrounds of floral patterns in gold, decorative bars, calligraphy, full-page representations of animals and plants
PROVENANCE: The manuscript was brought back as booty from the Turkish wars and passed into the possession of Prince Eugene of Savoy (1663–1736); it entered the Hofbibliothek in 1737.
SHELFMARK: Vienna, ÖNB, Cod. A. F. 50

these "biblical" figures are found in the present Ottoman genealogy, along with portraits of Muhammad, the last and greatest of the prophets of Islam, who is portrayed in traditional fashion with his face veiled, and Alexander the Great – this hero, too, is mentioned in the Koran (fol 8r). The information provided in the accompanying texts is based either on legend or, in the case of later, historically-documented individuals, on their lives.

The manuscript contains just one female portrait, the miniature of Eve (ill. p. 296); depictions of the Virgin, as found in another Ottoman genealogy (Vienna, ÖNB, Cod. A. F. 17), are entirely absent. The only reference to the Virgin is found in a small text medallion beside the miniature of Jesus, which reads: "Jesus, son of Mary" (ill. p. 298/299). Medallions decorated in gold bear the names of the daughters of the Prophet Muhammad.

The illustrations of the figures obey certain formulae: thus the prophets are identified by a nimbus of gold flame and Muhammad and his direct descendants by green turbans. The Persian kings are frequently depicted as soldiers with bracers and weapons (fol. 5r); the fratricidal Cain is portrayed as a fire worshipper (ill. p. 296, below right). The attributes of "biblical" figures are at times familiar to the Christian viewer: Jesus is shown as bare-headed, with long hair and simple robes, holding a book (ill. p. 298/299); Noah probably has a Koran lectern in front of him; the Ark is visible in the background (fol. 5r).

The genealogy was probably executed by dervish Mahmûd ibn Ramadân and dedicated to Sultan Suleiman the Magnificent († 1566). The present manuscript continues the genealogy up to Mehmed IV (deposed in 1687). The closing pages each show two to four large portrait medallions of Ottoman sultans; hidden at the foot of Sultan Mehmed's throne on the last page is the artist's signature: Hasan from Istanbul. *S. R.-D.*

Fol. 4v: Adam and Eve; below them to the left Abd al-Hârith, according to Islamic legend one of their sons, and Gayûmard, ancestral father of the legendary Persian kings. On the right, Abel, and beneath him Cain. The medallions in a vertical row down the centre contain the names of Seth and his descendants.

▸ **Detail from fol. 8r:** left: Alexander the Great, Jesus; right, Zechariah, John the Baptist.

شابور

قراجا خان

اكبر اردوان

اردشير

اصغر اردوان

بلاوش

كى

شابور

بهرام

يزدجرد

اسكندر ذو القرنين

جارسوغا خان

حضرت عيسى عليه السلام

قرى

عليه السلام

المنتصر اوغلی

مالك اوغلی

فهسر اوغلی

غابر اوغلی

غالو اوغلی

عرسطوس

مردوس

طلیموس

ایره اوغلی

سنیف

نجاشی ملك

صبلح اوغلی

ایره اوغلی

حضرت زكريا عليه السلام

برجيس

يونس

شمشون

ملك

ملك

ملك

ملك

ملك

حضرت

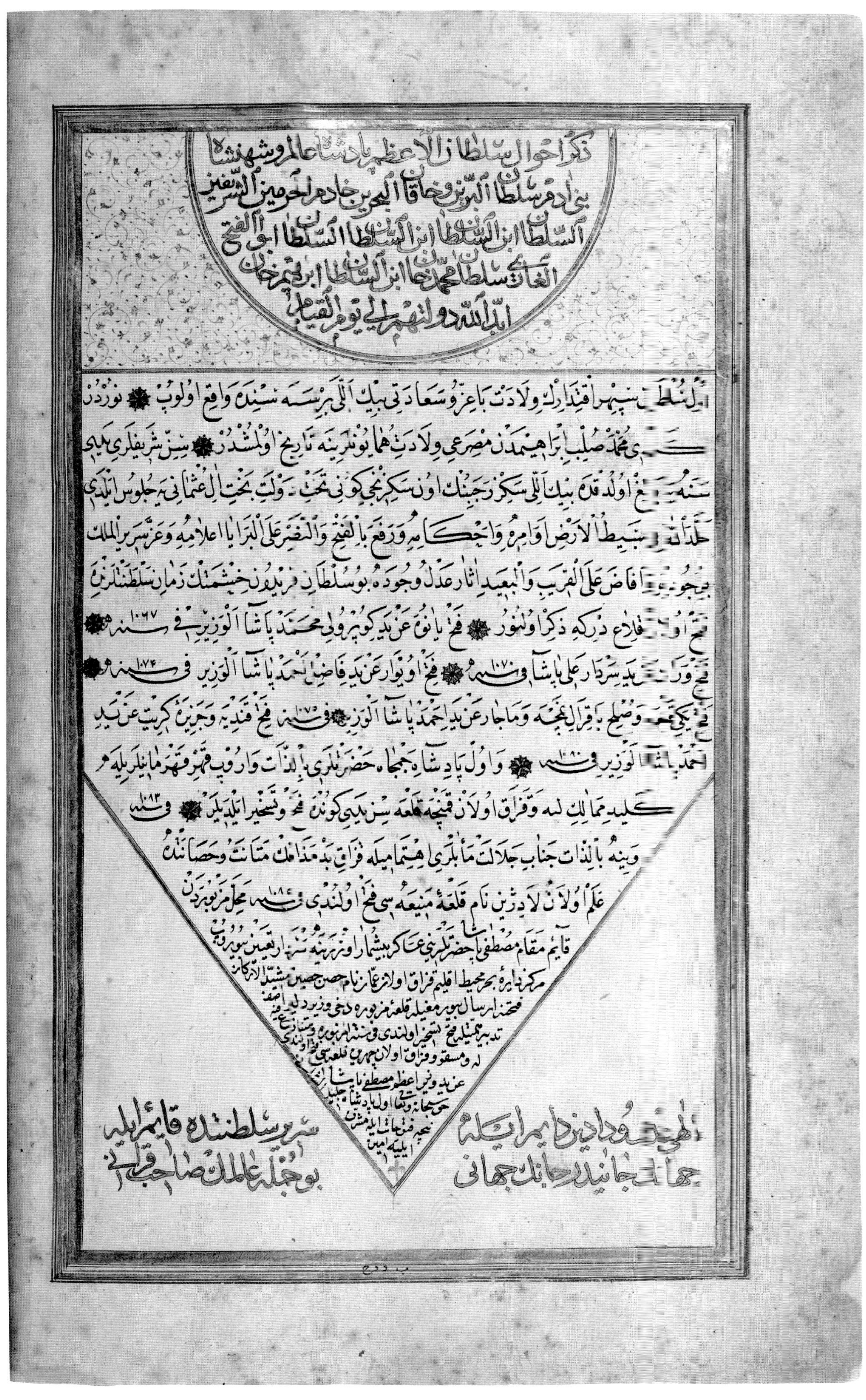

ذکر احوال سلطان الاعظم پادشاه عالم وشهنشاه
بنی آدم سلطان البرین وخاقان البحرین خادم الحرمین الشریفین
السلطان ابن السلطان ابن السلطان ابو الفتح
الغازی سلطان محمد خان ابن السلطان ابراهیم خان
ابد الله دولتهم الی یوم القیام

◂ Detail from fol. 17r: Fabulous beast and plants.

Fol. 16v: Closing chapter with a short biography of Sultan Mehmed IV. The title of the chapter is inscribed in gold calligraphy within a semicircle at the top of the page. The calligraphic verse at the bottom of the page requests God's succour for the Sultan.

Index of manuscripts and monuments

Cited according to catalogue number, bold type indicates a main description, italic type indicates the introductory chapters.

Concordance of biblical books

(based on the Vulgate)

Vetus Testamentum – Old Testament

Gn – Genesis – Genesis
Ex – Exodus – Exodus
Lv – Leviticus – Leviticus
Nm – Numeri – Numbers
Dt – Deuteronomium – Deuteronomy
Ios – Iosue – Joshua
Idc – Iudicum – Judges
Rt – Ruth – Ruth
I Rg – I Regum – 1 Samuel
II Rg – II Regum – 2 Samuel
III Rg – III. Regum – 1 Kings
IV Rg – IV Regum – 2 Kings
I Par – I Paralipomenon – 1 Chronicles
II Par – II Paralipomenon – 2 Chronicles
I Esr – I Esra – Ezra
II Esr – II Esra – Nehemiah
III Esr – III Esra – Nehemiah
IV Esr – IV Esra – Nehemiah
Tb – Tobias – Tobit
Idt – Iudith – Judith
Est – Esther – Esther
Iob – Iob – Job
Ps – Psalmi – Psalms
Prv – Proverbia – Proverbs
Ecl – Ecclesiastes – Ecclesiastes
Ct – Canticum canticorum – Song of Songs
Sap – Sapientia – The Wisdom of Solomon
Sir – Jesus Sirach (Ecclesiaticus) – Ecclesiasticus
Is – Isaias – Isaiah
Ier – Ieremias – Jeremiah
Lam – Lamentationes Ieremiae – Lamentations of Jeremiah
Bar – Baruch – Baruch
Ez – Ezechiel – Ezekiel
Dn – Daniel – Daniel
Os – Osea – Hosea
Ioel – Ioel – Joel
Am – Amos – Amos
Abd – Abdias – Obadiah
Ion – Ionas – Jonah
Mi – Micha – Micah
Na – Naum – Nahum
Hab – Habacuc – Habakkuk
So – Sophonias – Zephaniah
Agg – Aggai – Haggai
Za – Zacharias – Zechariah
Mal – Malachi – Malachi
I Mcc – I Maccabeorum – 1 Maccabees
II Mcc – II Maccabeorum – 2 Maccabees

Novum Testamentum – New Testament

Mt – Matthaeus – Matthew
Mc – Marcus – Mark
Lc – Lucas – Luke
Io – Iohannes – John
Act – Acta apostolorum – Acts
Rm – (Epistula Pauli) ad Romanos – Romans
I Cor – (Ep. Pauli) ad Corinthios I – 1 Corinthians
II Cor – (Ep. Pauli) ad Corinthios II – 2 Corinthians
Gal – (Ep. Pauli) ad Galatas – Galatians
Eph – (Ep. Pauli) ad Ephesios – Ephesians
Phil – (Ep. Pauli) ad Philippenses – Philippians
Col – (Ep. Pauli) ad Colossenses – Colossians
I Th – (Ep. Pauli) ad Thessalonicenses I – 1 Thessalonians
II Th – (Ep. Pauli) ad Thessalonicenses II – 2 Thessalonians
I Tim – (Ep. Pauli) ad Timotheum I – 1 Timothy
II Tim – (Ep. Pauli) ad Timotheum II – 2 Timothy
I Tit – (Ep. Pauli) ad Titum – Titus
Phlm – (Ep. Pauli) ad Philemonem – Philemon
Hbr – (Ep. Pauli) ad Hebraeos – Hebrews
Laod – (Ep. Pauli) ad Laodicenses – Laodiceans
Iac – (Epistula) Iacobi – James
I Pt – (Epistula) I Petri – 1 Peter
II Pt – (Epistula) II Petri – 2 Peter
II Io – (Epistula) I Iohannis – 1 John
II Io – (Epistula) II Iohannis – 2 John
III Io – (Epistula) III Iohannis – 3 John
Iud – (Epistula) Iudae – Jude
Apc – Apocalypsis – Apocalypse (Revelation)

▸ **Slavonic Liturgical Apostolos, Co. slav. 6, fol. 292v:** Crucifixion group: the grieving Virgin Mary to the left of the Cross, above her Archangel Gabriel, the grieving apostle John to the right of the Cross, above him Archangel Michael, in the centre Jesus Christ on the Cross.

ІѠ БГОСЛОВ

Bibliography

Literature cited in abbreviated form

Ayres = L. M. Ayres, A Fragment of a Romanesque Bible in Vienna (ÖNB, Cod. ser. nov. 4236) and its Salzburg Affiliations. *Zeitschrift für Kunstgeschichte* 42 (1982), pp. 130–144

Birkfellner = G. Birkfellner, Glagolitische und kyrillische Handschriften in Österreich (*Österr. Akad. der Wiss., Phil.-hist. Kl., Schriften der Balkankomm., Linguist. Abt.* XXIII). Vienna 1975

Bischoff = B. Bischoff, Die südostdeutschen Schreibschulen und Bibliotheken in der Karolingerzeit Part II: Die vorwiegend österreichischen Diözesen. Wiesbaden 1980

Buberl–Gerstinger = P. Buberl, H. Gerstinger, Die byzantinischen Handschriften II (*Beschreibendes Verzeichnis der illuminierten Handschriften in Österreich*, new series, vol. 4/2). Leipzig 1938

Cahn = W. Cahn, Die Bibel in der Romanik. Munich 1982

De Hamel = C. de Hamel, The Book. A History of the Bible. London 2001

Euw–Plotzek = A. v. Euw and J. M. Plotzek, Bibel, in: *ibid.*, Die Handschriften der Sammlung Ludwig, vol. 1. Cologne 1979

Fillitz = H. Fillitz (ed.), Geschichte der Bildenden Kunst in Österreich, vol. I: Früh- und Hochmittelalter. Munich, New York 1998

Fingernagel–Roland = A. Fingernagel and M. Roland, Mitteleuropäische Schulen I (ca. 1250–1350) (*Österr. Akad. der Wiss., Phil.-hist. Kl., Denkschriften* 245. *Veröff. der Komm. für Schrift- und Buchw. des Mittelalt., Reihe I: Die illuminierten Handschriften und Inkunabeln der Österreichischen Nationalbibliothek*, vol. 10). Vienna 1997

Fingernagel–Simader = A. Fingernagel and F. Simader, Ergänzungen und Nachträge zum Katalog der deutschen romanischen Handschriften. Online catalogue, Vienna (since 2001): http://www.onb.ac.at/sammlungen/hschrift/kataloge/ergaenzungen/ergaenzungen.htm

Fritzsche = G. Fritzsche, Die Entwicklung des "Wiener Realismus" in der Wiener Malerei, 1331 bis Mitte des 14. Jahrhunderts (*Dissertationen zur Kunstgeschichte* 18). Vienna, Cologne, Graz 1983

Hermann 1 = H. J. Hermann, Die frühmittelalterlichen Handschriften des Abendlandes (*Beschreibendes Verzeichnis der illuminierten Handschriften in Österreich*, new series, vol. 1). Leipzig 1923

Hermann 2 = H. J. Hermann, Die deutschen romanischen Handschriften (*Beschreibendes Verzeichnis der illuminierten Handschriften in Österreich*, new series, vol. 2). Leipzig 1926

Hermann 3 = H. J. Hermann, Die romanischen Handschriften des Abendlandes mit Ausnahme der deutschen Handschriften (*Beschreibendes Verzeichnis der illuminierten Handschriften in Österreich*, new series, vol. 3). Leipzig 1927

Hermann 5/3 = H. J. Hermann, Die italienischen Handschriften des Duecento und Trecento 1. Bis zur Mitte des XIV. Jahrhunderts (*Beschreibendes Verzeichnis der illuminierten Handschriften in Österreich*, new series, vol. 5/3). Leipzig 1928

Hermann 6/1 = H. J. Hermann, Die Handschriften und Inkunabeln der italienischen Renaissance. 1. Oberitalien: Genua, Lombardei, Emilia, Romagna (*Beschreibendes Verzeichnis der illuminierten Handschriften in Österreich*, new series, vol. 6/1). Leipzig 1930

Hermann 6/2 = H. J. Hermann, Die Handschriften und Inkunabeln der italienischen Renaissance. 2. Oberitalien: Venetien (*Beschreibendes Verzeichnis der illuminierten Handschriften in Österreich*, new series, vol. 6/2). Leipzig 1931

Hermann 6/3 = H. J. Hermann, Die Handschriften und Inkunabeln der italienischen Renaissance. 3. Mittelitalien: Toskana, Umbrien, Rom (*Beschreibendes Verzeichnis der illuminierten Handschriften in Österreich*, new series, vol. 6/3). Leipzig 1932

Hermann 7/2 = H. J. Hermann, Die westeuropäischen Handschriften und Inkunabeln der Gotik und Renaissance. 2. Englische und französische Handschriften des

XIV. Jahrhunderts (*Beschreibendes Verzeichnis der illuminierten Handschriften in Österreich,* new series, vol. 7/2). Leipzig 1936
Hunger-Lackner-Hannick = H. Hunger, W. Lackner, C. Hannick, Katalog der griechischen Handschriften der Österreichischen Nationalbibliothek, Teil 3/3: Codices theologici 201–337 (*Museion,* Österreichische Nationalbibliothek publication, new series, no. 4, vol. 1). Vienna 1992
Iorga = N. Iorga, Les arts mineurs en Roumanie. I. Icônes. II. Argenterie. III. Miniatures. Bucharest 1934
Irblich = E. Irblich (ed.), Thesaurus Austriacus. Europas Glanz im Spiegel der Buchkunst. Handschriften und Kunstalben von 800 bis 1600. Vienna 1996
Krása = J. Krása, Die Handschriften König Wenzels IV. Prague 1971
Mazal = O. Mazal, Catalogue of the Western manuscripts in the Österreichische Nationalbibliothek, "Series Nova" (new acquisitions), Part 4: Cod. Ser. n. 4001–4800 (*Museion,* Österreichische Nationalbibliothek publication, new series, no. 4, vol. 2). Vienna 1975
Mazal-Unterkircher = O. Mazal and F. Unterkircher, Katalog der abendländischen Handschriften der Österreichischen Nationalbibliothek "Series Nova" (Neuerwerbungen), Teil 3: Cod. Ser. n. 3201–4000 (*Museion,* Österreichische Nationalbibliothek publication, new series, no. 4, vol. 2). Vienna 1967
Pächt-Jenni = O. Pächt and U. Jenni, Holländische Schule, vol. 3 (*Öster. Akad. Wiss., Phil.-hist. Kl., Denkschriften* 124. *Veröff. der Komm. für Schrift- und Buchw. des Mittelalt., Reihe I: Die illuminierten Handschriften und Inkunabeln der Österreichischen Nationalbibliothek* vol. 3). Vienna 1975
Petschar = H. Petschar (ed.), Alpha und Omega, Geschichten vom Ende und vom Anfang der Welt. Exhibition catalogue, Österreichische Nationalbibliothek, Vienna. Vienna, New York 2000
Pfändtner = K.-G. Pfändtner, Die Psalterillustration des 13. und beginnenden 14. Jahrhunderts in Bologna, Herkunft – Entwicklung – Auswirkung. Neuried 1996
Schmidt = G. Schmidt, Die Armenbibeln des XIV. Jahrhunderts. Graz, Cologne 1959
Sörries = R. Sörries, Christlich-antike Buchmalerei im Überblick. Wiesbaden 1993
v. Bloh = U. v. Bloh, Die illustrierten Historienbibeln (*Vestigia Bibliae* 13/14, 1991/92). Berne (et al.) 1993

Introduction Füssel (pp. 6–18):
O. Mazal, Geschichte der Handschriftenkunde. Wiesbaden 1986 (= Elemente des Buch- und Bibliothekswesens 10). – V. Trost, Skriptorium: Die Buchherstellung im Mittelalter (= Heidelberger Universitätsschriften 25). Heidelberg 1986 (Stuttgart [2]1991). – F. Mütherich (et al.), Regensburger Buchmalerei. Catalogue of an exhibition mounted in Regensburg (= Bayerische Staatsbibliothek. Ausstellungskataloge 39). Munich 1987. – C. de Hamel, Medieval Craftsmen: Scribes and Illuminators. London 1992. – J. Kirmeier, A. Schütz, E. Brockhoff, Schreibkunst. Mittelalterliche Buchmalerei aus dem Kloster Seeon. Exhibition catalogue. Augsburg 1994. – J. M. Plotzek (et al.), Glaube und Wissen im Mittelalter. Catalogue to an exhibition in the Erzbischöfliches Diözesanmuseum. Cologne. Munich 1998. – C. Stiegemann (et al.): 799 – Kunst und Kultur der Karolingerzeit. Karl der Große und Papst Leo III. in Paderborn. 2 vols. Mainz 1999. – M. Brandt, Abglanz des Himmels. Romanik in Hildesheim. Catalogue to an exhibition in Hildesheim Cathedral Museum. Regensburg 2001. – C. de Hamel, The British Library Guide to Manuscript Illumination: History and techniques. London 2001. – Ralf M. W. Stammberger, Scriptor und Scriptorium. Das Buch im Spiegel mittelalterlicher Handschriften (= Lebensbilder des Mittelalters). Graz 2003.

Introduction Fingernagel (pp. 20–33):
J. Stummvoll (ed.), Geschichte der Österreichischen Nationalbibliothek (*Museion,* Österreichische Nationalbibliothek publication, new series, no. 2, vol. 3, Part 1). Vienna 19[illegible]. – Bibliotheca Eugeniana. Die Sammlungen des Prinzen Eugen von Savoyen. Exhibition in the Österreichische Nationalbibliothek and the Graphische Sammlung Albertina, Vienna 15.5.–31.10.1986. Vienna 1986. – O. Mazal, Königliche Bücherliebe. Die Bibliothek des Matthias Corvinus. Graz 1990. – Natur und Kunst. Handschriften und Alben aus der Ambraser Sammlung Erzherzog Ferdinands II. (1529–1595). Exhibition by the Kunsthistorische Museum and the Österreichische Nationalbibliothek in Ambras Castle, Innsbruck 23.6–24.9.1995. Vienna 1995. – Irblich. – A. Fingernagel, Zum Ursprung der Wiener Hofbibliothek, in: M. Csáky, P. Stachel (eds.), Speicher des Gedächtnisses. Bibliotheken, Museen, Archive, Part 2: Die Erfindung des Ursprungs. Die Systematisierung der Zeit. Vienna 2001, pp. 31–42.

Introduction Chapter I:
G. Sed-Rajna, The Image as Exegetical Tool. Paintings in Medieval Hebrew Manuscripts of the Bible, in: The Bible as Book. The Manuscript Tradition, ed. by J. L. Sharpe III and K. van Kampen. New Castle 2002 (reprint), pp. 215–221. – P. H. Brieger, Bible Illustration and Gregorian Reform, in: Studies in Church History, vol. 2. London 1965, pp. 154 ff. – H. L. Kessler, The Illustrated Bibles from Tours (*Studies in Manuscript Illumination* 7). Princeton 1977. – B. Smalley, The Study of the Bible in the Middle Ages. Notre Dame 1978. – Euw-Plotzek, pp. [illegible]. – W. Cahn, Die Bibel in der Romanik. Munich 1982. – K.-G. Pfändtner, Zwei Bologneser Bibeln des 13. Jahrhunderts in der Staatsbibliothek Bamberg (136. *Bericht des Historischen Vereins Bamberg*). Bamberg 1[illegible]9[illegible], pp. [illegible]. – R. Gameson (ed.), The Early Me-

dieval Bible, Its Production, Decoration and Use. Cambridge 1994. – PFÄNDTNER. – Louvain Database of Ancient Books by Willy CLARYSSE (first issued on CD in 1998, now accessible at the regularly updated website http://ldab.arts.kuleuven.ac.be/index2.html"). – R. H. and M. A. ROUSE, Manuscripts and their Makers, Commercial Book Producers in Medieval Paris, 1200–1500. Turnhout 2000. – DE HAMEL, pp. 12–39.

Introduction, Chapter II: EUW-PLOTZEK, pp. 25–41. – CAHN. – J. KRÁSA, Der hussitische Biblizismus, in: Von der Macht der Bilder. Beiträge des CIHA Kolloquiums „Kunst und Reformation". Leipzig 1983, pp. 54–59. – O. PÄCHT, Illustration der Bibel, in: Buchmalerei des Mittelalters. Eine Einführung. Munich 1984, pp. 129–154. – SÖRRIES. – H. HEGER, Philologischer Kommentar zur Wenzelsbibel (Das "Buch der Bücher", Die Bibel im Mittelalter, Die Problematik von Übersetzungen, Deutsche Bibelübersetzungen des Mittelalters und der Frühen Neuzeit), in: Die Wenzelsbibel. Complete facsimile edition of Codices Vindobonenses 2759–2764, Österreichische Nationalbibliothek, Vienna. Commentary volume. Graz 1998, pp. 51–57. – S. FÜSSEL, Gutenberg und seine Wirkung. Frankfurt am Main 1999. – DE HAMEL.

Introduction, Chapter III: B. ALTANER, A. STUIBER, Patrologie. Leben, Schriften und Lehre der Kirchenväter. Freiburg, Basle, Vienna ^{7}1966. – H. RIEDLINGER, Bibel in der christlichen Theologie, Lateinischer Westen, Geschichte der Auslegung, in: *Lexikon des Mittelalters* 2 (1983), pp. 47–58. – H. DE LUBAC, Medieval Exegesis. The Four Senses of Scripture. Edinburgh 1998. – S. DÖPP, W. GEERLINGS (eds.), Lexikon der antiken christlichen Autoren. Freiburg, Basle, Vienna ^{3}2002. – DE HAMEL, esp. pp. 92–113.

Introduction, Chapter IV: (GENEALOGY, WORLD CHRONICLES; A. F.): H. GRUNDMANN, Geschichtsschreibung im Mittelalter. Gattungen – Epochen – Eigenart. Göttingen 1965. – W. LAMMERS, Geschichtsdenken und Geschichtsbild im Mittelalter. Darmstadt 1965. – A.-D. VON DEN BRINKEN, Die lateinische Weltchronistik, in: A. RANDA (ed.), Mensch und Weltgeschichte. Zur Geschichte der Universalgeschichtsschreibung. Salzburg and Munich 1969, pp. 43–58. – K. H. KRÜGER, Die Universalchroniken. Turnhout 1976. – M. HAEUSLER, Das Ende der Geschichte in der mittelalterlichen Weltchronistik. Cologne 1980. – U. KNEFELKAMP (ed.), Weltbild und Realität. Einführung in die mittelalterliche Geschichtsschreibung. Pfaffenweiler 1992. – K. SCHNITH, Chronik, in: *Lexikon des Mittelalters* 2 (1999) 1956–1960. (HISTORY BIBLES; K. H.): H. VOLLMER, Materialien zur Bibelgeschichte und religiösen Volkskunde des Mittelalters, vols. 1–4. Berlin 1912–29. – CH. GERHARDT, Historienbibeln (deutsche), in: *Die deutsche Literatur des Mittelalters. Verfasserlexikon* 4 (^{2}1983), pp. 67–75. – G. KORNRUMPF, Die österreichischen Historienbibeln IIIa und IIIb, in: H. REINITZER (ed.), Deutsche Bibelübersetzungen des Mittelalters (*Vestigia Bibliae* 9/10, 1987/88). Berne (et al.) 1991, pp. 350–374, here p. 350 f., 368. – N. H. OTT, Historienbibel, in: *Lexikon des Mittelalters* 5 (1991), p. 45. – U. v. BLOH, Die illustrierten Historienbibeln (*Vestigia Bibliae* 13/14, 1991/92). Berne (et al.) 1993.

Introduction, Chapter V: (TYPOLOGY; A. F.): H. HOEFER, Typologie im Mittelalter. Göppingen 1971. – F. OHLY, Skizzen zur Typologie im späten Mittelalter, in: Medium Aevum deutsch. Beiträge zur deutschen Literatur des hohen und späten Mittelalters. Festschrift für Kurt Ruh zum 65. Geburtstag. Tübingen 1979, pp. 251–310. – S. SCHRENK, Typos und Antitypos in der frühchristlichen Kunst. *Jahrbuch für Antike und Christentum*, suppl. vol. 21 (1995). (BIBLE MORALISÉE) see below, cat. V:1–2 (BIBLIA PAUPERUM; V. P.-A.): H. CORNELL, Biblia pauperum. Stockholm 1925. – G. SCHMIDT, Die Armenbibeln des 14. Jahrhunderts. Graz, Cologne 1959. – K.-A. WIRTH, Biblia pauperum, in: *Die deutsche Literatur des Mittelalters. Verfasserlexikon* 1 (^{2}1978), pp. 843–852. – G. SCHMIDT, Bibbia dei poveri, in: *Enciclopedia dell' Arte medievale*, vol. 3. Rome 1992, pp. 487–491. – J. BACKHOUSE, J. H. MARROW and G. SCHMIDT, Biblia Pauperum. Facsimile edition of Kings Ms. 5, British Library, London. Commentary. 1994. – N. H. OTT, Biblia pauperum, in: Katalog der deutschsprachigen illustrierten Handschriften des Mittelalters, vol. 2 (*Veröff. Komm. für Deutsche Lit. des Mittelalters der Bayer. Akad. der Wiss.*). Munich 1996, pp. 249–327. (SPECULUM HUMANAE SALVATIONIS; V. P.-A.): J. LUTZ, P. PERDRIZET, Speculum humanae salvationis. Mulhouse 1907. – E. BREITENBACH, Speculum humanae salvationis. Eine typengeschichtliche Untersuchung. Strasbourg 1930. – A. WILSON, J. L. WILSON, A medieval mirror. Speculum humanae salvationis, 1324–1500. Berkeley, Calif. (et al.) 1984. – M. NIESNER, Das Speculum Humanae Salvationis der Stiftsbibliothek Kremsmünster. Edition der mittelhochdeutschen Versübersetzung und Studien zum Verhältnis von Bild und Text. Cologne, Vienna (et al.) 1995. – H.-W. STORK, B. WACHINGER, Speculum humanae salvationis, in: *Die deutsche Literatur des Mittelalters. Verfasserlexikon* 9 (^{2}1995), pp. 52–65. – B. CARDON, Manuscripts of the speculum humanae salvationis in the Southern Netherlands (c. 1410–c. 1470). A contribution to the study of the 15th century book illumination and of the function and meaning of historical symbolism. Louvain 1996.

Introduction, Chapter VI: SÖRRIES. – N. L. COLLINS, The Library in Alexandria and the Bible in Greek (*Supplements to Vetus Testamentum*, vol. LXXXII). Leiden, Boston, Cologne 2000. – H. and H. BUSCHHAUSEN, Codex Etschmiadzin. Complete facsimile edition of Codex 2374 in the Matenadaran Mesrop Maštoc' in Yerevan. Graz 2001. – W. BAUM, Äthiopien und der Westen im Mittelalter (*Einführungen in das orientalische Christentum 2*). Klagenfurt 2001. – S. G. RICHTER, Studien zur Christianisierung Nubiens (*Sprachen und Kulturen des Christlichen Orients*, vol. 11). Wiesbaden 2003 – cf. also the individual essays on the Lemmata Bible translations I, II in: *Theologische Realenzyklopädie* 6 (1980), pp. 160–228 and in the introduction to F. D'AIUTO, G. MORELLO, A. M. PIAZZONI, "I Vangeli dei Popoli. La parola e l'immagine del Cristo nelle culture e nella storia". Exhibition catalogue. Vatican City 2000.

I.1: A. KRAFFT, S. DEUTSCH, Die handschriftlichen hebräischen Werke der k. k. Hofbibliothek zu Wien. Vienna 1847, pp. 17–19 (no. 13). – A. Z. SCHWARZ, Die Hebräischen Handschriften der Nationalbibliothek in Wien (*Museion*. Nationalbibliothek publication, Vienna, essay, vol. 2). Vienna, Prague, Leipzig 1925, pp. 17–19 (no. 19).

I.2: P. BUBERL, Die byzantinischen Handschriften (*Beschreibendes Verzeichnis der illuminierten Handschriften in Österreich*, new series, vol. 4/1). Leipzig 1937, pp. 67–129. – O. MAZAL, Wiener Genesis. Illuminierte Purpurhandschrift aus dem 6. Jahrhundert. Facsimile of Codex theol. gr. 31 from the Österreichische Nationalbibliothek. Frankfurt/Main 1986. – SÖRRIES, pp. 45–55 with pl. 18–29 (with extensive bibliography). – B. ZIMMERMANN, Die Wiener Genesis im Rahmen der antiken Buchmalerei. Illustrationsverfahren, Darstellungsweise, Aussageintention. Wiesbaden 2003.

I.3: BUBERL-GERSTINGER pp. 63–67. – HUNGER-LACKNER-HANNICK, pp. 336–341. – L. PROSDOCIMI, Codici di Andrea Contrario nel testamento di Michele Salvatico, in: G. P. MANTOVANI, L. PROSDOCIMI, E. BARILE, L'umanesimo librario tra Venezia e Napoli. Contributi su Michele Salvatico e su Andrea Contrario (*Istituto Veneto di Scienze, Lettere ed Arti. Memorie della classe di scienze morali, lettere ed arti* XLV). Venice 1993, pp. 27–52 (with extensive bibliography on Andreas Contrarius).

I.4: HERMANN 1, 66–72. – BISCHOFF, p. 262 – B. FISCHER, Lateinische Bibelhandschriften im frühen Mittelalter (*Vetus latina. Die Reste der altlateinischen Bibel. Aus der Geschichte der lateinischen Bibel*, vol. 2). Freiburg 1985, pp. 46, 69, 150, 158, 227 f., 230, 232–235, 237, 249, 392. – J. VINTR, Die tschechisch kirchenslavischen Glossen des 12. Jahrhunderts in der Bibel Sign. 1190 der Nationalbibliothek in Wien (sog. Jagic-Glossen). *Wiener Slawistisches Jahrbuch* 32 (1986), pp. 77–113.

I.5: HERMANN 7/2, pp. 61–62, 58–60. – R. BRANNER, Manuscript Painting in Paris during the Reign of Saint Louis. A Study of Styles. Berkeley, Los Angeles, London 1977, p. 85, cat. 223, fig. 242. – F. AVRIL, A quand remontent les premiers ateliers d'enlumineurs laics à Paris? *Les dossiers de l'archéologie* 16 (1976), pp. 36–44. – L. LIGHT: French Bibles, c. 1200–1230: a New Look at the Origins of the Paris Bible, in: R. GAMESON (ed.), The Early Medieval Bible: its production, decoration and use (= *Cambridge studies in palaeography and codicology* 2). Cambridge 1994, pp. 155–176. – R. H. ROUSE and M. A. ROUSE, Illiterati et uxorati. Manuscripts and their Makers. Commercial Book Producers in Medieval Paris 1200–1500, 2 vols. Turnhout 2000.

II.1: P. BUBERL, Die illuminierten Handschriften in Steiermark. 1. Teil: Die Stiftsbibliotheken zu Admont und Vorau (*Beschreibendes Verzeichnis der illuminierten Handschriften in Österreich*, vol. 4). Leipzig 1911, pp. 27–33. – H. SWARZENSKI, Two Unnoticed Leaves from the Admont Bible. *Scriptorium* 10 (1956), pp. 94–96. – T. WEHLI, Die Admonter Bibel. *Acta historiae artium* 23 (1977), pp. 173–285. – E. MAZAL, Wie kam die Admonter Bibel nach Ungarn? *Codices manuscripti* 7 (1981), pp. 43–51. – Admont Giant Bible: the complete manuscript with a codicological and art-historical introduction by A. FINGERNAGEL on CD-ROM. Purkersdorf 1998. – A. FINGERNAGEL, Die Admonter Riesenbibel (*Codices illuminati* 1). Graz 2001.

II.2: MAZAL-UNTERKIRCHER, pp. 2[illegible]1–2[illegible]3. – E. MÜLLER, Geschichtlicher Abriß des Stiftes Lilienfeld seit 1700. Lilienfeld 1979, p. 36. – M. ROLAND, Buchschmuck in Lilienfelder Handschriften (*Studien und Forschungen aus dem Niederösterreichischen Institut für Landeskunde* 22). Vienna 1996, pp. 18–2[illegible] passim. – FINGERNAGEL-ROLAND, pp. 3–5. – A. HAIDINGER and F. LACKNER, Die Handschriften des Stiftes Lilienfeld. Anmerkungen und Ergänzungen zu Schimeks Katalog. *Codices manuscripti* 18/19 (1997), pp. 49, 57 ff.

II.3: Die Gotik in Niederösterreich. Kunst und Kultur einer Landschaft im Spätmittelalter. Exhibition in Krems-Stein. Vienna 1959, nos. 92 and [illegible]. – G. SCHMIDT, Italienische Buchmalerei in Österreich. *Alte und moderne Kunst* 6, vol. 48 (1961), p. 3. – IRBLICH, no. 12. – FINGERNAGEL-ROLAND, pp. 65–78 and 286–289 (with extensive bibliography).

II.4: J. V. SCHLOSSER, Die Bilderhandschriften Königs Wenzel I. *Jahrbuch der Kunsthistorischen Sammlungen des Allerhöchsten Kaiserhauses* 14 (1893), pp. 214–317. – KRÁSA. – M. THOMAS, G. SCHMIDT, M. KRIEGER, Die Bibel des Königs Wenzel. Graz 1989. – H. HEGER, I. HLAVÁČEK, G. SCHMIDT, Commentary volume accompanying the facsimile edition of the Wenceslas Bible. Graz 1998. – K. HRANITZKY, Die schönsten

Bilder aus der Wenzelsbibel. Graz 1998.

II.5: K. HOLTER, Die Korczek-Bibel der Österreichischen Nationalbibliothek, *Die Graphischen Künste*, new series 3 (1938), p. 81. - K. STEJSKAL, Votivní obraz v klášterní knihovně v Roudnici. *Umění* 8 (1960), pp. 568 f. - G. SCHMIDT, Malerei bis 1450, in: Gotik in Böhmen. Munich 1969, pp. 244, 245 - KRÁSA, pp. 216, 278. - H. HLAVÁČKOVÁ, Die Buchmalerei des Schönen Stils, in: Prag um 1400. Vienna 1990, pp. 128, 129.

II.6: A. BRÄM, Illuminierte Breviere. Zur Rezeption der Anjou-Monumentalkunst in der Buchmalerei, in: T. MICHALSKY (ed.), Medien der Macht. Kunst zur Zeit der Anjous in Italien. Berlin 2001, pp. 295-317 (with further bibliography). - E. IRBLICH, G. BISE, Die Bibel von Neapel (Altes Testament), Handschrift aus dem 14. Jahrhundert. Geneva 1978. - M. ROLAND, Apokalypse-Zyklus einer neapolitanischen Bibel, in: PETSCHAR, pp. 186-193.

II.7: W. WALTHER, Die deutsche Bibelübersetzung des Mittelalters. Braunschweig 1889, pp. 250, 254, 401-413. - K. ESCHER, Die "Deutsche Prachtbibel" der Wiener Nationalbibliothek und ihre Stellung in der Basler Miniaturmalerei des XV. Jahrhunderts. *Jahrbuch der kunsthistorischen Sammlungen in Wien* 36 (1923-25), pp. 47-96. - H. MENHARDT, Verzeichnis der altdeutschen literarischen Handschriften der Österreichischen Nationalbibliothek. Berlin 1960/61, pp. 272 f.

II.8: G. SCHMIDT, Buchmalerei, in: Gotik in Österreich, Exhibition catalogue. Krems a. d. Donau 1967, pp. 169 f. - K. HOLTER, Buchmalerei, in: J. GASSNER (ed.), Spätgotik in Salzburg. Die Malerei 1400-1530. Exhibition catalogue. Salzburg 1972, p. 240 (no. 276). - F. UNTERKIRCHER, Die datierten Handschriften der Österreichischen Nationalbiblitohek von 1451 bis 1500 (*Katalog der datierten Handschriften in lateinischer Schrift in Österreich* III). Vienna 1974, p. 25. - G. SCHMIDT, Ein unbekanntes Werk Ulrich Schreiers in Polen, in: Von Österreichischer Kunst, Festschrift Franz Fuhrmann, published by the Institut für Kunstgeschichte der Universität Salzburg. Klagenfurt 1981, pp. 37-41.

II.9: PÄCHT-JENNI, pp. 16-23 (with older bibliography). - The Golden Age of Dutch Manuscript Painting. Catalogue to the exhibition in the Rijksmuseum Het Catharijneconvent, Utrecht, 10.12.1989-11.2.1990, and in The Pierpont Morgan Library, New York, 1.3.1990-6.5.1990. Stuttgart and Zurich 1989. - K. VAN DER HORST, Masters and miniatures: proceedings of the Congress on Medieval Manuscript Illumination in the Northern Netherlands, (Utrecht, 10-13 December 1989) (*Studies and facsimiles of Netherlandish illuminated manuscripts* 3). Doornspijk 1991.

III.1: HERMANN 6/3, pp. 110-120. - P. D'ANCONA, La miniatura fiorentina nei secoli XI-XVI. Florence 1912, vol. 1, pl. LXXXIV, vol. 2, no. 1410. - E. GAMILLSCHEG, B. MERSICH, O. MAZAL, Matthias Corvinus und die Bildung der Renaissance. Handschriften aus der Bibliothek und dem Umkreis des Matthias Corvinus aus dem Bestand der Österreichischen Nationalbibliothek. Catalogue of an exhibition mounted by the Österreichische Nationalbibliothek (Manuscripts and Incunabula Department), 27.5 - 6.10.1994. Graz 1994, pp. 87 f. (with further bibliography).

III.2: M. REEVES, The Influence of Prophecy in the Later Middle Ages. Oxford 1969 (reprinted Notre Dame 1993). - M. REEVES, B. HIRSCH-REICH, The *Figurae* of Joachim of Fiore. Genuine and Spurious Collections. *Mediaeval and Renaissance Studies* 3 (1954), pp. 170-199. - M. REEVES, B. HIRSCH-REICH, The *Figurae* of Joachim of Fiore. Oxford 1972. - H. GRUNDMANN, Ausgewählte Aufsätze 2. Joachim von Fiore (*Schriften der Monumenta Germaniae Historica* 25, 2). Stuttgart 1977. - R. E. LERNER, Joachim von Fiore, in: *Theologische Realenzyklopädie* 17 (1988), pp. 84-88.

III.3: HERMANN 6/1, pp. 59-74. - C. HUTER, Cristoforo Cortese at the Bodleian Library. *Apollo* (January 1980), p. 14. - W. BAIER, K. RUH, Ludolf von Sachsen, in: *Die deutsche Literatur des Mittelalters. Verfasserlexikon* 5 ([2]1984), pp. 967-977 - G. MARIANI CANOVA, Miniatura e pittura in età tardogotica (1400-1440), in: M. LUCCO (ed.), La pittura nel Veneto. Il Quattrocento I. Milan 1989, pp. 193-222, esp. 199 ff.

IV.1: HERMANN 6/2, pp. 38-42. - P. S. MOORE, The Works of Peter of Poitiers. Notre-Dame, Ind. 1936. - MAZAL, p. 100. - A. FINGERNAGEL, *De fructibus carnis et spiritus*. Der Baum der Tugenden und der Laster im Ausstattungsprogramm einer Handschrift des *Compendiums* des Petrus Pictaviensis (Wien, Österreichische Nationalbibliothek, Cod. 12 538). *Wiener Jahrbuch für Kunstgeschichte* 46/47 (1993/94), pp. 173-185. - Magister Petrus Pictaviensis, Genealogia Christi. Barcelona 2000.

IV.2: HERMANN 7/2, pp. 168-177. - K. KOSHI, Die Wiener "Histoire universelle" (Cod. 2576) unter Berücksichtigung der sogenannten Cottongenesis-Rezension. Doctoral thesis. Vienna 1971. - K. KOSHI, Die Genesisminiaturen in der Wiener "Histoire universelle" (Cod. 2576). (*Wiener kunstgeschichtliche Forschungen* I). Vienna 1973. - D. OLTROGGE, Die Illustrationszyklen zur "Histoire ancienne jusqu'à César" (1250-1400). (*Europäische Hochschulschriften*, series XXVIII, Kunstgeschichte, vol. 94). Frankfurt/Main (et al.) 1989, pp. 43, 320-323 and passim. - M. DE VISSER-VAN TERWISGA, Histoire ancienne jusqu'à César (Estoires Rogier), 2 vols. (*Medievalia* 19; 30). Orleans 1995, 1999. - K. KOSHI, Die Miniaturen der heidnisch-antiken Mythologie und Geschichte in der Wiener "Histoire universelle". *Bulletin of The Faculty of Fine Arts, Tokyo National University of Fine Arts and Music* 34 (1999), pp. 3–97.

IV.3: H. MODERN, Die Zimmern'schen Handschriften der k. k. Hofbibliothek. *Jahrbuch der kunsthistorischen Sammlungen des allerhöchsten Kaiserhauses* 20 (1899), pp. 113–180, esp. 144 f. (no. 22). – H. VOLLMER, Materialien zur Bibelgeschichte, vol. I/1: Ober- und mitteldeutsche Historienbibeln. Berlin 1912, pp. 95–104 (no. 33), pl. XI. – J. A. ASHER, Der übele Gêrhart, in: H. BACKES (ed.), Festschrift für Hans Eggers zum 65. Geburtstag (*Beiträge zur Geschichte der deutschen Sprache und Literatur* 94, special ed.). Tübingen 1972, pp. 16–427 (on the scribe). – M. and H. ROOSEN-RUNGE, Das spätgotische Musterbuch des Stephan Schriber. Wiesbaden 1981, vol. 2: Commentary, pp. 179–200, esp. 187–190, ill. pp. 218 f. (entry by the scribe and list of expenses). – V. BLOH, pp. 278 f. and passim, ill. 84–86.

IV.4: H. VOLLMER, Materialien zur Bibelgeschichte und religiösen Volkskunde des Mittelalters, vol. I/1: Ober- und mitteldeutsche Historienbibeln. Berlin 1912, pp. 156 f. (no. 63), pl. XVI. – K. HOLTER, Die Wiener Buchmalerei, in: Geschichte der bildenden Kunst in Wien, vol. 2: R.K. DONIN (ed.), Gotik. Vienna 1955, p. 226. – G. KORNRUMPF, Die österreichischen Historienbibeln IIIa und IIIb, in: H. REINITZER (ed.), Deutsche Bibelübersetzungen des Mittelalters (*Vestigia Bibliae* 9/10, 1987/88), Berne (et al.) 1991, pp. 350–374, here 359–365. – IDEM, Die "Weltchronik" Heinrichs von München, in: P. STEIN, A. WEISS, G. HAYER (eds.). Festschrift für Ingo Reiffenstein zum 60. Geburtstag (*Göppinger Arbeiten zur Germanistik* 478). Göppingen 1988, pp. 508 f. – V. BLOH, pp. 318 f. and passim, ill. 82 f.

IV.5: A. W. BYVANCK and G. J. HOOGEWERFF, Noord-Nederlandse miniaturen in handschriften der 14e, 15e, 16e eeuwen. 3 vols. The Hague 1922–1925. – J. G. HOOGEWERFF, De Noord-Nederlandse schilderkunst, vol. I. S'Gravenhage 1936, pp. 535 ff., ill. 296–304, 306–307, 309–311, 316–318. – P. J. H. VERMEEREN, De Nederlandse Historiebijbel der Oestenrijkse Nationale Bibliotheek, Codex 2771 en 2772. *Het Boek* 32 (1955–57), pp. 101–189. – J. DESCHAMPS, Middelnederlandse handschriften uit Europese en Amerikaanse bibliotheken. Leiden ²1972, no. 50. – PÄCHT–JENNI, pp. 43–85, ill. 80–261, colour pl. IV–VII.

V.1–2: R. BRANNER, Manuscript Painting in Paris during the Reign of Saint Louis. A Study of Styles. Berkeley, Los Angeles, London 1977, Cod. 2554: pp. 3, 6, 33 passim, fig. 26c, 39–46; Cod. 1179: pp. 3, 33 passim, fig. 2 (p. 34), 3 (p. 35) 25a, b, 27–38. – Bible moralisée: Codex Vindobonensis 2554 der Österreichischen Nationalbibliothek. Commentary by R. HAUSSHERR. French Bible text transl. by H.-W. STORK. Graz 1992. – S. LIPTON, Images of intolerance: the representation of Jews and Judaism in the Bible moralisée. Berkeley 1999. – J. LOWDEN, The making of the bibles moralisées, 2 vols. Pennsylvania 2000.

V.3: H. CORNELL, Biblia pauperum. Stockholm 1925, pp. 83 f. – G. SCHMIDT, Der Codex 370 der Wiener Nationalbibliothek. *Wiener Jahrbuch für Kunstgeschichte* 17 (22) (1956), pp. 15–48. – SCHMIDT, pp. 15 f. – Krumauer Bildercodex. Österreichische Nationalbibliothek Codex 370. Facsimile edition (*Codices selecti* 13). Commentary volume by G. SCHMIDT and F. UNTERKIRCHER. Graz, Vienna, Cologne 1967. – G. SCHMIDT, Die Fresken von Strakonice und der Krumauer Bildercodex. *Umění* 41 (1993), pp. 145–152.

V.4: SCHMIDT, pp. 10 f., 60 ff. (with older bibliography). – [Facsimile edition:] Die Wiener Biblia pauperum. Codex Vindobonensis 1198. Ed., transcribed and transl. by F. UNTERKIRCHER. Introduction by G. SCHMIDT (3 vols.). Graz, Vienna, Cologne 1962. – FRITZSCHE, pp. 5 f. – FINGERNAGEL – ROLAND, pp. 261–264 (cat. 105) (M. ROLAND). – G. BRUCHER (ed.), Geschichte der Bildenden Kunst in Österreich, vol. II, Gotik. Munich 2000, pp. 511–512 (cat. 248) (M. ROLAND).

V.5: G. SCHMIDT, Die Malerschule von St. Florian. Beiträge zur süddeutschen Malerei zu Ende des 13. und im 14. Jahrhundert. Graz, Cologne 1962, esp. pp. 37 f., 150 ff. – F. UNTERKIRCHER, Ambraser Handschriften. Ein Tausch zwischen dem Kunsthistorischen Museum und der Nationalbibliothek im Jahre 1936. *Jahrbuch der kunsthistorischen Sammlungen in Wien* 59 (1963), pp. 225–264, here 235 (on older bibliography). – Die Zeit der frühen Habsburger. Exhibition, Wiener Neustadt 1979. Vienna 1979, cat. 248 (G. SCHMIDT). – FRITZSCHE, pp. 91–92. – FINGERNAGEL–ROLAND, pp. 293–302 (cat. 123) (M. ROLAND).

VI.1: A. Z. SCHWARZ, Die Hebräischen Handschriften der Nationalbibliothek in Wien (*Museion*. Nationalbibliothek publication, Vienna, essay vol. II). Vienna, Prague, Leipzig 1925, p. 11 (no. 11). – T. METZGER, Les arts du livre (calligraphie, décoration, reliure) chez les juifs d'Espagne, à la veille de l'expulsion 1492, in: R. GOETSCHEL (ed.), L'expulsion des juifs d'Espagne. Maisonneuve et Larose 1996, pp. 163–182, esp. 166 note. 13.

VI.2: K. WEITZMANN, Die byzantinische Buchmalerei des 9. und 10. Jahrhunderts (*Österr. Akad. d. Wiss., Phil.-hist. Kl., Denkschriften 243, Veröff. d. Komm. für Schrift- und Buchw. des Mittelalt. series IV, vol. 2, part 1*). Vienna 1996 (= reprint of the Berlin edition of 1935). – BUBERL–GERSTINGER, pp. 7–13. – H. BUCHTHAL, A Byzantine Miniature of the Fourth Evangelist and its Relatives. *Dumbarton Oaks Papers* 15 (1961), p. 130. – HUN-

GER-LACKNER-HANNICK, pp. 134-136.

VI.3: BUBERL-GERSTINGER, pp. 50-58. - H. HUNGER, C. HANNICK, Katalog der griechischen Handschriften der Österreichischen Nationalbibliothek, Teil 4: Supplementum graecum (*Museion*, Österreichische Nationalbibliothek publication, new series, vol. 1, Part 4). Vienna 1994, pp. 97-100. - I. SPATHARAKIS, A Dove whispers in the Ear of the Evangelist. *Jahrbuch der Österreichischen Byzantinistik* 49 (1999), pp. 267-288.

VI.4: IORGA, pp. 45-53, fig. 27-76. - Mittelalterliches Bulgarien. Exhibition of manuscripts and maps held in the Österreichische Nationalbibliothek, 24.5-15.10.1977. Vienna 1977, pp. 20-22. - BIRKFELLNER, pp. 113-116. - C. COSTEA, Ilustraţia de manuscris în mediul cărturăresc al mitropolitului Anastasie Crimcovici. Apostolul (Viena, Nationalbibliothek cod. sl. 6), in: Studii şi cercetări de istoria artei, *Seria Artă Plastică* 39 (1992), pp. 41-57.

VI.5: IORGA, pp. 45-53, pl. I-VI. - S. HAFNER, B. Kopitar und die slawischen Handschriften der Athosklöster. *Südost-Forschungen* 18/1 (1959), pp. 89-122. - BIRKFELLNER, pp. 86-88. - P. Ş. NĂSTUREL, Le Mont Athos et les Roumains. Recherches sur leurs relations du milieu du XIVe siècle à 1654 (*Orientalia Christiana Analecta* 227). Rome 1986, pp. 180-202. - J. PROLOVIČ, Tetraevangeliar aus Studenica, in: Studenica et l'art byzantin autour de l'année 1200 (*Colloques scientifiques de l'Académie Serbe des Sciences et des Arts*, vol. XLI, Classe des sciences historiques, vol. 11). Belgrad 1988, pp. 525-533. - W. LUKAN, Bartholomäus Kopitars "Bibliothekarischer Bericht" - Ein Dokument des Austroslawismus und die Probleme seiner Veröffentlichung. *Österreichische Osthefte* 37/1 (1995), pp. 147-194.

VI.6: S. GRILL, Vergleichende Religionsgeschichte und Kirchenväter. Beigabe: Die syrischen Handschriften der Nationalbibliothek in Wien (*Heiligenkreuzer Studien* 11). Horn, Lower Austria 1959, p. 54. - W. STROTHMANN, Die Anfänge der syrischen Studien in Europa (*Göttinger Orientforschungen* 1). Wiesbaden 1971, pp. 11-15. - B. ALAND, Bibelübersetzungen I. (4. Die Übersetzungen ins Syrische) 4.2. Neues Testament, in: *Theologische Realenzyklopädie* 6 (1980), pp. 189-196. - A. BREYCHA-VAUTHIER, Description du manuscrit de Vienne, in: C. ABOUSSOUAN (ed.), Le livre et le Liban jusqu'à 1900. Paris 1982, pp. 126-127. - D. G. K. TAYLOR, S. P. BROCK, The Hidden Pearl: The Syrian Orthodox Church and its Ancient Aramaic Heritage, vol. III. Rome 2001, pp. 163-164.

VI.7: H. and H. BUSCHHAUSEN, Armenische Handschriften der Mechitharisten-Kongregation in Wien. Catalogue to a special exhibition in the Österreichische Nationalbibliothek. Vienna ^{2}1981. - C. BURCHARD (ed.), Armenia and the Bible, Papers Presented to the International Symposium Held at Heidelberg, July 16-19, 1990 (*University of Pennsylvania Armenian Texts and Studies* 12). Louvain 1993. - W. SEIBT (ed.), The Christianization of the Caucasus (Armenia, Georgia, Albania). Lectures at the International Symposium in Vienna, 9-12 December 1999 (*Österr. Akad. der Wiss., Phil.-hist. Kl., Denkschriften* 296.; *Veröff. der Komm. für Byzantinistik*, vol. IX). Vienna 2002. - M. K. KRIKORIAN, Die armenische Kirche, Materialien zur armenischen Geschichte, Theologie und Kultur. Frankfurt/Main, Berlin (et al.) 2002. - M. E. STONE, D. KOUYMJIAN, H. LEHMANN, Album of Armenian Paleography. Aarhus 2002.

VI.8: Aethiopien - Buchmalereien. Introduction by J. LEROY, texts by S. WRIGHT and O. A. JÄGER. Paris 1961. - E. HAMMERSCHMIDT, Äthiopien - Christliches Reich zwischen Gestern und Morgen. Wiesbaden 1967. - E. HAMMERSCHMIDT, O. A. JÄGER, Illuminierte äthiopische Handschriften (*Verz. der Orient. Hss. in Deutschland* 15). Wiesbaden 1968 - E. ULLENDORF, Ethiopia and the Bible. Oxford 1968. - P. BRANDT, Geflecht aus 81 Büchern: Zur variantenreichen Gestalt des äthiopischen Bibelkanons. *Aethiopica* 3 (2000), pp. 79-115.

VI.9: G. FLÜGEL, Die arabischen, persischen und türkischen Handschriften der Hofbibliothek zu Wien, vol. 3. Vienna 1865, cat. no. 1544. - G. GRAF, Geschichte der christlichen arabischen Literatur, vol. 1. Vatican City 1944. - S. H. GRIFFITH, The Gospel in Arabic. An Enquiry into its Appearance in the First Abbasid Century. *Oriens Christianus* 69 (1985), pp. 126-167. - J.-D. THYEN (ed.), Bibel und Koran. Eine Synopse gemeinsamer Überlieferungen. Cologne 1989.

VI.10: P. WITTEK, Der Stammbaum der Osmanen. *Der Islam* 14 (1925), pp. 94-100. - Muhammad ibn Ramadan, Darwis: Subhatu'l-Ahbar (Haberler Tesbihi). Vienna, Österr. Nationalbibliothek, Cod. A. F. 50. Facsimile edition of the Dogan Kardes (with accompanying texts by S. RADO, Y. ÖZTUNA und K. HOLTER). Istanbul 1968. - Muhammad ibn Ramadan, Rosenkranz der Weltgeschichte. Complete reprint of Codex Vindobonensis A. F. 50 in the original format. Graz 1981. - PETSCHAR, pp. 210-211 (RUMPF-DORNER).

▸ **Vienna Genesis, Cod. theol. gr. 31, detail from fol. 1r:** The Fall in three scenes: Eve offers Adam the apple.

Glossary

(Sources: *Imagination – Zeitschrift für Freunde des alten Buches* (vol. 1993, issue 1, pp. 28–31, and issue 2, pp. 19–23), edited by Manfred Kramer and chief editor Norbert Cziep. Akademische Druck- und Verlagsanstalt, Graz; *Lexikon des gesamten Buchwesens*; *Lexikon des Mittelalters*; *Lexikon für Theologie und Kirche*

AMBO
(Medieval Lat., from Gk. *ámbon*, perhaps becoming *anabaínein* = to go up.) Pulpit or lectern in a church from where parts of the service were performed.

ANTITYPE ▸ TYPE

APOCALYPSE
(Gk. *apokalypsis* = revelation.) Text in which the course and end of the world are prophetically disclosed in visions, as in the (Secret) Revelation of John, the last book of the New Testament. Describes the imminent collapse of the world, followed by the defeat of Satan and the advent of the kingdom of heaven.

ARISTOTELIANISM
Term used to describe various philosophical models based on the writings of Aristotle (384–322) from Stageira (Macedonia). Aristotle was known to the West in the Middle Ages above all through translations of his works from the Arabic; his philosophy formed the foundation of western Scholasticism.

BIBLE MORALISÉE
(Fr. = "moralizing Bible".) A type of picture Bible consisting of short biblical passages and related commentaries and accompanied by an extensive cycle of illustrations, comprising up to 2,700 pairs of typological pictures, the majority in the shape of medallions. Early examples of the genre featured 8 picture medallions per page (= 4 pairs).

BIBLIA PAUPERUM
(Lat. = "Bible of the poor".) From the end of the 13th century onwards, a widely-used devotional book in which the life of Christ was portrayed from a typological point of view and illustrated accordingly. The illustrations in such "Bibles of the poor" thereby represent the most important source for our understanding of typology. In their entirety they provide a compendium of a tradition which reaches back to early Christian times and within which the instructional and pictorial system of Christian art evolved.

BLIND LINES ▸ BLIND TOOLING

BLIND STAMPING ▸ BLIND TOOLING

BLIND TOOLING
Method of decorating a book binding, whereby lines or ornamental designs were imprinted into the leather with a heated hand tool or stamp (blind stamping), leaving a permanent impression. As well as single stamps, rollers and plates were also used. The technique was employed chiefly in the Middle Ages.

CALLIGRAPHY
(Gr. *kalligraphia* = beautiful script.) Fine writing by a scribe or artist (calligrapher).

CATENA
(Lat. *catena* = chain.) Collection of commentaries by the Church Fathers on passages from the Bible, which are written around the actual biblical text (in their most extensive form, in the margins on all four sides of the page) and which are cross-referenced to the corresponding passage in the main text. In terms of page design, catena commentaries are usually written in a smaller script and are clearly distinguished from the main text.

COLOPHON
(Gk. = final writing.) Concluding remarks in a manuscript or incunabulum giving details of the scribe or printer and the title, place and date of production.

CORRUPTION
(Lat. *corrumpere* = break into pieces, destroy.) Term used in textual criticism to describe a word or sequence of words that, in the course of being transcribed from

one manuscript to the next, has been rendered incorrectly or altered; we also speak of "corrupt" passages of text.

DROLLERY
(Fr. *drôlerie* = amusing idea.) Hybrid figures of men or beasts and other fabulous creatures, appearing in the scrollwork on the pages of Gothic manuscripts and also in initials and borders. They inhabit the edge of the page and often form self-contained scenes. Not only do they reveal – particularly in the drolleries of the late Middle Ages – a tendency towards satire (and thereby towards a critique of society?), but they also offer an ironic commentary on the official practices of art, particularly in their representation of demons.

EPISTOLARIUM
(Lat. *epistola* = letter.) Collection of letters.

FLEURONNÉE
(Fr. *fleuronné* = flowered.) A form of decoration characteristic of manuscript illumination in the Gothic era, chiefly used with initials. In most cases combined with the body of a letter which has been developed out of the shape of a Lombard initial. Depending on their degree of elaboration, *fleuronnée* forms are essentially abstract; they commonly employ the stylized forms of palmettes and buds as well as filigree and pearls, which embroider the main body of the letter and spill into the margin beside it. This form of decoration probably evolved out of the French and English silhouetted initials of the Late Romanesque era.

FLORATOR
Artist responsible for painting the *fleuronnée* initials in manuscripts. In highly developed scriptoria, a specialist, but sometimes one and the same person as the scribe or artist executing the miniatures.

FLORENSIAN ORDER
The Order formed when Joachim of Fiore (*c.* 1130–1202) left the Cistercian order in around 1190 and founded his own monastery of S. Giovanni di Fiore in the Sila mountains in Calabria. Joachim was granted papal approval for his new Order which embraced a strict version of the Benedictine Rule. The monastery had numerous affiliates. The Order expanded only within Italy and existed until 1570.

GOSPEL BOOK
(Lat. *evangelium*, from Gk. *euangelion* = good news.) Liturgical book which contains the complete texts of the four Gospels. It also includes the various prefaces and other theological matter (canon tables, divisions into sections and chapter lists). The capitularies accompanying the Gospel texts helped the reader locate the pericopes to be read during divine service throughout the liturgical year. The Gospel Book was equated in notional terms with Christ and its text commanded the same reverence as Christ himself.

GRADUAL
(Lat. *gradus* = step.) Service book containing the variable and unchanging antiphons sung during the Mass.

HAPHTARAH (PL. HAPHTAROTH)
(Heb. = conclusion.) Reading selected from the Prophets, read in the synagogue service on the Sabbath.

ICONOCLASTIC CONTROVERSY
In the 6th century the veneration of icons of Christ assumed the form of an imperial cult in the Byzantine Empire. This veneration was intensified by legends of miracles worked by individual icons. In 726, as part of an opposition movement, Emperor Leo III declared the use and veneration of icons a punishable offence. With this, the iconoclastic controversy broke out in full strength. Countless works of art were destroyed and monks supportive of icon-worship were martyred. The first phase of the iconoclastic controversy ended in 787; a second phase lasted from 815 until 843.

ICONOGRAPHY
(Gk. *eikón* = image.) Study of images; academic method concerned with the factors by which subjects are represented in art, as opposed to the history of form or style. Knowledge of the subject-matter portrayed and its religio-historical, literary and social significance is seen as a prerequisite for understanding a work of art.

ILLUMINATOR
The artist responsible for the decoration of a manuscript (with miniatures, ornamental initials, borders).

IMPRESE
(It. *impresa* = emblem.) Comparable with more general emblems and devices, imprese employ a combination of word and image to create a personalized statement of an individual's goals and values. These brief and often puzzling emblems were first introduced at the Burgundian court and later spread to Italy.

INITIAL
(Lat. *initium* = introduction, beginning.) Opening letter of a section of text in manuscripts or incunabula, emphasized by its size, script and decoration. Fish and bird motifs, interlace and scrollwork often feature in initials. In the Gothic era initials also incorporated miniatures, mostly of biblical scenes and sometimes occupying a full page.

LEONINE VERSE
A special type of hexameter employed in Latin verse of the Middle Ages, in which each line has a rhyme in the middle (caesura at the third stress) and at the end, as in *Aethiopum terras iam fervida torruit aestas* (Eclogue Theoduli).

LIMP BINDING
A type of binding particularly common in the later Middle Ages, in which the covers are made not of wooden boards, but of soft, flexible material. The gatherings were attached to the limp binding using

a special technique (kettle stitching).

LOMBARD INITIALS
Simple decorative initials found in Gothic manuscripts and in printed books of the Late Gothic era. Usually executed in either red or blue, they are sometimes ornamented by means of gaps in the body of the letter. They display a characteristically round-bellied form.

MAJUSCULE
(Lat. *littera maiuscula* = slightly larger letter.) Capital letter. Script type whose letters are the same height and can be fitted between two parallel horizontal lines. By the High and Late Middle Ages, employed only as a display script.

MARTYROLOGY
(Lat. *martyrologium*.) Ecclesiastical calendar of Christian martyrs, organized by feast day; the Greek pendant, containing the saints of the liturgical year, is the menology (Gk. *menologion* = list of months).

MASORAH
(Heb. = tradition.) The body of critical notes made by Jewish scholars in Babylonia and Palestine from the 7th to the 10th century and designed to ensure the correct handing down of the Old Testament text. The word is derived from the Hebrew root *masar*, "to hand over, transmit".

MATUTINAL
(Lat. *matutinus* = of the morning.) Book containing the morning prayers.

MENOLOGY ▸ MARTYROLOGY

MIAPHYSITISM
Theological position within the christological dispute which divided the Eastern Church in the 5th and 6th century, and which held that in the person of Christ there was only one single, divine nature; Jesus the man had transformed himself into the divine Christ. An attempt to reach a compromise at the Council of Chalcedon in 451 failed. The excommunication of the Miaphysites in the first half of the 6th century led them to break away from the main body of the Church. In Egypt, Syria and Mesopotamia, the Miaphysites held on to their schismatic position throughout the dispute.

MINUSCULE
Quattrolinear script of lower case letters, with ascenders and descenders filling the line spaces.

MISSAL
(Middle Lat. *missale* = Mass book.) Service book containing all the variable and unchanging texts of the Mass for the liturgical year. It was a compilation of several, originally separate liturgical books which each had a specific function. The first Missals appeared at the end of the 10th century and in the 12th century – as quiet, private saying of the Mass became increasingly popular – displaced the Sacramentary used in ceremonial, public worship. The Missal contains the complete liturgical cycle from the first Sunday of Advent until the last Sunday after Pentecost and the feasts of the saints. It also includes the daily prayers, the prefaces, the canon, the Common of Saints and various votive Masses.

MOROCCO (BINDING)
Term referring to a goatskin primarily used for book-binding and originally made chiefly in Morocco.

MOSAICIST
A mosaicist is an artist who works with mosaic gold or produces mosaics.

OCTATEUCH
(Gk. *oktáteukhos* = eight scrolls.) In the Eastern Church, the name by which the first eight books of the Old Testament (? Pentateuch plus Joshua, Judges and Ruth) are commonly known.

ORATIO MANASSE (PRAYER OF MANASSEH)
Psalm-like prayer of penitence, which according to 2 Chronicles 33:11 ff. is attributed to the converted King Manasseh, but which was probably written in the Greek language in Palestine around the beginning of the Christian era.

PANDECT
(Gk. *pan* = all, *déchesthai* = to receive.) Complete Bibles, i. e. manuscripts containing all the books of the Old and New Testament.

PARASHA SYMBOLS
(Heb. = explanation.) Symbols, sometimes ornamental, usually noted in the margin, indicating the portion from the Torah read in the synagogue service.

PENTATEUCH
(Gr. *pentáteukhos* = five scrolls.) The first five books of the Old Testament.

PERICOPES
(Gr. *perikopé* = a shortening.) The selected passages from the Old and New Testament read out during the Mass over the course of the liturgical year.

PRAXAPOSTOLOS
(Gk. *Praxapóstolos*.) Lectionary used exclusively in the Eucharist and containing all the non-Gospel readings from the New Testament (with the exception of Revelation).

PREFIGURATION ▸ TYPE

PSALTER
(Gk. *psaltérion* = zither-like stringed instrument.) In the 9th century the Psalter was almost the only liturgical book in the hands of the laity. It remained so until the arrival of the first Books of Hours at the end of the 13th century. The Psalter played a prominent role in the life of the laity and even more so in the life of the clergy. In the Middle Ages the Psalter was recited daily, outside the hours of divine service; every priest and monk had to know it by heart.

PSEUDO-CUFIC
Form of writing which outwardly resembles the Cufic script but

which elaborates it into an ornamental script which pays no attention to the meaning of the words.

QUATREFOIL
A primarily Gothic decorative motif in which four semicircular arches describe a roughly square central field. Quatrefoils are chiefly found as framing elements in architecture, but are also employed in stained glass, wall painting and manuscript illumination.

RECTO
Recto (r) describes the right-hand page of a book which is lying open, i. e. the front side of a leaf in a codex. Manuscripts are numbered according to leaves, or folios, rather than pages. For example, 43 recto is the front side of the 43rd folio in the manuscript.

RITUAL
Book of rites used by a bishop, priest or deacon officiating at a sacrament.

SEPTUAGINT
The oldest and most important translation of the Old Testament into Greek. The name derives from a legend, according to which 72 Jews completed the translation in 72 days.

SQUARE SEPHARDIC SCRIPT
Hebrew script which is almost square in outline, used in the Sefarad sphere (Spain and southern France).

SUPRALIBROS
Decoration of a binding with a coat of arms impressed onto the cover, also serving as an indication of ownership.

TREE OF JESSE
The representation of the ancestry of Christ according to Isaiah (11:1), in the form of a tree growing up out of the sleeping Prophet's body and bearing in its branches pictures (busts and full-length portraits) of the forefathers of Christ.

TYPE
Person or event in the Old Testament considered to prefigure a person or event (antitype) in the Christian world of the New Testament

VERSO
Verso (v) describes the left-hand page of a book which is lying open, i. e. the reverse side of a leaf in a codex. Manuscripts are numbered according to leaves or folios, rather than pages. For example, 43 verso or 43v is the back of the 43rd leaf in the manuscript.

VESPERAL
(Lat. *vesper* = evening.) Book containing the words and hymns to be used at vespers.

VULGATE
The Latin translation of the Bible made by St Jerome at the end of the 4th and beginning of the 5th century.

Index of authors

Dr. Christine Beier (C. B.)
Österreichische Akademie der Wissenschaften
Institut für Kunstgeschichte der Universität Wien,
Pächt-Archiv

Dr. Andreas Fingernagel (A. F.)
Österreichische Nationalbibliothek
Handschriften-, Autographen- und Nachlass-Sammlung

Prof. Dr. Stephan Füssel (S. F.)
Johannes Gutenberg-Universität, Mainz
Institut für Buchwissenschaft

Dr. Christian Gastgeber (C. G.)
Österreichische Akademie der Wissenschaften
Zentrum Mittelalterforschung
Institut für Byzanzforschung

Dr. Katharina Hranitzky (K. H.)
Österreichische Akademie der Wissenschaften
Institut für Kunstgeschichte der Universität Wien,
Pächt-Archiv

Dr. Ulrike Jenni (U. J.)
Österreichische Akademie der Wissenschaften
Institut für Kunstgeschichte der Universität Wien,
Pächt-Archiv

Erzbischof Hon.-Prof. Dr. Mesrob K. Krikorian (M. K. K.)
Patriarchal-Delegat für Mitteleuropa und Schweden
Armenisch-apostolische Kirche Wien

Dr. Clemens Leonhard (C. L.)
Universität Wien
Institut für Liturgiewissenschaft der katholisch-theologischen Fakultät

Gabriele Pinkava (G. P.)
Universität Wien
c/o Institut für Ethnologie, Sozial- u. Kulturanthropologie

Dr. Veronika Pirker-Aurenhammer (V. P.-A.)
Österreichische Akademie der Wissenschaften
Institut für Kunstgeschichte der Universität Wien,
Pächt-Archiv

Dr. Karl-Georg Pfändtner (K.-G. P.)
Österreichische Akademie der Wissenschaften
Institut für Kunstgeschichte der Universität Wien,
Pächt-Archiv

Dr. Mihailo Popović (M. P.)
Österreichische Akademie der Wissenschaften
Zentrum Mittelalterforschung
Institut für Byzanzforschung

Ao. Universitätsprofessor Stephan Procházka (S. P.)
Universität Wien
Institut für Orientalistik

Mag. Solveigh Rumpf-Dorner (S. R.-D.)
Österreichische Nationalbibliothek
Sammlung von Inkunabeln, alten und wertvollen Drucken

Mag. Friedrich Simader (F. S.)
Österreichische Nationalbibliothek
Handschriften-, Autographen- und Nachlass-Sammlung

Mag. Maria Theisen (M. T.)
Österreichische Akademie der Wissenschaften
Institut für Kunstgeschichte der Universität Wien,
Pächt-Archiv

Dr. Martin Wagendorfer (M. W.)
Universität Wien
Institut für Österreichische Geschichtsforschung

Acknowledgements

The editors and publisher wish to thank all the authors who have contributed to the making of this book. We are especially grateful to the University of Vienna, the Austrian Academy of Sciences and the University of Mainz for their constructive co-operation.
Our thanks also go to the many members of staff at the Austrian National Library for their unstinting support in the Photographic Studio, the Institute of Restoration, the Department of Reprography, the Incunabula and Valuable Prints Collection, and lastly the Manuscripts, Autographs and Bequests Collection.
The editors would like to take this opportunity to thank the publisher once again for the energetic commitment and scrupulous attention to detail brought to this project.

Page 2:
Greek Gospels and Praxapostolos, Cod. suppl. gr. 52, detail from fol. 1v: Representation of the Trinity, surrounded by an angelic host.

To stay informed about upcoming TASCHEN titles, please request our magazine at www.taschen.com/magazine or write to TASCHEN America, 6671 Sunset Boulevard, Suite 1508, USA-Los Angeles, CA 90028, contact-us@taschen.com, Fax: +1-323-463.4442. We will be happy to send you a free copy of our magazine which is filled with information about all of our books.

Hohenzollernring 53, D–50672 Köln
www.taschen.com

Project management: Petra Lamers-Schütze, Cologne
Editorial co-ordination: Juliane Steinbrecher, Cologne
Translation: Karen Williams, Whitley Chase
Design: Catinka Keul & Angelika Taschen, Cologne
Cover design: Sense/Net, Andy Disl and Birgit Reber, Cologne
Production: Horst Neuzner, Cologne

Printed in China
ISBN 978–3–8365–0299–3